My GEORGIA home

INTRODUCTION BY ARTHUR BLANK

The compelling stories of famous and noteworthy Georgians
who have brought great pride to their home state.

published by
IMAGE PUBLISHING, INC.

My GEORGIA home

Georgia calls us home. Whether we lived in the mountains, the heartland, or the coast, and no matter where we live now, we still call Georgia home. Neighbors are friendly and spring offers up a rush of beautiful dogwoods and azaleas blooming across the landscape. The heat of summer can be remediated with a juicy Georgia peach—the fuzzy red and gold skin, a cozy and familiar texture for any native's fingertips. Fall offers a burst of color before the chilly winter, which—thankfully—is brief (just how Georgians like it). Just as the coastal wind scatters sand across the dunes, small towns are scattered throughout the state, coating the land in culture and comfort. We can't help but love the hustle and bustle of Atlanta nightlife: people rushing faster than the flowing waters that carve out the mountains and red hills of Georgia. There is no place like home, and there is definitely no home like Georgia. ∎

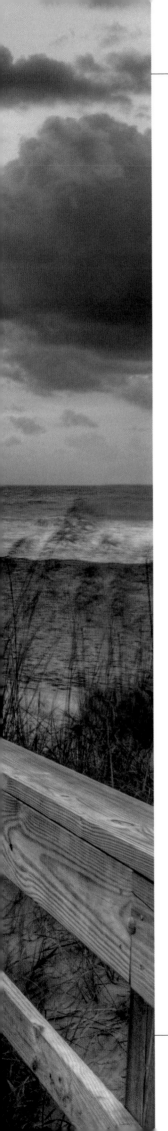

TYBEE ISLAND *at sunrise. Photo by Jesse Kunerth.*

Beautiful autumn FOREST ROAD *winds in the mountains.*
Photo by Balazs Justin.

Why I Call Georgia Home

Georgia is my home of choice. At this stage in my life I could live anywhere, and I choose to live in this place. Five of my six children and my grandchildren live here, and we're all proud to call Georgia home.

I grew up in the Sunnyside neighborhood of Queens, New York, and when I was eleven, my family moved to Flushing. My parents and my brother and I lived in a one-bedroom apartment. I spent my recreational time playing stickball and running around with my friends on the streets of our neighborhood. Georgia was not on my mind at the time, ▶

BY ARTHUR BLANK

and little did I know that my adult career path would lead me there not once, but three times.

My path to Georgia started under unfortunate circumstances. My father died suddenly at the age of 44. I was just fifteen. My mother Molly, with no real business experience of her own, took over Dad's mail-order pharmaceutical company. Despite the odds, she did a good job of expanding the business. Not surprising, my mother was tenacious about doing the right thing, and she instilled this in us at a very young age. I think that's what made her successful in business.

I remember one time when a man came to the door with a gun, which he aimed at my father's head. He tied up my brother and my mother and me while demanding money from my father. All the time he was there robbing us, my mother ▶

A young Arthur Blank posing with his mother, Molly (left). Pathway to TALLULAH GORGE *(right).*

lectured him that he was doing the wrong thing and that his mother would

not be proud of him. He eventually left without harming us, but it showed us

that my mother is fearless and always

wants everyone to do what's right, no

matter the circumstances.

My brother joined my mother in

the family business after he earned a

Arthur (center) in Flushing, New York, with HIS FATHER, MAX, *and his older brother, Michael. Blank credits his father with teaching him the importance of customer service and the human element in business dealings.*

degree in pharmacy from the University

of Michigan. After graduating from

Babson College with an accounting

degree in 1963, I worked for Arthur Young & Company for a few years

before deciding to join the family business, too.

Several years later, my mother sold the business to Daylin Corporation. I

stayed with the business for a while longer, and Daylin offered me a position

with   Elliott's Drug Stores/Stripe Discount Stores, a division of Daylin. Thus

began my journey to Georgia. ▶

After several years of living in Savannah where I owned my first home — one that I told my wife we'd never be able to fully pay for — I became president of Elliott's/Stripe and relocated the company and my wife and three children to Griffin, Georgia. At the time Griffin was called "The First City South of Atlanta." My, how the times have changed.

Partners Arthur Blank and Bernie Marcus pose in their Home Depot aprons.
A small waterfall in FREEMAN MILL PARK *in Atlanta.*

Fast forward to 1974, when Bernie Marcus, who also worked for a division of Daylin, asked me to join him at Handy Dan Home Improvement Centers, based in California. At that time it was the most successful home improvement retailer in the U.S. That move played a pivotal role in both of our futures.

I often wonder if Home Depot would have happened had we both not been fired by Handy Dan in 1978. Bernie, who was CEO of Handy Dan, got caught in a political power struggle with the CEO of Daylin, and he ▶

and I, along with Ron Brill, were the casualties. By that time, Bernie and I had already figured out that there was a retailing concept that would be successful in competing against Handy Dan: a big-box, no frills, low-price, customer-focused home improvement retailer.

Bernie and I spent many hours in a local coffee shop, our "office" midway between

Aerial CITYSCAPE OF DOWNTOWN *Atlanta, Georgia, with a full moon. The Millennium Gate (right) at Atlantic Station in Midtown Atlanta. Photo by Sean Pavone.*

our homes in California, hatching a plan. One of the key questions was, "Where do we plant our roots?" We narrowed our choices to four cities: Atlanta, Boston, Dallas and Los Angeles.

Being familiar with Georgia and the Atlanta area in particular, I drove Bernie around the I-285 perimeter highway. As we drove the tree-lined roadway, Bernie commented many times that there were "no people here." So, we'd exit the interstate and view the neighborhoods surrounding the downtown area. ▶

Those and many more neighborhoods are part of the metro area today. Coupled

with attractive real estate, prospects of business, population and economic growth,

and the quality of life the region offered, Atlanta was our choice for headquartering

our business and

opening our first

stores.

SAVANNAH HISTORIC DISCTRICT *includes august waterfront buildings and gracious antique homes.*

Lucky for us. We faced the challenges

of most business start-ups: finding willing

investors, gaining recognition and legitimacy

in the marketplace, and generating the cash

flow needed to continue our dream. But

looking back, I think the fact that we chose Georgia helped ensure our success.

This is a state rich in resources — for businesses, tourists and families alike.

We boast the busiest airport in the world with convenient access to and from a

myriad of other airports. The Port of Savannah provides logistical capabilities

second to none. We have major universities that provide an attractive talent pool

to the Fortune 500 and other businesses that call Georgia home. ▶

From its abundance of natural wonders across the state — extending

from seacoast to mountaintops — to its stunning springs

and major tourist attractions, we receive visitors from

around the world every year. And for families, we offer

a competitive quality of life, including housing and

Georgia is alive with natural beauty, from sunsets at Brasstown Bald Mountain to the RUSHING FALLS *at Dicks Creek in the Chattahoochie National Forest. Photo by Christopher Mobley.*

schooling choices, an affordable cost of living, arts and

cultural choices, and of course, professional sports.

Today, well after Bernie's and my retirement,

Home Depot continues to lead the industry. Bernie and I

have moved on to our next respective journeys; his in making possible the world's

largest aquarium in our state, along with continuing his other philanthropic

works, and mine in owning the Atlanta Falcons football team and a number of

other businesses based in Georgia. ▶

I'm proud to represent my family as chairman of our family foundation, which focuses the vast majority of its grant-making in Georgia. Consistent with the values instilled by my mother, I am proud to honor and perpetuate her lifelong efforts to be her "brothers' keeper" by sharing our blessings to help

Arthur Blank, proud owner of the ATLANTA FALCONS. *First half action as the Falcons visited the Chiefs to open the 2012 season.*

others. If not for founding Home Depot in Georgia, none of this may have been possible.

I am also proud to represent Georgia through my ownership of the Atlanta Falcons. I love sports and competition. When I bought the Atlanta Falcons in 2002, my goal was to make the Atlanta Falcons part of the fabric of the community and a source of pride — on and off the field — throughout the state of Georgia. By listening and responding to our fans, ▶

and by building a team based equally on talent and character, we have done

and continue to do that. We are a club and team with increasing relevance in

the National Football League as business

partners and as competitors.

We are also committed to being

winners off the field. Our Falcons

players, coaches, cheerleaders and

associates are among the most active

community citizens in the NFL,

The Atlanta FALCONS FITNESS ZONES *partner with the Boys and Girls Clubs of*
Metro Atlanta to serve as a direct youth obesity intervention initiative.

contributing an average of 3,000 hours of their collective personal time each

season to community outreach. In addition, the Atlanta Falcons Youth Foundation

invests millions of dollars to improve youth fitness and reduce childhood obesity

across Georgia. Central to this effort is our Falcons Fitness Zones, ▶

where through grant partners, we engage more

than 10,000 kids a year in more than one million

hours of physical therapy.

Now, well past a normal retirement

age, I continue to run my businesses

and personal life based on the notion

that there is no finish line —

you're either getting better or

you're going backwards, there

is no in between.

RISE UP ATLANTA *is a joint venture of the Atlanta Falcons and the Blank family of businesses that encourages all Falcons fans to "rise up" and join in to improve the Atlanta community.*

I think the same could be said about

Georgia. We are a state filled with business

leaders who are not afraid to tackle difficult ▶

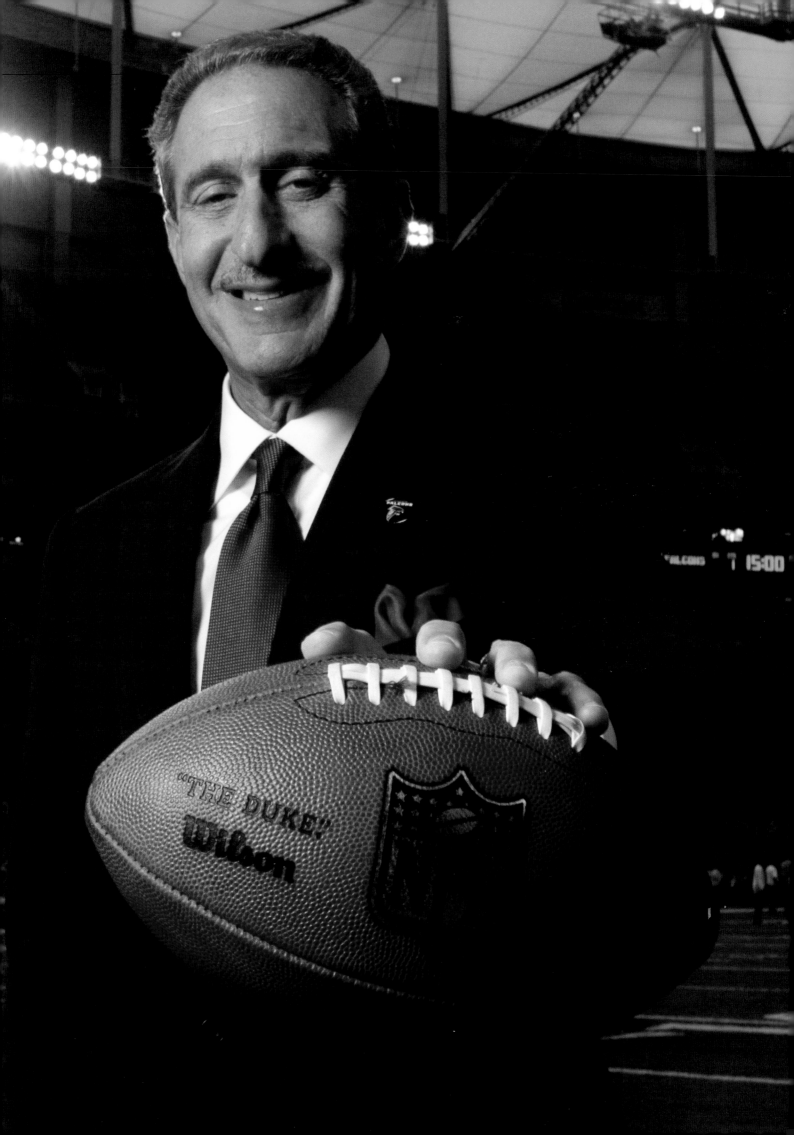

issues and who work together to enhance communities and the quality of life for our citizens. We also have a successful track record of using public-private partnerships in many areas to secure the long-term prospects of our state.

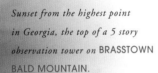

Sunset from the highest point in Georgia, the top of a 5 story observation tower on BRASSTOWN BALD MOUNTAIN.

Michelangelo once said, "The greater danger for most of us lies not in setting our aim too high and falling short; but in setting our aim too low, and achieving our mark." I believe in setting our aim high, and I believe Georgians feel the same way.

And that's why I call Georgia home. ∎

My Georgia home

My Georgia Home is a celebration of the fascinating people who are proud to call Georgia home.

The celebrities profiled in this book are extraordinary and we celebrate their stories of hard work and accomplishments that many people may have forgotten or simply did not know. We honor these Pulitzer Prize winning authors, playwrights, and journalists along with award-winning actors, legendary athletes, and forward thinking entrepreneurs.

The visionaries are "unsung heroes" who worked for positive change in Georgia making life better for future generations.

Our hope is that this book will be a role-modeling tool and a source of inspiration for Georgians, their children, and grandchildren. It is also a chance to let others outside the state know why "my home is in Georgia."

There was much research and effort involved in selecting the most appropriate individuals to be profiled in this book. Individuals were chosen not only for their accomplishments but also for the number of years they have spent in the state. They have to call Georgia home and have a certain level of involvement in the community. It is inevitable to have omissions of some deserving Georgians. The committee and publisher regret any such omissions.

Starr's Mill near Atlanta, Georgia, photo by Sean Pavone.

My Georgia home

Celebrities

THE FASCINATING PROFILES

OF THESE ACCOMPLISHED

AND TALENTED

GEORGIA CELEBRITIES

INSPIRE US TO REALIZE

THAT NO DREAM IS TOO BIG AND

NO GOAL IS IMPOSSIBLE.

"Separate we come, and separate we go. And this be it known, is all that we know."

Conrad Aiken

POET, AUTHOR & ESSAYIST . SAVANNAH . 1889 – 1973

CONRAD AIKEN, POET AND NOVELIST, RECEIVED numerous prestigious awards for his work, including a Pulitzer Prize. He served as the Poetry Consultant at the Library of Congress. Aiken never achieved the fame of his contemporaries because of his fear of performing readings in public. His fear of public speaking also led him to reject numerous offers of honorary degrees. During his life, he wrote or edited more than fifty-one books.

Conrad Potter Aiken was born in Savannah, Georgia, on August 5, 1889. His father was a wealthy and highly respected physician and brain surgeon. In February 1901, tragedy struck, suddenly and with no apparent reason, when his father murdered Aiken's mother and then shot himself. Aiken, eleven years old at the time, heard the gunshots and discovered the bodies. In his autobiography, *Ushant* (1952), he describes the circumstances of that morning: "…where

Aiken dodged serving in the armed forces during World War I by claiming the "essential industry" exemption because he was a poet. In 1921, he and his wife Jesse moved to England where she gave birth to their three children. However, the two divorced in 1929. In 1927-1928, Aiken tutored English at Harvard. Aiken married again twice but had no more children.

In 1930, Aiken was awarded the Pulitzer Prize for his *Selected Poems* collection. Aiken also produced some works of fiction that included the novels *Blue Voyage* (1927) and *King Coffin* (1934) and a collection of short stories entitled *Bring! Bring!* (1925). His *Among the Lost People* (1934) included the classic "Silent Snow, Secret Snow." His "Mr. Arcularis" from the same collection was adapted to a play in 1957. Aiken's poem "Music I Heard" has been set to music by a number of composers.

Much of Aiken's work is symbolic. His writing includes Freudian concepts as he felt that literature was a means to self-awareness.

the two bodies lay motionless, and apart, and, finding them dead, found himself possessed of them forever." It has been said that Aiken's interest in psychology and the themes found in his work stemmed from that incident.

Aiken was sent to Massachusetts where he was raised by relatives. There he attended private schools before enrolling at Harvard where he met the man who would become his lifelong friend and mentor, T.S. Eliot. Aiken, along with Eliot, was an editor for Harvard's *Advocate*. Placed on academic probation for irregular class attendance during his senior year, Aiken left for Europe but returned and graduated in 1912. After graduation, he married Jesse MacDonald, a graduate student from Canada.

In 1914, he published his first collection of poetry entitled *Earth Triumphant and Other Tales in Verse*. Aiken said he learned his style and what "he felt poetry to be" from George Santayana, a philosopher at Harvard. Between 1916 and 1922, he became a reviewer for *New Republic*, *Poetry*, *Chicago Daily News*, *Poetry Journal* and *Dial*. At *Dial* he was a contributing editor from 1917 to 1918. He published a collection of essays in 1919 entitled *Skepticisms* that dealt with his commitment to literature as a way to reach his own self-understanding.

In 1947, Aiken settled in Brewster, Massachusetts. He became a consultant in poetry for the Library of Congress from 1950 to 1952. In 1953, he published his *Collected Poems*. Aiken enjoyed wintering in Savannah, Georgia, where he stayed next to his childhood home. He died on August 17, 1973, in Savannah. Two daughters became well-known authors.

Much of Aiken's work is symbolic. His writing includes Freudian concepts as he felt that literature was a means to self-awareness. His novel *Great Circle* (1933) was one of Freud's favorites. In his own autobiography (*Ushant*, 1952), he speaks openly about his attempted suicides and fear of insanity as well as his many affairs and marriages.

Aiken received the National Medal for Literature (1969) and the Gold Medal for Poetry (1958) from the National Institute of Arts and Letters. He received a National Book Award (1954) and the Bollingen Prize for Poetry from Yale (1956). He was the first winner of the Shelley Memorial Award given in 1929 by the Poetry Society of America. In 2009, The Library of America included his "Mr. Arcularis" in its *American Fantastic Tales*.

In 1973, the state of Georgia honored him with the title of Poet Laureate. He will always be remembered by his native state as the first Georgia-born author to win a Pulitzer Prize. ■

Gregg Allman

MUSICIAN . RICHMOND HILL

GREGG ALLMAN SAYS THE TERM "Southern rock" is repetitious since rock-and-roll's pioneers hailed from the Deep South—"so 'Southern rock' is like saying 'rock rock' "—but that's the name of the hard-driving, bluesy-rock-jazz sound that he and The Allman Brothers Band pioneered in the early 1970s.

Forty years later, Allman has survived drug and alcohol addictions, is engaged to his future seventh wife, and has developed a solid solo career while also touring with The Allman Brothers Band.

Allman lives on a 4.5-acre estate in Richmond Hill, about 20 miles south of Savannah. "I love Savannah, I love where I live and I also love the people," he told the *Savannah Morning News* in 2011. "I hope I take my last breath here."

middle-aged rockers no longer have the energy to perform. "We'd play for six hours sometimes, start late and end with someone opening the doors and the morning sun shooting into your eyes," he told *USA Today.* "Uncle Bill (Bill Graham, the late promoter and owner of the Fillmore East and West) would just say, 'Hey, go for it, guys.' And we did."

Shortly after *At Fillmore East* was released, 24-year-old Duane was killed in a motorcycle accident in Macon. A year later, Oakley died the same way, just three blocks from where Duane's accident had occurred.

Eat A Peach, a double album released in 1972, was dedicated to Duane. It contained studio sessions recorded before his death,

"I love Savannah, I love where I live and I also love the people, ... I hope I take my last breath here."

Gregory Lenoir Allman was born in Nashville on Dec. 8, 1947, 13 months after his brother Duane. Their father, who was in the U.S. Army, moved the family to Norfolk, Virginia in 1949, and shortly afterwards, was slain by a hitchhiker. That left Geraldine "Mama A" Allman to raise the children. She trained to be an accountant, then moved the family to Daytona Beach, Florida.

Allman—who plays the Hammond organ, guitar and sings—learned at age nine to play chords on a neighbor's guitar, then taught Duane. "Duane and I caught it like an illness," Allman told *Southern Living* magazine. "We didn't eat, we didn't sleep, we didn't think about anything except music."

By 1969, Duane was a session musician playing slide guitar at Fame Studios in Muscle Shoals, Alabama, and had met several future members of The Allman Brothers Band, including Dickey Betts, Berry Oakley, Butch Trucks and Jai Johanny Johanson. Allman was intending to leave music and attend medical school, with hopes of becoming a dental surgeon, but Duane talked him into joining his newly formed band.

Their first two albums didn't sell well, but the third, the double live *At Fillmore East* in 1971, proved to be their breakthrough and was certified gold. Critical acclaim flowed for the band's improvisational style, which featured long jams that often reflected jazz and classical influence.

Allman still reminisces about those long concerts, which the

including Duane's moving "Little Martha" guitar solo, as well as live cuts left over from the Fillmore East session. "Melissa" and "Blue Sky" became instant classics. *Brothers and Sisters* (1973) yielded two more concert favorites, "Ramblin' Man" and "Jessica".

The Allman Brothers Band was considered one of the country's top bands by the mid-1970s. Drug problems and personality differences, however, were tearing the band apart. The band officially broke up in 1976 when Allman testified against his road manager in a federal drug case in exchange for immunity. "The band was long gone before this whole trial thing hit," he told *People* magazine later.

Also fueling tabloid headlines was Allman's marriage to pop singer Cher, who filed for divorce after nine days of marriage because she couldn't deal with his drug and liquor problems. Accounts vary as to whether they divorced, then remarried, but by 1979 the marriage was officially over after having produced one son, Elijah Blue.

Today, Allman is a much-lauded elder statesman of rock. The singer of "I'm No Angel" stopped boozing and drugging in 1996, but nonetheless had to undergo a liver transplant four years later.

He and the band, who eventually reconciled, are in the Rock and Roll Hall of Fame and have received a Grammy Lifetime Achievement Award. Gregg's also in the Georgia Music Hall of Fame, which gave him a Lifetime Achievement Award. ∎

Azkena Rock Festival, 2011.

B-52s

AMERICAN ROCK BAND . ATHENS

THE B-52s ARE CONSIDERED one of the most original bands in the music business. They are credited with launching the Athens music scene, which later introduced a long list of musical groups to the world. R.E.M., Wide Spread Panic and Elephant 6 are only a few. There is no question that the B-52s made their mark on the music industry and are arguably the world's greatest party band.

Their unique presentation sets them apart. *Rolling Stone* described their party music as "stripped-down, off-kilter funk, topped by chirpy vocals and lyrics crammed with 1950s and 1960s trivia." On stage, the group dressed in thrift store apparel and adlibbed lyrics along with recorded music. Most reviewers agreed; the B-52s were the most unlikely pop stars the world had seen.

The B-52s soon developed a cult following in Athens and pressed 2,000 copies of the single "Rock Lobster" that quickly sold out.

Early in 1979 the band signed with Warner Bros. Their first album, *The B-52s*, sold over half a million copies and the band successfully toured North America and Europe, performing for sold-out crowds. 1980's *Wild Planet*, their second album, sold even better and featured songs that were remixed to sound more danceable and reappeared on *Party Mix*, an extended play effort and the group's third major recording.

The B-52s followed up with *Mesopotamia* in 1982 and *Whammy* the following year. Both were critical and commercial successes. In 1985, while recording *Bouncing off the Satellites*,

The B-52s developed a cult following in Athens and pressed 2,000 copies of the single "Rock Lobster" that quickly sold out.

The beehive hairdos of the two female vocalists inspired the name of the band. It was simple: the tops of the women's heads resembled the nose cone of B-52 aircraft.

The group claims it was formed early in 1977 in an Athens Chinese restaurant after the five original members consumed several Flaming Volcano drinks. In the party were: Cindy Wilson, vocalist; her brother Ricky Wilson, guitarist; organist and vocalist Kate Pierson; drummer Keith Strickland and cowbell player/vocalist Fred Schneider. After a few drinks they gave an impromptu performance and some of the diners seemed impressed.

The B-52s, as they were originally known (they would later drop the apostrophe) gave their first concert on February 14, 1977, at a Valentine's Day party. The five soon started borrowing the Wilson family station wagon for gigs at New Wave clubs; their first official paid gig was at Max's Kansas City in New York.

The group's onstage presence was something no one had seen. The women wore thrift shop mini skirts and go-go boots to complement their wild mile-high hair and the men demonstrated impromptu dance steps while the entire band played toy instruments.

Ricky Wilson died of AIDS and the remaining band members were devastated by his death. The album was released in 1986 but did not sell as well; the B-52s did not record again for three years.

The next album, *Cosmic Thing*, released in 1989, gave the band their largest commercial success. Three singles received substantial radio airplay: "Deadbeat Club," "Love Shack" and "Roam." *Cosmic Thing* sold more than five million copies and made it to number three on the Billboard chart.

The B-52s came back to Athens to perform a 34th anniversary concert in February of 2011 at the Classic Center. The concert was filmed and recorded. The result, *With the Wild Crowd! Live in Athens, GA* was released in October of the same year and the DVD was released in 2012.

The band still has a heavy touring schedule and play 50-60 live shows in large venues each year. The touring band features: Sterling Campbell, former member of Duran Duran, on drums; Paul Gordon on keyboards and guitar and Tracy Wormworth on bass.

After more than thirty years, The B-52s are soaring into their fourth decade of entertaining crowds. ∎

Photo courtesy of the B52s.

Kim Basinger

ACTRESS . ATHENS

FOR A WOMAN WHO WAS SO WITHDRAWN as a child that her parents had her tested for autism and who has said she would face the wall in a restaurant rather than the other people eating there, Athens native Kim Basinger's life has been anything but private. In an industry that often overlooks actresses past the age of 40, Basinger remains one of Hollywood's elite—and working—stars.

Born December 8, 1953, Basinger's father Donald was a big band musician and a loan manager and her mother Ann was a model, actress and swimmer who appeared in several Esther Williams films. Basinger studied ballet from her toddler years until her mid-teens. At 16, winning the Athens Junior Miss contest and the title "Junior Miss Georgia" jump-started a modeling career. She competed in the national Junior Miss pageant and was offered a modeling contract with the prestigious Ford Modeling Agency, turning it down at first but reconsidering and finally signing with the firm. Over the next several years in the early 1970s, while living in New York City, she appeared on dozens of magazine covers and in hundreds of ads, best known perhaps as the Breck Shampoo Girl. All the while, she was taking acting lessons at the Neighborhood Playhouse and performing in Greenwich Village nightclubs with ambitions to become an actress.

In 1976, Basinger left Ford and moved to Los Angeles to pursue that acting career. Living in a low-rent apartment with a view of the freeway, she survived on her savings while trying to find work. Initially she landed roles in television shows including *The Six Million Dollar Man, McMillan and Wife*, the original *Charlie's Angels* and a starring role on the very short-lived *Dog and Cat*, in which she played a rookie female cop. After a few made-for-television movies and posing in a nude pictorial for *Playboy*, she starred in the 1981 low-budget film *Hard Country* with Jan Michael Vincent, portraying a young, small-town Texas woman desperate to move to the big city. While filming, she met and married one of the make-up crew's workers, Ron Britton.

Basinger continued working in B films for the next couple of years until finally getting her big break playing James Bond girl Domino Petachi opposite Sean Connery in his last Bond film, *Never Say Never*. The following year, she won a Golden Globe Award nomination for Best Supporting Actress in the blockbuster baseball film *The Natural* with Robert Redford and Glenn Close. In 1986, Basinger made more headlines when she starred with Micky Rourke in the controversial, sexually charged drama *9 ½ Weeks*, playing a SoHo art gallery dealer who becomes involved in a sadomasochistic relationship with a Wall Street broker who eventually drives her into an emotional breakdown. She enjoyed more success playing the lead role in 1987's *Nadine* with Jeff Bridges and Vicki Vale in Tim Burton's 1989 *Batman*. It was the next year, however, that would change her life forever.

"In, 1989, Basinger paid $20 million for the town of Braselton, about 10 miles outside Athens."

Having divorced Britton in 1989, Basinger met actor Alec Baldwin on the set of *The Marrying Man* in 1990 and married him in 1993. She starred with him the following year in a remake of *The Getaway*. Basinger and Baldwin were one of the hottest couples in Hollywood, their lives scrutinized by the tabloids. When their daughter Ireland was born in 1995, Baldwin famously scuffled with a photographer but was later acquitted of misdemeanor battery charges. Basinger grabbed more headlines in 1997 when she won the Academy Award for Best Supporting Actress, playing a high-priced call girl based on Veronica Lake in *L.A. Confidential*.

In 1989, Basinger paid $20 million for the town of Braselton, about 10 miles outside Athens, at the urging of her family and with the intent to restore many of the structures and build a movie studio in order to increase tourism and industry. Not long after this, she made news again when she was sued for $8.1 million for breach of contract for backing out of the movie *Boxing Helena*, in which she would have played a woman whose arms and legs were amputated by a doctor who was obsessed with her. She filed for bankruptcy, sold off parts of the town, and eventually settled with the studio for $3.1 million.

Basinger and Baldwin divorced in 2002 and have since been in one of the nastiest public custody battles in Hollywood history over their daughter Ireland. Basinger continues acting and campaigning against animal cruelty and the use of fur in clothing. ■

Kim Basinger at the Los Angeles premiere of her movie Cellular. *September 9, 2004*

Alton Brown

AUTHOR, CHEF, TELEVISION PERSONALITY . ATLANTA

ALTHOUGH BORN IN LOS ANGELES, Alton Brown has lived in Atlanta for most of his professional life. Known best as the creator, writer and star of *Good Eats*, the Peabody Award winning show airing on the Food Network in production from 1999–2011, he is also a multiple award winning author, a commentator on another of the Food Network's most successful offerings, *Iron Chef America*, and the co-host of another of the network's shows, *The Next Iron Chef*.

Brown says his interest in cooking began early in life as he enjoyed cooking with both his mother and grandmother. Watching them at work kindled his interest in the science of cooking—or how things work in the kitchen.

Brown's first career was in the film industry, where he spent more than a decade as a cinematographer and video director. His

which won a James Beard Foundation Award. His book *Alton Brown's Gear for Your Kitchen*, published by Stewart, Tabori and Chang (STC), was nominated for both a James Beard and IACP Cookbook Award the following year. Not one to be idle with his time, in 2003 STC released *I'm Just Here for More Food: Food x Mixing + Heat = Baking*, which soon became a *New York Times* Best Seller.

An avid motorcycle enthusiast, his fourth book, *Feasting on Asphalt*, was published in 2008 by CST and documented his motorcycle trip from New Orleans to Minnesota, in which he sampled roadside eateries along the footprint of the Mississippi River.

Living by his motto "There is no bad food, only bad food habits," Brown lost more than 50 pounds in 2009 and, to date, has kept it off for more than three years. In 2011, he documented his weight loss in an episode of *Good Eats,* "Live and Let Diet" in which he

Brown says his interest in cooking began early in life as he enjoyed cooking with both his mother and grandmother. Watching them at work kindled his interest in the science of cooking—or how things work in the kitchen.

work seemed boring and he filled his free time watching cooking shows. Thinking he could improve on the genre, he entered the New England Culinary Institute at the age of 34.

Although he graduated in 1995, in culinary school he reportedly annoyed his instructors by interrupting lectures and demonstrations with questions of how ingredients worked within individual recipes. This inquisitiveness eventually led to Brown's science-based approach to cooking. His entertaining yet educational style resulted in him being labeled "The Culinary Version of Mr. Wizard."

The New England Culinary Institute reports they now get applications from potential students stating they "want to learn to cook like Alton Brown."

In 2004, *Bon Appétit* named him "Cooking Teacher of the Year."

Brown's successful writing career begin in 2002 with his first book, *I'm Just Here for the Food*, published by Tabori & Chang,

divided all food into four basic groups: those to eat every day, three times a week, once a week, and those to never consume. Brown says adhering to those simple rules helped him to lose more than 50 pounds without going on a diet.

Although *Good Eats* aired it's last episode in 2011, Brown has written three cookbooks based on the show: *Good Eats: the Early Years* in 2009, *Good Eats 2: The Middle Years* in 2010 and *Good Eats 3: The Later Years* in 2011.

Brown is currently living in Atlanta wife Deanna, daughter Zoey and his beloved basset mix Matilida. He has signed a contract extending his relationship with the Food Network for three years, and is currently working, as usual, on many other projects. He is a frequent contributor to *Bon Appétit, Atlanta Magazine* and *Men's Journal*.

Who knows what he'll cook up next? ∎

Alton Brown's Blueberry Buckle, shown above.

James Brown

SINGER, SONGWRITER, MUSICIAN, & RECORDING ARTIST . AUGUSTA . 1933 – 2006

James Brown during the concert at the castle of Vigevano on July 21, 2006 in Milan, Italy.

"I FEEL GOOD!" sang James Brown, "the hardest working man in show buisness," "soul brother number one" and "the godfather of soul." This highly influential soul singer, who grew up in Augusta, Georgia, made his audiences feel good. So good, in fact, that he was a charter inductee into the Rock and Roll Hall of Fame in 1986.

Born into an impoverished family in South Carolina (dates of his birth vary from the late 1920s to 1933), Brown moved with his father to Augusta at a young age. As a boy, Brown employed himself in various ways: performing music, shining shoes and stealing. At 16, he was convicted of robbery and sentenced to several years in a juvenile prison.

Brown believed in giving his audience its money's worth, and more.

While incarcerated, Brown met a visiting musical performer, Bobby Byrd. Byrd was impressed with Brown's musical talent and Byrd's family helped secure Brown's release from prison. After that, Brown and Byrd performed in a gospel group for a time but, after attending a pop music concert, they renamed their band the Flames and shifted to pop music.

The Flames, later named the Famous Flames, toured the South, performing for African-American audiences and establishing a following. In 1956, the Flames were signed to Federal Records and began recording. Influenced heavily by Little Richard, they cut the single "Please, Please, Please" which was a big seller. More hits were to follow.

In 1962, Brown disagreed with his record label about the wisdom of recording a live album. The label said "no" so Brown financed the project himself, recording "Live at the Apollo" in the famed venue in Harlem and earning for himself a big hit.

Brown's musical style originally was gospel but he soon moved to rhythm and blues, eventually creating his own style of music: "funk." His music was to influence different genres of pop music, from jazz to R&B to soul to rock. *Rolling Stone magazine* called him the most important musician in rock music, period. Michael Jackson said Brown was his greatest influence. Brown's musical style highly influenced hip hop (or rap) music.

Brown believed in giving his audience its money's worth, and more. He dressed dramatically wearing a cape and dancing with seemingly endless energy and employed a band dressed "to the nines" and dancing as well. In many of his shows, Brown would feign exhaustion or fainting and be taken from the stage, only to throw off his cape and return to the microphone for more entertaining.

In the mid-'60s, "I Got You (I Feel Good)" and "Papa's Got A Brand New Bag" went to the top of the R&B charts and high on the pop charts. Brown, for some time, was considered the most successful African American in America, with high earnings from his recordings and performances and the purchase of radio stations and a private airplane.

When Dr. Martin Luther King, Jr. was assassinated on April 4, 1968, Brown was credited with quelling rioting by allowing his concert in Boston to be televised and by calling for calm. He also spoke to people about working hard to provide for themselves.

In the late 1960s, he recorded "Say It Loud (I'm Black and I'm Proud)," lending his voice to the Civil Rights movement and the pride and dignity of African Americans. Brown was invited to the White House by President Lyndon Johnson. He later was honored for his lifetime achievements in an event at the Kennedy Center.

Among Brown's hits over the years, in addition to those already mentioned, were: "Bewildered," "I Don't Mind," "Lost Someone," "Out of Sight," "It's a Man's, Man's, Man's World," "Mother Popcorn" and many more.

The popularity of Brown's music waned in the late 1970s with the arrival of disco. Brown rolled with the punches, making his own recordings with a disco sound. In 1986, director and actor Sylvester Stallone requested that Brown contribute a song to his "Rocky IV" movie. The resulting "Living in America" earned Brown a Grammy Award.

A controversial figure, Brown was arrested and imprisoned for crimes including spousal abuse, resisting arrest and drug possession. Upon release from incarceration, however, he continued his musical career. In 2006, he and his band went on a world tour.

On Christmas Day 2006, James Brown died of congestive heart faulure. A memorial service was held in Harlem and a public service was held later in Augusta. His influence on the world of pop music is securely established. ■

Ray Charles

SINGER, PIANIST, COMPOSER . ALBANY . 1930 – 2004

ROLLING STONE MAGAZINE ranked Ray Charles as number two on their 2008 list of the "100 Greatest Singers of All Time." An accomplished singer, pianist, composer and bandleader, he gave soul music to the world.

Ray Norman Charles was born in Albany, Georgia, on September 23, 1930. His family moved to Greenville, Florida, when Charles was an infant. When he was five, he began playing the piano at a local restaurant. Tragedy struck when his younger brother drowned in the bathtub and when Charles himself became completely blind by age seven as a suspected result of glaucoma. His mother always insisted that Ray continue to do his chores amid protests from neighbors. She told them her son was blind, not stupid, and needed to learn to take care of himself.

Charles attended the Florida School for the Deaf and Blind (1937-1945) where he developed his musical talent as the school's premier musician. Although learning classical music, Charles longed to play the jazz and blues sounds that he heard on the radio. When Charles was ten, his father died. His mother died from cancer when he was fifteen. An orphan, he lived with friends of his mother.

Charles left school and played for bands around the area. He played with The Florida Playboys where began his habit of wearing sunglasses. Charles decided to leave Florida and moved to Seattle in 1947. His first friend was a young man named Quincy Jones. In 1949, Charles recorded for the Down Beat label, achieving his first hit with "Confession Blues." He moved to Swing Time Records recording the hits "Baby, Let Me Hold Your Hand" (1951) and "Kissa Me Baby" (1952).

Charles moved to Atlantic Records where he garnered national acclaim in 1954 with "I Got a Woman." He went on to score big with such hits as "The Night Time Is the Right Time" (1958). His combination of the blues with the sounds of gospel marked the beginning of a new field of music—"soul."

Charles' next hit, "What'd I Say" (1959), became a pop crossover success. ABC Paramount Records made him a financial offer he could not refuse, plus ownership of his masters. In 1960, he won Grammy Awards for "Georgia on My Mind" and "Hit the Road Jack." By 1961, Charles had expanded his back-up ensemble into a large road band as a result of the creative control he was given, which was not the norm for black musicians of that era.

In 1962, his albums *Modern Sounds in Country and Western*

Music (Vol. 1 & 2) brought country music into the mainstream. His version of "I Can't Stop Loving You" remained on the pop charts for five weeks and was number one on the R&B charts for ten weeks. That same year, he founded Tangerine Records where he produced major hits such as "Busted" (1963).

In the mid-1960s, Charles was arrested for the third time for possession of cocaine. He avoided jail time by entering rehab for his nearly twenty-year-long addiction. He was on parole when his single "Crying Time" (1966) reached number six on the charts.

In 1986, he founded The Ray Charles Foundation to provide support in education and hearing disorders for young people.

In the late 1960s and early 1970s, his hits became sporadic even though he worked with singers like Stevie Wonder. His popular version of "Georgia On My Mind" was designated as the state song on April 24, 1979, and he was asked to perform it for the state legislature.

To attract a younger audience, Charles hosted *Saturday Night Live* in 1977. In 1980, he made a cameo appearance in *The Blues Brothers* and in 1986, he sang "America the Beautiful" at *Wrestlemania 2*. His Pepsi commercial made him a hit with the catchphrase, "You Got the Right One, Baby!"

In 1986, he founded The Ray Charles Foundation to provide support in education and hearing disorders for young people. Charles received seventeen Grammys and the Grammy Lifetime Achievement Award. He received Sweden's most prestigious music award (Polar Music Prize) and the National Medal of Arts. In 1986, he was inducted into the Rock and Roll Hall of Fame and received The Kennedy Center Honors. A statue of him is located in the Ray Charles Plaza in Albany, Georgia.

Ray Charles was married twice and had twelve children with nine different women. He died in June 2004 at age 73 from liver disease. His album, *Genius Loves Company*, was released posthumously in 2004 and won eight Grammy Awards. In 2010, the Ray Charles Memorial Library opened its doors as a tribute to the music and life of the "father of soul." ■

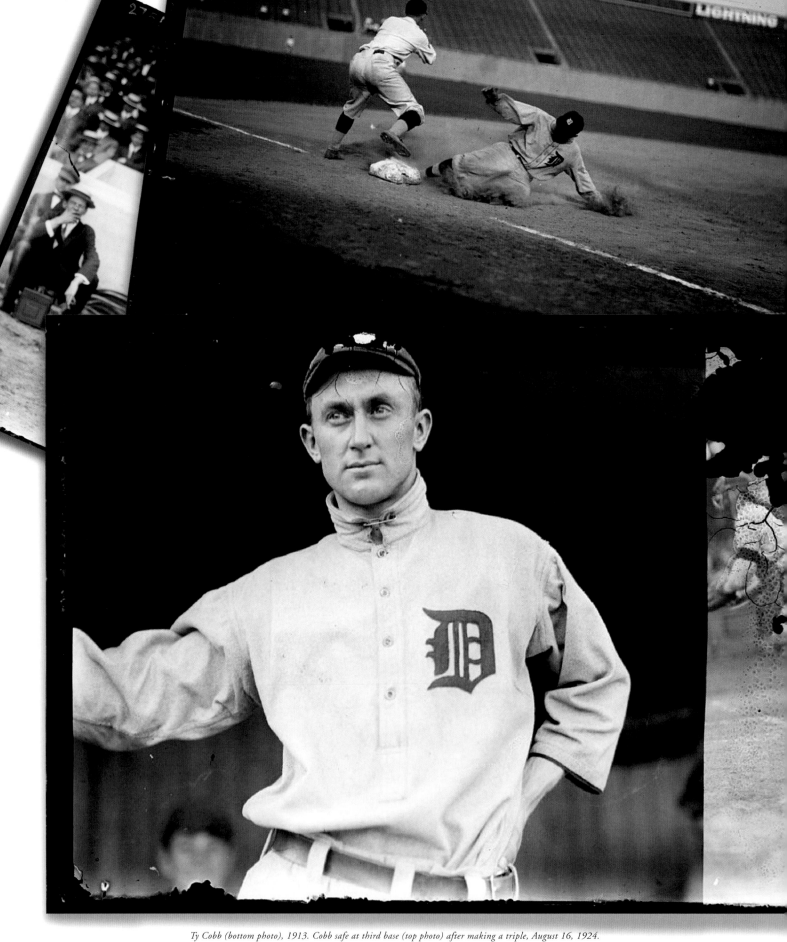

Ty Cobb (bottom photo), 1913. Cobb safe at third base (top photo) after making a triple, August 16, 1924.
Courtesy of the Library of Congress Prints & Photographs Division (Gift from Herbert A. French, 1947).

Ty Cobb

BASEBALL LEGEND . NARROWS . 1886 – 1961

TY COBB, NICKNAMED "THE GEORGIA PEACH," is considered to be the greatest baseball player of all time and is credited with setting ninety baseball records during his career. Even though his teammates disliked him personally, they respected his skills as a teammate. Cobb was born in Narrows, Georgia, on December 18, 1886.

Cobb's mother came from a prominent family and married his father before she was sixteen. His father was a school teacher and state senator who expected Cobb to attend college and become a professional. Young Ty preferred baseball to books, and his

achieve this success, he practiced sliding into bases until his legs were raw and during the winter months, he would hunt wearing weighted boots to strengthen his legs.

From 1921 to 1926, Cobb was the player/manager of the Detroit Tigers. Even though the team improved under his management, it was never a contender in the pennant race. When Cobb retired in 1926, it was amidst allegations that he conspired, along with the manager and former pitcher of the Cleveland Naps, to throw a game. In 1927, the baseball commissioner ruled there was not enough evidence to support the allegations.

"Baseball is a red-blooded sport for red-blooded men. It's no pink tea, and mollycoddles better stay out. It's a struggle for supremacy, survival of the fittest." — Ty Cobb

father relented and let him choose his own path. Tragedy struck in 1905 when his mother shot his father, thinking he was a burglar. Suspecting infidelity, his father was reportedly spying on her from the roof of the home when he received the fatal gunshot wound.

That same year, Cobb was playing for the South Atlantic League in Augusta, Georgia. He was traded to the American League and sent to Detroit where he did not take well to the hazing given to all rookie players and got into several fights with his teammates. Cobb appeared to hate anyone who was different from him, including Catholics, blacks, and northerners. As a player, he was aggressive and intimidating with an obsessive need to succeed.

In 1907, Cobb had a season high with a .350 batting average, 212 hits, 49 steals, and 119 RBI's. In 1907-1909, Cobb helped lead Detroit to three American League pennants. He became the youngest player to win a batting championship at age twenty. In 1909, the same year he won the Triple Crown, he received death threats from Cleveland A fans for spiking one of their players at third base. He was also arrested for assaulting the black night watchman at the Cleveland Hotel. On May 15, 1912, he dove into the stands to attack a heckler who was disabled. He was suspended by AL President Ban Johnson.

Despite his anger issues, from the time Cobb won the Triple Crown until Babe Ruth came on the scene in 1914, he was acknowledged as the best man to ever play the game of baseball. Two of his best years included 1911 when he led the league in every offensive category, and in 1915 when he stole 96 bases. To

Afterwards, Cobb signed on with the Philadelphia Athletics where he stayed for two years before retiring. Cobb was able to live a life of leisure because of his shrewd investments. One of these investments was the purchase of stock in a small company called Coca-Cola. However, in spite of his wealth, his life after baseball was less than ideal. He and his first wife Charlie Cobb divorced after 39 years of marriage. He remarried in 1949—divorced in 1956. His relationship with the five children from his first marriage was always strained. Sadly, two of his three sons died young.

Cobb was inducted in the Baseball Hall of Fame in 1936 receiving 222 of the 226 votes, outpolling Babe Ruth. By this time Cobb had started smoking and drinking heavily. By 1950, his health was extremely poor. In 1959, he was diagnosed with a degenerative kidney disorder, prostate cancer, diabetes and high blood pressure. It was at this time that he and writer Al Stump wrote Cobb's autobiography, *My Life in Baseball: The True Record* (1961).

Cobb died on July 17, 1961, at Emory University Hospital. His estate was reported to be worth twelve-million dollars. Part of his estate went to fund the Cobb Educational Fund, established in 1953, to provide academic scholarships for needy students of Georgia. The Cobb Memorial Hospital was built as the result of a $100,000 donation in memory of his parents and has grown into the Ty Cobb Healthcare System. In 1998, the Ty Cobb Museum opened in Royston, Georgia.

As of 2012, Cobb still holds several records including the highest career batting average and the most career batting titles. ■

Pat Conroy

WRITER . ATLANTA

Photo courtesy of Mariia Kravtsova at Kalamazoo Valley Community College.

PAT CONROY WRITES ABOUT SURVIVORS. He writes about abusive fathers, corrupt institutions, overly protective mothers and a gamut of issues that challenge the status quo. Many of his novels and memoirs have made the *New York Times* Best Seller list and two were made into Oscar-nominated films.

Donald Patrick Conroy was born in Atlanta, Georgia, on October 26, 1945. Growing up in a military family and one of seven children, he moved twenty-three times before he was eighteen. His father, a Marine Corp pilot, was physically and emotionally abusive to his family. Evidence of this appears in much of his writing, especially *The Great Santini*.

Conroy graduated from The Citadel Military School in South Carolina where he got the inspiration for his first novel, *The Boo* (1970). The self-published novel is a tribute to his favorite teacher and centers on cadet life. After the Citadel, Conroy taught English in Beaufort, South Carolina, where he met and married Barbara Jones, a widow with two young sons whom he adopted. Conroy then accepted a position teaching underprivileged children in a one-room schoolhouse on Daufauskie Island.

Conroy was fired from this position for his unconventional teaching practices, lack of respect for the administration and his refusal to administer corporal punishment. However, Conroy got the last word with the publication of the book *The Water is Wide* (1972) in which he exposed the racism and distressing conditions at the school. The book was made into a feature film entitled *Conrack*, starring Jon Voight. Conroy received a humanitarian award from the National Education Association.

After the birth of their daughter, the Conroys moved to Atlanta. In 1976, he wrote the autobiographical novel *The Great Santini*. Reflecting on his life, Conroy told interviewer Amy Reichert of the *San Francisco Focus* (December 1991): "What got left out of my childhood is that no one taught me how to love. Love in my family came with fists…I don't have a clue what love is about."

The book caused dissention within the Conroy family and eventually led to the failure of his marriage in 1977. His mother presented the book to the judge at her own divorce proceedings against Conroy's father. Ironically, the book helped to mend Conroy's relationship with his father. In 1979, the novel was made into a film with actor Robert Duvall in the lead role.

Conroy's next book, *The Lords of Discipline* (1980), exposed the Citadel's harsh military discipline. Even though he had success academically and athletically, the school reminded him of his father's abusive and domineering actions. This book also caused friction and upset many of the school's graduates. It was also made into a feature film.

Conroy remarried in 1981 and moved to Rome, Georgia. His second wife also had two children, and she and Conroy had a daughter together. This marriage too ended in divorce in 1995. In the meantime, Conroy published what is considered his most acclaimed novel, *The Prince of Tides* (1986). Barbra Streisand directed and starred in the film based on the book. Her co-star, Nick Nolte, received an Oscar nomination. The book has over five million copies in print.

"What got left out of my childhood is that no one taught me how to love."

Conroy's next book, *Beach Music* (1995), also became an international best seller. While on book signings throughout the country, members of his former Citadel basketball team began to show up. The result of these reconnections inspired him to write *My Losing Season*, a non-fiction novel based upon his last year as an athlete and the game that changed his life.

The following book was a departure from the trauma and insecurities of his own upbringing. The novel *South of Broad* (2009) presents a central character with a lovable father figure and celebrates lifelong friendships. One of his projects, *The Pat Conroy Cookbook* (2004), is a collection of his favorite recipes, stories of his life growing up in South Carolina and the people, places and great meals he has encountered.

In 1999, Conroy received the Stanley W. Lindberg Award for his significant contributions to the literary heritage of Georgia. In 2005, he was inducted into the Georgia Writers Hall of Fame. He was inducted into the South Carolina Hall of Fame in 2009. In 2010, he released *My Reading Life*, which takes readers on a journey showing how books shaped his life and world-view and created the consummate storyteller that we know today.

Pat Conroy married best-selling novelist Cassandra King in 1997. They presently live on Fripp Island in South Carolina. ■

Ossie Davis

ACTOR, DIRECTOR, ACTIVIST . COGDELL . 1917 – 2005

OSSIE DAVIS WAS A MAN OF many accomplishments. In a career that spanned more than 50 years, he was a gifted actor, director, producer, screenwriter and playwright. He was admired for his social and civil rights activism.

Born Raiford Chatman Davis on December 18, 1917, in Cogdell, Georgia, he got the name "Ossie" when a county clerk misunderstood his mother's pronunciation of the initials R.C. when registering his birth. The name stuck. Davis experienced racism early in life when his father, a railroad engineer, suffered threats from the Ku Klux Klan who believed he had a job too advanced for a black man.

At his parents' request, Davis enrolled in Howard University in Washington, D.C., but dropped out in 1939 to pursue an acting career in New York. In 1942, he enlisted in the army and was honorably discharged after three years. While in the army, he wrote and acted in shows for the troops.

Davis made his acting debut in the Broadway play *Jeb* in 1946. Here he met the vibrant and talented Ruby Dee whom he married in 1948. The two acted together frequently and were credited with providing opportunities for generations of minority actors through the production company Davis founded in the 1970s—Third World Cinema. Davis made his screen debut, along with Sidney Poitier, in the movie *No Way Out* (1950).

Like most black actors at that time, Davis met with the usual typecasting. He was offered roles as a porter or butler. However, in the 1960s, when television began to feature more black actors, Davis appeared in *Seven Times Monday* (1962) and *The Outsider* (1967). He also made regular guest appearances on *The Defenders* (1961-1965). His film career also on the rise, Davis appeared in *The Cardinal* (1963), *The Hill* (1965), *Shock Treatment* (1965) and *A Man Called Adam* (1966).

Davis wrote the successful Broadway musical *Purlie Victorious* (1961) in which he starred with his wife Ruby. He later adapted the musical to a screenplay for the film *Gone Are the Days* (1963) in which he played a leading role. He wrote and also directed the films *Cotton Comes to Harlem* (1973) and *Countdown to Kusini* (1976).

During the 1960s, Davis and wife Ruby were active in the civil rights movement and counted Jesse Jackson, Malcolm X and Martin Luther King, Jr. among their friends. They were leading organizers in the March on Washington in 1963. Davis helped raise money for the Freedom Riders and was arrested himself in the South for violating segregation laws. He also sued in federal court to secure voting rights for African Americans. Davis delivered a eulogy at the funeral of Malcolm X and gave a stirring tribute to Dr. Martin Luther King, Jr. in New York City following King's death in 1968.

In the 1970s, Davis published a children's play entitled *Escape to Freedom: A Play about Young Frederick Douglas*. In later years he published *Langston, a Play* (1982) and *Just Like Martin* (1992).

Davis' rich baritone voice kept him in demand as a voice-over artist.

Davis had a role in the popular miniseries *Roots: The Next Generation* (1979) and collaborated with Spike Lee on several films including *Do the Right Thing* (1989) and *Malcolm X* (1992) where Davis recreated the eulogy he had given at the funeral of the civil rights leader.

Davis' rich baritone voice kept him in demand as a voice-over artist. In the 1990s, he served as the narrator of the popular sitcom *Evening Shade*, starring Burt Reynolds. Davis' last role was in Showtime's controversial sitcom, *The L Word* (2004-2009). Davis' character died in an episode that was his final performance before his own death, and the episode was dedicated to him.

Ossie Davis died in February 2005 while working on a film in Miami Beach. He was 87. Davis and wife Ruby Dee received the National Medal of Arts award in 1995 and the Kennedy Center Honors in 2004. They were inducted into the NAACP Image Awards Hall of Fame in 1989. In 2001, Davis and Dee were awarded The Lifetime Achievement Award by the Screen Actors Guild.

Davis and Dee had three children. Their son Guy Davis is an actor and blues musician. On their 50th wedding anniversary, the couple published their autobiography, *In This Life Together* (1998).

Burt Reynolds on Davis' death: "Since the loss of my father, no other man has come close to representing the kind of man I hope to be some day. I know he's sitting next to God now, and I know God envies that voice." ∎

Ossie Davis promotional photo.

Paula Deen

CULINARY QUEEN OF MULTIMEDIA . SAVANNAH

BUBBLY, DOWN-HOME PAULA DEEN OVERCAME poverty, divorce and agoraphobia to burst onto television screens in 2002 with *Paula's Home Cooking*. Ten years later, the sassy Albany native has written 14 cookbooks, has a bimonthly magazine, multiple television shows, more than 15 product lines and owns several Southern-style restaurants.

"No one had better get between a fat girl and her food," the ample Paula has quipped during her cooking demonstrations on Food Network, delighting audiences with her genuineness.

The butter-loving chef has been criticized by health advocates for the high-calorie comfort food she whips up, but Paula has retorted, "I'm your cook, not your doctor" and "You know, I am so sick of cuttin' on my television and everyone on it is obsessed with livin' forever. Well, I have a news flash: Ain't none of us gettin' out of here alive."

Born Jan. 19, 1947, Deen grew up living behind her family's gas station and souvenir shop in Albany. They had no plumbing, so the family bathed in the gas station's restrooms. By the time she was 23, both of her parents had died. Then, her marriage to her high school sweetheart began crumbling and Deen developed agoraphobia, making her afraid to leave the house. After a 1989 divorce left her with two sons and little money, Paula knew she had to do something. Her solution was "The Bag Lady," a home-based catering service with sons Jamie and Bobby serving as sandwich deliverymen.

As the business grew, Deen moved from her kitchen to a full-service restaurant named The Lady at a Best Western hotel. There, daily interaction with guests eventually helped her overcome the agoraphobia. She left the Best Western in 1996 to open The Lady & Sons in downtown Savannah.

Deen's hungry customers followed her to the new location and she developed new fans with the publication of *The Lady & Sons Savannah Country Cookbook*. The cookbook led to a television appearance on QVC, where her warmth shone through.

Paula's Home Cooking, which showcased her cooking and lively personality, was such a hit after its 2002 launch that Food Network signed Deen to do a second show, *Paula's Party*, in 2006. Jamie and Bobby appeared on their mother's shows and eventually were given their own, *Road Tasted*, in which they drove around the country in search of delectable food. Her personal life was also flourishing; Deen married tugboat captain Michael Groover in 2004.

In the book *Paula Deen: It Ain't All About the Cookin'*, Deen attributes her early television success to the fact that "I was not a size two, but instead a sassy, roundish, white-headed cook. Women could identify with me... I could be them, and they could be me."

Today, trying to count Deen's numerous business interests is like trying to count the number of times she says "y'all" during a taping. The two-time Emmy winner stays busy appearing on *Paula's Home Cooking* and *Paula's Best Dishes*. She still owns The Lady & Sons as well as co-owns Uncle Bubba's Oyster House in Savannah with her brother, Earl "Bubba" Hiers. Then there's Paula Deen Buffets at Harrah's Tunica in Mississippi and Horseshoe in southern Indiana, as well as full-service restaurants at Harrah's Cherokee and Harrah's Joliet. Fans can live the full Paula Deen lifestyle by buying her own cookware, bakeware, dishes, furniture, greeting cards, T-shirts and candles!

The one dark spot in her empire came in early 2012, when Paula told *The Today Show* that she had had type 2 diabetes, a disease often caused by eating the many high-calorie, fat-filled meals that

"I was taught (to cook) by my grandmother and nothing I can do would change that."

she famously cooks, for three years and that she was endorsing a diabetes drug. That revelation prompted some people to accuse Deen of being a hypocrite for continuing to promote fattening meals and for profiting from her disease.

She acknowledged the critics in another *Today* interview a month later. "I think [the criticism] was from a few people that were kinda mean about it and wanted to hold it against me, but you know what? The people that care for me, Al, they came out like you wouldn't believe and they are the people that I care about."

Deen told *The Associated Press* that she was not going to change her cooking style, and that people should practice moderation. "I'm Southern by roots," she said. "I was taught (to cook) by my grandmother and nothing I can do would change that." ∎

Photo courtesy of Scripps Network.

AWARD-WINNING AUTHOR James Dickey achieved great fame in 1972 when his first novel, *Deliverance,* was made into a gripping hit movie starring Burt Reynolds and Jon Voight. His forte, however, was poetry, which Dickey taught at various U.S. colleges before settling down to a decades-long stint as the University of South Carolina's poet-in-residence.

"Hunger, time and the moon:/The moon lying on the brain/as on the excited sea as on/The strength of fields. Lord, let me shake/With purpose," he recited at the 1977 presidential inauguration of Georgia would have two sons. Dickey taught for a year at the University of Florida before abandoning academia for a more lucrative career in advertising. At age 33, he became a copywriter for McCann-Ericson in Manhattan, then jumped among several Atlanta ad agencies. The future Library of Congress poetry consultant (later referred to as poet laureate) churned out prose hailing the virtues of Coca-Cola, potato chips, fertilizer and Delta Airlines while continuing to write poetry in his spare time.

Dickey's first poetry collection, *Into the Stone and Other Poems,*

James Dickey

WRITER . ATLANTA . 1923 – 1997

native Jimmy Carter. "Wild hope can always spring/From tended strength. Everything is in that./That and nothing but kindness. More kindness, dear Lord/ Of the renewing green. That is where it all has to start:/With the simplest things. More kindness will do nothing less/ Than save every sleeping one/And night-walking one/Of us./My life belongs to the world. I will do what I can."

Dickey, the son of an attorney, was born Feb. 2, 1923, in Buckhead, then an Atlanta suburb. After graduating from North Fulton High School in 1941, he attended a semester at Clemson A&M (now Clemson University) where he was a tailback on the football team. An avid risk-taker, Dickey also pursued archery, canoeing and weight lifting as well as guitar and banjo playing.

In 1942, Dickey enlisted in the Army Air Corps and joined the 418th Night Fighter Squadron, for which he flew about 100 combat missions in the South Pacific. Upon his return stateside, Dickey attended Vanderbilt University, where he began writing poetry and was published in the campus literary magazine.

Armed with bachelor's and master's degrees in English from Vanderbilt, he taught English for a short time at Rice Institute (now Rice University) in Houston before being recalled to active military duty during the Korean War.

His wartime experiences were a theme often explored in Dickey's poetry. *The Firebombing,* for example, was told from the perspective of a World War II pilot: "...when those on Earth/Die there is not even sound; one is cool and enthralled in the cockpit/Turned blue by the power of beauty/...this detachment/The honored aesthetic evil..."

In 1954, Dickey received the first of many literary honors when the *Sewanee Review* awarded him a $3,500 fellowship that funded a year of poetry writing in Europe.

By this time, he was married to Maxine Syerson, with whom he was published in 1960. After he left advertising, a Guggenheim Fellowship took Dickey to Italy, where he wrote *Drowning with Others. Buckdancer's Choice* received the National Book Award in 1966.

Poets on Poetry, edited by Howard Nemerov, quotes Dickey as saying: "I came to poetry with no particular qualifications. I had begun to suspect, however, that there is a poet...buried in every human being...and that the people whom we are pleased to call poets are only those who have felt the need and contrived the means to release this spirit from its prison."

Dickey was a poet-in-residence at Reed College, San Fernando Valley State College, the University of Wisconsin and Washington University before he settled into a 29-year stint as an English professor and poet-in-residence at the University of South Carolina in Columbia.

Various profiles describe Dickey as a big, swaggering, hard-drinking professor who was particularly popular among women—an athlete and intellectual as well as a teller of tall tales.

His 20 volumes of poetry probed death and grief, civilization's alienation from nature, the worlds of football players and hunters, as well as the meaning of existence. "Poetry is, I think, the highest medium that mankind has ever come up with," Dickey stated in a 1981 interview. "It's language itself, which is a miraculous medium which makes everything else that man has ever done possible."

The 1970 publication of *Deliverance,* a best-selling novel about four middle-class Atlantan men on a weekend canoe trip that turns violent, and a subsequent movie based upon it, put Dickey on the map of popular culture. None of his other books ever received the same critical or commercial acclaim.

Dickey's wife died in October 1976. He married one of his students, Deborah Dodson, two months later and the couple had one daughter. Dickey died Jan. 19, 1997, at age 73. ∎

"Poetry is, I think, the highest medium that mankind has ever come up with.
It's language itself, which is a miraculous medium which makes everything else that
man has ever done possible."

Dickey behind his desk, 1984.

Vince Dooley

LEGENDARY FOOTBALL COACH . ATHENS

Photo courtesy of the University of Georgia.

GEORGIA FOOTBALL, VINCE DOOLEY. VINCE DOOLEY, Georgia Football. The two are synonymous. Dooley is considered the architect of all things "dawg." He spent his entire head-coaching career at the University of Georgia (UGA), producing 201 victories, twenty bowl games, six Southeastern Conference Championships, and one National Championship.

Vincent Joseph Dooley was born on September 4, 1932, and grew up in Mobile, Alabama, where he was a basketball star at McGill Catholic High School. He was an undergraduate student at Auburn University and played football under Ralph "Shug" Jordan. After graduating with a degree in business management, he spent two years in the U.S. Marine Corps. After the Marines, he returned to Auburn to work in the football program and earn his master's degree in history.

In December 1963, he accepted the head coaching position at UGA. Dooley was thirty-one and untested; Bulldog fans were not welcoming. It was not long, however, before Dooley distinguished himself. His 1968 team went undefeated but was declared National Champions by only one poll because the team had two ties. In 1980 the team won the National Championship against Notre Dame in the Sugar Bowl with celebrated player Hershel Walker. During his coaching tenure, Dooley was named NCAA Coach of the Year twice and SEC Coach of the Year seven times. In his 25 years, Dooley pitted his coaching skills against some of the best coaches and players in the business: Bear Bryant, Steve Spurrier, Joe Namath, Archie Manning and Kenny Stabler to name a few.

After the 1980 championship, Dooley retired from coaching and became the athletic director at UGA. Under his guidance, UGA sports teams won eighteen national championships and seventy-five Southeastern Conference championships. He broadened the program to twenty-one sports, which included female teams.

His fundraising abilities produced two million dollars for UGA's athletic department. The monies helped to build and expand many facilities on campus including an Academic Achievement Center, SkySuites at the football stadium and an indoor practice facility. Under his guidance, three 1996 Olympic Game events were brought to Athens. He also served on the Olympic organizational committee.

Not without its rocky moments, Dooley's forty years included a scandal regarding a former teacher who sued for wrongful termination after she criticized the University for recruiting and maintaining student-athletes unable to perform academically. In 2003, another scandal involving financial and academic improprieties regarding the men's basketball team resulted in Dooley's disallowing the team from competing in the Southeastern Conference and NCAA. Dooley told Athens Magazine (2003): We've had bruises, black eyes and strong winds of criticism, but we've always landed on our feet because we had a solid foundation of integrity as a base value."

In the 1980s, Vince Dooley made headlines when he considered running for governor of Georgia or possibly U.S. Senator. He never followed through and said in a 2000 interview (Tim Gardner, *DawgPost.com*): "At one point, I did consider it. My mind wanted to do it, but my heart was not totally in it, and I think a career in politics would require one's total self involved in order to be successful. I have always had my heart and soul totally in athletics."

In 2004, after forty-two years at the University of Georgia, Vince Dooley retired. That same year, the U.S. Sports Academy presented Dooley with the Carl Maddox Sport Management Award for his contribution to the growth and development of sports through management practices. He was also inducted into UGA's Circle of Honor—the school's highest tribute to former athletes and coaches.

Dooley was inducted into the Georgia Sports Hall of Fame (1978) and the College Football Hall of Fame (1994). He is also a member of the Alabama Sports Hall of Fame. In 2001, Dooley received the Amos Alonzo Stagg Award from the American Football Coaches Association. In 2007, Dooley was presented the Homer Rice Award—the highest honor given by the Division 1-A Athletic Director's Association. In 2011, he was inducted as a Georgia Trustee, an honor bestowed by the Georgia Historical Society and the Office of the Governor.

Dooley and wife Barbara, married 50 plus years, live in the same home they purchased in Athens in 1964. They have four children and eleven grandchildren. His son Derek is head football coach at the University of Tennessee. Dooley has published his memoir, *Dooley: My 40 Years at Georgia* (2005); two children's books and a gardening book entitled *Vince Dooley's Garden: A Horticultural Journey of a Football Coach* (2010). Dooley is a master gardener; UGA's Department of Horticulture named a rose in his honor. ∎

Bill Elliott

RACING LEGEND . DAWSONVILLE

BILL ELLIOTT HAS BEEN AROUND THE TRACK more than once. His three decades of racing have earned him fame, money, and a cover of *Sports Illustrated*. Elliott has participated in over 700 races, collected 44 wins, achieved 55 career poles, and amassed winnings close to $73 million. His devotion to the sport of racing has made him popular with race teams and race fans alike.

"Being under the car and behind the wheel has always given me a lot of satisfaction and a lot of joy, but the best thing about my career has been the fans."

"Awesome Bill from Dawsonville" was born William Clyde "Bill" Elliott on October 8, 1955, in Dawsonville, Georgia. His father, George, loved racing and created a speed shop where Bill's older brothers, Ernie and Dan, worked and where he sold parts for race cars, exposing Elliot to the sport of racing at an early age. In 1976, Elliott began racing on a regular basis at the Dixie Speedway in Woodstock, Georgia. After he won a few races, his father noticed his natural talent and encouraged him to pursue the sport.

Elliott started in first NASCAR Winston Cup Series race at Rockingham, NC, in 1976 where he qualified 34th out of 36. In 1977, he earned his first top 10 finish in the Southern 500 at Darlington, NC. In 1979, he finished in the Top 5 in the same race. Elliot gained his first major sponsorship in the fall of 1980 in the form of $500 from Harry Melling. Melling Racing eventually bought the team from Elliott's father in 1981.

In 1983, Elliott won his first Winston Cup race at the Winston Western 500 in Riverside, CA. Elliott soon received $400,000 in sponsorships from Coors. In 1984, he won three races, collected four poles and finished third in the championship standings. In 1985, he garnered eleven wins and eleven poles out of twenty-eight races and won Winston's first million-dollar bonus in the Southern 500 at Darlington. This win earned him the nickname "Million Dollar Bill." He also set an unprecedented NASCAR record of winning five consecutive pole qualifying sessions.

In 1987, Elliott set the NASCAR speed record at 210.364 miles per hour at Daytona International Speedway. Later that year, at Talladega Superspeedway, he broke his own speed record at 212.809. When Bobby Allison crashed at Talladega injuring several fans, NASCAR mandated the use of restrictor plates at Talladega

and Daytona, making it likely that Elliott's speed records will never be broken. In 1988, Elliott had six wins, six poles, eleven Top 5 and twenty-two Top 10 finishes in twenty-nine races. Fittingly, he earned NASCAR's Winston Cup championship.

Elliott left Melling and joined Junior Johnson, where in 1992, he just missed his second Winston Cup championship. From 1995 to 2000, Elliott put together his own Winston Cup race team. Even though he failed to win any races, he did have two Top 10 finishes in the championship standings in 1995 and 1997. In 1996 he missed seven races due to a broken hip.

In 2001, Elliott became the lead driver for Ray Evernham and Dodge. During this time, he captured the pole at the Daytona 500 and won the pole and the race at Homestead-Miami Speedway in November, his first victory since September 1994. In 2002, he won four poles, finished four times in the Top 5 and eleven times in the Top 10 and captured the checkered flag twice in a row. By 2003, Elliott had won the NMPA's "Most Popular Driver" Award sixteen times. He retired his name from the contest.

Starting in 2005, Elliott began a part-time driving schedule, preparing for retirement. However, his passion for racing and NASCAR continued to lure him back to the track, working in later years with Wood Racing, Phoenix Racing, NEMCO Motorsports and Turner Racing for the 2012 July race at the Daytona International Raceway.

Bill Elliott is an enduring race car legend with one of the most distinguished records in NASCAR history. In 2005, Georgia Governor Sonny Purdue declared October 8 as Bill Elliott Day in the state of Georgia. In Dawsonville, a stretch of road was renamed Elliott Family Parkway. He was inducted into the Motorsports Hall of Fame of America in 2007.

Elliott and wife Cindy have two daughters and one son. His son is following in his father's footsteps. In 2008, Elliott founded the Bill Elliott Driver Development Program through which he continues to mentor young racecar drivers, sharing his principles of teamwork, a strong work ethic, and the power of a positive attitude. ∎

Dakota Fanning

ACTRESS . CONYERS

AT SEVEN YEARS OLD, Dakota Fanning became the youngest person to be nominated for a Screen Actors Guild Award. When she won the award for Best Young Actor/Actress from the Broadcast Film Critics Association for her role in *I Am Sam*, presenter Orlando Bloom had to lift her up so that she could reach the microphone.

Hannah Dakota Fanning was born on February 23, 1994, in Conyers, Georgia. Her mother was a professional tennis player and her father played minor league baseball. A very active child, Fanning was part of a local playhouse that put on weekly plays. Managers of the playhouse, impressed by Fanning's talent, suggested that her parents consider taking her to a professional agency.

After being cast in a Tide commercial at age five, Fanning declared to everyone that she wanted to be an actress.

After being cast in a Tide commercial at age five, Fanning declared to everyone that she wanted to be an actress. Subsequently, the whole family moved to Los Angeles. Signing with a professional agency, Fanning was soon cast in the movie *Tomcats* (2001) and a smaller project called *Father Xmas* that same year.

Fanning's big break came when she signed to act in *I Am Sam* (2001) opposite Sean Penn and Michelle Pfeiffer. Highly sought after, 2002 was a banner year for Fanning as she played in *Trapped* with Charlize Theron and then portrayed a young version of Reese Witherspoon in *Sweet Home Alabama*. She took on the lead child role in the mini-TV series *Taken* as well as narrating the ten episodes. She also played Katie in the movie *Hansel & Gretel*.

In 2003, Fanning starred in *Uptown Girls* and *The Cat in the Hat*. She did voice over work for four animated projects including a young Wonder Woman in Cartoon Network's *Justice League*. Roles continued to pour in as Fanning appeared with Denzel Washington in the thriller *Man on Fire* (2004), with Robert De Nero in *Hide and Seek* (2005) and with Kurt Russell in *Dreamer: Inspired by a True Story* (2004) for which she won the Young Artist Award for Best Performance in a feature film. After Fanning worked with Glenn

Close in *Nine Lives* (2005), Close remarked: "She's definitely an old soul. She's one of those gifted people that comes along every now and then."

In 2005, she starred with Tom Cruise in *War of the Worlds*. In 2006, she became a fan favorite following her performance in *Charlotte's Web* and earned a Kid's Choice Award for Favorite Female Movie Star. However, her next role as a troubled youth in *Hounddog* (2007) created controversy because of a rape scene, depicted only through facial expressions. The movie was banned in many cities. Fanning redeemed her reputation with the feel-good movie *The Secret Life of Bees* (2008). In 2009, she provided the voice for the animated character in *Coraline,* which earned over $120 million dollars at the box office.

Fanning took on a supporting role in the five film installments of *The Twilight Saga,* based on the best-selling young adult vampire novels. In 2010, she teamed up with *Twilight* star Kristen Stewart in *The Runaways* in which she played the lead singer in a 1970s hard rock band. In 2011, she played Tessa in *Now is Good* and the starring role in *Effie*, which was written by and co-starred Emma Thompson. In 2012, she acted in *The Motel Life* and *The Twilight Saga: Breaking Dawn, Part Two.*

Fanning, by age 16, had acted in more than fifteen films. Her television credits include *CSI, Spin City, Ally McNeal* and her television debut in 2000 in an episode of *ER*, which she says remains one of her favorite roles.

Fanning has been praised for her maturity and professionalism by actors and directors alike. In 2007, she ranked number fourteen on the Forbes List of The Top Earning Young Superstars, reportedly earning $4 million dollars. In 2008, she was ranked number four in *Moviefone's* list of The 25 Hottest Actors under 25. In 2006, at age twelve, she was invited to join the Academy of Motion Picture Arts and Sciences.

Fanning was home schooled until her high school freshman year. She graduated from Campbell Hall School in Hollywood, California, in June 2011 where she was a cheerleader and voted homecoming queen. She presently attends New York University. When not acting, she plays the violin and piano, is a Girl Scout, a member of the Red Cross, loves to knit, collects dolls, rides horses and enjoys ballet. ∎

Dakota Fanning at the world premiere of her new movie The Twilight Saga: New Moon at Mann Village & Bruin Theatres, Westwood. November 16, 2009 Los Angeles, CA.

Laurence Fishburne III

ACTOR, PLAYWRIGHT, DIRECTOR & PRODUCER . AUGUSTA

KNOWN FOR HIS LOW, authoritative voice and the gap between his front teeth, Laurence Fishburne is a multi-award winning film, television and stage actor and a respected playwright, screenwriter, director and producer.

Fishburne was born in Augusta on July 30, 1961. His mother moved the family to Brooklyn shortly after her divorce. He started acting early in life when he was cast on television's *One Life to Live* at age 12 and made his film debut in *Apocalypse Now* at 15. "I was always actively in pursuit of mentors and father figures," Fishburne explained as he described people important to him during his development as an actor. "The ones who've influenced me the most are: Roscoe Lee Brown, Martin Sheen and Sidney Poitier, who has become my mentor. There is also Francis Coppola, the great Lloyd Richards and August Wilson, all because of the wealth of their experiences."

two sequels released in 2003, *The Matrix: Reloaded* and *The Matrix: Revolutions*. Reportedly, his appearance in the two sequels made him $15 million and 3.75 percent of the films' gross profits.

His film direction and screenwriting debut was in *Once in the Life* in 2000. He also starred in the film adaptation of the play he penned and staged in 1995, *Riff Raff*. In 2008 he joined the cast of one of television's most successful crime dramas, *CSI: Crime Scene Investigation*.

Off screen, Fishburne is an avid motorcycle enthusiast and is a founding member of the Guggenheim Motorcycle Club, a group inspired by the famed museum's 1998 exhibit. The Guggenheim Motorcycle Club organizes rides to museums throughout the country.

He is also a Goodwill Ambassador for UNICEF, the United Nation's Children's Fund, and travels the globe to raise awareness and funds for children's rights, survival and protection. Fishburne is particularly

His portrayal of Morpheus in The Matrix launched him into superstardom and identified him as one of the most recognizable movie characters of the decade.

His defining film roles began with *Boyz N The Hood* in 1991. The next years were full of accolades and strong roles. Fishburne was nominated for an academy award for his role of Ike Turner in *What's Love Got to Do With It?*, won a Tony Award for his role of Sterling Johnson in August's Wilson's *Two Trains Running* and was awarded an Emmy for his appearance in the premier episode of Fox TV's *Tribeca*.

Fishburne was the Executive Producer and starred in *Miss Evers' Boys (1997)*, an HBO drama based on the Tuskegee Study, a four decade long medical experiment during which the U.S. Government Public Health Service withheld treatment from African American men with syphilis. *Miss Evers' Boys* was awarded five Emmys, including the "President's Award" and "Outstanding Made for Television Movie." The program also garnered a NAACP Image Award in 1998.

Another of his outstanding roles was that of Henry II in a multi-racial version of *The Lion in Winter* in 1999. Later the same year, his portrayal of Morpheus in *The Matrix* launched him into superstardom and identified him as one of the most recognizable movie characters of the decade. He returned to play the role in

interested in the organization's HIV/AIDS awareness and education programs. He is also active in the 21st Century Leaders Foundation, an organization dedicated to raising money to support humanitarian and environmental issues and Artists for a New South Africa, a group formed in 1989 to support the efforts to end apartheid.

Fishburne had two children, Langston and Montana, with his first wife, actress Hanja Moss. He married Gina Torres in 2002; the couple has one child, Delilah, born in 2007. They currently live in Los Angeles.

"Stardom is one of the challenges of being a very well known person," he explained as he described his attempts to live humbly. "You get praise and attention from strangers and it makes you susceptible to believing you're the greatest thing since sliced bread. But at the beginning and end of the day, you are a human being, a child of God with faults and weaknesses. We live in a society that's obsessed with celebrity. The trap is 'believing it.' You have to practice to remain humble and grounded, to remain human."

Fishburne is currently grounded and working on *Man of Steel*, a Superman film in which he plays Perry White, the Editor of *The Daily Planet*. ■

Lawrence Fishburne at the 63rd Annual Primetime Emmy Awards held at Nokia Theater L.A. LIVE on September 18, 2011 in Los Angeles, California.

Jeff Foxworthy

COMEDIAN, AUTHOR, TELEVISION & RADIO PERSONALITY . ATLANTA

"YOU MIGHT BE A REDNECK IF..." This phrase became a catchword and catapulted Jeff Foxworthy's album of the same name to number three on the country charts in 1995, selling over four-million copies and making it the biggest selling comedy album of all time. His wry southern musings on human nature have caused reviewers to liken him to Mark Twain. He is the biggest selling comedy recording artist in history.

Jeffrey Marshall Foxworthy was born in Atlanta, Georgia, on September 6, 1958. He graduated from Hapeville High School and attended Georgia Tech for a short while before dropping out and going to work as a mainframe computer technician with IBM where his father was an executive.

In 1984, at the insistence of his coworkers, Foxworthy entered and won the Great Southeastern Laugh Off at Atlanta's Punchline Comedy Club. Foxworthy went on to receive the Best Stand-up Comic Award at the 1990 American Comedy Awards. However, it was not until 1993 when his "You Might Be a Redneck If..." jokes were released on his *Laughing Hyena* album that he caught the eye of Warner Brothers whose promotional savvy propelled Foxworthy to fame.

Foxworthy's next album, *Games Rednecks Play,* debuted in 1995 and soared to number two on the country charts. The album also crossed over to the pop Top Ten, selling over two million copies. In 1995, Foxworthy was offered his own sitcom by ABC. The show was cancelled after its first season, picked up by NBC, then cancelled again after one season. Foxworthy felt that the networks did not know how to market his humor to a larger audience. However, he did receive a People's Choice Award as "Favorite Male Newcomer" for the sitcom.

Foxworthy branched out into musical satire with his *Crank It Up: The Music Album* (1996), which made the country Top Five and went gold. His 1998 HBO live standup album, *Totally Committed,* was certified gold and received a 1999 Grammy nomination. The Foxworthy Countdown, a weekly three-hour radio show of music and conversation with some of country's superstars, premiered in April 1999. The show, which ended in December 2009, was broadcast by close to 300 country stations nationwide. Foxworthy received a CMA nomination in 2001 for "Broadcast Personality of the Year." That same year, he received a nomination at the 43rd Annual Grammy's for "Best Spoken Comedy Album."

In 2000, Foxworthy and comrades Bill Engvall, Ron White and Larry the Cable Guy, teamed up for the record-breaking *Blue Collar Comedy Tour* (2003-2006), which turned into the television series, *Blue Collar TV* (2004-2006), produced by Foxworthy. The television show was the second most watched show in that time period with over 5.4 million viewers. *The Blue Collar Tour: The Movie* (2003) soundtrack has been RIAA certified gold and has sold over 2.5 million DVD's.

"You might be a redneck if you have started a petition to change the National Anthem to 'Georgia On My Mind.'"

In 2004, Foxworthy released his solo comedy CD, *Have Your Loved Ones Spayed or Neutered.* It debuted at number one on the Billboard Comedy Charts and became his second highest selling album. In 2006, he made an attempt to resurrect the *Blue Collar TV* format with *Foxworthy's Big Night Out,* but the show was cancelled after one season. Foxworthy's next big success was the game show *Are You Smarter Than a 5th Grader?* (2007-2009/syndication to 2011). In March 2012, The Game Show Network announced *The American Bible Challenge* where Foxworthy will serve as host and producer.

Foxworthy has authored eleven books including his autobiography, *No Shirt, No Shoes, No Problem!* (1996). His children's books include *Dirt On My Shirt* (2008), *Silly Street* (2009) and *Hide!!!* (2010). His most recent venture is a line of outdoor living products that includes hunting and camping gear as well as a line of travel trailers. He also has a line of greeting cards, calendars and other specialty items.

Foxworthy's charities include the Atlanta Mission, Atlanta Community Ministries, Young Life Christian Youth organization and serving as celebrity host for the Duke Children's Classic Golf Tournament. He also dedicates time to the USO.

A devout Christian, Foxworthy and his wife Pamela have been married since 1985 and have two daughters. They reside in Fulton County, Georgia. ∎

Jeff Foxworthy arriving at the Comedy Central Roast of Larry the Cable Guy in Los Angeles, California on March 1, 2009.

Walt Frazier

BASKETBALL LEGEND . ATLANTA

"IT'S CLYDE'S BALL!" FANS WOULD SHOUT FOR YEARS at Madison Square Garden where Walt Frazier set many records for the New York Knicks, led them to championships, and converted many new fans to the game. He was much more than a basketball star; he was considered one of the finest professional guards in the late 1960 and early 1970's.

His nickname was given to him by a Knicks trainer to pay homage to Frazier's ability to steal the ball. "Clyde" referred to Clyde Barrow, the folk hero bank robber whose infamous life was made widely known in the 1967 film *Bonnie and Clyde* starring Fay Dunaway and Warren Beatty in the title roles.

He spent the next decade with the team and proved to be popular both on and off the court. He brought a sense of style to the game never seen before and was known to arrive at Madison Square Garden in a Rolls Royce wearing a full-length mink.

During his time with the Knicks he helped them win two World Championships and was named to the NBA's All Star Team seven of his ten years with the team. He held multiple records for the Knicks for years, including most games played, field goals, free throws, steals and assists. Later the Knicks' Center Patrick Ewing would break most of Frazier's records but his amazing 4,791 assists still prevails.

"Born in Atlanta, the eldest of nine children, Frazier said leading a team came naturally to him."

As a player, Frazier did more than steal the ball for the Knicks. When he left the team in 1977 he held team records for points scored, games played and assists.

During his decade with the Knicks, he built numbers that defined him as a legend. Scoring an average of 19.3 points per game, arguably his most memorable performance was in 1970 when he led the team to victory in the seventh and deciding game against the Los Angeles Lakers in the NBA final game.

Born in Atlanta, the eldest of nine children, Frazier said leading a team came naturally to him. He was the quarterback at Howard High School and was the catcher on the baseball team. Howard didn't have a basketball court so Frazier learned the sport on a dirt playground.

Frazier, best known for his quarterback abilities, received scholarship offers from Kansas and Indiana for football. Not seeing a future for himself as a black quarterback, Frazier accepted a basketball scholarship from Southern Illinois (SIU). He quickly became a college star in the game and was named a Division II All-American in both 1964 and 1965. Frazier led SIU when they won the National Invitational Tournament (NIT) in 1967; he was also named the Most Valuable Player in the NIT.

Frazier left college a year early and was drafted in the first round by the New York Knicks in 1967.

After a game-changing decade with the Knicks, Frazier was traded to the Cleveland Cavaliers in October of 1977. His famous line about his two years in Cleveland was, "I couldn't find a place to park my Rolls." Along with foot injuries, he seemed to miss the excitement of the city. He retired three games into the 1979-80 season.

After retirement from the NBA, Frazier became a player agent and soon moved to the U.S. Virgin Islands where he became a charter boat captain. After losing both his house and boat to Hurricane Hugo, he moved back to New York and became an analyst for the Knicks broadcasts. Along with his broadcasting work he has been a long-term spokesperson for Just for Men hair products.

The Knicks retired "Clyde's" number 10 uniform on October 15, 1979. His college number 52 jersey has also been retired by SIU.

Frazier was elected to the Basketball Hall of Fame in 1986 and named one of the "Fifty Greatest Players in NBA History" the same year. He has also been honored with a plaque at both the Georgia and Madison Square Garden's walks of fame.

Frazier has two children, Walt III and Angel. He currently lives in Manhattan but still spends much of his time in St. Croix in the Virgin Islands where he owns a bed and breakfast. ∎

Amy Grant

SINGER & SONGWRITER . AUGUSTA

FROM TOE-TAPPING POP TUNES to epic songs of faith, Amy Grant's smooth and mature alto voice is known across the music charts. Six-time Grammy winner Amy Grant has been called the Christian Queen of Pop and has been writing songs and singing for more than 30 years. She signed a record deal at 16 and her do what she loves. "I've sung in front of 40,000 people and I've sung on a street corner with my guitar case open hoping to make enough money for dinner," Grant said. "It's equally exciting, no matter the size of the audience. I have a job that makes people feel good and I love what I do."

"I've sung in front of 40,000 people and I've sung on a street corner with my guitar case open hoping to make enough money for dinner."

first Christian album came out in 1977. To pursue her new music career, she left Vanderbilt University to sing and write full-time. She is now a multi-platinum record holder, selling more than 30 million albums worldwide.

In 1982 she married songwriter Gary Chapman. That same year she released *Age to Age* which helped her win a Grammy for Best Gospel Performance. She also won the first of 26 Dove awards received in her career, including Performer of the Year (which Grant has since won a total of four times), from the Gospel Music Association. Grant is one of the few artists who have had No. 1 hit songs in each of the last three decades. With six No. 1 hits, her success in the 80s helped open doors for other artists who also wanted to sing about faith.

With her 1985 album *Unguarded*, she had her first crossover success on the pop charts and a music video on MTV. *CCM Magazine* voted her 1988 hit album, *Lead Me On*, the No. 1 Contemporary Christian Music Album of All Time in 2002. Her 1991 album *Heart in Motion* included "Baby, Baby" which hit No. 1 on the Billboard music chart that year. She wrote this song after being inspired by the birth of her first daughter, but the music video showed it as a romantic tune. Some gospel fans claimed she forgot her roots.

Her 1994 album *House of Love* included both love songs and songs about her faith. She sang the hit title song in a duet with country music star Vince Gill, whom she married in 2000, a few years after her divorce from Chapman. She and Gill have one child together and share four from their first marriages.

Throughout her career Grant has amazed audiences around the world with her passion for music and is thrilled that she can still

She was inducted into the Gospel Music Hall of Fame in 2003 and four years later received a star on the Hollywood Walk of Fame, one of only two Christian musicians to be so honored.

People magazine named her one of the World's Most Beautiful People in 1992, and *Style Bistro* named her one of the 50 Most Beautiful Women Over 50.

In 1999 she turned to acting and starred in the television movie *A Song From the Heart* and later had a show called *Three Wishes*. She wrote her autobiography, *Mosaic: The Pieces of My Life So Far* in 2008. The book details her life as a singer, wife, mother, believer and caregiver. She also shared how she and her three sisters took care of their aging parents who both suffered from dementia. Because of her experiences as a caregiver, in 2012 she served as spokesperson for the National Association of Insurance Commissioners to encourage other baby boomers to plan for their and other family members' long term care needs. She said she and her sisters were fortunate that her parents had made their own long-term care plans many years before they needed help. She and Gill have done the same thing and hope their children will take that same advice and plan for their future.

She continues to write new songs, tour and raise funds for her foundation, Amy's Helping Hands, which supports organizations like the Nashville Rescue Mission, HOPE Clinic For Women, Blood: Water Mission and With This Ring (Clean Water Wells). Her summer 2012 "Weekend with Amy" at her farm in Nashville raised more than $50,000 for her foundation. She has recently completed another European tour and plans to continue her annual Christmas concert with her husband in Nashville each December. ■

Amy Grant and Vince Gill perform a live Christmas concert onstage at Ovens Auditorium celebrating the 70th anniversary of the Charlotte Rescue Mission, North Carolina, 2008.

Lewis Grizzard

SOUTHERN WRITER & HUMORIST . MORELAND . 1946 – 1994

IN LEWIS GRIZZARD'S BRIEF 47 YEARS, he battled alcoholism, survived three divorces and suffered from a congenital heart defect. However, Grizzard's newspaper columns, books and live performances made him one of the best loved writers and Southern humorists of the 20th century.

Lewis McDonald Grizzard, Jr. was born on October 20, 1946, in Fort Benning, Georgia. His father, a highly decorated veteran of World War II, returned from the Korean War and began to drink heavily and borrow large sums of money. His mother, no longer able to cope, moved the six-year old Grizzard to her parent's home in Moreland, Georgia, the town frequently referred to in his writings.

"It's difficult to think anything but pleasant thoughts while eating a homegrown tomato."

Grizzard's mother was a school teacher and an influence in his chosen profession: "Mama taught me that an education was necessary for a fuller life," he wrote. "She taught me an appreciation of the language. She taught a love of words, of how they should be used and how they can fill a creative soul with a passion and lead it to a life's work." On the other hand, Grizzard never felt he measured up to his father. His book, *Daddy Was a Pistol and I'm a Son of a Gun* (1987), reflected those feelings.

Grizzard, a staunch Georgia Bulldog supporter, left the university early, needing only one course to graduate. In later years, the University of Georgia awarded him a journalism degree. Grizzard worked as sports editor of the *Athens Daily News* when he was 19, and at 23 he became the youngest person ever to hold the position of sports editor of the *Atlanta Journal Constitution.* In 1975, he became an assistant city editor at *The Journal* but soon left to free-lance for *Sports Illustrated.*

Grizzard's next job took him to the *Chicago Sun-Times* as executive sports editor. He disliked Chicago immensely, especially the cold winter months. He refers to those years as "exile" in his book, *If I Ever Get Back to Georgia, I'm Gonna Nail My Feet to the Ground* (1990).

He returned to *The Journal* in 1977 as a sports columnist. In 1978, he switched to the humor/life column that soon made him famous. The column was so popular that it led to national syndication with collections of his columns hitting the *New York Times* bestseller list. Grizzard typed his columns on his vintage Royal manual typewriter.

When he wrote, he said he "liked to hear some noise."

Grizzard's column was syndicated in 450 newspapers. He was soon performing on television shows and doing stand-up comedy. He appeared on the *Johnny Carson Show, Designing Women* and *Larry King Live* and had his own TV special: *Love, Sex and Romance.* The alternative newspaper in Atlanta, *Creative Loafing,* in its annual Best of Atlanta poll, included the categories "Best Columnist" and "Best Columnist besides Lewis Grizzard."

Grizzard's 20 books and syndicated columns reflected his own style of down-home Southern redneck humor. He enjoyed attacking Yankees, liberal politicians, feminists and draft dodgers. Newspaper colleagues were fair game for characters. Reporter Bill Robinson, a longtime friend, became Billy Bob Bailey, the world's most obnoxious Alabama fan.

He wrote that women's activities should be limited to rubbing his back, baking pies and washing his clothes. He also waded into the area of social commentary—not without controversy. While many people delighted in his humor, others became enraged. One of his favorite targets was football rival Georgia Tech. As a fixture at his beloved "Dawgs" Sanford Stadium, Coach Vince Dooley was one of his closest friends. Dooley and his wife Barbara gave Grizzard his best companion, a black lab he named Catfish.

In his books and columns, many of his reader's favorite fictional characters emerged: Weyman C. Wannamaker, Jr., Kathy Sue Loudermilk and Cordie Mae Poovey. His first book was a collection of columns entitled *Kathy Sue Loudermilk, I Love You* (1979). It sold over 75,000 copies the first week. His second book, *Elvis Is Dead And I Don't Feel So Good Myself* (1980), made *The New York Times* best-seller list.

Lewis Grizzard wrote about his passions: patriotism, cowboys, country music, trains, pick-up trucks and his dog Catfish. He wrote about Moon Pies, homegrown tomatoes and barbeque. He wrote about his first open-heart surgery in *They Tore Out My Heart and Stomped That Sucker Flat* (1982). His third surgery in 1993 is recounted in *I Took a Lickin' and Kept on Tickin' (and now I Believe in Miracles).*

Grizzard died from massive brain damage during his fourth open-heart surgery in March 1994. He married his fourth wife Dedra Kyle in the hospital four days before his death. As requested, part of his ashes were scattered over the 50 yard line at Sanford Stadium. Grizzard's bucket list of things to do, made in his last year of life, included "See Rock City." ∎

Lewis Grizzard promotional photo, 1989, courtesy of Dedra Grizzard.

Oliver Hardy

COMIC ACTOR . HARLEM . 1892 – 1957

A TALL, 300-POUND MAN from Georgia and a thin, shorter man from Great Britain teamed up to create side-splitting laughter. The two comedians were captured on film from the 1920s to the 1950s. Oliver Norvell Hardy from Harlem, Georgia, teamed up with Stan Laurel to form one of the most successful comedy duos of all time.

Hardy, whose given name was Norvell Hardy, was born to an attorney and his wife. When Hardy was very young, his father, Oliver Hardy, died. His mother, Emily Norvell Hardy, began running boarding houses to provide for the family.

Hardy had a troublesome streak as a boy and was sent to military school. He also loved to sing and began to perform in public.

Eventually, Hardy went to Jacksonville, Florida, which had a burgeoning movie industry and began to appear in films. He traveled to New York City and acted in films there, as well. Hardy later moved to Los Angeles to pursue acting in the epicenter of the industry.

At that time, he went by the name Oliver Norvell Hardy, in honor of his late father. He also had the nickname "Babe." In his early film career, Hardy appeared in short films. In Los Angeles he acted for the Hal Roach Studio, an important film company of that day.

Over 6 feet tall and weighing about 300 pounds, Hardy had frequently been cast as a "heavy." His weight limited the roles he could play. But at the Hal Roach Studio, Hardy crossed paths with Stan Laurel, who not only acted but also directed movies. The two played together in one film but didn't interact in front of the camera.

Hal Roach had a sense that these two actors would work well together in comedic roles. He could not have been more right. The comedic chemistry Laurel and Hardy achieved was based on people Hardy had seen in his mother's boarding houses. With two friends, he observed one would often be dumb, and the other one would seem intelligent, but this second fellow would be dumb in his own right—he just wouldn't know it.

Laurel and Hardy began making movies as a team in the late 1920s, kicking off a string of films that would establish them as household names. In 1932, their short film *The Music Box* won an Academy Award, the only one the two would ever win. Other notable Laurel and Hardy films included *Big Business, Way Out West, Flying Deuces* and *Saps at Sea*.

Hardy was known for a number of signature mannerisms. When Laurel would make a big mistake, creating a real problem for the two men, Hardy would resort to one of two measures: either he would tell Laurel, "This is another fine mess you've gotten us into," or he would turn to the camera, look full into the lens and strike an exasperated, at-wits-end facial expression. Another famous Hardy mannerism was to twiddle his tie in boyish shyness.

"This is another fine mess you've gotten us into."

In the 1940s, the two left Hal Roach Studio for 20th Century Fox and later MGM. At these larger studios, short films—Laurel and Hardy's forte—were replaced by feature films. With Roach, Laurel could write the scripts to suit their comedic acting style but other writers penned the scripts at the larger studios. Adlibbing, with which the comedic pair had improved their earlier films, was replaced by a strict adherence to the scripts. The result was disheartening. Their success waned. Laurel and Hardy stopped making films together in 1951. Their last picture not measuring up to their earlier high standards.

Over his lifetime, Hardy had three wives. Divorced from the first two, he was married happily to his third wife, Virginia Lucille Jones, until his death.

He enjoyed a number of pastimes, including golf. On the golf course, he could frequently be seen in foursomes with fellow celebrities.

Toward the end of his life, Hardy dropped a huge amount of weight, going from about 300 pounds to about 150. He suffered a heart attack and a number of strokes and died August 7, 1957.

It was after his death that the popularity of Laurel and Hardy revived. Fan clubs sprang up around the world. The two even ended up, along with other icons of entertainment, on the cover of the Beatles' album *Sgt. Pepper's Lonely Hearts Club Band*.

Laurel and Hardy movies can be seen in many countries, the voices of the big man and the skinny man dubbed. No doubt, the visual, slapstick humor of two men in derbies getting into all kinds of "fine messes" translates into any language. ∎

Promotional photo of Oliver Hardy, circa 1921, State Archives of Florida, Florida Memory.

Photo courtesy of the Library of Congress Prints & Photographs Division, by Francies Benjamin Johnston, circa 1890.

Joel Chandler Harris

WRITER . EATONTON . 1845 – 1908

JOEL CHANDLER HARRIS ENTERTAINED scores of children and became one of the country's most renowned authors. His folktales about Br'er Rabbit, Br'er Fox and other inhabitants of the Briar Patch were beloved by children and their parents worldwide.

Uncle Remus, a kindly old former slave, narrated the allegorical stories in which the mischievous, cunning Br'er Rabbit outsmarted the larger, more powerful animals. His stories, told to the plantation master's young son, were related in a Deep South dialect, which was praised by 19th- and early 20th-Century folklorists.

"My purpose has been to preserve the legends themselves in their original simplicity…and I have endeavored to give to the whole a genuine flavor of the old plantation," Harris wrote in his introduction. (By the 1990s, that idyllic portrayal would be labeled as "politically incorrect" by some.) Harris was born Dec. 9, 1845, in Putnam County, to an unwed mother, Mary Harris, who took in sewing to support them. The small, shy red-haired boy loved to read and write and was remembered as being impish. At 16, Harris was hired as an apprentice by printer Joseph Addison Turner, who owned Turnwold Plantation and published what is believed to be the country's only plantation newspaper, *The Countryman.*

Under Turner's guidance, Harris learned to hand-set type and published dozens of book reviews and poems. Harris also visited Turnwold's kitchen and slave quarters, where he spent many hours listening to African-American folklore spun by Uncle George Terrell, Aunt Crissy and Old Harbert. Years later, these stories would form the basis of the Uncle Remus tales.

The young journalist had a front-row seat for Gen. William Sherman's March to the Sea, in which large swaths of Georgia, including Turnwold Plantation, were pillaged. Turner suspended his operations, and, at 20, Harris left to work for a string of newspapers in Macon, New Orleans, Forsyth and Savannah. While in Savannah, Harris met and married Esther LaRose, the daughter of a ship captain, with whom he would eventually have nine children.

Harris' writing career was going well. His humor pieces and essays about rural Georgia attracted a loyal following and were reprinted around the state. In 1876, he joined the staff of the *Atlanta Constitution*, where he would remain for 24 years. Harris soon became an associate editor, joining the likes of Henry W. Grady in chronicling the rise of the post-Civil War New South. He also wrote many editorials promoting regional and racial reconciliation.

International prominence, however, came after Harris invented a character named Uncle Rem*us,* who would visit the *Atlanta*

Constitution offices and humorously expound on daily life in Atlanta. In 1880, *Uncle Remus: His Songs and His Sayings* was published to great commercial and critical acclaim and eventually translated into more than 40 languages. Five more Uncle Remus books followed: *Nights with Uncle Remus* (1883), *Uncle Remus and His Friends* (1892), *Mr. Rabbit at Home* (1895), *The Tar-Baby and Other Rhymes of Uncle Remus* (1904), and *Uncle Remus and Br'er Rabbit* (1906).

Most of his 29 other books, such as *Free Joe and Other Georgia Sketches* (1887), portrayed a more complicated side to life in the post-Reconstruction South for former slaves, poor whites and aristocrats.

His folktales about Br'er Rabbit, Br'er Fox and other inhabitants of the Briar Patch were beloved by children and their parents worldwide.

Harris' many admirers included his friend Mark Twain, who also used local stories to illuminate universal truths. In 1882, Twain invited Harris to join him and George Washington Cable on a series of story readings around the country. Harris declined, perhaps because he was afflicted with a stutter.

Harris retired from the *Atlanta Constitution* in 1900, but continued to write novels and articles for such magazines as *The Saturday Evening Post*. In 1905, he was elected to the American Academy of Arts and Letters. Harris died July 3, 1908, of acute nephritis and complications from cirrhosis of the liver.

His literary legacy today is complicated. In 2008, a *PasteMagazine.com* article noted that the same attributes that made his work so compelling—the use of dialect, mischievous animals and the Uncle Remus character—also drew the most criticism in later years. "But Harris saw it as a means of preserving black culture, and he documented the specific rhythm and pitch of his characters' speech patterns with a sophisticated, finely tuned ear," the article said.

Many of the Uncle Remus stories were written on the front porch of the Wren's Nest, a Queen Anne Victorian house in Atlanta's West End that today is a museum. Eatonton also has an Uncle Remus Museum, which comprises two former slave cabins and numerous Harris memorabilia. ∎

Susan Hayward

ACTRESS . CARROLLTON . 1917 – 1975

"BROOKLYN BOMBSHELL" Susan Hayward was a shining star of the Golden Age of Hollywood—when men were men and women were smart, beautiful and sassy. Even though much of her work consisted of B-rated movies, Hayward hit Oscar nomination gold five times.

Hayward was born Edythe Marrenner on June 30, 1917, in Brooklyn, New York. Her family, living in a tenement, struggled to survive. Hayward was the youngest of three children. She and her brother Wally collected recyclable materials and sold them in order to buy extra food and sometimes clothes for the family. Hayward was hit by a car when she was six, suffering hip and leg fractures that left her with a limp. The limp, coupled with the poverty, made life difficult at school.

Hayward, however, found her solace in acting in school plays. Any extra money she made selling bottles and newspapers she used to buy movie tickets. She once said, "I learned at a very early age that life is a battle. My family was poor; my neighborhood was poor. The only way that I could get away from the awfulness of life, at that time, was at the movies. There I decided that my big aim was to make money. And it was there that I became a very determined woman."

Hayward began her career as a model. Color photography had become popular and a modeling agency felt that her fiery red hair and beautiful complexion and eyes would be a hit. They were right. Hayward was invited to audition for the coveted part of Scarlet O'Hara in *Gone With the Wind*. Even though she did not get the part, she was offered a six month contract with Warner Brothers.

It was then that she took the stage name Susan Hayward. At first, her inexperience and rough Brooklyn accent proved problematic. Hayward overcame these obstacles and secured a seven year contract with Paramount. Her first films, made in 1939, failed to make box office history: *Beau Geste, Our Leading Citizen,* and *$1000 Touchdown.* In 1941, on loan to Columbia Pictures, she made her mark in the film *Adam Had Four Sons* and was signed to act in two more films that year.

In 1942, she landed a role in the Technicolor film *Reap the Wild Wind*, playing opposite John Wayne. Once again her red hair, creamy complexion, and beautiful eyes caught attention. She finished four more movies that same year, and from 1943 to 1946, she made nine additional movies. She was on the fast track to becoming an A-list star.

During the war, Hayward volunteered at the Hollywood Canteen, serving coffee and dancing with the military men. She was already a favorite pin-up of the soldiers. At the canteen, she met actor Jess Barker to whom she was married for ten years (1945-1954). The couple had twin boys. After the war, Hayward became a favorite leading lady, and in 1947 she received the first of five Academy Award nominations for her role in *Smash-up, the Story of a Woman*.

Hayward was invited to audition for the coveted part of Scarlet O'Hara in Gone With the Wind.

In 1949, she earned another Academy Award nomination for *My Foolish Heart*. Hayward then began working with producer Daryl Zanuck on more substantial films and was cast with such popular leading men as Gregory Peck, Clark Gable and Charlton Heston. In 1952, she received her third Academy nomination for *With a Song in my Heart*. That same year, she and John Wayne were named the "Two Most Popular Stars in the World" by the Foreign Press Association. In 1955, she received her fourth Academy Award nomination for *I'll Cry Tomorrow*.

In 1957, Hayward met and married Georgia native Floyd Eaton Chalkley. She settled down to a quiet life on his ranch in Carrollton, only making one movie for which she won the coveted Oscar for Best Actress. *I Want to Live* (1958) is considered by many to be one of the finest acting performances of all time. She continued to make occasional film and television appearances. Following her husband's death in 1966 from hepatitis, she retired to Florida. She made her last film in 1972, *The Revengers,* and appeared in a made for TV drama *Say Goodbye, Maggie Cole.*

Hayward was diagnosed with brain cancer in March 1972, allegedly as the result of being exposed to radioactive toxins while making the movie *The Conquerer* (1956) in Utah. Speculation exists as all the leads in the movie eventually died from cancer. Hayward made her last public appearance as a presenter at the 1974 Academy Awards. Supported by Charlton Heston, she received a standing ovation.

Susan Hayward died in 1975 at age 57. She was laid to rest next to her husband in Carrollton, Georgia. Her tombstone modestly reads, "Mrs. F. E. Chalkley." ■

Holly Hunter

ACTRESS . CONYERS

HOLLY HUNTER IS AN ACTRESS appearing in films, television and on stage. She is one of the elite 11 actors to be nominated for an Academy Award in both lead and supporting roles in the same year. 1993 was an important year in Hunter's career; she won the Oscar for best actress for her portrayal of Ada McGrath in *The Piano* and was nominated for best supporting actress for her role in *The Firm*.

Holly Paige Hunter was born on March 20, 1958, in Conyers, a city 25 miles east of Atlanta. Her parents encouraged her love of performing from an early age. She started playing piano at the age of nine and starred in her first play, *Helen Keller*, in the fifth grade.

After high school Hunter went to Carnegie Mellon University in Pittsburgh, where she received her degree in drama in 1980. She moved to New York and achieved success rather quickly due to several serendipitous meetings.

The first of these meetings occurred when she was stuck in an elevator with playwright Beth Henley, another Southerner in New York trying to make her mark on Broadway. The two started collaborating on works about Southern life and the meeting led to Hunter's 1992 Broadway debut in *Crimes of the Heart*, Henley's play that won her, among other awards, the Pulitzer Prize.

While living in the North Bronx with roommate Frances McDormand, Hunter was seen in *Crimes of the Heart* by the Coen brothers who offered her a starring role in their film *Blood Simple*. Hunter turned down the role due to commitments to her current play, *The Wake of Jeremy Foster*. The Coen's offered the role to her roommate who went on to star in the film and eventually married Joel Coen.

The Coen brothers reportedly wrote the character of Edwina "Ed" McDunnough in *Raising Arizona* with Hunter in mind. Although she had appeared in films earlier, she considers the 1987 role of Ed to be the one that launched her career.

Hunter was critically acclaimed for her role in the film but it was her portrayal of Jane Craig, the news producer in 1987's *Broadcast News* that launched her into stardom. Her performance garnered nominations for both the Academy Award and the Golden Globe for Best Actress and won the Boston, Los Angeles and New York film critic's awards.

Better roles were soon offered including the leading roles in *Miss Firecracker*, based on another play written by Beth Henley, Steven Spielberg's *Always* and the made for television docudrama, *Roe vs. Wade*.

Hunter was awarded the Oscar for Best Actress in 1993's *The Piano*, a drama written and directed by Jan Campion. Hunter actually received three credits for the film as she played her own piano pieces and was also the sign language teacher for Anna Paquin, the 11 year old who won for Best Supporting Actress. *The Piano* also won the year's Academy Award for Best Original Screenplay.

Hunter was awarded the Oscar for Best Actress in 1993's The Piano, a drama written and directed by Jan Campion.

"I think that an Academy Award has a certain kind of business shelf life. People have different speculations but definitely for a couple of years, your price is raised and there are more plentiful offers. Which only makes sense—it is a business," Hunter explained in an interview following her win. "I think the most significant thing for me was, one, it was presented to me by Al Pacino, which I just loved. And two, that it was given to me for a role and experience that I felt was a profound influence on my life."

Hunter went on to win accolades for her performances on film and television, most notably 2003's *Thirteen*, a film directed and co-written by Catherine Hardwicke and *Saving Grace*, a television series that ran from 2007-2010 in which she played the title character.

She is in a long-term relationship with British actor Gordon MacDonald, who also acted in *Saving Grace*. The couple has twin boys, whose names are believed to be Claude and Press, born in 2006. Hunter stated in a 2009 interview that she does not discuss her children with the media. She has held true to that statement.

MacDonald, Hunter and their twins spent most of their time in Los Angeles until the end of the filming of *Saving Grace*. Their permanent home is in New York. ∎

Holly Hunter at the Women In Film 2009 Crystal And Lucy Awards. Hyatt Regency Century Plaza, Century City, California, 2009.

Alan Jackson

COUNTRY MUSIC SINGER . NEWNAN

ALAN JACKSON, originally from Newnan, Georgia, is one of the most successful and respected singer-songwriters in music. He is known for such hit songs as "Livin' On Love," "Gone Country," "Here in the Real World," "Where Were You (When the World Stopped Turning)," "Don't Rock the Jukebox" and many others.

Jackson is in the elite company of Paul McCartney and John Lennon among songwriters who have written more than 20 songs they've recorded and taken to the top of the charts. Jackson is one of the 10 best-selling artists since the inception of SoundScan, ranking alongside the likes of Eminem and Metallica. His latest hit, "So You Don't Have to Love Me Anymore," was released in 2012.

Jackson has sold nearly 60 million albums worldwide, topped the country singles charts 35 times and scored more than 50 Top-10 hits. He has written or co-written 24 of his 35 No. 1 hit singles.

Jackson is a 17-time ACM Award winner, a 16-time CMA Award recipient and a two-time Grammy-winning artist whose songwriting has earned him the prestigious ASCAP Founders Award and an induction into the Nashville Songwriters Hall of Fame as a 2011 Songwriter/Artist inductee.

Jackson was born to Eugene and Ruth Jackson Oct. 17, 1958. His first performance was lip-synching "Little Red Riding Hood" in a school play. Before he hit it big in the music world, he worked a number of jobs. At age 12, he took a job in a shoe repair shop. He later worked as a car salesman, a furniture salesman, a carpenter, a home-builder, a garage worker, a forklift driver for K-Mart and a mailroom worker at TNN.

Jackson's first band was Dixie Steel (the name brand of a box of nails) and he began writing songs in 1983. In 1986, he signed as a songwriter with Glen Campbell's publishing company. Three years later, he signed with Arista/Nashville as its first country artist.

Jackson's first album, *Here In The Real World*, was released in 1990. He received the Academy of Country Music's Top Male Vocalist award the same year. In 1991, Jackson became a member of the Grand Ole Opry, inducted by Roy Acuff and Randy Travis. He also released his second album, *Don't Rock The Jukebox*. Jackson reaped many awards that year.

As the 1990s rolled on, Jackson kept putting out the hits and collecting prestigious awards. By 1997, he had become such an icon that he was a national spokesman for Ford Trucks.

Jackson's "Murder on Music Row," performed with George Strait, was the CMA Vocal Event of the Year in 2000. Jackson collaborated with another musical great, Jimmy Buffett, to record "It's Five O'Clock Somewhere" in 2004. In 2006, Jackson's DVD, *Precious Memories – Live at the Ryman*, was released. In 2008, Jackson was honored at a celebration commemorating 50 million albums sold.

Jackson's first album, Here In The Real World, *was released in 1990. He received the Academy of Country Music's Top Male Vocalist award the same year.*

As the first decade of the new millennium neared an end in 2009, Jackson topped the charts with "Country Boy," the third No. 1 single in a row from his smash "Good Time" album. The next year, Jackson was honored with a star on the Hollywood Walk of Fame.

His star power continued in 2011 as he won a Grammy Award for "As She's Walking Away" with the Zac Brown Band. He also performed "Where Were You (When the World Stopped Turning)" in front of a crowd that included President Barack Obama, Vice President Joe Biden and their wives at a remembrance event for the 10th anniversary of 9/11 at the Kennedy Center in Washington, DC. Also in 2011, Jackson opened a new career chapter by entering into a joint venture to record and release new music with Capitol/EMI Records in Nashville.

Jackson and his wife, Denise, met at the Dairy Queen in Newnan. The couple married in 1979, and they have three children.

The people and things that Jackson loves are close to the hearts of many; his favorite clothes, a T-shirt and jeans; his favorite TV show, *The Andy Griffith Show*; his favorite sports, going fishing or pulling for the Tennessee Titans, his favorite foods, pineapple and mayonnaise sandwiches or Brunswick stew, his favorite song, "He Stopped Loving Her Today" by George Jones. Many can relate to these things that are dear to Alan Jackson which may explain his powerful appeal to fans all across the nation. ∎

SOME BOYS DREAM OF JOINING A CIRCUS; Henry Haag "Harry" James was born in one and was a showman all his life. James' mother was a trapeze artist and horse rider and his father the bandleader in a traveling circus and they were touring when James was born in a hotel room in Albany, Georgia. The child began playing the drums at 7 and the trumpet at 10 with the Christy Brothers circus band. Although he lacked much formal education, James studied the trumpet with his father, a hard taskmaster who

popularity did not extend to the rest of the country, as financially devastating trips to Los Angeles and Chicago proved. James' jazz sound was highly respected by other musicians but not appreciated by the general public. In 1941, James signed with Columbia Records and added a string section to the band that then recorded ballads and semi-classical selections. The public listened and the band was on its way. James had gone through a succession of vocalists, but when he hired Helen Forrest in 1941, she added her emotional voice

Harry James

ACTOR & MUSICIAN . ALBANY . 1916 – 1983

assigned him a page of music each day. James learned early that achievement meant approval. By 16, James was playing with local bands in Beaumont, Texas, where the family had settled.

James owned several thoroughbred racehorses that won races such as the California Breeders' Champion Stakes (1951) and the San Vicente Stakes (1954).

James moved fast. In 1935, he joined a popular band and less than two years later moved up to Benny Goodman's sensationally popular orchestra where his colorful trumpet playing became a favorite of jazz fans. He soon earned the nickname "The Hawk" which paid tribute to his ability to sight-read. The joke among musicians was that if a fly landed on a piece of music, James would play it.

By February 1939, James had his own band in Philadelphia and in June hired a young vocalist named Frank Sinatra. On the fateful day of December 7, 1941, James' tune "You Made Me Love You" was in the Top 10. James was 23. He had developed some bad habits during his quick rise to success and was plagued life-long by heavy drinking, gambling and compulsive promiscuity.

Although James' band was a big hit in New York City, his

to his trumpet and the band peaked. Movie offers rolled in.

James had married singer Louise Tobin in 1935 and the couple had two children, but, in Hollywood, James met actress and famous pin-up girl Betty Grable. James divorced Tobin and he and Grable were married a few months later. This marriage, which lasted until 1965, also produced two children. James had a fifth child, from a brief marriage to Las Vegas showgirl Joan Boyd in the late 60s.

James and his band were very popular during the war years but lost members to the war effort. James himself, expecting to be drafted in 1944, gave warming to his remaining band members and cancelled his radio program. However, he was classified 4-F and the band reunited.

The band's popularity continued during the war years, but James became less interested. He signed on as a regular member of the cast of Danny Kaye's radio series and he and Betty became more involved in raising racehorses. In 1946, James dissolved the band.

This "retirement" proved to be only a hiatus. James' habits took a huge toll on his finances and he soon formed a new band and continued to play until nine days before his death in 1983. He is buried at the Bunkers Eden Vale Memorial Park in Las Vegas.

Although driven by his additions, and described by acquaintances and band members as cold and aloof, James and his trumpet undeniably gave great pleasure to numberless big-band enthusiasts for three decades. ∎

Photo courtesy of Wordpress.

Jasper Johns

ARTIST . AUGUSTA

JASPER JOHNS and Robert Rauschenberg changed the art world. In the 1950s, when Johns arrived in New York City, the art scene was dominated by abstract impressionists led by the powerful figures of Pollock and de Kooning. Rauschenberg's work was becoming known and noticed. When Alfred Barr, founding director of New York's Museum of Modern Art (MOMA), bought 4 of Johns' works in 1958, Johns' career was launched and the art world changed.

Jasper Johns was born in Augusta, Georgia, on May 15, 1930, and moved to South Carolina as a very young child. Although Johns began to draw when he was three, he was, as he has said, "alone with his art." "In the place where I was a child, there were no artists and no art, so I really didn't know what that meant." It was not until he moved to New York City in 1949 for a few semesters at the Parsons School of Design that he met kindred spirits who shared his interests. The Korean War took him to Japan in 1952 and 1953, but when Johns returned to New York, he met Robert Rauschenberg, a fellow artist, and a new era began for Johns and the art world.

painted surface was sufficient. This method paved the way for future movements such as Pop, Minimal and Conceptual art. In 1980, the Whitney Museum of American Art paid $1 million for *Three Flags*; by 2006, Johns' *False Start* sold for $80 million, making it the most expensive painting by a living artist.

Johns' interest in the process of a work of art led him to printmaking which he enjoyed because the process lent itself to experimentation with repeated variations on a subject. His new techniques in lithography, screen printing and etching transformed the field. Johns used the handfed offset lithographic press to produce *Decoy*, an image that was first produced as a print before being made into a drawing or painting.

Collaboration was important to Johns as he felt it helped to advance his own art. He often worked with other artists, including Andy Warhol and Bruce Naumann and in the 70s, illustrated the poet Frank O'Hara's book, *In Memory of My Feelings*.

Also in the 70s, Johns collaborated with writer John Beckett to create prints to accompany Beckett's work, *Fizzles*.

Since his early paintings in the 50s, Johns has created a body of work that is represented in almost every major museum collection.

In contrast to the spontaneity and emotionality of the abstract impressionists, Johns paints easily recognized and iconic subjects: flags, targets, numerals, letters, maps. His surfaces are lush and richly worked, often including encaustic and plaster relief. He was influenced by Marcel Duchamp, whose work Johns saw on a trip to Philadelphia with Rauschenberg when both artists were at the beginning of their careers and working together on window displays for Tiffany's.

Johns' early work, notably the oil on paper *Flag* (1954), the large monochrome *White Flag* (1955) and *Three Flags* (1958) reintroduced a concept art viewers had not seen in some time: utterly familiar objects that neutralized the subject so that the

In 1984, Johns was elected a Fellow of the American Academy of Arts and Sciences and in 1990 was awarded the National Medal of Arts. He received the Presidential Medal of Freedom from President Barack Obama, becoming the first painter or sculptor to receive this medal since Alexander Calder in 1977.

Since his early paintings in the 50s, Johns has created a body of work that is represented in almost every major museum collection. He has set the standard for current American art and challenged the technical possibilities in painting, printmaking and sculpture preparing the way for younger artists.

Johns now divides his time between his home in Sharon, Connecticut, and St. Martin. ∎

Three Flags by Jasper Johns, 1958. Displayed in Whitney Museum of American Art in New York.

Bobby Jones swings (upper left) and pictured with his wife (upper right), Atlanta, circa 1920. The Attorney General flips a coin (bottom) to decide privilege of first to tee off.

Left to right: Roger Whiteford, Washington Attorney; Bobby Jones, Attorney General Cummings, and John McClure, Washington lawyer, Congressional Country Club, 1938.

Above left, courtesy of the Library of Congress; center, Bain News Service, courtesy of the Library of Congress; below, by Harris & Ewing, courtesy of the Library of Congress.

Bobby Jones

GOLF PRO . ATLANTA . 1902 – 1971

BOBBY JONES HAS BEEN CALLED the greatest golfer of all time.

Born in Atlanta in 1902, the son of a lawyer, Jones began to play the game early in life, but golf was not his only pursuit. Jones was an intellectual who graduated with a mechanical engineering degree from Georgia Tech and an English literature degree from Harvard. He attended law school at Emory University and, before graduation, withdrew from school to pass the bar exam.

Jones was a sickly child before his parents moved near a golf course in the Atlanta area. There, he began playing golf and baseball. Jones never had formal golf lessons but followed at St. Andrews, Jones played badly, and, after one poor shot, picked up his ball without finishing that hole. Although he played the 18 holes, his actions on that hole equated to withdrawal from the tournament. Jones regretted his conduct at St. Andrews. He went on from there to excel at the game, perhaps like no one else ever has. However, after winning the Grand Slam, he shocked the golfing world by ending his competitive career.

Aside from Jones' unparalleled winning streak, another remarkable aspect of his golf career was the fact that he always played as an amateur. He played golf only about three months

In one year, Jones won the four major tournaments: the U.S. Open, the U.S. Amateur, the British Open and the British Amateur. No one in golf since then, not Tiger Woods, Arnold Palmer or Jack Nicklaus, has duplicated Jones' feat.

the club's Scottish pro, emulating his golf swing and developing his own smooth and effective swing. As he grew, his golf game improved.

When he was 14, the father of a friend took his own son and young Bobby to the 1916 U.S. Amateur competition. Bobby qualified for the tournament, leading in the first qualifying round, and advanced far into the tourney. This focused the attention of the golfing world on the young man from Georgia. Jones began playing in major tournaments.

Until 1923, he experienced what was called the seven lean years, failing to win a major tournament. Following those difficult years were the seven fat years, when Jones won tournament after tournament. There were many high points during that time, but the ultimate—and the one that led to his being considered one of the greatest athletes of all time—was winning the Grand Slam of 1930. In one year, Jones won the four major tournaments: the U.S. Open, the U.S. Amateur, the British Open and the British Amateur. No one in golf since then, not Tiger Woods, Arnold Palmer or Jack Nicklaus, has duplicated Jones' feat.

Yet Jones faced challenges in playing the game he loved. He was inwardly driven and, during a tournament, he would often lose as much as 15 pounds. He also had to overcome his temper. In a tournament of the year, about as much golf as a weekend warrior, yet he won more major tournaments than anyone else in the game. In eight years, he won 13 national championships.

Jones entered the U.S. Army Air Corps during World War II and arrived in Europe the day after D-Day. He was stationed in Europe for some time before returning home.

Having retired from competitive golf, Jones practiced law, but he bestowed on the game of golf a great gift. He wanted to design a great golf course—and he did. He collaborated on the design of the Augusta National Golf Club in Augusta, Georgia, the home of the Masters, one of the Grand Slam tournaments of today. Jones played in the Masters himself but never finished near the top.

Later in life, Jones developed a disease of the spinal cord that eventually confined him to a wheelchair. It was said of Bobby Jones that what made him great was not only his winning ways in golf but also his character. One man observed that Jones graciously accepted the best that life had to offer early, not an easy feat. Later, wheelchair-bound, Jones endured some of the worst life had to offer. He handled both with courage and nobility.

Jones died in 1971 at the age of 69. He was later inducted into the World Golf Hall of Fame. He was a great athlete, an accomplished intellect and an example of sportsmanship and character. ■

Stacy Keach

ACTOR & NARRATOR . SAVANNAH

STACY KEACH IS CELEBRATED AS ONE OF America's finest Shakespearean actors. The *New York Times* called him "The finest American classical actor since John Barrymore." He is, in addition, a respected film and television actor.

Walter Stacy Keach, Jr. was born on June 2, 1941, in Savannah, Georgia. The night he was born lightning hit the chimney, catching it on fire. His parents referred to it as "a sign of someone special coming into the world." Keach was born with a cleft palate, undergoing numerous operations. He would later sport a mustache to hide the scars.

Keach's father, Stacy Keach, Sr., was a successful actor, producer and writer. He moved the family to Pasadena, California, where young Keach, Jr. grew up. After graduating from high school in 1959, he enrolled in the University of California at Berkeley graduating in 1963 with two bachelors' degrees, English and dramatic arts. He also earned a Master of Fine Arts degree from the Yale School of Drama and was a Fulbright Scholar at the London Academy of Music and Dramatic Art.

Keach made his Broadway debut with the New York Shakespeare Festival in 1964 in a production of *Hamlet*. However, he attracted notice when he starred in the off Broadway political satire *MacBird*. His character was a blend of MacBeth and Lyndon B. Johnson.

In 1968, Keach made his first film appearance in *The Heart Is a Lonely Hunter*. He followed that with films *End of the Road* (1970) and *Doc* (1971). But it was his portrayal of the boxer "Tully" in *Fat City* (1972) that earned him acclaim. Also in 1972, he played a rookie cop in *The New Centurions* with George C. Scott.

In 1973, he narrated the Formula One racing documentary *Champions Forever, The Quick and the Dead*. It was here that his talents as a narrator received international exposure. *National Geographic*, *The Discovery Channel* and *Nova* have utilized his narrative abilities. He narrated *The Kennedys* for PBS and his voice can be heard narrating the *American Greed* series. Keach's Shakespearean readings are among the nation's best-selling classical CDs.

In 1980, Keach played the elder brother of Jesse James in *The Long Riders* (1980). His own brother James played Jesse. His film credits continued to mount over the years even though he never quite reached the status of "movie star."

His television roles have also been numerous. His earliest role was in 1958 when he starred with Barbara Eden in *How to Marry a Millionaire*. He acted in the 1977 series *Caribe*, played Barabbas in the 1977 *Jesus of Nazareth* miniseries and played a spy in the 1982 miniseries *The Blue and the Gray*. He is most known for his character Mike Hammer in the CBS television series *Mickey Spillane's Mike Hammer*. He won a Golden Globe for that role and then starred in *The New Mike Hammer* from 1984 to 1986. Keach was temporarily ousted from the show when customs officials found cocaine in his shaving cream container. He spent six months in prison. *Mike Hammer, Private Eye* aired from 1997 to 1998.

Keach's Shakespearean readings are among the nation's best-selling classical CDs.

Keach won a Golden Globe and an Emmy nomination as Best Actor for his 1988 television portrayal of *Hemingway*. His role as the father in the series *Titus* (2000) helped rejuvenate his career and introduced him to a new TV generation.

However, it is Keach's stage performances that have made him a mainstay with critics and fans alike. He has won Drama Desk Awards, three Obie Awards, three Vernon Rice Awards and three Helen Hayes Awards. In 2007, he was presented with the Prestigious Millennium Recognition Award for his outstanding contribution to classical theatre. He has played Hamlet in three separate productions, portrayed King Lear, Merlin, and Richard M. Nixon in the play *Frost/Nixon* to name a few. His recent endeavors include the Broadway production of *Other Desert Cities* (2011).

Most recently, Keach starred as a retired boxing trainer in FX's new series *Lights Out* (2011), which was cancelled after one season. Continued offers of work after 40 years in show business are a testament to his talent. He has more than sixty films and more than fifty television credits in his resume.

Keach presently serves as the honorary chairman for the Cleft Palate Foundation and works on the Artistic Advisory Board for the National Foundation for the Advancement in the Arts. In 1995, he won the Celebrity Outreach Award for his charitable work. He and his fourth wife Malgosia have been married for over 25 years and have two children. ∎

Martin Luther King Jr.

CIVIL RIGHTS LEADER . ATLANTA . 1929 – 1968

ON THE EVENING OF APRIL 3, 1968, IN MEMPHIS, Tennessee, a storm so strong that the thunder was rattling the windows and the wind was making shutters in the Mason Temple slam open and shut was raging through the city. At the pulpit in the standing room only church, Dr. Martin Luther King Jr., in town to support the city's striking African-American sanitation workers and help them get better pay and working conditions, told the crowd in what proved to be an eerily prophetic speech, "I've seen the promised land. I may not get there with you. But I want you to know tonight that we, as a people, will get to the Promised Land." It would be the last speech of his life.

As a young man, King didn't set out to become a minister and Civil Rights leader. In fact, as an adolescent he rebelled against his deeply religious minister father. In college at Morehouse College in Atlanta at just 15 years old, he drifted through school, questioned religion, drank beer and played pool, all to his father's dismay. But in his junior year he took a Bible class and had a change of heart.

After receiving his sociology degree from Moorehouse and studying at the liberal Crozer Theological Seminary in Pennsylvania, King began working on his Ph.D. at Boston University. It was there that he met and married his wife Coretta Scott and, while still in school working on his dissertation in 1954, became pastor of Dexter Avenue Church in Montgomery, Alabama. He was just 25 years old and one year later he would become a Civil Rights pioneer when he organized the Montgomery Bus Boycott in the wake of Rosa Parks' arrest for not giving up her seat at the front of a city bus.

From that point on, King was the most active and important nonviolent Civil Rights leader in American history, staging protests, marches, campaigns and other activities which many times landed him in jail and led the FBI to wiretap his phones, home, and hotel rooms. During this time, he received numerous death threats. His work in leading the March on Washington caused Congress to pass the Civil Rights Act of 1964, essentially ending legalized segregation in the United States and the Voting Rights Act of 1965 that eliminated the barriers to voting for African-Americans. In 1964, at 35 years old, he became the youngest person to win the Nobel Peace Prize.

Between 1965 and 1968, King shifted his focus toward economic justice and international peace, which he championed by speaking out strongly against the Vietnam War. His work in these years culminated in the "Poor Peoples Campaign," which was a broad effort to assemble a multiracial coalition of impoverished Americans who would advocate for economic change.

All of that came to a halt, however, on the evening after his famous speech in Memphis. While standing on the balcony of the Lorraine

"I've seen the promised land. I may not get there with you. But I want you to know tonight that we, as a people, will get to the Promised Land."

Motel with friends and colleagues, he was assassinated. His work carries on today, however, at the Martin Luther King Jr. Center for Nonviolent Social Change, founded by his widow Coretta Scott King shortly after the murder as a living memorial aimed at continuing King's work on important social ills around the world. His accomplishments are now taught to American children of all races and his teachings are studied by scholars and students worldwide. He is the only non-president to have a national holiday in his honor and is the only non-president memorialized on the Great Mall in the nation's capitol. He is honored by hundreds of statues, parks, streets, squares, churches and other public facilities around the world as a leader whose teachings are increasingly relevant to the progress of humankind. ■

Dr. Martin Luther King, Jr. (left), courtesy of the Library of Congress through Instrument of Gift, World Telegram & Sun photo by Dick DeMarsico, 1964. The Lorraine Motel balcony where Dr. King was assassinated (above) at the National Civil Rights Museum, Memphis, Tennessee. Photos by Jencie LaVae Escue.

Gladys Knight

SINGER-SONGWRITER, ACTRESS, HUMANITARIAN & AUTHOR . ATLANTA

Not many singing sensations who began their careers as children in the 1950s South are as popular now as they've ever been, but such is the case for Georgia native Gladys Knight, still known as the "Empress of Soul."

BORN MAY 28, 1944, IN ATLANTA, Knight began singing in Atlanta's Mount Mariah Baptist Church when she was four years old and performed as a guest soloist with the Morris Brown College Choir. Just a few years later, she won the grand prize on television's *Ted Mack's Amateur Hour* and was catapulted into national fame. The following year, she, along with her brother Bubba, her sister Brenda and her cousins William and Elenor Guest, formed The Pips, the most famous background singers in soul music. In 1959, after Brenda and Eleanor left the group and were replaced by cousin Edward Patten and friend Langston George, they took on the new moniker, Gladys Knight & The Pips, and set out on a career that would lead to their becoming one of the most successful musical acts in the world.

By the late 1950s and early 1960s, Gladys Knight and the Pips were regulars in the segregated South "Chitlin' Circuit," touring as the opening act for Sam Cooke, Ike and Tina Turner, Otis Redding, Wilson Pickett and Little Richard. They released their first album in 1960, when Knight was just 16 years old. With Knight singing lead and The Pips providing lavish harmonies and graceful choreography, the group (on Motown and later Buddah Records) went on to record some of the most memorable songs of the 1960s, 1970s, and 1980s. Smash hits including "I Heard it Through the Grapevine" (1967, later recorded by Marvin Gaye), "If I Were Your Woman" (1970), "Neither One of Us (Wants to be the First to Say Goodbye)" (1973), "I've Got to Use My Imagination" (1974), "Best Thing to Ever Happen to Me" (1974) and the Number one classic "Midnight Train to Georgia" (1973) cemented the group as soul royalty with one Top 20 and Top 10 hit after another. Knight enjoyed another Number One hit in

1985 when she teamed with Stevie Wonder, Elton John and Dionne Warwick on "That's What Friends are For."

During her career, Knight has recorded more than 38 albums over the years, both solo and with The Pips. To date, as a solo artist and with The Pips she has had more than 20 Top 20 hits, with many of those in the Top 10, and has won a total of seven Grammy Awards and seven American Music Awards. She has starred in several televisions shows including *The Jeffersons, New York Undercover, Charlie & Co.* with Flip Wilson, many television specials and her own musical variety show, *The Gladys Knight and The Pips Show*, which ran four seasons from 1975 until 1979.

The list of awards and accolades Knight has received in her lifetime is a long one. Among the dozens of them, she earned a star on the Hollywood Walk of Fame, was inducted in 1996 into the Rock 'N' Roll Hall of Fame, won the Lifetime Achievement Award from the Rhythm and Blues Hall of Fame, received the BET Lifetime Achievement Award, the Soul Train Heritage Award and was inducted in the Vocal Group Hall of Fame and the Apollo Theater Hall of Fame.

A humanitarian and philanthropist, Knight has donated to various worthy causes including the American Diabetes Association, for which she is a national spokesperson, the American Cancer Society, the Minority AIDS Project, amFAR and Crisis Intervention. She has been honored by numerous organizations as well, including the NAACP Legal Defense Fund, Congress of Racial Equality (CORE) and B'Nai Brith. Knight is also a mother, grandmother, and great-grandmother.

Today, Knight lives in Las Vegas, where she operates her personal entertainment corporation, Shakeji, Inc. ∎

Lady Antebellum

CONTEMPORARY MUSIC GROUP . AUGUSTA

IT TOOK ONLY A FEW short years for the group Lady Antebellum to accumulate numerous awards, including seven Grammies and Best New Artist of the Year from the County Music Association in 2008. The country pop group which came together in Nashville in 2006 consists of Dave Haywood, Charles Kelley and Hillary Scott.

Dave Wesley Haywood was born on July 5, 1982, in Augusta, Georgia, and plays the piano, guitar and mandolin. Haywood learned to play the piano from his mother and the guitar from his father, Van, a dental professor well known for his invention of a teeth-whitening method. Haywood and his family lived in North Carolina before moving

2007. Shortly afterwards, they signed with Capitol Records and released "Love Don't Live Here" from their first album entitled *Lady Antebellum* (2008). "I Run to You" from the same album became their first number one hit in 2009 on the Hot Country Songs Chart and the trio won the Best Country Performance by Duo or Group at the 52nd Grammy Awards.

In 2009, "Need You Now" was released from their second album of the same name and became their second number one single, winning Single of the Year at the 44th ACM Awards and Song of the Year and Record of the Year at the 53rd Grammy Awards. The

"I hope people realize we aren't taking it all for granted. Twenty years later I hope people will talk about us and say, 'They were just genuine people who made genuine music based upon their life experiences.'" says David Haywood.

back to Augusta where Haywood met Charles Kelley at Riverside Middle School. Haywood graduated from the University of Georgia in 2004. He has written for other artists including the track "Love Song" for Miranda Lambert.

Charles Kelley was born on September 11, 1981, in Augusta, Georgia. As a teenager, he joined his brother, Josh, also a musician and singer, and their oldest brother, John, in forming a band called Inside Blue. They released a CD that grabbed the attention of a major recording label. When Kelley met Haywood in middle school, the two wrote their first song together. Kelley also graduated from the University of Georgia in 2004 with a degree in finance. He worked in construction and as an accountant before moving to Nashville in 2005 to live with his brother Josh.

Hillary Scott was born in Nashville, Tennessee, on April 1, 1986, to Lang Scott, a musician and entrepreneur, and Linda Davis, a country music artist. Scott's first performance was with her mother for a family Christmas show at Opryland. At the time, Scott was a junior in high school at Donelson Christian Academy. Hillary Scott unsuccessfully auditioned twice for *American Idol*. In 2006, she ran into Kelley and Haywood in Nashville and the rest, as they say, is history.

The trio performed at local hot spots around Nashville before appearing as vocalists on Jim Brickman's single "Never Alone" in

album also won Best Country Album at the 54th Grammy awards. To date, the album has sold over five million copies worldwide. "We never expected to be thrust into the international spotlight in the way that we were...from the success of just one song," said Kelley.

"American Honey" from the same album was released in 2010 and became their third number one hit; the album's third single, "Our Kind of Love" (2010), became their fourth consecutive number one hit. That same year, Lady A performed on *American Idol*, sang the national anthem at game two of the World Series and launched their first tour: "Need You Now 2010."

In September 2011, Lady Antebellum released their third studio album, *Own the Night*, and launched their 2011-2012 tour of the same name. Lady A took home an award for Video of the Year for "We Owned the Night" at the 2012 County Music Television Awards, an award they received for group video for the last two years. The 54rd Grammy Awards saw them taking home five Grammies. At the 2012 Academy of Country Music Awards, they won Top Vocal Group.

On a personal note, Scott married the band's drummer, Chris Tyrrell, on January 7, and Haywood married longtime friend Kelli Cashiola on April 14, 2012. Fans can connect and get an up-close and personal view of Lady Antebellum and their activities through the short video clips shown on "Webisode Wednesdays" on Lady A's homepage. ∎

Lady Antebellum at the 2010 American Country Awards Arrivals, MGM Grand Hotel, Las Vegas, Nevada.

Brenda Lee

ENTERTAINER . AUGUSTA

"LITTLE MISS DYNAMITE" Brenda Lee is known to thousands of fans, not only for her petite 4-foot, 9-inch, body but also for her powerhouse performances on stages around the world. She is one of the few female singers who has sold more than 100 million records. Entertaining crowds of all sizes and ages, she has performed for more than six decades and still continues amazing crowds with her energy and powerful voice.

Nominated four times for a Grammy for her top hits including "I'm Sorry" in 1960, "Johnny One Time" in 1970, "Tell Me What It's Like" in 1980 and, in 1989, for "Honky Tonk Angels Medley" with K.D. Lang, Loretta Lynn and Kitty Wells. She received a Lifetime Achievement Grammy Award in 2008.

Born Brenda Mae Tarpley on December 11, 1944, she began singing in front of audiences at 5. Her father died in a construction accident in 1953 and she grew up with little money. She lived in Georgia until 1955 when her mother remarried and the family moved briefly to Cincinnati and later Nashville, before settling in Augusta, Georgia.

At 10, she changed her name to Brenda Lee, after Sammy Barton, the producer of *The Peach Blossom Special* on WJAT-TV where she had been singing, recommended changing from Tarpley to Lee because "Brenda Lee" would be much easier for audiences to remember.

Her stepfather, George Rainwater, opened the Brenda Lee Record Shop in Augusta. WRDW held a weekly radio program in the shop featuring Brenda Lee singing country songs. Her family moved to Missouri in 1956 so she could be a regular on the *Ozark Jubilee*.

Nationally known by age 11, she sang on the *Steve Allen Show, The Perry Como, American Bandstand* and many other television programs over the next five years.

In May 1956, she signed a recording contract with Decca Records and recorded seven songs, including "Jambalaya," "Your Cheatin' Heart" and "Bigelow 6-200." It wasn't until 1957 that she saw some chart success with "One Step at a Time" which hit No. 43 on the Billboard chart, peaking at No. 4 on the country chart. The next year she recorded "Rockin' Around the Christmas Tree" which has been used in many movies as well as numerous television shows. The song did not move up the charts until its re-release in 1960. Today, it remains No. 4 on the Top 10 All Time Christmas Songs.

Lee moved to the international arena with her first concert in Paris in early 1959. The local press there kept asking her manager for updated photos not realizing that she was still a young teenager and the photos were indeed recent. Held over for five additional weeks after her initial three-week run, she continued conquering Europe with concerts in Italy, Germany and England before heading to South America. In 1961 she began recording in other languages, releasing hit songs in German, Italian and French. By 1965, just before turning 21, she recorded her first song in Japanese.

"She has the greatest rock and roll voice of them all." – John Lennon of The Beatles

She also began acting in movies in 1961, performing with Eddie Albert and Jane Wyatt in *Two Little Bears*. She had a small role in *Smokey and the Bandit* and later often played herself in both movies and television shows throughout the 1980s, 90s and 2000s. Her songs, especially "Rockin Around the Christmas Tree" and "I'm Sorry," have been in numerous movies and shows during the last 50 years.

With 29 gold records and five gold albums, including *Little Miss Dynamite*, which went triple gold in the United Kingdom, Holland and Germany, Lee has received many awards throughout her long history. She has also hit the charts in more categories than any female singer in history with hit songs on the Rock, Pop/Rock, Easy Listening and Country charts.

She is a member of the Rock and Roll Hall of Fame, the Country Music Hall of Fame, the Rockabilly Hall of Fame and the Grand Ole Opry. She was inducted into the Georgia Hall of Fame in 1982.

The late John Lennon said about Brenda Lee: "She has the greatest rock and roll voice of them all."

She and her husband of 50 years, Ronnie, live in Nashville. They have two daughters, Julie and Jolie, and two granddaughters.

Little Miss Dynamite, whose 2002 autobiography has the same title, has been a beloved entertainer for more than six decades and still entertains audiences with her distinctive style. ■

Spike Lee

FILM ACTOR, PRODUCER, DIRECTOR & AUTHOR . ATLANTA

BEST KNOWN FOR CREATING FILMS that may be controversial, Spike Lee is not afraid to confront political issues, race relations and urban crime and violence. His award winning films, commercials and music videos have transformed the business of independent cinema and helped to enlighten minds along the way.

Born March 20, 1957, in Atlanta, Shelton Jackson Lee and his family soon moved to Brooklyn, New York, where he continues to live and conduct business through his film company, 40 Acres and a Mule Filmworks. His mother, Jacquelyn, gave him the nickname of Spike as a young child; she said it was because of his adventurous spirit and attitude.

Jacquelyn Lee taught at a private primarily white school and Spike and his three siblings were all offered the opportunity to attend with discounted tuition. He opted to go to public schools and learned to appreciate the arts from both his parents. His mother urged all of her children to attend museums, art galleries and plays. She also fostered an interest in African American art and literature. Lee's father, Bill, was a noted jazz musician and inspired a love of music in all of his children. Spike would frequently accompany his father to clubs where he played.

After graduation from John Dewey High School in Brooklyn, Lee went back to Atlanta to attend Moorehouse College, as his father and grandfather had done, and graduated with a degree in mass communications. His time at Moorehouse created his interest in directing films. His first student film, *Last Hustle in Brooklyn,* was completed while he was still an undergraduate student.

Lee moved back to New York after graduating from Morehouse and enrolled in the Tisch School of the Arts graduate film program at New York University. His 45-minute thesis film, *Joe's Bed-Stuy Barbershop: We Cut Heads*, won the 1983 Motion Picture Arts and Sciences' Student Academy Award.

Within a year, Lee produced his first feature film, *She's Gotta Have It,* filmed in two weeks with a budget of under $200,000 and partially funded by his maternal grandmother, Zimmie Shelton. Shelton was an alumna of Spelman College, the all-female college affiliated with the all-male Morehouse College in Atlanta attended by Lee, his father and grandfather.

Island Pictures agreed to distribute *She's Gotta Have It.* The film grossed over $7 million in the U.S. and Lee was on the radar of cinematic circles as both a director and comic actor. The film also received the Prix de Jeunesse Award at the Cannes Film Festival in 1986.

To date, Lee has directed and produced 48 films and written and/or acted in 28 of them. Most are critically acclaimed and admired for taking on subject matter many producers would avoid. His most recognized are his 1989 film, *Do the Right Thing*, which received an Academy Award nomination for Best Original Screenplay and won the Los Angeles Film Critic Associations' Best Film and Best Director Awards and *Malcolm X*, which received two Academy Award nominations in 1993, one for Denzel Washington for Best Actor and one for Best Costume Design.

It was the first documentary to focus on the life of Americans stranded in New Orleans after Hurricane Katrina.

Lee has also written and produced many award-winning documentaries—again taking on controversial issues. He produced *When the Levees Broke: A Requiem in Four Acts* in 2005. It was the first documentary to focus on the life of Americans stranded in New Orleans after Hurricane Katrina. He followed it up with *If God is Willing and Da Creek Don't Rise* in 2010, documenting the lack of assistance from governmental agencies and political leaders. Lee has also produced many music videos for a diverse group of artists including Tracy Chapman, Miles Davis, Bruce Hornsby and Michael Jackson.

His commercial work has garnered him awards and recognition, most notably his Nike Air Jordan Campaign and his work with Levi's 501 button fly jeans, AT&T and ESPN. In 1997, he partnered with DDB Needham to create a full-service advertising agency, Spike/DDB, a group dedicated to producing advertising that is literally out of the box. Like most projects in his life, Lee likes to create advertising that stands out from the competition.

Lee has authored or coauthored eight books and is currently the Artistic Director of the graduate division of the Kanbar Institute of Film and Television at New York University's Tisch School of the Arts.

He is married to Tonya Lewis Lee. The couple live in Brooklyn and have two children, Satchel, born in 1994, and Jackson, born in 1997. ■

Spike Lee at the 12th Annual Critics' Choice Awards at the Santa Monica Civic Auditorium, 2007 Los Angeles, California.

Chris Lowell

ACTOR, PHOTOGRAPHER & AUTHOR . ATLANTA

ALTHOUGH BEST KNOWN AS AN ACTOR, CHRIS LOWELL is also a photographer, writer and singer. He was born in Atlanta and attended the Atlanta International School (AIS) where he studied drama and theater. While at AIS, he founded the Video Yearbook and Film Program, giving students the opportunity for hands-on experience, from the script to the screen, in the filmmaking procedure.

After graduation he went to the University of Southern California to continue his studies and focus on photography. He was spotted while playing beach volleyball in his freshman year and connected with the casting director of *Life as We Know It*, a television show featuring life through the eyes of three teenage boys. The series ran for two seasons on the ABC network.

"I think the show's portrayal of sex through the eyes of teenage boys delivers a very unique message about the emotional attachment that should be involved in sex, but rarely ever is," he explained about his first big break in television in 2004.

Lowell was cast as a regular on *Veronica Mars,* a series with a cult following which aired on CW in 2006-2007. He also appeared on several episodes of *Grey's Anatomy* and landed a reoccurring role on the show's spin-off, *Private Practice*, in 2008. The show ran for two years.

His first role in film was as Kevin, George Clooney's assistant in the 2009 comedy, *Up in the Air*. His second film appearance was as Emma Stone's boyfriend in *The Help* in 2011. His role was considered the male lead of the primarily female cast. *The Help* won the 2011 Screen Actors Guild Award for Outstanding Performance by a Cast in a Motion Picture.

In 2012 Lowell played Peter in *Love and Honor*, a romantic drama about a soldier going AWOL to win back his hometown girlfriend during the Vietnam War, and "The Boy" in *Light Years*, a drama written and directed by Maggie Kiley.

With all of his success in television and film, his real passion remains photography. His work has been shown several times at Jackson Fine Art, an internationally known photography gallery in Atlanta, and he has had two gallery showings in Los Angeles, "Rendering the Ordinary Extraordinary," in 2007 at the Walter Maciel Gallery and "Dreamers" at the Stephen Cohen Gallery in 2010. Photographs by Lowell are included in The Sovereign Collection in Atlanta and the Sir Elton John Collection.

Lowell often lends his photography talent to charitable organizations. He worked as a photojournalist for Project Medishare in rural Haiti and donated all the proceeds from his Haitian photographs to the project. He supports its mission of achieving quality healthcare and development services for all Haitians. Project Medishare is actively involved with training health professionals and establishing health programs for rural communities. The project also provides technology, supplies and equipment to affiliated programs throughout Haiti.

With all of his success in television and film, his real passion remains photography.

He also dedicates all proceeds from his photographs of Uganda to Invisible Children Uganda (ICU), a charity headquartered in San Diego that began working in Uganda in 2005. The organization is dedicated to ending the use of child soldiers in the country's rebel war and to restoring previously affected communities in central Africa to peace and prosperity.

Lowell came back to Atlanta in the summer of 2012 to be a guest instructor and speaker at CampFlix, a week-long professional film camp designed to give children aged 11 to 17 the chance to work with industry professionals.

Lowell's current project is the independent film, *Beside Still Waters*. The film is being shot in Michigan and stars Ryan Eggold (of *Beverly Hills 90210* fame). It is a drama concerning a young man who is losing his family home shortly after the death of his parents. Lowell co-wrote the screenplay and is directing and producing the film. ∎

Photo this page, Lowell arrives at the "Hilarity For Charity" Benefit at Vibiana in Los Angeles, 2012. Lowell, left page, arrives at the BAFTA Award Season Tea Party 2012 at Four Seaons Hotel in Beverly Hills, California.

Carson McCullers

WRITER . COLUMBUS . 1917 – 1967

"If you would not be forgotten as soon as you are gone, either write things worth reading or do things worth writing." —Carson McCullers

CARSON MCCULLERS WAS A PIONEER of the Southern Gothic genre. Her work dealt with lonely, sad and misfit characters, in many ways reflections of herself. Because of lifelong ill health, McCullers was not able to "do things worth writing," but she spent her life "writing things worth reading."

Southern to her core, McCullers was born on February 19, 1917, to Lamar Smith and Vera Marguerite Waters, comfortably well off residents of Columbus, Georgia. She attended Columbus schools and graduated from Columbus High School in 1934. Her family sent her to New York City, expecting her to attend the Julliard School of Music as she was a more than proficient pianist, but McCullers had other plans. In fact, she studied creative writing at Columbia University and Washington Square College of New York University.

Forced back to the family home in 1934 to recover from a respiratory infection, McCullers began work on her first novel, *The Heart is a Lonely Hunter*, and wrote her first published short story, "Wunderkind," which appeared in the December 1936 issue of *Story* magazine.

In 1937, McCullers married James Reeves McCullers, an Alabama native, and began a tumultuous relationship that included a divorce in 1941 and a remarriage in 1945. Reeves eventually took his own life in the early 50's. The marriage was tormented by the bisexuality and alcoholism of both partners and Reeves' envy of his wife's abilities.

While separated from her husband in the early 40s, McCullers shared a house in Brooklyn Heights owned by George Davis, the literary editor of *Harper's Bazaar*, with W. H. Auden. The house became a haven for the more bohemian artists and writers of the time. In 1944, after her father's death, her mother bought a home in Nyack, New York, and it was here that McCullers spent many of the remaining years of her life. Shortly after moving to the house, McCullers met the great director, John Huston, who recounts the meeting in his autobiography. "…one day when Buzz (Burgess Meredith) and I were out for a walk, she (McCullers) hailed us from her doorway. She was then in her early 20s, and had already suffered the first of a series of strokes. I remember her as a fragile thing with great shining eyes, and a tremor in her hand as she placed it in

mine. It wasn't palsy, rather a quiver of animal timidity. But there was nothing timid or frail in the manner in which Carson McCullers faced life. As her afflictions multiplied, she only grew stronger."

Following World War II and after remarrying Reeves, McCullers lived in Paris. During this period, her close friends were fellow Southerners Tennessee Williams and Truman Capote.

However, the early strokes were followed by others. Her health and the traumatic life she had with Reeves caused her to return to New York where her health continued to decline and eventually she became bedridden. She died in Nyack in 1967 and is buried in Oak Hill Cemetery.

McCullers principal works are *The Heart is a Lonely Hunter* (1940) and *The Member of the Wedding* (1946), both novels, and "Ballad of the Sad Café," a short story that first appeared in *Harper's Bazaar* (August, 1943) and later was included in *The Ballad of the Sad Café: The Novels and Stories of Carson McCullers*. This story is considered by many to be her finest work. It recounts a love triangle involving the hunchback midget, Miss Amelia—one of McCullers "grotesque" characters whose anguish all can share—and depicts characters who are frail and vulnerable. Its Southern Gothic setting does not disguise the feelings of loneliness and despair that are universal.

Her greatest financial success was her stage adaptation of *The Member of the Wedding*, which opened on Broadway in 1950 and ran for 501 performances. The play won the 1950 New York Drama Critics Circle Award and the Donelson Award. Both *The Member of the Wedding* and *The Heart is a Lonely Hunter* were adapted to major motion pictures.

She received two Guggenheim fellowships, an Arts and Letters grant from the American Academy of Arts and Letters and other honors. In 1952, she was inducted into the National Institute of Arts and Letters and was named as a Georgia Woman of Achievement in 1994. She became a charter member of the Georgia Writers Hall of Fame in 2000.

Carson McCullers was acclaimed by critics and readers in her lifetime and continues to be a major influence on writers and readers today. ■

Johnny Mercer

LYRICIST, SONGWRITER & SINGER . SAVANNAH . 1909 – 1976

IF THE THEORY IS TRUE THAT THERE ARE ONLY six degrees of separation between everyone in the world touching one another's lives, it would likely be .6 degrees for lyricist, singer and record industry legend Johnny Mercer. Thank everyone, from Frank Sinatra, Bing Crosby, Nat King Cole and Judy Garland, all of whom sang his famous lyrics, to Snoop Dogg, Katie Perry, Coldplay and Beastie Boys.

John Herndon "Johnny" Mercer was born on November 18, 1909, in Savannah, Georgia. From the time he was a small child, Mercer was fascinated with music. Unlike many of his contemporaries, he was exposed to the African-American and Creole cultures and listened to fisherman, playmates, servants and others sing and speak in the Geechee dialect. He was also allowed to attend black church services and began memorizing the songs he heard there. While attending the Woodberry Forest boys' prep school in Virginia, Mercer attempted to learn to play the trumpet and piano without much success. An avid fan of poetry and classical literature, it soon became apparent that Mercer's genius was in writing and singing in addition to becoming an authority on jazz.

Mercer had intended to attend Princeton University but the Great Depression caused his father financial problems and Princeton had to be put on hold. Instead, he remained in Savannah for a while working for his father and listening to new heroes like blues artists Ma Rainey and Bessie Smith, whose records he shopped for in the black–run stores. But by age 19, Mercer decided he'd had enough and moved to New York to become an actor with money his father gave him to keep him afloat for a year.

New York City's Harlem and Tin Pan Alley scenes were booming in 1928 when Mercer arrived and he was eager to get himself in the thick of both. He found a day job at a brokerage house, acted in bit parts and wrote music at night in his tiny Greenwich Village apartment. Mercer traveled to Hollywood the following year and got his foot in the door by writing lyrics for movie soundtracks. Back in New York, he had a hit with the song "Lazy Bones," for which his new friend Hoagy Carmichael wrote the music. It landed the broke Mercer a $1,250 royalty check and the admiration of successful Tin Pan Alley songwriters Irving Berlin, George Gershwin and Cole Porter.

It was in 1935, however, when Mercer and his new wife Ginger Meehan moved to Hollywood, that he landed the first big break that would catapult him into the ranks of the lyric writing elite. His now famous song "I'm an Old Cowhand from the Rio Grande" was performed by Bing Crosby in the movie *Rhythm on the Range* in 1936 and was such a hit that suddenly Mercer found himself in great demand and working with some of the most renowned composers in the film industry, penning songs that would become a part of America's culture.

The first of his staggering 19 Academy Award nominations, of which he won four, came in 1938 for "Jeepers Creepers," performed by Louie Armstrong in the film *Going Places* with Ronald Reagan. That same year his "You Must Have Been a Beautiful Baby" was recorded by Bing Crosby and performed in the movie *Hard to Get* by Dick Powell. It has since been recorded by more than a dozen artists, from Tommy Dorsey and Dean Martin to Toni Tennille and Michael Buble.

Having hit his stride writing lyrics for musical films, Mercer co-founded Capitol Records in 1942 and within four years the label had sold more than 40,000 million records. Issuing wax on popular, classical and jazz artists, the Capitol roster read like a who's who through the 1940s and '50s: Les Paul, Peggy Lee, Stan Kenton, Miles Davis, Benny Goodman, Nat King Cole, Frank Sinatra, Judy Garland, The Andrews Sisters, Dinah Shore, Dean Martin, The Kingston Trio and dozens of other top-tier singers, including, of course, Mercer himself. Capitol is now a fully owned subsidiary of EMI Records, one of the largest labels in the world, which represents the aforementioned current pop artists.

It's hard to imagine that anyone who grew up in America hasn't heard a few of Mercer's lyrics from his more than 1,500 songs, including "That Old Black Magic" (1942), "Skylark" (1942), "Ac-Cent-Tchu-Ate the Positive" (1944), "On the Atchison, Topeka and the Santa Fe" (1946), "Come Rain Or Come Shine" (1946), "Satin Doll" (1953), "Something's Gotta Give" (1954), "Days of Wine and Roses" (1962) and the classic "Moon River" (1961), which he wrote for Audrey Hepburn to sing in the blockbuster film *Breakfast at Tiffany's*. So popular was the song and so closely associated with Mercer that the city of Savannah renamed The Back River, near which Mercer grew up, Moon River.

There's one Mercer song, however, that perhaps has been played more than any and sums up Mercer's life best. It is played every year at the Academy Awards and has been used in countless films, commercials and television shows; the 1937 song: "Hooray for Hollywood." ■

Johnny Mercer publicity photo, ca. mid-1940s. Special Collections and Archives, Georgia State University Library.

Photo of Margaret Mitchell courtesy of Atlanta Historical Society, circa 1936, by Asasno. Fifty years after Gone With the Wind *hit bookshelves, the U.S. Post Office would issue a 1-cent stamp to commemorate the event and in 1990, a 25-cent commemorative stamp honoring the movie.*

MARGARET MITCHELL PUBLISHED ONLY ONE BOOK—it received the Pulitzer Prize in 1937. *Gone With the Wind* sold over one million copies in the first six weeks of publication. Over 75 years later, more than 250,000 copies are still sold each year. The film adaptation broke all box office records and received ten Academy Awards.

Margaret Munnerlyn "Peggy" Mitchell, a fourth generation Atlantan, was born on November 8, 1900. She learned about the Civil War on the laps of relatives as a young child. She was ten before discovering the South lost. Mitchell had a love for storytelling before she could even write and would make up stories and dictate them to her mother.

with Macmillan publishing in New York City, asked to see Mitchell's manuscript. After reading part of the manuscript, Macmillan offered her a contract with a $500 advance and ten percent of the royalties.

Mitchell edited and revised her work, even changing the name of her main character, originally called Pansy. Titles she considered for the book included *Tomorrow is Another Day, Bugles Sang True* and *Ba! Ba! Blacksheep.* She eventually chose the now famous title because it was in a line from one of her favorite poems.

When the book was published in June 1936, Mitchell became an overnight celebrity and was in great demand for interviews and

Margaret Mitchell

WRITER . ATLANTA . 1900 – 1949

Margaret Mitchell's talents extended into writing and directing plays that the neighborhood children acted out on her front porch. At Washington Seminary, a prestigious Atlanta finishing school, she was a founding member of the drama club. She was also the literary editor of the high school yearbook and president of the Washington Literary Society.

When America entered World War I, the Seminary girls attended dances for young servicemen stationed at local military bases. It was at one of these dances that Mitchell met Clifford Henry, a wealthy and socially prominent New Yorker, to whom she became engaged. However, Henry was killed in October, 1918, while fighting in France.

That same year, Mitchell entered Smith College in Massachusetts to study medicine. She also began to use the nickname "Peggy." The next year when her mother died from influenza she returned home to take care of her father and brother. As a member of Atlanta's upper class, she scandalized polite society by performing a provocative dance at the last debutante ball of the season.

In 1922, she married Red Upshaw who came from a prominent North Carolina family. The ex-football player and bootlegger left Atlanta four months later. The marriage was annulled two years later. In 1922, Mitchell also became a reporter for the *Atlanta Journal Sunday Magazine* using Peggy Mitchell as her byline and earning $25 a week. In four years at the magazine, she wore many hats: proofreader, book reviewer, reporter and writer. There she produced some of her most popular work, profiles on Civil War Generals.

In 1926, she left *Sunday Magazine* due to complications from a broken ankle. To relieve her boredom, Mitchell began writing *Gone With the Wind* in the small apartment she occupied with her second husband, John Marsh. She wrote the last chapter first and the remaining chapters in no particular order. Harold Latham, an editor

speaking engagements. Constantly in the spotlight throughout the making and premiere of the film held at Loew's Grand Theater in Atlanta on December 15, 1939, Mitchell eventually declined requests for public

Gone With the Wind sold over one million copies in the first six weeks after publication.

appearances and stopped autographing copies of her book. Also, at her request, the original manuscript, except for pages validating her authorship, was destroyed along with other writings.

The financial rewards Mitchell received from the success of the book and movie allowed her to support various philanthropic endeavors including medical scholarships for African Americans at Morehouse College. When the USS Atlanta sank during battle in World War II, she raised $65 million to build a replacement ship.

In August 1949 when Mitchell was hit by an off-duty cab driver when crossing Peachtree and 13th Street. She died five days later.

The Margaret Mitchell House, located in Midtown Atlanta, is a leading tourist attraction. A museum dedicated to the book and the film called Scarlett on the Square, is located in Marietta. Clayton County, the setting for the fictional plantation, maintains The Road to Tara Museum in Jonesboro.

Lost Laysen, a real-life romance set in the South Pacific and written by Mitchell when she was 15 years old, was discovered in a shoebox kept by a former beau, Henry Love Angel, after his death. The novella was published in 1996 complete with photographs and copies of letters. It was a last gift to those left wanting more from one of America's most beloved storytellers. ■

PHIL NIEKRO'S MOVE TO ATLANTA with the Braves baseball team was the beginning of a long relationship between the player and the city during which Niekro became one of the most popular players in franchise history and a favorite of Atlantans. Niekro, known as "Kuncksie," a tribute to his famous knuckleball, played for the Atlanta Braves for eighteen years.

faithfulness endeared him to Atlantans, as did his contributions to local charities. At the end of his career with the Braves, Niekro's number, 35, was officially retired, making him one of only four players so honored by the team.

Niekro, a great all-around player as well as an outstanding pitcher and winner of 5 Golden Glove awards, played with the

Phil Niekro

MAJOR LEAGUE BASEBALL PITCHER . ATLANTA

Phillip Henry Niekro was born in Blaine, Ohio, and attended high school in Bridgeport. He and his younger brother Joe, who would also become a major league pitcher, learned to play ball in the

"Hitting Niekro's knuckleball is like eating soup with a fork."
- Richie Hebner

backyard with their dad. Niekro senior taught young Phil how to throw a knuckleball, the most difficult of pitches. The knuckleball floats with no spin or rotation and dips or swoops as it gets to the batter, making it almost impossible to hit. As it is equally difficult to throw, most knuckleball pitchers succeed with the pitch only about half the time, but Niekro's command of the ball allowed him to rely on the pitch for 300+ victories. Unlike most pitchers, Niekro held the ball with only two fingers of his right hand touching the top of the ball. The pitch, while difficult to master, is easier on the arm, allowing Niekro to continue to play the game well into his 40s.

In 1959, just out of high school, Niekro signed with the Milwaukee Braves. He played in their minor league farm system until 1963 and then spent a year in the military. In 1964, Niekro made his major league debut with the Braves and moved with the team to Atlanta in 1966.

The Atlanta team's record over the following years was not outstanding. Often, Niekro was the only star on the team and his

Braves until 1983. In 1969, Niekro's pitching abilities shot the Braves into a National League West title and helped earn another division title in 1982. In October 1982, Niekro pitched a complete game shutout against the San Diego Padres and hit two home runs, further endearing himself to Atlanta fans.

Following his career with the Braves, Niekro played briefly for the New York Yankees, the Cleveland Indians and the Toronto Blue Jays. At the age of 48, he ended his baseball career as a player with one last late season start for the Braves.

During his career, Niekro pitched 5,404 1/3 innings, the most innings pitched by one pitcher post 1920. Niekro's 318 victories are the most by any knuckleball pitcher. He was a five-time All Star with 3,342 career strikeouts and was elected to the National Baseball Hall of Fame in 1997. The Bridgeport, Ohio, baseball field is named Niekro Diamond in honor of Phil and his brother Joe.

Niekro managed Atlanta's AAA farm club and later the Colorado Silver Bullets women's pro team, after retiring. He has now fully retired from the game and lives in Flowery Branch, Georgia.

Fans who fondly remember the great knuckleball pitcher can go to a restaurant known as "Knucksie's" near the Gwinnett Braves' stadium in Lawrenceville, GA and and enjoy a barbeque and coleslaw sandwich on a corn muffin, said to be the star's favorite. ∎

Phil Niekro's photo (right) courtesy of the Greater Knoxville Sports Hall of Fame.

Jessye Norman

OPERA SINGER . AUGUSTA

TWO WORDS THAT COULD BE USED to describe opera singer Jessye Norman are "stellar" and "unclassifiable."

Norman, who was born September 15, 1945, in Augusta, Georgia, sang in a church choir early in life and rose to operatic stardom. An African-American, she has sung for presidents and royalty, in opera houses across Europe and in Carnegie Hall and has won a myriad honors.

Although considered a soprano, Norman can sing at any female voice register with a quality worthy of the most celebrated opera houses in the world. Included in her vocal range are mezzo-soprano and contralto. She also sings genres of music other than classical. Norman has said her voice could not be classified; she consciously chose to sing in a variety of ranges. She also has said that pigeonholes are only good for pigeons.

Norman absorbed music in her home; both parents were amateur musicians. One of five children, she was encouraged to sing at an early age. She also heard a radio broadcast of the Metropolitan Opera at age 9 and, although she didn't fully understand it, she loved it. The singing of Marian Anderson and Leontyne Price inspired her. At age 16, she participated in the Marian Anderson Vocal Competition and, though Norman did not win it, she received a scholarship to Howard University.

Upon graduation from Howard, Norman entered the Peabody Conservatory in Baltimore and later studied at the University of Michigan, earning a master's degree.

In 1968, Norman entered the International Music Competition of the German Broadcasting Corporation in Munich and took first place. In 1969, she made her debut at the Deutsche Oper in Berlin.

In 1972, she sang at La Scala, the renowned opera house in Milan, Italy. Later that year, she sang in the Hollywood Bowl, at the Tanglewood Festival in Massachusetts and at the Royal Opera House in London. In the ensuing years, she performed across Europe, in Argentina and in the United States.

In 1975, Norman relocated to London and didn't sing in opera halls for five years, allowing her voice to develop fully. She sang in concerts and recitals during this period. Though, up to that time, she had met with tremendous success, she would reach greater heights in the years to come.

She returned to the opera stage in 1980 in Richard Strauss' *Ariadne auf Naxos* at the Hamburg State Opera in West Germany.

Two years later, Norman made her American operatic debut in Stravinsky's *Oedipus Rex* with the Opera Company of Philadelphia. In 1983, she made her Metropolitan Opera debut, celebrating the 150th anniversary of the Met. By the middle of that decade, she had achieved worldwide renown. In 1985, she sang at the second presidential inauguration of Ronald Reagan. The next year, she sang for the 60th birthday of Queen Elizabeth II. In 1989, she sang

Norman is the youngest person, at age 51, to receive the Kennedy Center Honor.

in Paris for the bicentennial of the French Revolution for which she was awarded the Legion of Honor. She sang during the 1996 Summer Olympic Games in Atlanta and for the second presidential inauguration of Bill Clinton in 1997. She sang at the event honoring those who died in 9/11 and to honor former President Jimmy Carter when he won the Nobel Peace Prize in 2002.

She was the youngest person, at age 51, to receive the Kennedy Center Honor. In 1996, her hometown renamed Riverwalk Amphitheater and Plaza after her. She is an inductee in the Georgia Music Hall of Fame. She has received more than 30 honorary doctorates, including one from Harvard In 2009, President Barack Obama awarded Norman the National Medal of Arts. She has won four Grammy Awards.

Norman has helped many causes, including arts education for children in her hometown. She is a member of the board of trustees of both Paine College and the Augusta Opera Association. Norman is a lifetime Girl Scout and is known for her purchase and generous gifts of the famous cookies.

She owns an estate near New York City. Although no longer appearing on the opera stage, she performs in concerts and recitals. Her memoir, *Stand Up and Sing!* is scheduled to be published by Houghton Mifflin Harcourt in 2013. Norman told the *New York Times*, "I am absolutely thrilled to be able to tell my own story, to celebrate my family's rich, diverse heritage, and to pay tribute to all those who have imbued my life with their resonance."

This daughter of Georgia has delighted audiences worldwide, received honors from all corners of the globe, and, with her magnificent voice and boundless spirit, enriched humanity. ∎

Mary Flannery O'Connor

WRITER . SAVANNAH . 1925 – 1964

MARY FLANNERY O'CONNOR, THOUGH SHE lived a short and largely secluded life and produced only a small body of work, was an American writer whose influence was broad and who continues to be revered. Her *Complete Stories* won the U. S. National Book Award in 1972, eight years after her death, and in 2009, was named "Best of the National Book Awards" in an internet survey.

O'Connor was born in Savannah, Georgia, on March 25, 1925, the only child of Edward F. O'Connor and Regina Cline. Both of her parents were from traditional Catholic families, a rarity in the largely Protestant South, and O'Connor attended parochial schools as a child. Her family later left Savannah to live on a farm, Andalusia, just outside of Midgeville. There, when she was 15, her father died of lupus. This would be a devastating loss for his only child. O'Connor often used the literary technique of foreshadowing—hinting at things to come—in her work. Ironically, her father's death was a sort of foreshadowing; she contracted the disease when she was 25.

O'Connor attended the Peabody Laboratory School and graduated in 1942. She completed a degree in Social Sciences at the Georgia State College for Women (now Georgia College and State University) in three years. After graduation, she received a scholarship to the Iowa Writer's Workshop at the University of Iowa. Although she intended to study journalism, she quickly switched to a master's program in creative writing, where she attended lectures led by such illustrious authors as Robert Penn Warren.

After leaving Iowa, O'Connor was accepted at Yaddo, an artists' retreat in Saratoga Springs, New York. She remained there and in New York City for several months before moving to live near friends in Ridgefield, Connecticut. However, this quiet and productive interlude ended in 1950 when O'Connor was struck with the disease that had taken her father's life. At that time, the only treatment was a regime of steroid drugs. Although she survived the first attack of the disease, O'Connor was forced to return to her family home, Andalusia, and remain there until her death in 1964. She was buried in Memorial Hill Cemetery in Midegeville beside her father.

O'Connor never lost her sense of humor, her ability to record the vagaries of human nature or her strong Catholic faith, in spite of a life spent constantly waging a losing battle with a devastating disease. She was a disciplined writer who spent time every morning at her desk, a bird lover who raised peacocks on the farm and an avid correspondent who enjoyed a lively exchange of letters with friends, critics and other writers. It is because of this correspondence that her admirers are able to know her thoughts during these years. Her letters to a close friend were edited by Sally Fitzgerald and published in 1979. Her readers saw in these letters her warm personality, her writing habits, her bright intelligence and keen wit and, above all, her strongly held religious beliefs.

In her life, O'Connor produced two carefully crafted novels, *Wise Blood* (1952) and *The Violent Bear It Away* (1960) and two short story collections, *A Good Man is Hard to Find* (1955) and *Everything That Rises Must Converge* (posthumously, 1965). Her essays and lectures, which she managed to occasionally present in spite of fragile health, were collected in *Mystery and Manners* (1965) and she wrote over one hundred book reviews.

Her work is often characterized as "darkly comic", "ironic" and "grotesque."

Her work is often characterized as "darkly comic", "ironic" and "grotesque." Her characters are from the rural South and her theme of the fall of humanity and its need for redemption is variously repeated. Her stark vision reveals human frailty, often with a comic overtone. She stated that she felt the good in the world was "under construction" and her characters pursue a spiritual quest. The reader finds an emphasis on guilt, sin and alienation. Although chiefly concerned with personal exploration, she was cognizant of the racial situation in the South at the time, and alluded to it in her work. Aware that her work was considered by some to be grotesque, O'Connor commented, "Anything that comes out of the South is going to be called grotesque by the Northern reader, unless it is grotesque, in which case it is going to be called realistic."

The work produced during Flannery O'Connor's short, quiet life has had and continues to have a profound effect on modern literature. She received many awards, including grants from the Ford Foundation and the National Institute of Arts and Letters and multiple O. Henry Awards. She was the first writer born in the twentieth century whose work was collected and published by the Library of America. The Georgia Press presents the Flannery O'Connor Award for Short Fiction yearly. In 1992 she was inducted into Georgia Women of Achievement and in 2000 into the Georgia Writers Hall of Fame. ∎

Ty Pennington

TELEVISION HOST, ARTIST, PHILANTHROPIST, CARPENTER & MODEL . ATLANTA

FROM CARPENTER TO MODEL, from author to television host, 47-year-old Ty Pennington loves what he does and is happy to share his success with people who need help. His most popular and longest running show, the Emmy and People's Choice Awards winner "Extreme Makeover: Home Edition," ended in January 2012 after nine seasons of shows that helped more than 200 families. The last episode featured the eight-person design team and hundreds of volunteers rebuilding seven homes in seven days for the people in Joplin, Missouri, who had lost everything in a devastating tornado that spring. Fans cried along with the families as Pennington called out his heartwarming "Welcome home."

Viewers will remember his dedication to the show's mission. In 2005, after suffering an acute appendicitis attack and undergoing an emergency appendectomy, viewers watched as he ran things via phone and email from his hospital bed to make sure the family whose house the team was rebuilding would have a new home by the end of the seven days.

In early 2012, Pennington joined a new daytime talk show called "The Revolution." He is one of the hosts who interview guests on the latest news about everything people need to know to have a healthy and happy life.

Hired in 2000 as the zany and tousle-haired carpenter on The Learning Channel's "Trading Spaces," Pennington garnered fans of all ages. The show featured two families willing to re-do a room or two in the other family's home in the way they thought the homeowners would like. Each family had two days, a carpenter, a designer and very little budget to finish the project. For four years, Pennington was a creative carpenter who could re-build anything in a home for practically no money.

Pennington expanded his television reach with a new series in Canada and Great Britain. "Homes for the Brave" showcases the lives of British soldiers who served in Afghanistan and who need help improving their lives and homes. He hosted and served as an executive producer for a community-improvement series called "Ty's Great British Adventure" which became UKTV Home's highest rated television series.

As an author, he wrote *Ty's Tricks: Home Repair Secrets Plus Cheap and Easy Projects to Transform Any Room* in 2003 and *Good Design Can Change Your Life: Beautiful Rooms, Inspiring Stories* in 2008. In 2007 he released the first issue of his quarterly magazine, *Ty Pennington at Home*, which offered advice and how-to instructions for home repair and design.

Pennington was born in Marietta, Georgia, and attended Sprayberry High School. He attended Kennesaw College, studying art and history, then transferred to The Art Institute of Atlanta where he graduated with a bachelor's degree. He attended the Atlanta College of Art to study art and sculpture while working his way through school as a carpenter and model for companies like J. Crew, Swatch, Body Glove and Land's End. He also appeared in commercials for Diet Coke, Macy's, Levi's and Sears.

"You have to be ready for anything that comes along and always open the door when someone knocks on it."

In June 2012, SCAD (Savannah College of Art and Design) awarded an honorary doctorate of humane letters to Pennington, who spoke at the graduation ceremony. He told the graduates that he has an emotional connection to the people he has helped and that they always changed the lives of the design team at the same time that he and his team were creating new homes for those families. He said he was thankful for the support of his mother and all his family, friends and design teams who have helped him get where he is today.

"It takes a lot of hard work to succeed, but you also need someone who believes in you like you believe in yourself," Pennington said. "You have to be ready for anything that comes along and always open the door when someone knocks on it."

Today, Pennington partners with Sears (Ty Pennington Style seasonal home décor), Lumber Liquidators (the Ty Pennington Collection flooring), Westminster Fabrics (Ty Pennington Impressions fabric line), Howard Miller (Signature Home Furnishings by Ty Pennington) and runs several businesses in Atlanta.

Still single, but now with a girlfriend and living in New York City, Pennington was named one of *People* magazine's Top 50 Bachelors in 2002. ∎

Ty Pennington attending the Silver Rose Awards Gala at Beverly Hills Hotel on April 17, 2011 in Beverly Hills, California.

Tyler Perry

WRITER, DIRECTOR, PRODUCER & ACTOR . ATLANTA

TYLER PERRY'S STORY IS TRULY A TALE of rags to riches. Born Emmitt Tyler, Jr. in New Orleans, his early childhood was marred by poverty and abuse from his father and resulted in Perry's suffering from depression that caused a suicide attempt. In spite of these beginnings, he never lost sight of his goal. He has become one of the most successful men in show business. In 2011, *Forbes* magazine named him number one on their "Highest Entertainment Earners" list—estimating his earnings from his plays, films and television at $130 million for the year.

At the age of 16 Perry changed his name to Tyler to distance himself from his father. He dropped out of high school and began working at various odd jobs. Inspired by an Oprah Winfrey show to write his feelings, he began writing letters to himself at 18. Those letters eventually evolved into a musical, *I Know I've Been Changed.* In 1992, at the age of 22, he went to Atlanta and used his life savings to stage his first play.

The first staging was not successful but Perry did not give up. After more odd jobs and stints of living out of his car, he convinced a promoter in 1998 to book the play in an Atlanta church. The play's sold out run attracted investors and eventually the musical was on stage at the city's famed Fox Theatre.

I Know I've Been Changed set the stage for one of the most successful careers in entertainment. He spent the next thirteen years writing a play a year but it was his 2000 play, *I Can Do Bad All by Myself* which introduced the character Madea, who not only would appear in future plays but would open the door for Perry's jump to the big screen. Perry played the Madea character himself dressed in drag and based her on his mother and several other women in his life. The character developed a strong following and made several appearances in Perry's future plays, including: 2002's *Madea's Family Reunion*, 2003's *Madea's Class Reunion* and *Madea Goes To Jail* in 2005. By this time, his eight plays had grossed over $75 million dollars in ticket and DVD sales. His empire was blossoming.

His first feature film, *Diary of a Mad Black Woman*, debuted at number one nationally early in 2005 and Perry appeared as three different characters, including the soon-to-be-legendary Madea. *Diary of a Mad Black Woman* grossed more the $50 million.

Perry directed, produced and played the leading role in 2006's *Madea's Family Reunion*, which grossed over $63 million and allowed him to establish his studio in Atlanta. Tyler Perry Studio's is now housed in Southwest Atlanta and employs 350 people.

"I live my life outside of the box because when I die they're going to put me into one!"

The 200,000 square foot studio features five sound stages, a post-production facility and a private screening room.

2006 was a busy year for Perry. Along with the success of *Madea's Family Reunion* and the launching of his studio, he also wrote his first book and produced his first television series. Both were, yet again, tremendous successes.

His book, *Don't Make a Black Woman Take Off Her Earrings: Madea's Uninhibited Commentaries on Love and Life*, was on *The New York Times* non- fiction best seller list for nine weeks and won Quill Book Awards in two categories, Humor and Book of the Year.

His first television series, *The House of Payne* on TBS, went into syndication within one year and was the highest rated first-run cable show of all time. His second television series, *Meet the Browns,* claimed second place in all time cable rankings.

Perry has utilized his success to help many organizations and social causes. He donates funds to charities dedicated to helping the homeless, including Feed the Hungry and Project Adventure. In 2006, he built Perry Place, a 20-home community for survivors of Hurricane Katrina and his charitable organization, The Tyler Perry Foundation, gave $1,000,000 in 2010 to help those affected by the earthquakes in Haiti.

He currently lives on a 12-acre estate along the Chattanooga River, just outside Atlanta. ∎

Tyler Perry at the 2nd Annual Black Movie Awards in Los Angeles, 2006.

Dwight Phillips

OLYMPIC GOLD MEDALIST . DECATUR

DWIGHT PHILLIPS, WHO STARTED OUT AS A SPRINTER, switched to the long jump and became the only long jumper to win four world titles. The story does not end there. His personal record for the 60 and 100 meter dashes ranks him among the top twenty fastest runners ever. In 2004, he brought home the first U.S. Olympic men's long jump gold medal since Carl Lewis won it in 1996 in the Atlanta Olympic Games.

2008 Olympic Trials, he finished fourth, which meant he would not be defending his Olympic Gold title.

In June 2009 at age 31, Phillips competed in the long jump at the Prefontaine Classic, a premier track and field meet that takes place at the University of Oregon. He won the long jump with his third jump that was his personal best. It was also the longest jump by an American since Mike Powell set the

By the 2004 Athens Olympics, Phillips was ranked number one in the world in the long jump. He defeated his opponent and won the gold medal by a margin of twelve centimeters.

Dwight Phillips was born on October 1, 1977, in Decatur, Georgia. At age 14, he was hit by a motorcycle while playing street football with his friends, and both his legs were broken. His injury required eight months of rehab, the use of a walker and two years before achieving full recovery. However, as a high school athlete, he became a 1996 All-American, setting school records in the triple jump.

Phillips attended the University of Kentucky where he was a triple jumper. In 2002, he transferred to Arizona State University and graduated with a degree in communications. While there, he focused on the long jump. In 2000, he competed in his first Olympics in Sydney. He finished eighth in the long jump but was considered the best American performer in the event.

Phillips participated in his first World Championships in 2001, finishing eighth. It was in 2003 that he made his mark when he won both the International Association of Athletes Federation (IAAF) and then the outdoor World Championships by beating his fellow runners by a margin of four centimeters. He won the indoor by beating Spain's Yago Lamela by a mere centimeter.

By the 2004 Athens Olympics, Phillips was ranked number one in the world in the long jump. He defeated his opponent and won the gold medal by a margin of twelve centimeters. His winning jump was the fourth longest in Olympic history behind Olympic greats Bob Beamon (1968) and Carl Lewis (1988, 1992).

Phillips went on to win the gold at the 2005 Helsinki World Championships and at the 2007 Osaka World Championships. In the

world record in 1991. The jump placed him in the top ten of all-time performers in track and field and was the eighth best outdoor mark in history, tying him with Larry Myricks and Erick Walder.

In 2009, Phillips won his third long jump World Championship in Berlin. He received his gold medal from Jesse Owen's granddaughter. Owen had won the medal in Berlin in 1936. Competing in Daegu in 2011, Phillips won his fourth outdoor World Championship. He held up his assigned bib number of "1111," appropriately signifying his fourth gold medal.

Phillips suffered back and neck injuries in an automobile accident right before the start of the 2012 outdoor season. Coupled with a recurring tendon injury, Phillips decided to forgo the London Olympics and have surgery in order to extend his athletic career.

Phillips is one of the founders of QuickTime Cinema located in Atlanta, Georgia. He and his partners are making a name for themselves in the area of film, commercials, reality shows and music videos. Dwight Phillips and his wife Valerie have been married since 2004 and have two boys, Dwight Jr. and Elijah.

A world-class athlete, businessman and family man, Phillips enjoys life in Georgia: "Until I lived in Arizona for seven years and returned to Georgia in 2004, I did not realize how much home truly meant to me. The great thing about Georgia is the beautiful greenery and the spectacular changing of the seasons. The Southern cuisine is pretty good too, especially the collard greens and macaroni and cheese!" ∎

VTB Bank World Athletics Final 2009 American athlete in the long jump, Dwight Phillips, on September 12, 2009 in Kaftatzoglio stadium, Thessaloniki, Greece.

Otis Redding

SOUL SINGER-SONGWRITER, RECORD PRODUCER & TALENT SCOUT . DAWSON . 1941 – 1967

SOUL MUSIC ICON Otis Redding could have lived anywhere in the world after rising to fame and success with Stax Records in Memphis, Tennessee, in the 1960s, but he loved his home state of Georgia so much that he bought a 300-acre ranch a few miles outside Macon, made that his home, and set about not only to further his career but also to raise a family, become one of Georgia's first black, successful entrepreneurs and make a difference in the lives of young people.

Born in Dawson in 1941, Redding's family moved to Macon when he was five years old and he soon began singing in his father's Vineville Baptist Church. He attended Ballard Hudson High School and participated in the school band but dropped out to help his family financially by working part time and competing in Douglass Theater talent shows for the $5 prize money. After 15 straight wins, he was no longer allowed to compete in order to give other singers and musicians a chance.

In 1960, Redding joined local band Johnny Jenkins and the Pinetoppers and sang with them while also singing at Macon's "Teenage Party" talent shows on Saturday mornings at the Douglass and the Roxy Theatres.

Redding's big break came in October 1962 when he drove Johnny Jenkins and the Pinetoppers to Memphis (Jenkins didn't have a driver's license) for a recording session at the relatively new Stax Records. At the end of the session, just as everyone was about to leave, owner Jim Stewart allowed Redding to sing a song. Redding broke out in his moaning rendition of "These Arms of Mine" and Stewart cut it on the spot. Redding, Stax and the world of soul music would never be the same.

As Redding continued to travel to Memphis and cut hit after hit at Stax including "I've Been Loving You Too Long" (1964), "Try A Little Tenderness" (1967), and "Respect" (1965), which was later covered by Aretha Franklin and became one of the most memorable songs in music history, and his smash hit "(Sittin' On) The Dock of the Bay" (released in 1968 after his death and now the sixth most aired song in American history), he toured throughout the United States, Canada, Europe and the Caribbean. His concerts were some of the biggest box office smashes of anyone touring at the time and earned him large sums of money. He became even more of an international sensation when, in 1967,

he performed before his first large, U.S., predominantly white audience at the Monterrey Pop Festival in California. He was a massive hit with the "Summer of Love" crowd, and it positioned him to become one of the industry's most successful crossover artists.

What set Redding apart from many in the soul music world at the time was that he had great business acumen. He and his manager Phil Walden founded Redwal Music Co., Inc. in Macon and, as president, Redding was responsible for the company's leadership in music publishing; to date, the company has

As popular as Redding's recordings were, his live performances and larger than life stage presence drove crowds wild.

copyrighted more than 200 songs and published many that have sold in excess of a million copies each. He also founded his own publishing and record label, Jotis Records, which was rare for a black recording artist in the 1960s. In fact, while it wasn't his prime motivation, he was a role model to blacks who admired him for getting paid and paid well without the usual problems of being cheated by promoters, agents or record company executives. In addition to the music business, Redding also had other business interests in Georgia, including real estate, investments, stocks and bonds and livestock that he raised on his beloved Big-O Ranch with his wife Zelma and children Karla, Otis III and Dexter (the Reddings also adopted a daughter, Demetria, after his death). He was already a philanthropist in Macon, staging fund-raisers and working in other ways to make sure children there stayed in school instead of dropping out as he had to do.

Just at the height of his career, on December 10, 1967, while en route to a concert in Madison, Wisconsin, the private plane Redding had recently purchased crashed into the freezing waters of Lake Monona, killing him, the pilot, his valet and all members of his band on board except one, Ben Cauley of the Bar-Kays. Redding was just 26 years old.

Today, his legacy lives on through the Big "O" Youth Educational Dream Foundation, which Zelma and daughter Karla Redding-Andrews operate from an office in Macon and from the Big O Ranch, where most of the family still lives. ∎

Early promotional photo (top), ca. 1966. Otis at Big O Ranch (left), September 1967. Photo by Paul C. Acree, Jr.
Otis and the Bar-Kays (right), 1967. All photos courtesy of Zelma Redding.

Jerry Reed

SINGER, SONGWRITER, ACTOR & GUITARIST . ATLANTA . 1937 – 2008

JERRY REED WAS KNOWN by many as Burt Reynold's sidekick in the zany *Smokey and the Bandit* movies. However, he was known in the music world as a gifted guitar player and songwriter. His finger picking guitar skills made him a highly sought after studio session player for many of the great country music stars.

Jerry Reed Hubbard was born in Atlanta on March 20, 1937. His parents separated shortly after his birth. He and his sister spent several years in and out of orphanages and foster homes until 1944 when they were reunited with their mother and stepfather.

He was also a regular on *The Glenn Campbell Goodtime Hour* and produced his biggest hit during that time, "When You're Hot, You're Hot" (1971), which sold over one million copies and was certified gold. It was also the title track of his first solo album and reached number nine on the pop charts and number six on the Billboard's Easy Listening charts. In 1972, his single "Lord, Mr. Ford" hit number one.

Reed earned a 1971 Grammy nomination for best male country vocal for "Amos Moses." He won the following year with "When

In 1967, he was invited by Elvis to play his distinctive "claw-style" guitar licks on one of his own songs that Elvis was recording, "Guitar Man."

He spent time with his grandparents in Rockmart, Georgia, and was quoted as saying while strumming on his guitar: "I am gonna be a star. I'm gonna go to Nashville and be a star." Toward this end, Reed started writing music and singing in high school, eventually dropping out to tour with Ernest Tubb and Faron Young. At 18, he was signed to cut his first record by record producer Bill Lowery: "If the Good Lord Willing and the Creek Don't Rise" (1955).

Reed recorded both rockabilly and country singles, and in 1958 Lowery signed him to the National Recording Corporation (NRC) where he recorded as an artist and as a member of the house band. In 1959, he made the Cashbox Country chart with the single "Soldier's Joy." However, disappointed in his lack of success, Reed joined the army. After he was discharged in 1961 he moved to Nashville to become a songwriter. His song "Misery Loves Company," recorded by Porter Wagoner, hit number one in 1962.

He was soon in great demand and wrote hit songs for Elvis Presley, Brenda Lee, Johnny Cash and others. In 1967, he was invited by Elvis to play his distinctive "claw-style" guitar licks on one of his own songs that Elvis was recording, "Guitar Man." He also played for Elvis' "Big Boss Man" that same year. Elvis later recorded three other Reed compositions: "U.S. Male" (1968), "A Thing Called Love" (1971) and "Talk About The Good Times" (1973).

In the 1970s and 1980s, Reed established himself on the pop and country charts with humorous hits such as "Amos Moses," "East Bound and Down," and "She Got the Goldmine (I Got the Shaft)." His music was a mainstay on the pop and country charts.

You're Hot, You're Hot." He and Chet Atkins received a Grammy in 1971 for their album *Me And Jerry*. Reed was named musician of the year in 1970 and 1971 by The Country Music Association. His last chart hit was in 1983—"I'm a Slave."

In 1974 he headed to Hollywood and starred with his good friend Burt Reynolds in the film *W.W. and the Dixie Dancekings*. He followed that up with *Gator* (1976), *High Ballin* (1978) and *Hot Stuff* (1979) and three *Smokey and the Bandit* films. He scored a number two hit with the soundtrack "East Bound and Down" (1977) from the first film. His shot at hosting his own variety show lasted only two episodes in 1976.

Reed enjoyed making movies and felt they kept his persona in front of the public long after his sixteen year string of 57 Top 100 country singles started to wane in the early 1980s. In 1983, he co-starred in the comedy *The Survivors* with Robin Williams and Walter Matthau. He acted in Danny Glover's 1988 movie *Bat*21* and starred in the 1998 Adam Sandler film, *The Waterboy*. He and Chet Atkins won a second Grammy in 1993 for their CD *Sneakin' Around*.

Reed married Priscilla Mitchell in 1959. She was a member of the folk rock group, the Appalachians. They had two daughters. Jerry Reed died on September 1, 2008, in Nashville from complications of emphysema.

Country music singer Steven Wariner told *The Tennessean* upon Reed's death: "He was a brilliant songwriter, a consummate singer/ entertainer and, of course, a world-class guitarist. Chet Atkins used to say—and I agree—'I don't think he even realizes how great he is.'" ∎

Jerry Reed performs live at the RCA Records show in October 1982 in Nasville, Tennessee.

R.E.M.

ROCK AND ROLL BAND . ATHENS

WHAT DO YOU GET when you mix a childhood ukulele player, a childhood sousaphone player, a record store clerk/guitar player, a punk rock cover song singer, an old church rented out as a communal residence, a young woman with a birthday, massive amounts of beer, 500 people and a town that had just been put on the musical map by the ultra-popular rock group the B-52s? You get the very first concert by a band in Athens, Georgia, that would shortly thereafter become R.E.M., one of the world's most beloved bands and one that all but created the genre of alternative music.

R.E.M. consisted of Georgia-born lead singer Michael Stipe, Minnesota-born drummer Bill Berry, California-born guitarist Peter Buck and California-born bass player Mike Mills. They all ended up in Athens by the late 1970s, attending the University of Georgia. They met on the Athens record-store and live music scenes, decided to form a band, and eventually dropped out of college.

On April 5, 1980, they had their first public performance; it was at a birthday party for their mutual friend Kathleen O'Brien, who lived in the old St. Mary's Episcopal church with Buck and some other friends and was largely responsible for introducing the musicians to each other. Against their own good judgment, feeling that they weren't prepared to perform yet, they played for the 500 guests, were a big hit and word began to spread about a new underground band with a style that didn't fit into any one category. Stipe had an eccentric on-stage charisma, often hurling himself around the stage and singing barely audible lyrics that he seemed to make up on the spot. The guitar sounds were harmonious and up beat, playing off a bass line driving like a force of nature. The new post-punk sound they created turned out to be infectious among college crowds. They began touring in college towns around the South in an old blue van eating on a $2 a day budget.

In 1981, they made their first single record at Mitch Easter's Drive-In studios in Winston-Salem, North Carolina, "Radio Free Europe." The critics loved it and The New York Times named it one of the 10 best singles of the year. The following year, having signed with I.R.S. Records, the band recorded an EP (extended play record; too short to be an album and too long to be a single), Chronic Town, which garnered mixed critical praise simply because no one quite knew what to make of it. Creem magazine writer Robot A. Hull wrote, "This EP is so arcane that I had to play it six times in a row to get a

"To anyone who ever felt touched by our music, our deepest thanks for listening."

handle on it – and even now, I'm still not sure." He finally concluded, however, that, "Despite its eccentricity, R.E.M.'s record is undoubtedly the sleeper EP of the year." Chronic Town was followed in 1983 by the release of the band's first full LP, Murmur, which Rolling Stone magazine named as its record of the year.

R.E.M. continued touring and recording, making music on their own terms and not bowing to the gimmickry many other bands used to gain mainstream success. In 1987, their LP Document turned out to be a major breakthrough success. It was their first million selling record and prompted Rolling Stone to feature them on that year's December cover, declaring them "America's Best Rock & Roll Band."

For the remainder of the band's existence, it remained comprised of only the original members and became more and more political and cause-driven as it cranked out monster hits like "It's the End of the World as We Know It (And I Feel Fine)" (1987), "Orange Crush" (1988), "Shiny Happy People" (1991), and their all-time highest selling single, "Losing My Religion" (1991). They were darlings of the music video world and were inducted into the Rock and Roll Hall of Fame in 2007. In 2011, after 31 years together and with 15 studio albums to their credit, almost all of them either gold or platinum, R.E.M. announced on their website that they were disbanding, writing, "To our Fans and Friends: As R.E.M., and as lifelong friends and co-conspirators, we have decided to call it a day as a band. We walk away with a great sense of gratitude, of finality, and of astonishment at all we have accomplished. To anyone who ever felt touched by our music, our deepest thanks for listening." ■

Burt Reynolds

ACTOR . CONYERS

BORN ON FEBRUARY 11, 1936, BURTON LEON REYNOLDS, JR., is a son of Conyers, Georgia. In high school he was a star football player and attended Florida State University on a sports scholarship. He became an All Star Southern League halfback and was drafted to play professional football by the Baltimore Colts in 1955 but a knee injury and an automobile accident ended his football career. Reynolds won the 1956 Florida State Drama Award that included a scholarship to the Hyde Park Playhouse, a summer stock theater in Hyde Park, New York.

Golden Globe in 1991 for his work on the television show. He went back to film in 1996 with a role as a drunken congressman in *Striptease*. The film was a financial disaster yet Reynolds received accolades for his performance. The following year, Paul Thomas Anderson cast him as the persnickety porn director in *Boogie Nights*. After seeing the first screening of the film, he fired his agent immediately. The New York Film Festival was held shortly after and the raves began for *Boogie Nights*. Reynolds was later nominated for a Best Supporting Actor Academy Award and won a Golden Globe Award.

It was 1972's Deliverance that propelled Reynolds into stardom. The controversial movie was filmed on Georgia's Chattooga River and was lauded as one of the years' best.

Reynolds met Joanne Woodward during his summer at Hyde Park in 1957 and she helped him find an agent and a part in another playhouse's production of *Tea and Sympathy*. His first big break came after he appeared in a revival of *Mister Roberts* at New York's City Center. He signed a television contract and had regular roles on several shows including *Riverboat, Gunsmoke, Hawk* and *Dan August*.

His big screen debut was in 1961 in *Angel Baby*, but it was 1972's *Deliverance* that propelled him into stardom. The controversial movie was filmed on Georgia's Chattooga River and was lauded as one of the years' best. *Deliverance* was the beginning of Reynold's passion for being involved with movies made in, or about, the South. His role firmly established him as a serious actor and a star.

In 1973, he appeared as a private investigator in *Shamus* and in Woody Allen's comedy *Everything You Wanted to Know About Sex But Were Afraid to Ask*.

Reynolds was featured as the first male centerfold in *Cosmopolitan* magazine in 1972. Throughout the decade and well into the 1980s, he was one of the most visible stars on film, appearing in films of all genres, ranging from *Smokey and the Bandit* in 1977, *Starting Over* with Candice Bergen in 1979 and with Dolly Parton in *The Best Little Whorehouse in Texas* in 1982.

Reynolds returned to television in the mid 1980s as the star of a very popular sitcom, *Evening Shade*. He won both an Emmy and a

"It's obvious why someone would be afraid of this project and I thought I had some baggage in terms of a lot of people who grew up with the movies I had done who would wonder why I would even be near a film like that," he said of his work on *Boogie Nights*. "I also felt like this thing would either crash and burn, be the biggest disaster of all time or the most talked about film of the year."

Reynolds is truly an American icon; he has won many awards and recognitions. He was named America's Favorite All Around Motion Picture Actor and received a Peoples Choice Award for a record six consecutive years. He was also the Most Popular Star for five straight years and voted Star of the Year by the National Association of Theater Owners. The same group voted him #1 Box Office Star for five years in a row—a record that still stands.

Reynolds was married to comedian and actress Judy Carne from 1963 to 1966 and to actress Loni Anderson from 1988 to 1993. He and Anderson adopted a son, Quinton, in 1988. He lives in Hobe Sound, Florida, and has established the Jupiter Theater, a college level drama training institute. He also supports his alma mater, Florida State University.

"I'm going to retire hopefully like Cary Grant did," he said as he described his future. "I'll be on stage telling a story, everyone's going to applaud and laugh and then I'll drop like a rock." ∎

Burt Reynolds, 2006.

Little Richard

SINGER, SONGWRITER, MUSICIAN, RECORDING ARTIST & ACTOR . MACON

WHILE DEPRESSION-ERA MACON, Georgia, may have been an eclectic place with interesting people, not just everyone had 11 brothers and sisters, lived in a rundown house on a dirt street, had a father who was a minister and sold moonshine on the side and was a young bisexual man who wore a high pompadour hairstyle and women's makeup and could bang the devil out of a piano and howl boogie-woogie songs, all the while worrying about just what Jesus would think of him. Such was the case, however, with Maconite Richard Wayne Penniman, better known as "Little Richard."

Penniman grew up in a Southern stew of religion, attending various family members' Baptist and African Methodist Episcopal (AME) churches and singing in other area churches with his siblings as the Penniman Singers. But it was the Pentecostal churches with their holy dancing and speaking in tongues that he found the most fun. By the time he was 10, he was already serving as a faith healer in the church, singing gospel songs and touching people who later said he made them feel better.

By 1945, in his early teens and kicked out of the family home by his father because of his effeminate sexual mannerisms, Penniman was out on the road entertaining audiences with a kind of act never seen before. His over-the-top singing style was filled with screams and moans and high-pitch screeching, all laid into his combination of gospel, boogie-woogie and rhythm and blues. "Little Richard," as he was calling himself by then, was well on his way.

Penniman began his recording career in October 1951, cutting jump blues records for RCA Camden. He soon signed with Peacock Records but commercial success eluded him. After forming a new R&B road band he called The Upsetters, he moved to Specialty Records and it was with that label that, in a 1955 recording session, Penniman began banging out a boogie-woogie riff on the piano and singing a song he had written years earlier and had been performing on the road. The song was "Tutti Frutti" and it would change the course of music history.

"Tutti Frutti," with its renegade cry of "Bop bopa-a-lu a whop bam boo!" which some critics say was the very beginning of rock and roll, reached number two on Billboard's R&B Chart and was quickly covered by Elvis Presley and Pat Boone. They were just two of the many singers who would cover Penniman's many hits, including "Lucille" (1956), "Keep-A-Knocking" (1957), and "Good Golly, Miss Molly" (recorded in 1956 and released 1958).

With the success of "Tutti Frutti," Penniman and his band swept across the United States selling out concert after concert at sports arenas and music venues. He performed in sequined capes under flickering lights, driving audiences into frenzies by running on and off stage, singing, yelling and just being Little Richard. Although most of his concerts started out segregated, by the end of the evening the crowd was usually all together, screaming, dancing, shouting for more, and not caring about the color of each other's skin. During this period Penniman was also partying hard on the road, even indulging in orgies in the hotels in which he stayed.

Little Richard was in the first group of inductees into the Rock and Roll Hall of Fame in 1986.

In 1957, at the zenith of his young career and with seven gold records to his credit, Penniman walked away from rock and roll. Citing what he interpreted as religious experiences that predicted his own damnation, he announced his retirement just days before he was scheduled to perform for 40,000 people in Australia. His decision sent shock waves through the music world.

For the next few years Penniman attended a Seventh Day Adventist Bible college and attempted but did not succeed at a gospel recording career and gaining a following in his newfound ministry. In 1964, he returned to rock and roll with a wildly successful European tour with the Beatles as his opening act. From that time until today, he has continued in both the secular and spiritual worlds—touring, starring in films and television, officiating at celebrity weddings and funerals, performing at presidential inaugurations and continuing to garner accolade after accolade as one of the most important entertainment figures in history.

He was in the first group of inductees into the Rock and Roll Hall of Fame in 1986. He is a member of the Songwriters Hall of Fame, Apollo Theater Legends Hall of Fame, Music City Walk of Fame, Louisiana Music Hall of Fame, NAACP Image Award Hall of Fame and has been given the Lifetime Achievement Grammy Award and the Rhythm and Blues Foundation Lifetime Achievement Pioneer Award. In 2004, *Rolling Stone* magazine ranked him number eight on their list of the 100 Greatest Artists of All Time." ∎

Richard performs at The Domino Effect, a tribute concert to New Orleans Rock 'n' Roll musician Fats Domino. Courtesy of Morning Journal, 2009, New Orleans, Louisiana.

Julia Roberts

ACTRESS . ATLANTA

JULIA ROBERTS, WITH HER WIDE AND WINNING SMILE, has charmed movie audiences since 1988, has won an Academy Award for Best Actress and has become one of the all time top stars at the box office.

Roberts was born into a family of actors. Her parents, Betty Lou and Walter Roberts, who met while performing for the armed services, co-founded the Atlanta Actors and Writers Workshop in Atlanta and were running an acting school for children when Roberts was born. Among their students were the children of Martin Luther and Coretta Scott King. Mrs. King was so pleased with her children's progress that she paid the hospital bills when baby Julia was born. Roberts' brother and sister, Eric and Lisa, also became actors. Roberts parents divorced and she, her mother and sister, moved to Symrna, Georgia, where Julia attended school and graduated from Campbell High School.

After graduation, Roberts was off to New York to pursue an acting career. After some modeling and small television and movie roles, Roberts was cast in *Satisfaction* and *Mystic Pizza* in 1988 and *Steel Magnolias* in 1989. The critics loved her and *People* magazine named her one of 1988's Newcomers. "The first time I felt famous was when I went to the movies with my mom. Someone in the bathroom said, 'Girl in stall number one, were you in *Mystic Pizza*?'" she told an interviewer for *People* magazine. She received an Academy Award nomination for Best Supporting Actress for *Steel Magnolias* and won a Golden Globe Award in the same category. Roberts was well on her way to stardom when she was cast opposite Richard Gere as the "pretty woman" in the film of the same name. That film solidified her position as a top star and America's sweetheart.

During the 90's, Roberts made several movies including favorites such as *My Best Friend's Wedding*, *Notting Hill* and *The Pelican Brief*. Also in the 90's, Roberts surprised her fans by marrying the country music star Lyle Lovitt but the marriage lasted only 21 months.

Pretty Woman, solidified her position as a top star and America's sweetheart.

In 2001, Roberts was cast in the title role of *Erin Brockovich*, a film about the woman who helped win a lawsuit against energy giant Pacific Gas and Electric. This role brought Roberts the Oscar for Best Actress in 2001. Her $20 million dollar salary for this film was a Hollywood milestone.

Following her Oscar win, Roberts starred in numerous films: *Ocean's Eleven, Full Frontal, Ocean's Twelve, The Mexican* and *Charlie Wilson's War* opposite box office favorites such as George Clooney, Brad Pitt and Tom Hanks. She lent her voice to two animated films in 2006, *The Ant Bully* and *Charlotte's Web*. With her sister Lisa, she served as executive producer for a series of American Girl films and made her Broadway debut in *The Days of Rain*. In 2010, Roberts returned to block-busting success in the film version of Elizabeth Gilbert's bestseller, *Eat, Pray Love.*

On July 4th, 2002, Roberts married Daniel Moder, a cameraman she had met on the set of *The Mexican*. The couple have three children, twins Hazel Patricia and Phinnaeus Walter born in 2004 and a younger child, Henry Daniel, born in 2007. Roberts now balances her life between her family and her search for compelling roles. ∎

Julia Roberts (left) arrives at the "Mirror, Mirror" Premiere at the Graumans Chinese Theater on March, 2012 in Los Angeles, California.
Julia Roberts and Javier Bardem (above) at the 58th International Film Festival in San Sebastian, Spain, 2010. Photo by Joe Seer.

Pernell Roberts

STAGE, TELEVISION & MOVIE ACTOR . WAYCROSS . 1928 – 2010

PERNELL ROBERTS IS BEST REMEMBERED FOR his roles as Adam Cartwright on the western series *Bonanza* and as a doctor on *Trapper John, M.D.* During his career, he guest starred on more than sixty television series. Athletically built and darkly handsome, Roberts was a Shakespearean actor before landing his role on *Bonanza*.

Pernell Elven Roberts, Jr. was born on May 18, 1928, in Waycross, Georgia, and was an only child. While in high school, he acted in school and church plays, played the horn and sang in local USO shows. After high school, he attended Georgia Tech but did not graduate. Instead he joined the Marines in 1948 where he was assigned to the Marine Corps Band. A skilled musician, Roberts also played the tuba, sousaphone and percussion.

After serving two years in the Marines, Roberts left and attended the University of Maryland on a G.I. Bill. While at Maryland, he acted in classical theatre and appeared in four productions including *Othello* and *Antigone*. Bitten by the acting bug, he decided to leave college to act in summer stock. While pursuing acting, he worked as a forest ranger, butcher and railroad riveter. He made his professional stage debut in 1949 in *The Man Who Came to Dinner* at the Olney Theatre in Maryland. He then spent eight weeks at Bryn Mawr College where he played in *Night Must Fall* and *Pygmalion*.

In 1950, Roberts moved to Washington, D.C., where he performed with the Arena Stage Theatre, appearing in such productions as *Burning Bright, The Glass Menagerie, Twelfth Night* and *Julius Caesar* among others. Afterwards, he acted with the Port Players in Milwaukee and with Brattle Theatre in *Othello* and *Henry IV, Part I*.

In 1952, he moved to New York City where he attracted acclaim for his roles in *Twelfth Night, Romeo and Juliet* and *Macbeth* for which he won a Drama Desk Award in 1955. In 1956, he was cast as Petruchio in *The Taming of the Shrew* and then returned to the Olney Theatre where he starred in *Much Ado About Nothing*.

Also in 1956, Roberts made his television debut in *Shadow of Suspicion*. He followed with guest roles in *Gunsmoke, Sugarfoot* and *Cheyenne*. A year later in 1957, he signed with Columbia Pictures and made his film debut with Burl Ives and Sophia Loren in *Desire Under the Elms* (1958).

Roberts continued his television work in roles on episodes of *Shirley Temple Storybook Theater, Zane Grey Theater*, *Northwest Passage* (1958), *Tombstone Territory* and *Have Gun Will Travel*. However, it was his role in the *Bonanza* series (1959-1965) that made him a television star. *Bonanza* was the second longest running TV western and the first to be filmed in color. Trained as a stage actor, Roberts found the transition to a television series confining and most difficult.

Roberts was also unhappy with his character and the fact that three grown men had to defer to their father for every decision. He allegedly referred to *Bonanza* as "junk television" and did not renew

Athletically built and darkly handsome, Roberts was an aspiring Shakespearean actor before landing his role on Bonanza.

his six-year contract. "I haven't grown at all since the series began ...I have an impotent role. Wherever I turn there's the father image," said Roberts to the *Washington Post* on May 1, 1963. During his time with *Bonanza*, Roberts used his singing talents in two episodes and on two *Bonanza* albums (1959). He recorded one solo album of folk music entitled *Come All Ye Fair and Tender Ladies* (1962).

After *Bonanza*, Roberts turned his attention to singing, musical theatre and TV appearances. In 1972, he returned to Broadway in *Captain Brassbound's Conversion* with Ingrid Bergman. In 1973, he was nominated for a Joseph Jefferson Award for his performance in *Welcome Home*.

He maintained his public image by guest starring in numerous big name TV shows including *The Virginian, The Big Valley* and *Mission: Impossible* and in TV movies such as *The Night Rider*. However, he soon regained his star status as the lead in *Trapper John, M.D.* (1979-1986) for which he received an Emmy nomination in 1981. He made his last TV appearance in 1991 in *Diagnosis Murder*.

Pernell Roberts spent his life fighting TV's racism, segregation and sexism. He was a civil rights activist in the 1960s. He was married four times but had only one child, Chris Roberts, who died in a motorcycle accident at age 38. Roberts was diagnosed with pancreatic cancer in 2007. He managed to outlive the *Bonanza's* Cartwright clan, dying at age 81 in 2010. ∎

Pernell Roberts as Adam Cartwright on "Bonanza".

Jackie Robinson

BASEBALL LEGEND . CAIRO . 1919 – 1972

JACKIE ROBINSON IS THE BASEBALL PLAYER who broke the color barrier in Major League Baseball, setting many records and opening the door for future players along the way. More than a baseball star who happened to be the first African American to play in the major leagues, Jackie Robinson was a man other players looked up to and fans adored. His legendary story is one of trials with racism, ultimately resulting in huge advancements in the cause of civil rights for black athletes.

In 1962 he became the first African American to be inducted into the Baseball Hall of Fame.

Born Jack Roosevelt Robinson in Cairo, Georgia, on January 31, 1919, Jackie Robinson was the youngest of five children. His parents were sharecroppers. His mother, Mallie Robinson, moved, with her children, to California after his father left the family.

Robinson excelled in sports from a very young age. He attended John Muir High School and Pasadena Junior College where he played four sports: baseball, basketball, football and track. He was named the region's Most Valuable Player in 1938. Later at UCLA, he became the first athlete to win varsity letters in all four sports and was named to the All-American Football team in 1941.

His college career was cut short due to financial difficulties. He enlisted in the U.S. Army in 1942 and advanced to second lieutenant. He left the Army in 1944 and played one season with the Kansas City Monarchs of the Negro Baseball League. Although the sport was segregated at the time, Robinson was approached by Branch Rickey of the Brooklyn Dodgers to help in efforts to integrate professional baseball. He soon joined the all white Montreal Royals, a farm team for the Dodgers, and played his first game on March 17, 1946.

Being the first African American in an all-white sport was not easy for Robinson. He endured racial slurs at games and some of his teammates objected to having him as part of their team. Robinson and his family received threats. Even with the abuse, Robinson had a great first year with the Royals. He led the league with a .349 batting average and a .985 fielding percentage.

Robinson was brought up to the Dodgers the next season. On April 15, 1947, he became the first African American in the major leagues. At the end of his rookie season with the team, he had scored 12 home runs and 29 steals and was named the National League's Rookie of the Year. In 1949 he was named the National League's Most Valuable Player of the Year while leading the league with an amazing .342 batting average.

Robinson become a hero and mentor for future major league players. He was the highest paid athlete in Brooklyn Dodgers history and the subject of a popular song "Did You See Jackie Robinson Hit that Ball?" recorded by Buddy Johnson in 1949 and later by Count Basie and his orchestra.

Robinson's success in breaking the color barrier in Major League Baseball paved the way for many future African American players, including Hank Aaron, Willie Mays and Satchel Paige.

In his ten years with the Dodgers, he led the team to win the pennant several times—four times losing to the New York Yankees in the World Series. Victory finally came to Jackie Robinson and the Dodgers in 1955 when the Dodgers bested the Yankees in seven games to win the team's first championship title.

Robinson was traded to the New York Giants in 1957 and retired from the sport soon after. In 1962 he became the first African American to be inducted into the Baseball Hall of Fame. The Dodgers retired his uniform number 42 a decade later.

Off the ball field, Robinson was a dominant figure in political and social issues. He testified on discrimination before the House Un-American Activities Committee in 1949, helped established the Freedom National Bank in Harlem, which at the time was the largest black-owned and operated bank in the state, and served on the board of the NAACP until 1967.

Robinson died from complications of diabetes on October 24, 1972. He was survived by his wife, Rachel Isum, and their three children, Jackie Jr., Sharon and David. After his death, Isum started the Jackie Robinson Foundation to not only honor his legacy but also to help young people with scholarships and mentoring programs. ■

Jackie Robinson poses in his Dodgers uniform, circa 1948. Robinson as an ABC broadcaster (lower photo) for Major League Championship Baseball, 1965. Jackie Robinson card (showing lower right) from the 2010 ©Topps bonus packs.

Sugar Ray Robinson

WORLD BOXING CHAMPION . AILEY . 1921 – 1989

CONSIDERED BY NEARLY EVERY BOXING FAN as the greatest boxer of all-time, Sugar Ray Robinson was a six-time world champion boxer and was virtually unbeatable in the ring. He reigned as the world welterweight champion from 1946-1951 and then won the world middleweight title five times between 1951 and 1960. Born as Walker Smith, Jr., in Ailey, Georgia, although his autobiography claims Detroit as his birthplace, his parents moved the family to Detroit to escape the prejudices in the South. He grew up in Detroit until he and his two sisters moved with their parents to Harlem in New York City in 1932.

"To be a champ you have to believe in yourself when no one else will."

He discovered boxing at a Harlem gym where he used a friend's Amateur Athletic Union boxing card. The friend's name was Ray Robinson. Crowds gathered to watch him box, and his future coach, George Gainford, called his style and fluid motions "as sweet as sugar." That nickname stuck.

After winning all 85 amateur bouts, 69 by knockout, 40 in the first round, Robinson won the New York Golden Gloves lightweight championship in 1939. At 19 years of age, Sugar Ray Robinson turned pro.

In 1941 Robinson fought 20 times, including two fights in August just two days apart. His schedule ground to a halt in the summer of 1943 when he began a brief time in the U.S. Army. He got an honorary discharge and resumed fighting in the fall of 1944. In his first 123 fights, he lost only once to Jake LaMotta on February 5, 1943. He had beaten LaMotta four times out of the five fights they had previously fought. On Valentine's Day, 1951, they met for a sixth fight with LaMotta's NBA middleweight title at stake. The boxing writers called the fight "another Valentine's Day Massacre" after Robinson beat LaMotta so severely that the doctor at ringside halted the fight in the 13th round. Robinson won the middleweight title. This fight was recreated in Martin Scorsese's 1980 movie *Raging Bull* with Robert DeNiro as Jake LaMotta. It provides an account of Robinson's epic battles in three title fights with LaMotta. Former boxer Johnny Barnes played Robinson in the movie.

For more than two decades Robinson dominated the boxing ring, traveling the world for both title and non-title fights, until his second retirement in 1965 at the age of 44. He had retired on December 18, 1952, but returned to the ring at the beginning of 1955. He regained his world middleweight champion title in December 1955.

Often seen driving in a flashy pink Cadillac convertible, new each year, he was known as a lavish tipper who wore diamonds with his custom-made suits, silk shirts and ties and lived in the best hotels. His large entourage traveled around the world with him for his fights.

He made an estimated $4 million in the ring, but spent it all by the mid-60s. The *New York Times Book of Sports Legends* recalled Robinson saying, "I went through $4 million, but I have no regrets. If I had the chance to do it over again, I'd do it the same way. I didn't gamble away my money. I used it to help people live. I took my family and my friends on trips with me. I loaned it to strangers to pay their bills and sometimes I didn't get it back."

He made the cover of the June 25, 1951, issue of *TIME* magazine. He was often quoted as saying, "To be a champ you have to believe in yourself when no one else will. I've always believed that you can think positive just as well as you can think negative." Changing careers and improving his finances in the mid-60s, Robinson moved to Los Angeles where Frank Sinatra helped him find roles as an actor in television shows and movies, including *Fantasy Island*, *The Mod Squad* and *Mission Impossible*. He also established the Sugar Ray Robinson Youth foundation in 1969 that funded and organized recreation for inner city children. It did not sponsor a boxing program.

In 1967 he was elected to the Boxing Hall of Fame and in 1990 he was inducted into the International Boxing Hall of Fame. In 2006, a $0.39 commemorative U.S. postage stamp was issued in his honor.

He suffered from Alzheimer's disease and diabetes, dying at age 67 on April 12, 1989, in Culver City, California, with his third wife, Millie, by his side.

His 202 fights ended in a record of 174 wins, 19 losses, 6 undecided and 2 no-contests. Of Robinson's 19 defeats, 15 came after he was 35 years old, 10 were after he turned 40, with five when he was 44. ■

Sugar Ray Robinson, circa 1965.

WHEN YOU THINK OF BILLY JOE ROYAL, THE FIRST SONG that probably pops into your head may be his hit, "Down in the Boondocks" or perhaps it is "Funny How Time Slips Away" from the 60s. Royal is one of the few musicians who successfully moved from pop to rock to country and entertained live audiences for more than four decades.

In a 2008 interview with *Rising Stars* online magazine, Royal recalled his first times as a performer.

"My uncles had a band and a radio show when I was a kid," Royal said. "My first ambition was to be a steel guitar player and at nine, I took steel guitar lessons to be in their band. Then I would sing a little bit, so they started letting me sing on their radio show."

Tahoe. He also continued acting in television and commercials. During his years in Las Vegas, he met and became friends with Elvis when they both played the Vegas strip in the early 70s. "I first saw Elvis on *The Tommy Dorsey Show* and when Elvis made it so big, all of us Southern boys thought we had a shot, too," Royal said of his early career.

In 1978 he recorded "Under the Boardwalk" which became a minor hit. In the 80s, Royal moved into the country arena. He recorded "Burned Like a Rocket" in 1984. Atlantic Records picked up the hit song and signed him to a contract. The song reached the country Top 10 in early 1986. He had a string of Top 40 hits over the next few years, including "I'll Pin a Note on Your Pillow,"

Billy Joe Royal

SINGER, SONGWRITER & MUSICIAN . VALDOSTA

"Most of the audience is from our own age group, and it takes them back to their youth. Everybody seems happy at the end of the show."

His family moved to Marietta, Georgia, when he was about 10. As a teenager, he had a band called the Corvettes and they played parties and private clubs during high school. He went to Savannah and worked in a club called the Bamboo Ranch for several years. It showcased country or rhythm and blues acts like Roy Orbison, Sam Cook, Chuck Berry, Marty Robbins and George Jones.

In his early 20s he kept playing music and began getting small parts in movies and television shows such as *Route 66*. He moved to Cincinnati in 1964, working for a local club called Guys and Dolls and playing radio promotions. Singer and songwriter Joe South told him about a song he had written called "Down in the Boondocks." Royal thought it was a strange name but South wanted him to record it as a demo. It became a Top 10 hit in 1965. He got a six-year deal with Columbia Records and Dick Clark called him to join the Dick Clark Caravan tour with stars like Tom Jones, Peter and Gordan and Mel Carter.

Royal returned to the U.S. Top 20 with "Cherry Hill Park" in 1969 and in the 1970s he became a regular artist in Las Vegas and Lake

"I Miss You Already" and a duet with Donna Fargo, "Members Only." But by 1990 his popularity waned. He had a few minor hits through 1992 and then toured the country for the next two decades.

He launched a comeback album in 1998 called *Stay Close to Home* on the Intersound label and followed it with the independent release *Now and Then, Then and Now* in 2001. Many of his recordings were then re-released.

By 2008 he was touring with B.J. Thomas throughout the United States. In their shows, they each did a set of songs and then sang some duets at the end. "This is all I've ever done," Royal said. "I had to stick to it, 'cause I've never done anything else."

After more than four decades of entertaining audiences of all ages, Royal has done what many entertainers have not been able to do for an extended time, make sure that the audience stays happy. "Most of the audience is from our own age group, and it takes them back to their youth," Royal said. "Everybody seems happy at the end of the show."

Royal was married twice and has a teenage daughter from his second marriage. He retired to North Carolina in 2012. ∎

Photo courtesy ©BillyJoeRoyal.com

Nipsey Russell

COMEDIAN & ACTOR . ATLANTA . 1924 – 2005

SUCH FOUR-LINE RHYMES brought quick-witted comedian Nipsey Russell to national fame on television in the 1960s and '70s, earning him the sobriquet "poet laureate of comedy."

The Atlanta native was born Julius Russell around 1924 or 1925; he said he was nicknamed Nipsey because his mother liked the way that name sounded. Russell began performing professionally at age six with the Ragamuffins of Rhythm, a song-and-dance troupe formed by Eddie Heywood Sr., father of the renowned jazz pianist.

Russell moved to Cincinnati to live with an aunt so he could attend the city university tuition-free. After one semester of studying classical literature, he enlisted in the U.S. Army and served as a medic during World War II. Accounts differ as to whether he obtained the rank of captain or second lieutenant.

"The girl who would make my life complete/ need not be young and fair/Just be a nymphomaniac/and a multimillionaire."

Upon returning to Atlanta, he became carhop #46 at The Varsity, the world's largest drive-in restaurant. Russell cleverly augmented his curbside delivery of chili dogs, burgers, fries and orange shakes with jokes that elicited laughs—and brought him bigger tips.

By the 1950s, he was performing comedy acts in "chitlin'-circuit" clubs along the East Coast. Russell's sophisticated, clean-mouthed patter, delivered while wearing a suit and tie, differentiated him from the raunchy, baggy-panted comedians usually featured at such clubs. Russell also "crossed over" during these days of segregation to perform for mostly white audiences at New York's legendary Apollo Theater and at popular Catskills resorts.

The opposite of 'pro' is 'con'/This fact is clearly seen/But if 'progress' means move forward/What does 'Congress' mean?

Performances at the Club Baby Grand led to a 1959 guest spot on *The Tonight Show* with Jack Paar which, in turn, led to numerous appearances on other talk and variety shows including *The Jackie Gleason Show, The Dean Martin Comedy Hour* and *Rowan & Martin's Laugh-In.*

As U.S. society slowly became integrated, Nipsey appeared on more and more shows. In 1961, Russell became one of the first black actors on "prime time" television when he played Officer Anderson on *Car 54, Where Are You?* Three years later, he became the first regular black game-show panelist on *Missing Links*, which led to a breakthrough moment.

As Russell's manager, Joe Rapp, recounted to National Public Radio in 2005, host Ed McMahon asked Russell as the show was ending to "say something to the audience for good night" so he recited an impromptu poem. McMahon did the same thing the next night, and once again Nipsey quickly came up with a funny verse. "He realized this was his hook," Rapp said. "Like Rodney Dangerfield had 'I don't get any respect,' he had the poems. A lot of the people used to call him the original rapper."

I am a bachelor, and I will not marry/Until the right girl comes along/But while I'm waiting, I don't mind dating/Girls that I know are wrong. Russell told the Los Angeles Times in 1993 that writing poems "is very simple to do. ... I start with the joke line and then write backward."

Nipsey's rhymes and one-liners entertained game-show audiences during the 1970s and '80s when he appeared on such television shows as *To Tell the Truth, Hollywood Squares, Password, $25,000 Pyramid* and *Match Game.* He also appeared frequently on *The Tonight Show Starring Johnny Carson,* co-starred in TV's *Barefoot in the Park* and performed in Las Vegas and Atlantic City nightclubs.

In 1978, he received favorable reviews for his portrayal of the Tin Man in the box-office bomb *The Wiz.* Russell also appeared in the movies *Dream One* (1984), *Wildcats* (1986), and *Posse* (1993).

Though game shows fell out of fashion in the 1980s, Nipsey hosted two: *Juvenile Jury* and *Your Number's Up.* His popularity among younger comedians also resulted in frequent appearances on *Late Night with Conan O'Brien* and *The Chris Rock Show.*

Hurricanes are named after women/Because they start on the very same plan/Start up over nothin', make a whole lotta noise/And can't be controlled by man!

He continued performing in Atlantic City and Las Vegas in the 1990s. Russell died of cancer on Oct. 2, 2005; friends said he was 80. He never married—"I have enough trouble living with myself, how could I ever live with anyone else?" he once quipped—and left no known survivors. After cremation, his ashes were scattered across the Atlantic Ocean. ∎

Publicity still of Nipsey Russell, 1966. Photo by John D. Kisch/Separate Cinema Archive/Getty Images.

Ryan Seacrest

REALITY & GAME SHOW HOST & RADIO PERSONALITY . DUNWOODY

BORN ON CHRISTMAS EVE, 1974, in Dunwoody, Georgia, Ryan Seacrest showed his parents at a very young age that he wanted to be a star. He used his favorite toy microphone to play radio host and later made the family cassette tapes to play in the car. He was the "voice" of Dunwoody High School, reading morning announcements. And while in high school, he interned at WSTR-Star 94 FM in Atlanta, where he soon moved into hosting the evening radio program. During the summer, he mowed lawns.

After graduating from high school, Seacrest studied journalism at the University of Georgia in 1992, quitting at 19 to move to Hollywood. His first television host job was in 1995 on the ESPN game show, *Radical Outdoor Challenge.*

It was *American Idol* that helped make Seacrest a household name and the highest paid reality television host in history. He he was managing editor of *E!News*. He joined the No. 1 nationally syndicated Los Angeles morning drive-time radio show in 2006.

Taking Dick Clark's advice to own the business, that same year he started Ryan Seacrest Productions which develops shows on the E! television network like *Keeping Up With the Kardashians,* and its spin-off shows, *Khloe & Lamar, Kourtney & Kim Take New York,* and *The Dance Scene,* plus the *Shahs of Sunset* for Bravo*, Melissa & Tye* on CMT and *Jamie Oliver's Food Revolution* on ABC.

In April 2012, he joined *The Today Show* as a special correspondent and helped cover the 2012 London Olympics and the 2012 elections for NBC.

He and his family started the Ryan Seacrest Foundation in 2010 to help seriously ill and injured children use multimedia and interactive platforms while in the hospital. By 2012, the foundation

> *He and his family started the Ryan Seacrest Foundation in 2010 to help seriously ill and injured children use multimedia and interactive platforms while in the hospital.*

hosted the show from its beginning in 2002. His charm and hugs helped soothe upset contestants and his trademark statement, "You're safe," became the best thing a contestant heard each week during the elimination judging. He bantered with the judges, smoothing over on-air squabbles. In twelve seasons, he hosted more than 400 episodes of the popular show.

Seacrest once told a *New York Times* reporter that the thought of being out of work frightened him and that helps explain his intense work history. He never has just one project or job and produces multiple television and radio shows. At the beginning of the new century, he hosted two game shows for kids, *Gladiators 2000* and *Click*. That same year, he hosted NBC's *Saturday Night at the Movies,* offering interesting facts and insights into the weekly movie. He later hosted the syndicated daytime television talk show, *On-Air with Ryan Seacrest*.

Not one to slow down, in 2004 he replaced the retiring Casey Kasem on the weekly *American Top 40* radio show still heard each week around the world. When Dick Clark suffered a stroke in 2004, Seacrest became executive producer and co-host of *Dick Clark's New Year's Rockin' Eve* in 2005. In 2006, he began co-hosting *E!News Live* and produced red carpet award shows while had created a broadcast media center in both Children's Healthcare of Atlanta and Children's Hospital of Philadelphia, with plans for other children's hospitals in the future.

Nominated for an Emmy nine times, Seacrest won a Creative Arts Emmy Award in 2010 for producing *Jamie Oliver's Food Revolution* on ABC.

In 2007, he moved in front of the movie camera in a cameo role in *Knocked Up*; he played himself as the host of *American Idol*. In 2010 he was the voice of the father of Butter Pants in *Shrek Forever After*, the third sequel in the Shrek movie series. He had also played a non-credited extra in *Crimson Tide*.

Always ready to start new ventures, he developed Ryan Seacrest Media in 2012 and re-branded HDNet/HDNet Canada to AXS TV. Eventually, he wants the cable channel to broadcast concerts and live events. His production company will develop shows for the channel.

He was No. 29 on the May 2012 *Forbes* magazine's World's Most Powerful Celebrities with $59 million in earnings.

Seacrest received a star on the Hollywood Walk of Fame in 2005. He lives in Los Angeles and is co-owner of Katana, a sushi bar on Sunset Boulevard in Hollywood. It celebrated its 10th anniversary in 2012. ■

Ryan Seacrest arrives at the City of Hope's Music And Entertainment Industry Group Event at The Geffen Contemporary at MOCA on June 12, 2012 in Los Angeles, California.

Steven Soderbergh

FILM ACTOR, DIRECTOR, PRODUCER & SCREENWRITER . ATLANTA

ONE OF THE MOST SUCCESSFUL producers in the film industry, Steven Soderbergh is the only director in history to have two films in the same year receive Best Director nominations from the Academy Awards, the Golden Globe and the Directors' Guild of America. The films, *Traffic* and *Erin Brockovich,* were both released in 2000.

He loves his work. "I think it's a real privilege to make a living doing this job," he said during an interview following his 2000 Academy Award nomination. "You walk into a room and say, 'I'm imagining this,' and they give you millions of dollars to go out and make it real. That's a pretty good gig."

He wrote the independent film, Sex, Lies and Videotape, in eight days and went on to edit and direct the film.

Born in Atlanta on January 14, 1963, to Peter and Mary Ann Soderbergh, Steven was the second of six children. The family soon moved to Baton Rouge, Louisiana, where Peter was a professor and the Dean of Education at Louisiana State University (LSU). Mary Ann, a parapsychologist, appeared frequently on the local ABC affiliate WBRZ-TV's morning show, as a call-in psychic. She also taught adult education and alternative education in parapsychology at LSU.

Steven graduated from Louisiana State University Laboratory School, a K-12 school directed by LSU. Before graduation, Steven enrolled in LSU's film animation class and began making 16mm short films. He completed his first short, *Janitor*, at the age of 15.

Soderbergh moved to Los Angeles soon after high school graduation in 1989 to try and get into the film industry. He found work as a cue card holder and later as editor for *Games People Play*, a television game show that was cancelled after six months.

He moved back to Baton Rouge and began to build a reputation for directing pop rock videos. In 1985 he directed the Grammy nominated concert video, *9012Live*, for the rock band Yes. In 1987,

Soderbergh was still in Baton Rouge when he made the short film, *Winston*, which laid the groundwork for the film which would set him on the road to success, *Sex, Lies and Videotape.*

He wrote the independent film, *Sex, Lies and Videotape,* in eight days and went on to edit and direct the film. *Sex, Lies and Videotape* won the Palme d'Or at the Cannes Film Festival in 1989 making Soderbergh the youngest person ever to receive the award; he was 26. The independent film received an Academy Award nomination for Soderbergh in the category of Best Screenplay.

The next decade was tough on Soderbergh. In 1991 he directed his second feature, *Kafka*, with Jeremy Irons as Franz Kafka. The film was poorly received and a financial flop. That film was followed by others—roughly one per year—all of which were disappointing.

Soderbergh's comeback started with 1999's *The Limey*, which starred Terrence Stamp and Peter Fonda. The film incorporated flashback scenes of Stamp's character in 1967's *Poor Cow*, a film directed by Ken Loach. The film received critical acclaim and set the pace for what would be his best year to date.

2000 would have been a great year for Soderbergh even if he had only directed Julia Roberts' Academy Award winning title role in *Erin Brodkovich*. He also directed *Traffic*, which won four Oscars, including Best Director, Best Supporting Actor, Best Film Editing and Best Adapted Screenplay. The $46 million budget film garnered almost $208 million worldwide.

Soderbergh formed Section Eight Productions with George Clooney the same year. The following year he directed the remake of the 1960's film *Ocean's Eleven* starring Clooney and Julia Roberts. The film's success led him to direct *Ocean's Twelve* in 2004 and *Ocean's Thirteen* in 2007. He was the executive director of 2005's *Good Night, and Good Luck*, which was nominated for six Academy Awards, including Best Picture. In 2012, he directed two commercial successes: *Haywire* and *Magic Mike.*

Soderbergh currently lives in New York and is working on *The Bitter Pill*, a psychological thriller starring Jude Law and Catherine Zeta-Jones. It is set for release in February of 2013. ∎

Director Steven Soderbergh at Le Moulin de Mougins restaurant for amfAR's Cinema Against AIDS 2003 Gala, 2003.

Sugarland

COUNTRY MUSIC DUO . ATLANTA

AS A TRIO OF SONGWRITERS from the Atlanta area, Sugarland became superstars in 2009 when their album *Love on the Inside* gained platinum status and won Grammy Awards for Best Country Song and Best Country Performance, yielding the group a prime-time television network special. The group has garnered over 50 nominations and many wins from the Academy of Country Music, Country Music Television and the Country Music Association.

Songwriter Kristen Hall, vocalist and multi-instrumentalist Kristian Bush and lead singer and songwriter Jennifer Nettles formed the group in 2002. The three were regulars in the folk-rock scene in Atlanta in the 1990s and early 2000s. Before becoming officially known as Sugarland, the group played frequently at Eddie's Attic in Decatur, Georgia.

Lead singer Nettles was born on September 12, 1974, and grew up in Douglas, Georgia. After graduating from Agnes Scott College in 1997, she formed the band Soul Miners Daughter with fellow student Cory Jones before forming her own band in 1999. Kristian Bush was born in Nashville and is the great grandson of A.J. Bush, known for his "Bush's baked beans."

In 2004, Sugarland signed on with Mercury Nashville Records and released the single "Baby Girl" from their multi-platinum debut album, *Twice the Speed of Life*. The single peaked at number two on *Billboard's* Hot Country Songs. The group had begun to attract quite a bit of attention when Kristen Hall left in 2005.

In 2006, now a duo, Bush and Nettles released the hugely successful *Enjoy the Ride*, which found fans in both the pop and country genre. The album also produced their first two number one singles with "Want To" and "Settlin," and charted at number two on the Top Country Album Charts, selling over 210,000 copies the first week. That same year, the duo performed at the 48th Annual Grammy Awards and the Country Music Television (CMT) Music Awards where they received nominations for Group/Duo Video of the Year, Breakthrough Video of the Year and Collaborative Video of the Year.

In 2007, the group appeared on *The Tonight Show* and later headlined their first concert tour. They won the award for Vocal Duo of the Year at the 41st Country Music Association (CMA) Awards.

In 2008, they co-produced their own album in Georgia instead of Nashville. *Love on the Inside* spawned three chart topping singles:

"All I Want to Do," "Already Gone," and "It Happens." In December 2008, Sugarland garnered three Grammy Awards. In 2009, they were nominated by the Academy of Country Music (ACM) for Top Vocal Duo and Vocal Event of the Year for their "Life in a Northern Town." That same year, they received five CMT award nominations, including one for Video of the Year.

In 2008, they co-produced their own album in Georgia instead of Nashville.

With the release of their fourth album, *The Incredible Machine*, in October 2010, Sugarland had now sold in excess of fourteen million records. The album, co-written and co-produced by Nettles and Bush, became the number five best selling country album of 2010 and the number three selling digital country track with the single released from the album entitled "Stuck Like Glue."

In 2011, they won Vocal Duo of the Year at the 46th annual Academy of Country Music Awards and CMT's Duo Video of the Year. In April 2011, Sugarland also branched out into owning a radio station. Nettles and Bush are responsible for the programming that gives fans a chance to hear about the singers' personal lives and their musical endeavors.

Tragedy struck in August 2011 at the duo's concert at the Indiana State Fair when an outdoor stage collapsed due to high winds, killing seven people and injuring dozens more. In October 2011, Sugarland held a free benefit concert in honor of the victims of the stage collapse. However, it was announced the next month that forty-four lawsuits had been brought against Sugarland and others associated with the show.

That same month on November 26, Nettles married her boyfriend of two years, Justin Miller, in a sunset ceremony in Nashville. She joined the reality show *Duets* which premiered in May 2012. Bush and his wife Jill have two children. He took part in the CMA Summer Songwriters Series in June 2012, which showcases some of Nashville's best of the best songwriting talent.

Sugarland took a brief hiatus at the end of 2011 but resumed touring in April 2012, jump-starting their "In Your Hands" tour. ∎

Kristian Bush and Jennifer Nettles of Sugarland at the 2012 Academy of Country Music Awards at MGM Grand Garden Arena on April 1, 2012 in Las Vegas, Nevada.

Travis Tritt

COUNTRY SINGER & SONGWRITER . MARIETTA

TRAVIS TRITT'S BLEND OF TRADITIONAL country and southern rock made him one of the top country singers in the 1990s, holding his own against the likes of Garth Brooks and Clint Black. A country singer without a cowboy hat, Tritt developed a fearless, outlaw image that helped him stand out from the rest.

James Travis Tritt was born in Marietta, Georgia, on February 9, 1963. He taught himself to play the guitar at eight and held his first performance in the fourth grade, singing "Annie's Song" and "King of the Road." He performed in the church band and for school classmates whenever possible. He attended Sprayberry High School where he wrote his first song, "Spend a Little Time," about a former girlfriend. In high school, Tritt founded a bluegrass group which won second place in a local tournament for their rendition of "Mammas Don't Let Your Babies Grow Up to Be Cowboys."

As a teenager, Tritt worked as a supermarket clerk and in a furniture store. His father did not encourage his musical aspirations and his mother wanted him to sing only gospel. He continued to play while working at various jobs and made attempts to settle down and have a family. However, Tritt was married and divorced twice before age twenty-two. It was through the encouragement of his boss at an air-conditioning company that he quit his job and pursued music full-time.

Working with a Warner Bros. record executive in 1982, Tritt began recording demos while playing the honkey tonk circuit. In 1987, a demo album called *Proud of the Country* got Tritt signed by Warner's Nashville division. He was also signed by Ken Kragen, a manager who had worked with stars such as Lionel Ritchie, Tricia Yearwood and Kenny Rogers. His first single, "Country Club" (1989), soared into the top 10, followed by his debut album of the same name which soon became platinum. His next two singles, "Help Me Hold On" and "I'm Gonna Be Somebody" both hit number one. Billboard named him "Top New Male Artist" in 1990.

As Tritt was known primarily as a country singer, radio deejays were reluctant to play his "Put Some Drive in Your Country" because of its rock and roll sound. The Nashville music industry was also hesitant to accept Tritt as they felt his music and stage show had too much rock and roll and his outlaw image of long hair and leather did not fit with the country singers of the time. However,

Tritt's manager helped market him in a way that appealed to fans on both sides of the country aisle. His second album, *It's All About to Change*, debuted in 1991 and soon was certified triple platinum.

Tritt admitted he was influenced by gospel singers and later on by Southern rock groups. Throwing in a little bluegrass, Tritt said that his influences were a mixture of country, rock and folk. "I never understood why you had to be broken down into these categories and be stuck in boxes," said Tritt.

Tritt's father did not encourage his musical aspirations and his mother wanted him to sing only gospel.

In 1991, Tritt won CMA's prestigious Horizon Award. In 1992, he was inducted into the Grand Ole Opry. He released his third album, *T-r-o-u-b-l-e*, in 1992 which spawned a number one single, "Can I Trust You With My Heart." He went on to score hits with "Here's A Quarter (Call Someone Who Cares)," "Ten Feet Tall and Bulletproof," "Foolish Pride," and dozens more. In 1995, he released *Greatest Hits: From the Beginning* which went platinum within six months of its release.

In 1992, Tritt won a Grammy for Best Vocal Collaboration of the Year ("The Whiskey Ain't Working") and in 1999 for Best Country Collaboration With Vocals ("Same Old Train") with Marty Stuart. His *Down The Road I Go* (2000) spawned four top ten hit singles, but his 2002 *Strong Enough* only hit with two top twenty singles. He released *Live in Concert* in 2007 and *My Honky Tonk History* in 2011.

Tritt's acting roles consist of *Rio Diablo* (1993, made for TV movie), *The Cowboy Way* (1994), *Sgt. Bilko* (1996), *Fire Down Below* (1997) and a starring role in *Fishers of Men* (2010), a Christian film.

Tritt and his third wife Theresa have been married since 1997 and he is a devoted father of two boys and one girl. His career has spanned 25 years and there seems to be no end in sight for this country outlaw singer/songwriter. As Tritt himself has said: "If you're gonna sing, sing loud."■

Travis Tritt smiling during his performance at the Food Lion Speed Street 600 event in Charlotte NC, 2008.

Ted Turner

MEDIA MOGUL & PHILANTHROPIST . ATLANTA

EVERYTHING TED TURNER DOES, he does in a over-sized way—a huge media empire, vast ranches, a billion dollar donation, winning the America's Cup, outrageous statements and a movie star wife.

Robert Edward Turner III was born on November 19, 1938, in Cincinnati, Ohio, but moved to Savannah when he was nine. He attended The McCallie School in Chattanooga, Tennessee, and Brown University and served in the United States Coast Guard.

Turner's father made a fortune in the billboard business, but when the business fell into debt, he committed suicide, leaving his

channel. What followed is media history. Turner bought MGM/UA Entertainment Company, he sold off most of its assets, but kept the huge film library. Using this material, and other acquisitions, he introduced Turner Network Television (TNT), Turner Classic Movies (TCM) and the Cartoon Channel and then added wresting to his offerings.

While managing his vast media empire, Turner still had time for other interests. Through Turner Enterprises, he owns 15 ranches located in several states making him one of the largest individual

Turner created Captain Planet, an environmental hero, and the Captain Planet Foundation to teach young citizens the value of cherishing our earth's resources.

son, at 24, to resolve the situation. The young Turner turned the business around, eventually using it as a springboard to his media acquisitions, and found spare time to successfully defend the America's Cup as captain of the yacht *Courageous* in 1977.

In the late 1960's, Turner used the profits from the billboard business to purchase Southern radio stations that he then sold to buy an Atlanta UHF television station. Turner had the foresight to understand the public would soon want more television choices. At first, he showed old movies, cartoons and second run television shows and acquired the right to televise Atlanta Braves baseball games. He shortly had a second station in Charlotte, North Carolina. In 1976, he bought the Atlanta Braves and Hawks, partially to provide programming. His choice to house his television business in downtown Atlanta was instrumental in promoting the area's revival.

In 1976, the breakthrough came when the FCC allowed Turner to distribute his programming to cable stations around the country using satellite transmission. Turner's stations, now christened "Super Stations," rose to two million subscribers and Turner's net worth to $100 million.

In 1978, Turner obtained the rights to the WTBS call sign which allowed him to use the acronym TBS for Turner Broadcasting System. In 1980, Ted Turner created CNN, the first 24/7 news

landowners in North America. These ranches raise bison, which fulfill the double aim of protecting this American species and supplying Turner's restaurant chain, Ted's Montana Grill.

Turner's interest in the environment is sincere. He created Captain Planet, an environmental hero, and the Captain Planet Foundation to teach young citizens the value of cherishing our earth's resources. Turner also founded the Goodwill Games, as a means of demonstrating peace through sports. He believes that the wealthy should share their resources and his foundation aids countless projects. His largest single contribution was one billion dollars to help support United Nations efforts.

Turner's many accolades include being named the American Humanist Association's Humanist of the Year in 1990 and *Time* magazine's Man of the Year in 1991, receiving the Governor's Award in 1992 from the National Academy of Arts and Sciences, the Albert Schweitzer Gold Medal for Humanitarianism and the Bower Award for Business Leadership from the Franklin Association in 2006.

Turner has been married three times, most notably to Jane Fonda, and has five children.

Ted Turner has been called many things, among them "mouth of the South" and "Captain Outrageous" for his outspoken views, but no one can deny his business acumen, vision and generosity. ∎

Ted Turner at the 76th Annual Academy Awards in Hollywood. February 29, 2004.

UGA

MASCOT . ATHENS

WHEREVER AND WHENEVER GEORGIA PLAYS FOOTBALL, he is there. At home games, he stays in an air-conditioned doghouse or sits regally atop a bag of ice. Who is this revered icon? Uga, NCAA's most well-known school mascot.

Frank W. "Sonny" Seiler is a prominent Georgia attorney and something of a celebrity because of his courtroom successes and movie roles in *Midnight in The Garden of Good and Evil, The Legend of Baggar Vance* and *Gingerbread Man*. However, his true claim to fame involves a four legged canine.

In 1955, Seiler and his wife Cecelia received a white bulldog as a wedding gift. His name was Hood's Old Dan and his bloodlines were said to be of historical significance. He was the grandson of the white English bulldog that accompanied the Georgia team to the 1943 Rose Bowl where Georgia shutout UCLA and earned their first National Championship.

Since the introduction of the white bulldog as a mascot in 1956, the Seiler family has maintained the unbroken line of white English bulldogs, taking each Uga to Sanford Stadium during football season from their Savannah home. "We've done the math," says Seiler in his book, *Damn Good Dogs*. "Counting home games, away games, bowl games, support for other Georgia athletic teams and public appearances, we've covered more than 50,000 miles with Uga."

Each Uga has a unique personality and leaves his own legacy. However, Uga V, born the only fully white male in a litter of three, stands out from the pack. He made the cover of *Sports Illustrated* when the magazine named Uga as the nation's best mascot in 1997. He played his father (Uga IV) in Clint Eastwood's film rendition of *Midnight in the Garden of Good and Evil*. He became a fan favorite when he lunged at an Auburn player who ended up on the Georgia sidelines during play in overtime. Uga V was also the first mascot to become a card-carrying member of the Georgia National Alumni Association.

Uga IV accompanied Hershel Walker to the Heisman Trophy Banquet and Uga VI flew to Washington in 2002 to attend a political reception. His appearance made headlines in a London newspaper. Uga IV was posthumously awarded the highest honor available to UGA mascots, the Georgia varsity letter. Vince Dooley declared him "Dog of the Decade" in 1991.

Uga's have appeared in ads, promotional posters, parades, *Newsweek, Time, ESPN's College Gameday* and even a "Dogumentary" by Athens filmmaker Erica McCarthy. Picture Day with Uga attracts so many admirers that the event is held indoors at Sanford Stadium.

To date, nine dogs have served as mascot, descending from the same line and in most cases each has been the son of the previous mascot. There are also replacement Uga's warming the bench. Interim dogs include Otto (1986), Magillicuddy (1989) and Russ who served as a substitute in 2009-10 for his half-brother Uga VII and then for Uga VIII who took over in 2010, but who died from lymphoma that same year at only seventeen months old.

Due to a groundswell of support from students and fans, Russ, the eight year old stand-in who was never groomed to be a full-time mascot, was inducted as Uga IX in 2012 during the pregame ceremony of the "passing of the collar" while fans chanted "damn good dog." The ceremony and chant are a tradition dating back to Uga I.

"If you can't appreciate the swaggering gait and churchillian physiognomy of Uga V, you must be a cat lover." (Sports Illustrated 1997)

Uga VIII, like all deceased Ugas before him, was buried in the "Georgia red" marble mausoleum at the southwest corner of Sanford Stadium. A bronze plaque engraved with the dog's tenure and an epitaph is in front of each tomb. Standing guard is a life-size bronze statue of Uga.

Even though the Ugas have an important job, they are also beloved family pets to the Seiler family. Sonny Seiler and Kent Hannon provide a very personal history of Georgia's famous mascot along with more than 500 colorful photos and many anecdotes in *Damn Good Dogs!*, now in its fourth printing. According to Seiler, "As long as there's a University of Georgia…there will always be an Uga." ∎

Sonny Seiler with Uga (above), photos courtesy of the University of Georgia, by Danny White.

Alice Walker

AUTHOR, POET & ACTIVIST . EATONTON

ALICE WALKER HAS USED HER prodigious talent to cast a gentle light on the undervalued, marginalized and castout and to rescue their insight and hard-earned wisdom and spirit for her readers. Her often intensely personal fiction and poetry reflect the trials and triumphs of those who otherwise might go unnoticed, including her young and sensitive self.

As a young woman during the 60s and 70s when the twin causes of civil rights and feminism became national issues, Walker began to crusade for civil and human rights. She was involved in the Civil Rights protests of the 60s and has continued to champion human rights, particularly for women, from the American South to Iraq and Africa. Her work often reflects her concern for women, especially black women, whose woes, strengths, abuses, courage, joy and sisterhood she

birth to her first novel, *The Third Life of Grange Copeland*, and her daughter, Rebecca Grant. After the marriage dissolved, Walker moved to California where she lives today.

Walker has served as a contributing editor of *Ms. magazine*, is a co-founder of Wild Tree Press, has continued to advocate for international women's rights and has taught African-American women's studies at Yale, Brandeis, the University of Massachusetts, Wellesley and the University of California. On teaching she commented, "I imagine good teaching as a circle of earnest people sitting down to ask each other meaningful questions. I don't see it as a handing down of answers..." In addition to her own work, Walker has been instrumental in bringing the work of Zora Neale Hurston to the attention of a new generation of readers.

"I imagine good teaching as a circle of earnest people sitting down to ask each other meaningful questions. I don't see it as a handing down of answers..."

celebrates in story and poetry. As she has said, "And so our mothers and grandmothers have, more often than not anonymously, handed on the creative spark, the seed of the flower they themselves never hoped to see—or like a sealed letter they could not plainly read."

Alice Malsenior Walker was born on February 9, 1944, to sharecropper parents Minnie Tallulah Grant and Willie Lee Walker. Her early life was marked by a lively spirit but when she was eight, her right eye was wounded in an accident while at play; she not only lost the vision in the eye but suffered disfiguring scarring. The scar tissue was removed six years later, but Walker had become shy and reclusive. Much of her former spirit returned, but the need for solitude, appetite for reading and writing and feeling of estrangement lingered.

She attended Spelman College where she became active in the Civil Rights movement, and, after two years, transferred to Sarah Lawrence in New York. After graduation, Walker married a civil rights attorney and moved to Jackson, Mississippi, where she worked with the Head Start program and was writer-in-residence at Jackson State College and Tugaloo. During this time, she gave

Her most famous novel, *The Color Purple,* was published in 1982 and won both the Pulitzer Prize and the National Book Award for Fiction. Her works are too numerous to list but include, *The Temple of My Familiar* and *By the Light of My Father's Smile*, both novels; the non-fiction works *In Search of Our Mother's Gardens: Womanist Prose* and *We Are the Ones We Have Been Waiting For*; poetry collections *A Poem Traveled Down My Arm: Poems and Drawings* and *Hard Times Require Furious Dancing: New Poems* as well as numerous short stories.

Among the many awards that Walker has received are: an Honorary Degree from the California Institute of the Arts, Guggenhem, Merrill and the Radcliffe Institute Fellowships, the Rosenthal Award from the National Institute of Arts and Letters, Humanist of the Year (1997) from the American Humanist Association and the Domestic Human Rights Award from the Global Exchange.

An Alice Walker quote: "The nature of this flower is to bloom." Walker continues to bloom in her work and through her actions and has helped others find their own blooming through her writing and the example of her life. ■

Herschel Walker

STAR RUNNING BACK . WRIGHTSVILLE

HERSCHEL WALKER PLAYED FOOTBALL for the University of Georgia and was a three-time All-American and winner of the 1982 Heisman Trophy. During his pro football career, which spanned fifteen years, Walker logged more yardage than any pro football player who ever lived.

Born on March 3, 1962, in Wrightsville, Georgia, Walker was an overweight child with a speech impediment. One of seven children from a blue collar family, Walker was taught by his mother that these challenges were not to be used as excuses in life. Following his mother's advice, he helped his Johnson County High School Trojans to their first state championship in 1979, rushing for over three-thousand yards. That same year, he was awarded the first Dial Award for the national high school scholar-athlete of the year.

Recruited by Vince Dooley, Walker played running back at UGA for three years before leaving to go pro. He set the National Collegiate Athletic Association's (NCAA) freshman rushing record and was the first true freshman to become a first team All-American. As a freshman, he also played a major role in helping Georgia go undefeated and win the National Championship in 1980. Walker won the Heisman in his junior year (1982) and was the only player to finish in the top three in Heisman voting each year he played.

During his time at Georgia, Walker set eleven NCAA records, sixteen Southeastern Conference records and forty-one UGA records. Walker's 5,259 yards, gained by the end of his three-year Georgia career, was the most ever by a college running back. He became the third leading rusher in NCAA history. Walker also competed on Georgia's track and field team where he twice drew all-American honors.

Walker left Georgia after his junior year to play for the New Jersey Generals of the United States Football League (USFL) where he set a single-season rushing record and was named USFL's Most Valuable Player. He also won the USFL's rushing title in 1983 and 1985.

Walker went to the Dallas Cowboys in 1986 where he shared duties with Tony Dorsett, a former Heisman winner from the University of Pittsburgh. He soon established himself as a premier NFL running back, and when Dorsett was traded in 1988, Walker reached NFL career highs while playing in several different positions. He became the tenth player in NFL history to accumulate more than 2,000 combined yards rushing and receiving in a season.

At the height of his NFL career, Walker was traded to the Minnesota Vikings in 1989 in exchange for five players. Walker was never utilized to his full potential by the Vikings, and after three seasons, he was traded to the Philadelphia Eagles in 1992. That year, he rushed for over one-thousand yards. In 1994, he became the first player in the NFL to have gained ninety or more yards in rushing, receiving and kick-off returns.

"Coming from a small town it was tough to dream big. When I grew up in a small town in Georgia, my biggest dream was one day to be able to go to Atlanta."

In 1995, Walker signed with the Giants but left after one season. He returned to the Cowboys where he played as a kick-off return specialist. At the end of the 1997, Walker retired from football. In the NFL, he had gained 8,225 yards rushing, 4,859 yards receiving and over 5,000 kick-off return yards.

At retirement, he was ranked second among NFL's all time leaders in total yardage. In 1999, he was chosen as a member of the *Sports Illustrated* NCAA Football All-Century Team. Fox Sports named him the best college football running back of all time in their Sports List. ESPN selected him as the greatest player in college football history. He was elected to the College Football Hall of Fame in 1999. UGA retired his number 34 jersey.

An all around athlete, Walker competed in the 1992 Winter Olympics two-man bobsled, achieving seventh place. In 1988, he danced with the Forth Worth Ballet for a season. He holds a fifth-degree black belt in tae kwon do.

Presently, Walker has a new career as a combatant in mixed martial arts. He begins his day at 5:30 a.m. doing up to 1500 push-ups and 2,000 sit-ups. He eats one meal a day and is a vegetarian. He also owns and runs Renaissance Man International with offices in Georgia and Arkansas. Herschel's Famous 34 division sells prepared chicken and appetizers to restaurants. A portion of his profits go to charitable organizations.

Walker published his autobiography in 2008 entitled *Breaking Free: My Life with Dissociative Identity Disorder*. He was diagnosed with the condition in 2002. A born again Christian, Walker is divorced and has one son, Christian. ∎

Herschel Walker speaks to the Class of 2016 during Basic Cadet Training in the U.S. Air Force Academy's Jacks Valley in Colorado Springs, Colo. July 17, 2012. Photo by Michael Kaplan.

Joanne Woodward

ACTRESS & PRODUCER . THOMASVILLE

WHEN A LITTLE GIRL DREAMS, she may see herself becoming a beauty queen or famous movie star. A young woman may dream of the man she falls in love with asking for her hand in marriage and becoming her lover and partner for the rest of their lives, dreaming of children and grandchildren. A young woman may dream, unrealistically, of having it all. So what was Joanne Woodward imagining when she was a young girl?

Born February 27, 1930, in Thomasville, Georgia, Joanne Gignilliat Trimmier had a mother who was so enamored of the movies she named her daughter after Joan Crawford. Typically Southern, she turned one syllable into two and the name became Joanne. Her mother was responsible for Joanne's first introduction to the movies and movie stars. When Joanne was seven, her family moved from Blakeley to Marietta and Mrs. Woodward took her daughter to the premiere of *Gone With The Wind* in Atlanta. There is a familiar story told about Joanne's determination to meet Laurence Olivier. After her parent's divorce, Joanne and her mother moved to Greenville where she spent much of her high school life on stage in theatrical productions. When she decided on Louisiana State University, she also decided to major in drama.

Woodward continued on to New York to perform, once again on stage, where she met her future husband in 1953. On the set of *Picnic,* she met Paul Newman with whom she shared an agent. Although he was married and she was unimpressed with his acting, the two were drawn to each other. He was divorced in 1958. After working together on *The Long Hot Summer*, the two were married.

Woodward had come to Greenville in 1955 for her feature debut movie, *Count Three and Pray,* but afterwards returned to the live stage. She filmed *No Down Payment* and won a nomination for the BAFTA Award for Best Foreign Actress in 1957. That was also the year she achieved true Hollywood star status with her Academy and Golden Globe Award winning performance in *The Three Faces of Eve. Eve* also won her the National Board of Review Award for Best Actress and a nomination for the BAFTA Award for Best Actress.

1958 began a rewarding ten years for Woodward as she and her new husband enjoyed successful personal lives and professional careers. Along with her marriage to Newman and nominations and awards from *Eve,* came the birth of their daughter Elinor Teresa in 1959. Woodward and Newman starred together in several films, including *From The Terrace* in 1960 and *Paris Blues* in 1961. 1961 also brought the birth of Melissa Stewart, their second baby girl,

who later gave them their two grandsons.

A New Kind of Love in '63 bought Woodward a nomination for the Golden Globe Award for Best Actress. Two years later marked the birth of their third daughter, Claire Olivia Newman, in 1965. Ten films later, in 1968, Joanne lost her leading man. He had become her director and producer in *Rachel, Rachel,* for which she received another Academy Award nomination for Best Actress. The film also received a nomination for best picture.

After 50 years of marriage, a rarity in Hollywood life, Paul and Joanne celebrated their golden anniversary in January, 2008.

Her film career continued and two of her last efforts, *The Effects of Gamma Rays on Man-in-the-Moon Marigolds* and *Summer Wishes, Winter Dreams,* earned Woodward several awards and nominations. In 1976, for her first television drama, *Sybil,* she won a Prime Time Emmy Award for Outstanding Actress that began her rewarding television career.

Woodward acted on stage and in film, has been a co-producer, producer and director and has written a teleplay. She is currently the artistic director for Westport County Playhouse. To say she loves the business is an understatement.

One of her most important achievements, the Hole in The Wall Gang, was founded in partnership with Newman in 1988. The program now has eleven camps and serves over 14,000 seriously ill children at no cost to them or their parents. The charity is now incorporated and replicated in Europe.

After 50 years of marriage, a rarity in Hollywood life, Paul and Joanne celebrated their golden anniversary in January, 2008. Paul died in their home in Westport, Connecticut, in December, 2008. Woodward continues to live in that home.

When a young woman dreams of her future, she dreams of a husband who makes her laugh—a "most considerate and romantic man." She sees a fabulous union that lasts and brings the joy of children and grandchildren into her life. She imagines a successful career for both, sharing hopes and dreams for each other and their children. She wonders if dreams do come true. She is wishing for a Joanne Woodward life. ■

Joanne Woodward publicity photo, circa 1960.

Trisha Yearwood

COUNTRY MUSIC ARTIST . JASPER COUNTY

TRISHA YEARWOOD IS A WOMAN of many talents. Not only is she a three time Grammy Award winner and a three time Country Music Award winner, she is also a two-time *New York Times* Bestselling Cookbook author. Add to this talk show host on the *Food Network* and there is a recipe for success.

Patricia Lynn Yearwood was born September 19, 1964, in Monticello, Georgia. Her mother was a schoolteacher and her father a local banker. Young Patricia enjoyed singing in musicals and talent shows in elementary school. She earned an associate's degree from Young Harris College before enrolling at the University of Georgia. In 1985, she transferred to Belmont College in Nashville and graduated with a BA in business administration in 1987.

While at Belmont, Yearwood worked as an intern with MTM Records and later as a full-time employee. A much sought after demo singer, she was hired as a backup vocalist by up and coming country singer Garth Brooks. In 1990, when performing live at the label showcase of Brooks' album *No Fences*, she was spotted by an MCA record producer who signed her with MCA Nashville Records.

Shortly afterwards, Yearwood served as the opening act for Brooks' 1991 nationwide tour. That same year, she released her self-titled debut album with the lead single "She's in Love with the Boy" reaching number one on the Billboard Country Chart. Three additional singles peaked in the top ten. The album sold a million copies making Yearwood the first female artist to have accomplished that feat with a first album. The album's success resulted in Yearwood being named "Top New Female Vocalist" (1991) by the Academy of Country Music Awards and voted "Favorite New Country Artist" by the American Music Awards (1992).

She released her second album, *Hearts in Armor* (1992), to critical acclaim. Two singles, "Wrong Side of Memphis" and "Walkaway Joe" made the top five. The album, a collaboration with other artists, went platinum. In 1994, Yearwood released a Christmas album entitled *The Sweetest Gift* and also married bassist Robert Reynolds of the Mavericks. This was her second marriage.

Yearwood's 1995 album *Thinkin' About You* and her 1996 album *Everybody Knows* leaned toward Country pop. Yearwood garnered three number one singles as a result of both albums. Her 1997 greatest hits album *Songbook: A Collection of Hits* was her first album to reach number one on the Billboard Top Country Albums and the single "Perfect Love" reached number one on the country

charts in 1998. The album sold four million copies and was certified 4x Multi-Platinum. In both 1997 and 1998, she won "Female Vocalist of the Year" from the Country Music Association and the Academy of Country Music.

Now a hit crossover artist, Yearwood released *Where Your Road Leads* (1998) with three singles hitting the top ten on *Billboard* Country. That same year, she tried her hand at acting with a recurring role in the hit drama *Jag*. Divorced in 2000, her next album *Real Live Woman* was a reflection of her heartbreak.

Yearwood was inducted into the Georgia Hall of Fame in 2000.

Yearwood released *Inside Out* in 2001, topping the country charts and yielding the number four hit "I Would've Loved You Anyway." She released *Jasper County* in 2005 and the hit single "Georgia Rain." The album, named for her home county, was her third to peak at number one on the *Billboard* Top Country Albums Chart, becoming the eleventh Gold certification of her career.

In November 2007, she released her tenth album, *Heaven, Heartache, and the Power of Love*, with a new independent label, Big Machine Records. The album gained her some of the most complimentary revues of her career.

In 2008, Yearwood released a cookbook written with her mother and sister, *Georgia Cooking in an Oklahoma Kitchen*. The trio released a second cookbook, *Home Cooking With Trisha Yearwood*, in April 2010. *Trisha's Southern Kitchen* premiered on the *Food Network* in April 2012.

Yearwood, who married Garth Brooks in 2005, believes in giving back. She is active with Habitat for Humanity for which she and Brooks helped build a flood wall in New Orleans after Katrina. Yearwood participated in a project with National Women Build Week (2009). Two hundred crews of women learned to build houses in Georgia and Oklahoma during that project. She is also the national spokesperson for Campbell's Labels for Education Program.

Yearwood was inducted into the Georgia Hall of Fame in 2000. She has performed at the Olympics, the White House and with Luciano Pavarotti. She and Brooks were named by Billboard.com as the 2012 Most Powerful Celebrity Couple in Music. ∎

Trisha Yearwood at the first CMT Giants concert honoring country star Reba McEntire, at the Kodak Theatre, Hollywood, California in 2006.

Georgia

POLITICAL HISTORY

GEORGIANS HAVE PLAYED A MEANINGFUL

ROLE IN SHAPING U.S. POLITICS.

WE DON'T HESITATE TO BOAST ABOUT THREE

PRESIDENTS AND ONE VICE PRESIDENT

FROM OUR HOME STATE.

THE INDIVIDUALS INCLUDED IN THIS SECTION

CONTRIBUTED TO OUR UNIQUE CHARACTER

AND HAD AN ENORMOUS IMPACT ON PAST,

PRESENT, AND FUTURE GENERATIONS.

THESE ELECTED OFFICIALS ARE INSPIRING,

SOMETIMES UNPREDICTABLE,

BUT ALWAYS FASCINATING.

*The **GEORGIA STATE CAPITOL** Building in Atlanta, Georgia. The building was constructed in 1889 and a restoration of the House chambers was performed in 1997. Photo by Rob Wilson.*

WHEN GOVERNOR NATHAN DEAL ENTERED the political arena after having spent 23 years practicing law, he was following in the footsteps of his parents, both of whom were teachers.

"They always regarded what they did as public service," Deal told the *Atlanta Journal-Constitution* in 2010. "And I've always appreciated the fact that people who do public service are some of the best citizens we have."

Nathan Deal

GOVERNOR OF GEORGIA . 2010 – PRESENT

Born in Millen in 1942, Deal grew up in Sandersville where he attended First Baptist Church and was a prominent member of his high school debate team. One of Deal's earliest hobbies was showing registered Duroc pigs at 4-H Club and Future Farmers of America competitions. "I've got a box full of ribbons and trophies over the years from that," he told *Atlanta Magazine*. "I saved up enough money to pay for my first year of college from winnings in livestock shows."

Deal received his bachelor and law degrees with honors from Mercer University, with an added bonus; it was there that he met his future bride, Sandra Dunagan, on a blind date. Today, they have four children and six grandchildren.

After graduation, Deal served as a captain in the U.S. Army for two years before entering private practice. He worked as an assistant district attorney and juvenile court judge, then, as a Democrat, served for 12 years in the Georgia Senate, where Deal was named president pro tempore during his last term.

By then, he had caught the political bug and Capitol Hill beckoned. In 1992, Deal was elected to the U.S. House, defeating incumbent Ed Jenkins in Georgia's Ninth Congressional District. He was re-elected in 1994, then switched political parties the next spring after the Republicans, led by fellow Georgian Newt Gingrich, won control of the U.S. House for the first time in 40 years.

In announcing his switch, Deal said the National Democratic Party had refused to admit that it "was out of touch with mainstream

NATHAN AND SANDRA DEAL *pose on the steps of the Georgia State Capitol in Atlanta, 2011.*

America." The political move codified his conservative values and those of his constituents, he later told the *Atlanta Journal-Constitution*. "They, too, had become more conservative over a period of time."

Gingrich said the party's "Contract with America," which vowed to shrink the federal government, reduce taxes, promote entrepreneurship and pursue welfare reform, had prompted Deal's change of parties. "Congressman Deal called me and said he'd had enough of liberalism and he'd had enough of being pressured by

left-wing Democrats," the former House Speaker said in a video in support of Deal's 2010 gubernatorial bid.

Deal, who served nine terms in the U.S. House, consistently pressed for immigration reform. He was the lead sponsor of four bills that would deny automatic citizenship for children born to illegal immigrants. None of those bills passed but Deal co-sponsored successful legislation that required the citizenship of Medicaid recipients to be verified.

The *National Journal Almanac* describes Deal's voting record in Congress as "mostly conservative, with an occasional deviation on foreign policy." His campaign platform included improving education and transportation infrastructure, increasing economic competitiveness, and a phase-in of zero-based budgeting, in which state agencies must defend their proposed budgets and each line-item must be approved annually. Deal defeated Democrat Roy Barnes in the November, 2010, election to become Georgia's 82nd governor. ∎

GEORGIA NATIONAL GUARD *senior leaders meet with Gov. Deal at the capitol. Saluting the colors at change of command ceremony, the incoming and outgoing Adjutants General stand on either side of Gov. Deal, Clay National Guard Center, Marietta, Georgia, 2011. (Photo by Sgt. 1st Class Roy Henry)*

★ Jimmy Carter

Thirty-Ninth President of the U. S. (1977-1981), Georgia Governor (1971-1975)

JIMMY CARTER was born in a mental institution. He has worked in nuclear physics. He has been a peanut farmer and an owner of a seed and farm supply store. He is one of only two native Georgians to win the Nobel Peace Prize. He is the author of 27 books, once filed a UFO Sighting Incident report, is a cousin of Motown founder Barry Gordy and served as the 39th President of the United States.

James Earl Carter Jr., Jimmy Carter, was born October 1, 1924, in Plains, Georgia, the son of a farmer and businessman and a registered nurse. He attended public schools in Plains and later attended Georgia Southwestern College and the Georgia Institute of Technology. In 1946 he received a Bachelor of Science degree from the United States Naval Academy and, on July 7th that same year, married Rosalynn Smith of Plains. In the Navy he became a submariner, rising to the rank of lieutenant and working in New York in reactor technology and nuclear physics.

Upon his father's death in 1953, Carter resigned his commission to move back to Georgia and take over the operation of his family's Carter Farms. He and Rosalynn also operated Carter's Warehouse, a seed and farm supply store. Because his inheritance from his father was very little, he and his family had to live in public housing for roughly a year, but he quickly became a leader in the community, serving on education, hospital and library boards. This led to a victorious Georgia Senate run in 1962, followed by a failed run for governor in 1966, losing to segregationist Lester Maddox. He won the next gubernatorial election and became Georgia's 76th governor on January 12, 1971. In his inaugural address, he surprised many by saying, "No poor, rural, weak, or black person should ever have to bear the additional burden of being deprived of the opportunity of an education, a job, or simple justice." He went on to appoint many African-Americans to statewide boards and offices.

On December 12, 1974, Carter announced his candidacy for president of the United States and was elected on November 2, 1976. He remains the only Georgian-born U.S. president.

Serving from January 20, 1977, until January 20, 1981, President Carter came into office during a recession and energy crisis. Carter famously referred to the energy crisis as "the moral equivalent of war" and set about putting energy reforms in place, including creating a new Department of Energy. His presidency was also marked by significant foreign policy accomplishments, including the Panama Canal treaties, the Camp David Accords, the peace treaty between Egypt and Israel, the SALT II nuclear arms reduction treaty with the Soviet Union and the establishment of U.S. diplomatic relations with the People's Republic of China. His final year in office was beleaguered by the Iran hostage crisis in which 52 Americans were held hostage for 444 days from November 4, 1979, to January 20, 1981, after Iranian extremists took over the American Embassy in Tehran. After unsuccessful negotiations and rescue attempts, officials in Algiers brokered a release deal and the hostages were set free just minutes after Ronald Regan replaced Carter as president on January 20, 1981.

In many circles, Carter is revered more for his work after leaving office than during his presidency. In 1982, he and wife Rosalynn founded The Carter Center and have consistently been involved in resolving conflict, promoting democracy, protecting human rights and preventing disease worldwide. On December 10, 2002, the Norwegian Nobel Committee awarded Carter the Nobel Peace Prize "for his decades of untiring effort to find peaceful solutions to international conflicts, to advance democracy and human rights, and to promote economic and social development." The only other Georgia native to win the prize was Dr. Martin Luther King, Jr., and while three U.S. presidents have been awarded the honor, Carter is the only one to receive it after leaving office. ■

Zell Miller ★

Seventy-ninth Governor of Georgia (1991-1999), Lt. Governor (1975-1991)

ZELL BRYAN MILLER is the only politician to give a keynote speech at both the Democratic and Republican National Conventions. He is a former marine sergeant, college professor, senator and governor.

Miller was born February 24, 1932, in the small town of Young Harris, Georgia. He was raised by his widowed mother, an art teacher. His father, dean of Young Harris College, died when Miller was an infant.

Miller received a master's degree in history from the University of Georgia. He attained the rank of sergeant in the U.S. Marine Corps and published a book on his experiences and the values he learned: *Corps Values: Everything You Need to Know I Learned in the Marines* (1997).

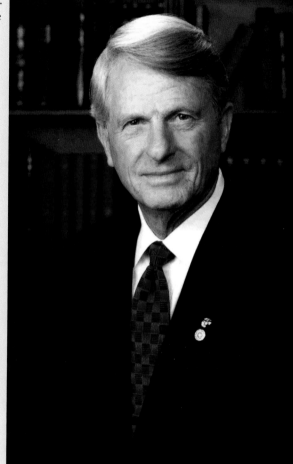

He began his political career as the mayor of Young Harris from 1959 to1960 and was then elected to two terms as a Georgia State Senator during the 1960s. In 1964 and 1966, he was unsuccessful in his bid for the Democratic nomination for a seat in the U.S. House of Representatives. He later served as Chief of Staff for Georgia Governor Lester Maddox.

Miller was elected Lieutenant Governor of Georgia in 1975 and served for 16 years. During this time, he unsuccessfully challenged Herman Talmadge in the 1980 primary for the United States Senate seat. In 1990, he defeated Atlanta Mayor Andrew Young in the primary and then Republican Johnny Isakson to become governor of Georgia for two terms.

As governor, he was a strong supporter of education and created the HOPE Scholarship program. Funded by the state lottery, which he also initiated, the program allows high school students who meet certain requirements to attend in-state universities tuition free. In addition, he developed a free pre-kindergarten program and brought technology to all the public schools in the state. Georgia became known as a national leader for innovative education programs. *The Washington Post* in 1998 called him the most popular governor in America.

After leaving the governor's office in 1999, he taught at Young Harris College, Emory University and the University of Georgia until his appointment to the U.S. Senate in 2000 after the untimely death of Paul Coverdell. He was elected to fill the seat for the remaining four years.

As a conservative southern Democrat, Miller soon began showing support for Republicans and increased his criticisms of the Democrats. He declared himself a conservative on all economic and social issues in his support of various bills and amendments. He strongly supported the estate tax and advocated drilling in the Arctic National Wildlife Refuge.

Miller's book *A National Party No More: The Conscience of a Conservative Democrat* (2003) spent nine weeks on *The New York Times* Best Seller list. In 2004, he was the keynote speaker at the Republican National Convention in support of President George W. Bush. That same year, he cosponsored the Federal Marriage Amendment to the U.S. Constitution which declared marriage consists solely of a man and a woman. Miller criticized the United States Supreme Court stating that it removed prayer from public schools and legalized the killing of unborn babies. He declared in 2008 that he would not support Obama or Hillary Clinton for president.

However, during his tenure, Miller did support some of his own party's positions such as the Bipartisan Campaign Reform Act (2002) and the Bipartisan Patient Protection Act to allow consumers to import cheaper prescription drugs from Canada.

After leaving the Senate in 2005, he worked in the National Government Affairs department of a Georgia law firm, became a Fox News Channel contributor, and published the best-seller *A Deficit of Decency*, which expands on his earlier criticisms of the Democratic Party. He currently serves with the American Battle Monuments Commission and on the board of directors of the National Rifle Association.

Miller and his wife Shirley have been married for 58 years and have two sons, four grandchildren and four great-grandchildren. They live in the rock home in Young Harris which his mother built with rocks she hauled out of a nearby stream; the home is a symbol of rugged independence to Miller. Retired from public service, he continues to write and enjoys walks in the mountains with his two yellow Labradors, Gus and Woodrow. ■

★ Herman Eugene Talmadge *(1913-2002)*

United States Senate (1957-1981), Governor of Georgia (1948-1955)

DEMOCRAT HERMAN TALMADGE served four terms in the United States Senate and as governor of Georgia for a partial and full term. He was born on August 9, 1913, in McRae, Georgia. His father Eugene was governor of Georgia in the 1930s and 1940s. Talmadge graduated from the University of Georgia in 1936 with a law degree.

He practiced law for several years and then joined the Navy during World War II where he saw extensive combat duty in the South Pacific. He left the service with the rank of lieutenant commander. When he returned home, he spearheaded his father's last successful run for governor in 1946. Sadly, his father died before he could be sworn in.

The Georgia General Assembly decided to appoint Herman Talmadge as governor amid controversy from other elected officials who felt they should be governor. Two months after Talmadge took office, the Georgia Supreme Court ruled his appointment unconstitutional. He vacated the office and signed on to run in the special election held in 1948. Talmadge won the election and was reelected governor for a full term in 1950.

Talmadge's tenure as governor included enacting the state's first sales tax, which helped the state's public education system. He worked to attract new industry to the state and was an advocate for the timber industry. Talmadge was considered a progressive in many ways except for his stance as a segregationist which marred his gubernatorial terms. He wrote a book in 1955 entitled *You and Segregation* in answer to the Supreme Court's decision to declare segregation as unconstitutional. Ironically, however, he made sure that the salaries of black teachers were equal to those of whites.

Talmadge was elected to the United States Senate in 1956. Still an opponent of civil rights, he took part in a boycott of the 1964 Democratic National Convention after President Lyndon B. Johnson signed the Civil Rights Act of 1964. While serving as chairman of the Agriculture Committee (1972-1981), Talmadge pushed through the Rural Development Act of 1972 to help farmers. He also helped to expand the school lunch and food stamp programs.

Talmadge also served on the Senate Finance Committee where he consistently advocated for a balanced budget. He supported bills which cut federal spending in order to achieve that goal. In 1973, Talmadge was asked to serve on the Senate Watergate Committee. He received recognition for his intelligent questions, and it was noted by the committee's chief counsel, Samuel Dash, that Talmadge's questioning "was among the best."

In 1978, Talmadge voted for the Panama Canal Treaties in support of President Jimmy Carter. The vote for the treaty, which gave control of the canal to the Panamanian government, was considered by Talmadge to be politically suicidal, but also the right thing to do.

Talmadge was defeated for reelection to the Senate in 1980. The combination of his alcoholism (which escalated after his son Bobby drowned in 1975), his bitter divorce, and the charge that he accepted more than $43,000 for the reimbursement of false expenses cost him his position and reputation. His wife Betty was called to testify against him before the Senate Ethics Committee. He lost the election to Republican Mack Mattingly.

Talmadge retired to his home in Henry County where he maintained a low profile. A lifelong Democrat, he supported Republican Johnny Isakson in the 1990 Georgia governor's race. Herman Talmadge died at home on March 21, 2002, at the age of eighty-eight. He was the father of two sons, Herman E. Talmadge, Jr. and Robert Shingler Talmadge. ■

Clarence Thomas ★

Associate Justice of the Supreme Court of the United States

CLARENCE THOMAS was born in Pin Point, Georgia, on June 23, 1948, and grew up in the small African American community that had been founded by freedmen after the Civil War. Thomas' father left the family when Thomas was two, and, although his mother struggled to keep the family together, she was forced to send her children to her parents in Savannah after a house fire left the family homeless. In Savannah, Thomas found the man who was to be the greatest influence on his life. His grandfather, who had built a thriving fuel business in spite of difficult times, impressed upon the boy the values that inspired him throughout his life.

One of the most respected and conservative justices in the history of our country, Thomas took a unique path to the Supreme Court. Raised a Catholic, he briefly attended St. John Vianney Minor Seminary in 1967 and Immaculate Conception Seminary in Missouri. After overhearing a classmate make a joke about the assassination of Martin Luther King, Jr., he left the seminary and moved north to attend Holy Cross College in Massachusetts. While pursuing a degree in English Literature, he became very active in social causes including protesting the Vietnam War and starting a campaign for civil rights. After graduating cum laude, he attended Yale University Law School and earned a Juris Doctor degree in 1974. He then moved back to Missouri to work as an assistant to the state Attorney General John Danforth.

After Danforth was elected to the Senate in 1976, Thomas worked as an attorney for the Monsanto Company for a short time but returned to Washington to work with Danforth in 1979. In 1981, he joined the Reagan administration and served as Assistant Secretary of Education for the Office for Civil Rights in the U.S. Department of Education and later as Chairman of the US Equal Employment Opportunity Commission. In 1989, President H. W. Bush nominated Thomas to be a Federal judge in the Court of Appeals. The Senate approved his nomination in 1990.

In 1991, President Bush nominated Thomas to replace the retiring Supreme Court Justice Thurgood Marshall. This nomination was hotly contested because of Thomas' conservative views and the allegations of sexual harassment made against him by Anita Hill; however, Thomas was confirmed as a Justice of the Supreme Court in 1991.

Justice Thomas is recognized as one of the most conservative members of the Court. His memoir, *My Grandfather's Son*, was published in 2007. Thomas is married to Virginia Lamp, an activist in conservative politics. ■

★ Newt Gingrich

U.S. Congress (1979-1999), Speaker of the U.S. House of Representatives (1995-1999)

IN 1994, NEWT GINGRICH became the first Republican Speaker of the House in forty years. His "Contract with America" helped bring the Republican Party to victory by capturing the majority in the U.S. House. As a result, *Time* named him Man of the Year in 1995. He was re-elected to Congress ten times.

Gingrich's tenure as Speaker was marked with success and controversy. Under his aegis, Congress passed its first balanced budget since 1969, decreasing the national debt by over $400 billion. Congress reformed welfare and cut taxes for the first time in sixteen years and restored funding to strengthen the defense program.

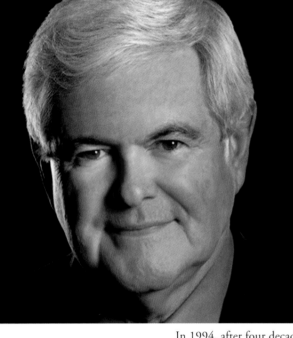

Newt Leroy McPherson was born in Harrisburg, Pennsylvania, on June 17, 1943. His parents divorced soon after his birth but he was later adopted by his mother's second husband, Army officer Robert Gingrich. Newt Gingrich graduated from Baker High in Columbus, Georgia, and received his bachelor's degree in history from Emory University in 1965.

As the son of a career soldier, Gingrich decided early to dedicate his life to the protection of freedom. He continued his studies at Tulane University earning an M.A. and Ph.D. in Modern European History in 1971. In the 1970s, he taught history and geography at West Georgia College.

Gingrich lost his bids for congress in 1974 and 1976. In 1978, he won a seat in the House and became an influential conservative member of the Republican Party. Gingrich formed the Conservative Opportunity Society, a group consisting of young conservative House Republicans.

In 1988, Gingrich enhanced his image in the party by leading the charge against Democratic Speaker of the House Jim Wright who had allegedly violated campaign finance rules. As a result, when Dick Cheney was appointed Secretary of Defense, Gingrich took his place as House Minority Whip in 1989.

When the House Banking Scandal broke in 1992, making it known that House members were allowed to overdraw their House checking accounts without being penalized, Gingrich was himself, with 22 overdrawn checks to his account, was included in the group. However, noting that more Democrats were involved in the scandal, Gingrich decided to let all names be made public. As a result, 77 representatives resigned or lost reelection.

In 1994, after four decades of congressional Democratic control, the GOP won the majority in the House and Gingrich was elected Speaker. Gingrich passed some major pieces of legislation including a capital gains tax cut and a balanced budget and gained President Clinton's signature on the welfare reform act.

In 1995, Gingrich's popularity took a decline due to his failure to compromise with Clinton on budget cuts, resulting in a partial government shutdown. He was also surrounded with ethics charges - all but one eventually cleared. His push for Clinton's impeachment in response to the Monica Lewinsky scandal created a backlash for Republicans who lost five seats to the Democrats in the 1998 midterm elections. In 1998, Gingrich resigned as Speaker of the House, and, in 1999, he resigned his seat in Congress.

Gingrich, widely known for his commitment to a better heath care system for all Americans, founded the Center for Health Transformation in 2003 to develop free market healthcare reforms centered on the individual. His past leadership helped save Medicare from bankruptcy and prompted FDA reforms.

An acknowledged expert on military issues, Gingrich served on the Defense Policy Board under President George W. Bush and was appointed to the U.S. Commission on National Security/21st Century. He teaches the Joint War Fighting course for Major Generals at Air University and is an honorary Distinguished Visiting Scholar and professor at the National Defense University. He also serves on the Terrorism Task Force for the Council on Foreign Relations.

Gingrich Productions, which he runs with his wife Callista, produces award winning documentary films. He has authored or co-authored twenty-three books. Thirteen have made *The New York Times* Best Seller list. In 2012, Newt Gingrich made an unsuccessful bid for the GOP nomination for the presidency. He and Callista live in McLean, Virginia. ■

Sam Nunn ★

U. S. Senate (1972-1997)

SAM NUNN SERVED as a U.S. Senator from Georgia, was mentioned as a possible vice-presidential nominee and cabinet-level appointee and considered a bid for the presidency himself.

He continues to use his influence to reduce the threat of weapons of mass destruction worldwide.

Nunn was born in Macon, Georgia, on September 8, 1938. As a Boy Scout, he earned the rank of Eagle Scout. He attended Georgia Tech, Emory University and Emory University Law School, where he earned a degree in 1962. He served on active duty in the U.S. Coast Guard and later in the Coast Guard Reserve.

Nunn's great-uncle, Carl Vinson, served in the U.S. House of Representatives and influenced Nunn to pursue politics with the aim of influencing U.S. military affairs. Nunn, a Democrat, began as a member of the Georgia General Assembly in 1968. In 1972, he successfully ran for a seat in the U.S. Senate. Nunn became a long-standing member of the Senate, winning reelection three times. He served as a Senator until 1997, when he retired, citing a decrease in his enthusiasm to continue in that role.

While in the Senate, Nunn chaired the Senate Armed Services Committee and the Permanent Subcommittee on Investigations. He cooperated with Republican Senator Richard Lugar to sponsor the Cooperative Threat Reduction Act, which helped remove nuclear weapons from the former Soviet Union.

In the Senate, Nunn was a moderate-conservative legislator who helped form the Democratic Leadership Council. This centrist arm of the Democratic Party contributed to the election of President Bill Clinton in 1992. Nunn voted to allow school prayer, for limiting punitive damage awards and for balancing the federal budget. In contrast, he voted with liberals on such issues as affirmative action, abortion and gun control.

Nunn was mentioned as a possible nominee as Secretary of Defense or Secretary of State during the Clinton administration. He also was mentioned as a possible cabinet member should Al Gore have been elected President. In 2008, Nunn considered a possible bid for the presidency but instead endorsed Barack Obama as the Democratic nominee.

In retirement, Nunn has remained active in business and politics. He serves on the boards of Coca-Cola, Dell Computer and General Electric. He is co-chair and CEO of the Nuclear Threat Initiative which seeks to decrease the threat of weapons of mass destruction around the globe. He is a distinguished professor in international affairs at Georgia Tech. He is retired as a partner from the King & Spalding law firm.

Nunn is married to the former Colleen O'Brien, and they have two children, Michelle and Brian. ■

★ Julian Bond

Georgia House of Representatives (1967-1975), Georgia Senate (1975-1986)

JULIAN BOND FOUGHT for equality for all Americans during his twenty years in the Georgia legislature. When he retired from the Georgia senate, he had been elected to office more times than any other black Georgian. He had been a social activist and leader in the civil rights movement from his early college days.

Horace Julian Bond was born on January 14, 1940, in Nashville, Tennessee. The family moved to Pennsylvania when his father became president of Lincoln University. There, he attended a white elementary school where he was named the brightest student in the sixth grade class. He watched and observed as his father fought against segregated facilities. Later, his father became president of Atlanta University and moved the family to Georgia.

Bond started at Morehouse College in 1957 but did not graduate until 1971, earning a degree in English. He dropped out of school for a few years to join the staff of the protest magazine *The Atlanta Inquirer*, later becoming the managing editor. When he attended Morehouse, Bond lettered in swimming, helped found a literary magazine called *The Pegasus* and served as an intern for *Time* magazine. Since graduating from Morehouse, Bond has been awarded twenty-one honorary degrees from various colleges and universities.

In 1966 Bond ran for the Georgia House of Representatives and won. However, he was not seated until 1967 because of outspoken statements he made against the Vietnam War that angered many Georgia legislators. He went on to serve four terms (1965-1975). During his time as a Georgia State Representative, Bond supported civil rights laws, a minimum-wage provision, welfare legislation, legislation to end the death penalty and antipoverty and urban renewal programs.

In 1971, he assisted the Student Nonviolent Coordinating Committee (SNCC), a grassroots organization he helped found when in college, conduct a highly publicized voter registration drive in the densely populated black areas of Georgia. In 1975, he was elected to the Georgia Senate and served for six terms. He organized the Georgia Legislative Black Caucus and became the first black chair of the Fulton County senate Delegation.

In 1986, Bond resigned his senate seat in an unsuccessful bid to be the Democratic nominee for congress. He lost to John Lewis amidst allegations made by his wife of drug use and infidelity.

His political career over, Bond served as a visiting professor at several prestigious universities, including Harvard. He hosted television's *America's Black Forum* and had his own nationally syndicated column called *Viewpoint*. He has authored and co-authored more than 20 books. A collection of his essays has been published under the title *A Time To Speak, A Time To Act* (1972, Touchtone). He narrated the critically acclaimed 1987 and 1990 PBS series, *Eyes on the Prize*.

Bond served as the chairman for the National Association for the Advancement of Colored People (NAACP) from 1998 until 2009. He distinguished himself in the Georgia General Assembly by sponsoring or co-sponsoring more than 60 bills which became law. One of these included a pioneering sickle cell anemia testing program. In 2002, he received the prestigious National Freedom Award.

Julian Bond continues to write and speak and is currently a Distinguished Scholar in Residence at the American University in Washington, D.C. and is a professor at the University of Virginia in the history department. ■

Andrew Young ★

Fity-fifth Mayor of Atlanta (1982-1990),

U. S. Ambassador to the United Nations (1977-1979), U. S. House of Representatives (1973-1977)

ANDREW YOUNG rose to prominence as an aide to Dr. Martin Luther King Jr. at the time of the civil rights movement. He went on to win election to Congress, to serve as U.S. ambassador to the United Nations, to be elected mayor of Atlanta and to work in many high-level business and humanitarian activities. He played a major role in advancing Atlanta to its present status of an international city.

Andrew Young was born March 12, 1932. He grew up in New Orleans, the son of a schoolteacher and a dentist whose patients included the jazz musician Louis Armstrong and the Olympian Ralph Metcalf. Young graduated from Howard University with a degree in biology and then earned a divinity degree from Hartford Theological Seminary.

Early in his career, Young pastored a church in Alabama. He then moved to New York City to work for the National Council of Churches. He later relocated to Atlanta to work for the Southern Christian Leadership Conference and Dr. King.

Young was in Memphis when Dr. King was assassinated in 1968. In the aftermath of that tragedy, Young ran for a seat in the U.S. Congress. He lost his 1970 bid for that office but ran again in 1972 and won. Young was the first African American elected to Congress from Georgia since Reconstruction. He was reelected in 1974 and 1976. In the House, Young helped secure funding for Atlanta's rapid transit system and served on a number of committees.

In 1977, Young was named as the U.N. ambassador by President Jimmy Carter. In that role, Young promoted human rights and Third World economic development. In 1979, he was asked by President Carter to resign after he spoke with a Palestine Liberation Organization representative. The U.S. had pledged to Israel not to hold talks with the Palestinians until the P.L.O. acknowledged Israel's right to exist.

In 1981, Young was elected mayor of Atlanta, succeeding another African-American, Maynard Jackson. As mayor, Young brought billions of dollars of investment to Atlanta, furthering the city's goal of becoming an international metropolis.

He campaigned in 1990 to become Georgia governor, failing in that effort, but, during that time, he was helping Atlanta's bid to host the 1996 Summer Olympic Games. With help from Young, the Olympics were held in Atlanta, boosting the city's reputation worldwide.

Young and his first wife, the former Jean Childs, had four children. She died of cancer in 1994. Subsequently, he married Carolyn McClain. Young is still active in international business deals, helping historically black colleges and sharing his political acumen. ■

★ Dean Rusk

U. S. Secretary of State (1961-1969) . Atlanta . 1909-1994

DEAN RUSK IS the second longest serving U.S. Secretary of State in U.S. history. He served from 1961 to 1969 under Presidents John F. Kennedy and Lyndon B. Johnson during the turbulent years of the Vietnam War.

Rusk believed in military action to combat communism and was the main architect of the United States' intervention in the Vietnam War. He was dedicated to arms-control, initiating the Nuclear Test Ban Treaty with the Soviet Union, and displayed his diplomatic skills during the Cuban Missile Crisis. He was a champion of aid to the poor in other countries.

David Dean Rusk was born in Cherokee County, Georgia, on February 9, 1909. He graduated from Boys High School in Atlanta and went on to play basketball at Davidson College in North Carolina where he graduated Phi Beta Kappa in 1931. He later attended St. John's College in England on a Rhodes scholarship where he earned his B.S. and M.A. degrees. While there, he also received the Cecil Peace Prize in 1933 for his essay on Britain's international relations.

Back in the United States, he taught international relations and politics at Mills College in Oakland, California, for six years (1934-40) and studied law at the University of California. It was at Mills that he met and married a student named Virginia Foisie with whom he had three children.

After serving in World War II, he returned to the U.S. as a highly decorated colonel. He worked briefly in the War Department before joining the Department of State in 1945. In 1950, he became the Assistant Secretary of State for Far Eastern Affairs where he played a part in the U.S. decision to become involved in the Korean War.

A Democrat, Rusk lost his position when Eisenhower was elected president. However, he served as head of the Rockefeller Foundation until he was appointed Secretary of State by President John F. Kennedy in 1961. During Kennedy's administration, Rusk dealt with the Cuban Missile Crisis and the country's ever growing involvement in Vietnam. He strongly believed in the use of military action to stop Communism.

After Kennedy's assassination, he remained as Secretary of State under President Lyndon B. Johnson, a person with whom he had more in common and with whom he enjoyed a closer working relationship. He remained in this post until the Republican Party regained power in 1969. When Johnson died in 1973, Rusk eulogized the former President as he lay in state.

Rusk returned to Georgia and taught law at the University of Georgia (UGA) in Athens, leading a quiet life and eschewing lucrative book deals and the lecture circuit; nevertheless, he did publish several books including *As I Saw It: A Secretary of State's Memoirs* (1990), co-authored with his son Richard.

Rusk always maintained his belief that the U.S. should have been in the Vietnam War even though at the time he became the target of protests at college campuses across the country. However, in his later years at UGA, he earned the admiration and respect of the students.

In 1969, Rusk received the Presidential Medal of Freedom and also The Sylvanus Thayer Award given each year by the United States Military Academy at West Point. He died in 1994 in Athens of congestive heart failure. The International Studies Program at Davidson College bears his name. Dean Rusk Middle School in Canton, Georgia, is named in his honor as well as Dean Rusk Hall on the campus of the University of Georgia. ■

Jefferson Franklin Long ★

U.S. House of the Representatives (1870-1871) . Macon . 1836-1901

JEFFERSON FRANKLIN LONG grew up in the heart of the south in the state of Alabama. Born on March 3, 1836, to a slave mother and a white father, Long was listed as a slave in the household of James C. Lloyd, a tailor.

By the age of 24, he was a self-educated, well-known tailor and married to Lucinda Carhart. Long and his tailoring skills were respected by everyone in Macon, and he was an active member of the African Methodist Episcopal Church of Macon, headed by renowned missionary Henry McNeal Turner.

Under the precise tutelage of Turner, Long made his first political appearance at a Georgia Educational Association meeting in 1867. It is believed that Long was a key cog in the development of Georgia's Freedman's Savings Bank, a major project led by Turner and the church.

By the end of 1867, everyone in the Republican party knew who the quick-witted, charismatic tailor from Macon was. He traveled throughout the Peach State and the rest of the south encouraging former slaves to register to vote. Because of Long's efforts, there were 37 African Americans elected to the state's constitutional convention and 32 to the state's legislature.

Jefferson Franklin Long made history in 1871. That December, he became Georgia's first African American congressman when he was chosen to fill the void in the 41st Congress. He was known all over the South as a supporter of education and his career as a congressman reflected that mission. He organized conventions and seminars that promoted public education and was also a supporter of higher wages for sharecroppers.

Long entered the record books once again in 1871 when he became the first African American to speak on the floor of the House of Representatives. After accomplishing so much for the radical Republican party, Long left the political scene in 1880. He spent the remainder of his days operating and owning several businesses, the most famous being the first dry-cleaning establishment in Macon.

The father of six children, Long managed to educate all of them before dying of influenza in 1901. Considered a trailblazer by most in the political realm, his "never say never" attitude and dedicated approach to Southern politics despite the obvious obstacles is unprecedented. ■

The Honorable Jefferson Franklin Long of Georgia, circa 1868, courtesy of the Library of Congress Prints and Photographs Division.

The interior of the Georgia STATE CAPITOL BUILDING *in downtown Atlanta.*

*A*tlanta, September 1864. Rhett, astride his horse and with the flames of burning Atlanta in the background, tells Scarlett that he is, at last, going to join the Confederate Army, now that all hope for victory is lost. Scarlett, for once in her willful life, is truly frightened.

The 150th anniversary of the American Civil War

Scarlett had every reason to be afraid and Rhett was correct in his assessment that the burning of Atlanta marked the beginning of the end for the Confederacy. The taking of Atlanta and Union general William Sherman's march to sea, spreading desolation in an area sixty miles wide and about 250 miles long, with the goal of conquering the port city of Savannah as a Christmas present for President Lincoln, ▶

THE ATLANTA CYCLORAMA, *a cylindrical panoramic painting of the American Civil War Battle of Atlanta (left), is the main attraction in The Atlanta Cyclorama and Civil War Museum. The painting at one time was the largest oil painting in the world. Union Major General William T. Sherman and his staff (above) in the trenches outside of Atlanta, circa 1864, courtesy of the Library of Congress Prints & Photographs Division.*

effectively put an end to the dream of a Confederate State although the aftermath dragged on for another year.

Sherman divided his 60,000 troops into two units, both of which marched toward Midgeville, then the state's capital, bypassing Macon and Augusta. His only opposition was 8,000 Confederate cavalry under Major General Joseph Wheeler and several Georgia militia units. Sherman's plan was as much psychological as strategic. "This may not be war but rather statesmanship," he said of the march. He left behind no food or resources and proved to the South that it could not defend its own ground. His foragers, called "bummers," swept up or destroyed everything of value in their path, burning when they met resistance. Finally, shortly before Christmas, Sherman's army reached Savannah; the city surrendered rather than experience Atlanta's fate.

Georgia had not seen much military action before 1863 although the state had sent nearly 100,000 soldiers to the conflict, most of whom served with the armies of Virginia. However, in the last two years of the war, nearly 550 battles and skirmishes were fought in the state. The most famous of these was the first; the Battle of Chickamauga in 1863 was ▶

Potter's House (top left) in Atlanta housed Confederate sharpshooters until Union artillery made a specific target of it, circa 1911. A street corner in Atlanta with a destroyed bank building (top right), intact neighboring buildings and shops, and covered wagons. Ruins of Atlanta depot (right bottom) after burning by General Sherman's troops, circa 1864, courtesy of the Library of Congress Prints& Photographs Division.

an understanding of the Civil War. ... I believed that firmly. It defined us. The Rec

Photo from nature By. G N. Barnard.

CITY OF ATLANTA. GA Nº2.

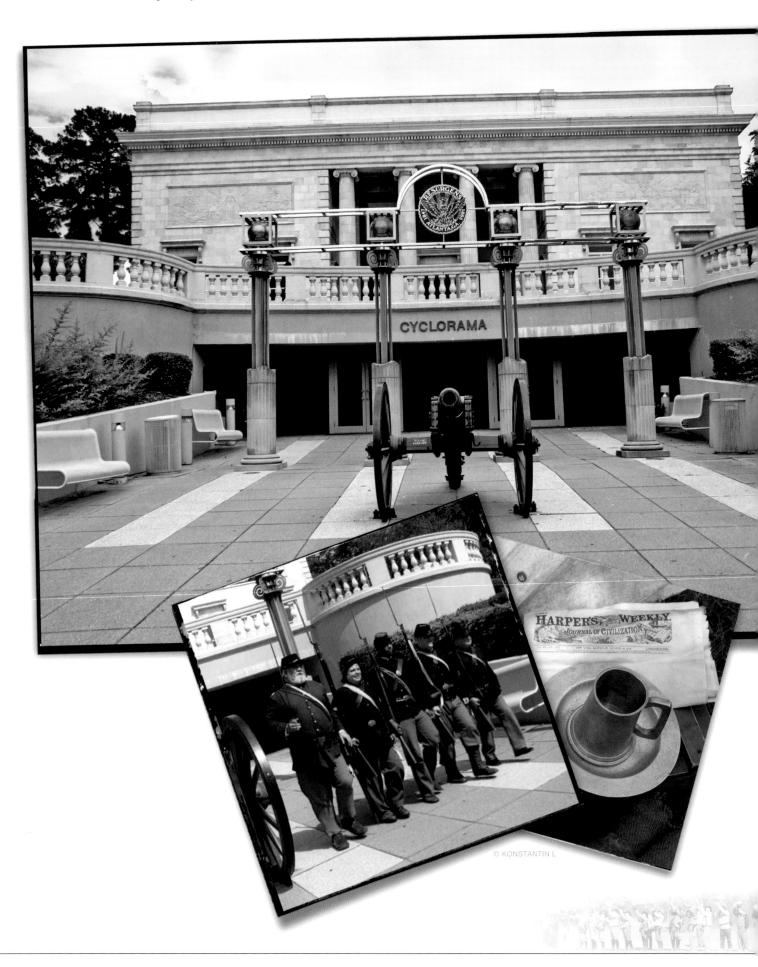

© KONSTANTIN L

the last major Confederate victory in the west.

In spite of the deprivations of war, an indomitable spirit survived in Georgia, often visible in its women, whose incarnation is Scarlett herself. One Georgian woman even dared to dispute General U. S. Grant. On November 27, 1863, after the Battle of Ringgold Gap, Grant established his headquarters in the nearby Whitman-Anderson home. Upon his departure the following morning, Grant offered Mrs. Whitman $50 in U.S. currency. Mrs. Whitman declined, saying she preferred to be paid in Confederate dollars. Grant remarked, "She certainly is not whipped yet" and the Union troops cheered her as they left.

Among the saddest sites of the misery the war brought to Georgia is Camp Sumter Military Prison at Andersonville, Georgia, commonly referred to as simply "Andersonville." Over 45,000 Union prisoners were held at the camp; thirteen thousand died there. Conditions at Andersonville were brutal. Much of the south was starving and the prisoners of war suffered more than any other group. The site of the infamous prison is now a memorial to all American prisoners of war. Andersonville National Historic Site is a part of the Nation Park system and visitors may explore its rural setting and learn about the original prisoners ▶

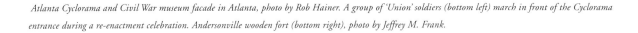

Atlanta Cyclorama and Civil War museum facade in Atlanta, photo by Rob Hainer. A group of 'Union' soldiers (bottom left) march in front of the Cyclorama entrance during a re-enactment celebration. Andersonville wooden fort (bottom right), photo by Jeffrey M. Frank.

as well as prisoners from all wars fought since by the United States.

There are over 350 Civil War sites across the state. At another National Military Park in northwest Georgia, visitors may retrace the action of the Battle of Chickamauga. The result of this key action was the fall of Chattanooga, a vital Confederate supply center, and pointed the way to the other large supply center, Atlanta. At Atlanta's Cyclorama, visitors sit at the center of the action during the battle of Atlanta and experience some of the sensations of the residents of that beleaguered city. Throughout the state, visitors may see stately ante-bellum homes and museums full of Civil War memorabilia and walk the sites of battlefields.

Before the war began, Georgia was known as "The Empire State of the South" as it had already begun to industrialize. The city of Roswell, a mill town about thirty miles north of Atlanta, had begun a thriving textile industry. Despite the desolation the war left behind, Georgians' struggle to reclaim their former standing has been successful. Today, Atlanta, the most devastated, is classified as an "alpha-world city" in a 2010 university study and the state prospers as a result of the industry of its citizens and their ancestors. ■

Reenactment and living history, "Civil War Expo," at the City of Helen Riverside Park and the Kennesaw Mountain National Battlefield Park. Features period villages, demonstrations, camps and sutlers. Skirmishes between the Union and confederate "armies" re-create some of the war's most interesting battles. The event features living history demonstrations and re-enactors from across the country. The rare Double Barrel Cannon (right) and City Hall in Athens, Georgia.

the crossroads of our being, and it was a hell of a crossroads." *Shelby Foote – 1990*

'CONFEDERATE' CAVALRY *ride horses at Civil War reenactment. The yearly reenactment honors the Americans who died during the Civil War.*

Visionaries

INDIVIDUALS WHO WORKED

FOR POSITIVE CHANGE IN GEORGIA,

MAKING A LIFE BETTER

FOR FUTURE GENERATIONS.

Dr. Ralph Abernathy

MINISTER & CIVIL RIGHTS LEADER . ATLANTA . 1926 - 1990

Dr. Ralph Abernathy endured beatings, arrests, murders of his colleagues and daily threats against his life and the lives of his family. He suffered the confiscation of his family's land and his automobile, which he had to re-purchase at a public auction. His home and church were bombed in 1957. Undaunted, he continued marching the streets of the South proclaiming, "Let my people go."

From a young age, Ralph Abernathy wanted to become a minister. Encouraged by his mother, Abernathy became a Baptist minister before finishing college. He preached his first sermon on Mother's Day 1948 in honor of his deceased mother.

It was this call to ministry that would bring him in contact with the man with whom he would help ignite the fires of change for people of color, the Reverend Martin Luther King, Jr.

Dr. Ralph David Abernathy, Sr. was born on March 11, 1926, to a former slave who saved enough money to buy his own 500-acre farm in Linden, Alabama. His father, William Abernathy, became the county's first African American to vote and the first to serve on a grand jury. A devout Baptist, he instilled in his son the divine responsibility of those who had been given much.

Taking his father's teachings to heart, Abernathy organized his first protest demonstration against Linden Academy's outdated science equipment, resulting in a refurbished laboratory. He graduated with a mathematics degree in 1950 from Alabama State University and earned a master's degree in sociology from Atlanta University in 1951. In college, he was elected president of the student council and led successful protests for better living quarters and better cafeteria conditions for students.

While in college, Dr. Abernathy worked as the first African American disc jockey at a white radio station in Montgomery, Alabama. After graduation, he began his professional career as the personnel director at Alabama State University and later became the dean of men and professor of social studies and mathematics. In 1952, at age 25, he was appointed senior pastor of Montgomery's largest black congregation, First Baptist Church. It was during this time that he and the pastor of Dexter Avenue Baptist Church, Martin Luther King, Jr., united in their mutual vision of bringing down the walls of segregation and discrimination. They would stand together for 13 years.

From 1955 until Dr. King's death in 1968, the two spearheaded nonviolent movements in cities all over the South and in Washington, D.C., and Chicago. They shared hotel rooms and jail cells. In 1955, in response to the arrest of Rosa Parks, they organized the successful Montgomery Bus Boycott, ending Alabama's bus segregation and beginning the Civil Rights Movement.

In 1957, the two founded the Southern Christian Leadership Conference (SCLC) to push for more effective civil rights laws. Their success in Birmingham in 1963 spurred desegregation programs in over 250 southern cities. Their work secured the passage of the Civil Rights Bill of 1964 and the Voting Rights Act of 1965.

Dr. Ralph Abernathy was honored with more than 300 awards and citations.

In 1961, at the urging of Dr. King, Dr. Abernathy assumed the pastorate of West Hunter Street Baptist Church in Atlanta where he remained until his death. In 1977, he ran unsuccessfully for Georgia's 5th Congressional District seat. That same year he resigned his decade long tenure as president of the SCLC.

Dr. Ralph Abernathy was honored with more than 300 awards and citations. He founded the nonprofit Foundation for Economic Enterprises Development to help workers of all races and ethnicities and co-founded the American Freedom Coalition in 1980. In 1989, Harper Collins published his autobiography, *And The Walls Came Tumbling Down*, Dr. Abernathy's final accounting of his friendship with Dr. King and their work in the Civil Rights Movement in a nonviolent struggle for freedom, justice and equality.

Dr. Abernathy died in 1990 at age 64 from a massive stroke. He was married to Juanita Odessa Jones of Uniontown, Alabama, for 37 years. They had five children. The Ralph David Abernathy Freeway (Interstate 20), Abernathy Road, and Ralph David Abernathy Boulevard of Atlanta were named in his honor. ∎

Ralph David Abernathy, April 1968. Flip Schulke/Corbis

George Washington Adair

REAL ESTATE DEVELOPER . ATLANTA . 1823 – 1899

Col. George Washington Adair was a pioneer in real estate development in Atlanta after the Civil War. Adair, of Scotch-Irish descent, was born in 1823 in Morgan County, Georgia. His ancestors can be traced back to about 1100 AD.

When Adair was young, his father moved the famly to an area near Decatur, Georgia. Times were hard—his mother died when he was a boy and his father, John F. Adair, a wheelwright, sent the young Adair to Decatur to work as a clerk in a store.

As young George Adair was bright, industrious, a quick learner and loyal to his store, he met with great approval from the store's owner. He also caught the attention of several prominent businessmen who sent him to Decatur Academy. After completing his studies at Decatur Academy, Adair attended law school in Covington, Georgia, and was admitted to the bar.

With his debts more than his income could erase, Adair took a job

Following General Sherman's notorious ride through Georgia, Atlanta was a broken city. Adair began selling real estate again. As Atlanta began its return to prosperity, Adair also prospered.

with the Georgia Railroad as a conductor. He held this job for four years and was the first conductor to enter Atlanta by the Georgia Railroad in 1845. He next tried other businesses, including the mercantile trade, but did not meet with success. His fortune turned when he went into the general trading, auction and real estate business in Atlanta, and profited handsomely. However, war was on the horizon.

Adair opposed secession, but when Georgia left the Union, he supported his state. As the war raged on, he ran a newspaper and speculated in cotton. He already owned one newspaper and bought a second one, merging the two. Not only was he the owner of the newspaper but also its editor, striving to provide his readers with accurate news from the battlefronts. During the last year of the Civil War, Adair served as an aide to Confederate General Nathan Bedford Forrest.

Following General Sherman's notorious ride through Georgia, Atlanta was a broken city. Adair began selling real estate again. As Atlanta began its return to prosperity, Adair also prospered. He was instrumental in forming the Atlanta Street Railway Company that took people to new real estate developments where Adair was selling land.

Adair served on the Atlanta city council, worked on many civic projects and was associated with high profile, successful business ventures, in some of which he partnered with other Atlanta businessmen. He developed Adair Park, a residential development southwest of Downtown Atlanta.

When the financial panic of 1873 hit, Adair had to relinquish his business holdings. When that crisis was over, he returned to the real estate business with a positive attitude and regained his fiscal well-

being. In the 1880s, he and his sons started Adair and Company, a real estate development firm. This company became the largest developer of real estate in Atlanta.

Adair was married to the former Mary Jane Perry. They had six children. He lived to see Atlanta grow from a town of about 2,000 people into a city with a population in six figures. Adair died in 1899 at 76. Two of his sons continued to develop the Adair Park area, offering lots for sale as late as 1910. ■

Ivan Allen, Jr.

CIVIC LEADER & BUSINESSMAN . ATLANTA . 1911 – 2003

Many white Atlantans complained about Ivan Allen Jr.'s liberal mindedness, but few could argue with his results. As mayor of "The City Too Busy to Hate" from 1962-70, Allen steered segregated Atlanta through the turbulent civil rights movement with minimal violence while ushering in tremendous economic growth.

"He really built this city," Sam Williams, president of the Metro Atlanta Chamber of Commerce, told the *Atlanta Journal-Constitution*. "He was what made us different from Birmingham and the rest of the South. He put us on the map of the world."

Born on March 15, 1911, Allen was the only child of state senator Ivan Allen Sr., who owned an office products company, and Irene Beaumont Allen. After graduating from the Georgia Institute of Technology, Allen joined the family company in 1933. Three years later, his marriage to Louise Richardson, granddaughter of Hugh T. Inman, once known as Georgia's richest man, was the social event of the year. They eventually had three sons.

During World War II, Allen was a supply officer in the U.S. Army. He later served as an aide to Govenor Ellis Arnall before becoming president of Ivan Allen Co. in 1946 when his father retired. Under his supervision, the company grew into the South's preeminent office supply store with 17 offices across the region.

Allen also embarked on a career of civic service. He chaired Atlanta's Community Chest drive in 1947 and was president of the Atlanta Area Council of Boy Scouts and the Georgia Tech Alumni Association before being elected president of the Atlanta Chamber of Commerce in 1960. Allen developed a Six-Point Program for the

"He really built this city," Sam Williams, president of the Metro Atlanta Chamber of Commerce, told the Atlanta Journal-Constitution. "He was what made us different from Birmingham and the rest of the South. He put us on the map of the world."

chamber that later would serve as a cornerstone of his mayoral campaign. The program called for new expressways, development of a rapid transit system and low-income housing for blacks, construction of a stadium and coliseum-auditorium and a national advertising campaign called "Forward Atlanta" to promote the city's image.

By carrying the black vote, which comprised 40 percent of the electorate, Allen defeated segregationist Lester Maddox in the 1961 mayoral race. On his first day in office, Allen ordered all "white" and "colored" signs out of City Hall, integrated City Hall's cafeteria and authorized black policemen to arrest any law-breaking whites.

The lifelong Democrat also boldly became the only elected Southern politician to testify before the U.S. Congress in 1963 in favor of the public accommodations section of civil rights legislation that was passed the next year.

With Allen's support, Atlanta quickly became home to the Atlanta Braves, Falcons and Hawks, major league sports teams fit for a major league city. Atlanta continued to boom with new infrastructure, buildings, jobs and people.

After serving two terms as mayor, Allen decided not to run for re-election in 1970 and instead returned to his office supply business. A decade later, Martin Luther King, Jr.'s widow, Coretta, presented him with the Martin Luther King Jr. Nonviolent Peace Prize. Allen died on July 2, 2003, at age 92. ■

Martha Berry

EDUCATOR . ROME . 1865 - 1942

In the early 1900s, motivated by a desire to help disadvantaged children in Georgia receive an education, Martha Berry dedicated her time and resources to developing schools. She was the founder of Berry College, located in Rome, Georgia, and is listed as one of Georgia's most prominent women of the first half of the twentieth century.

Martha McChesney Berry was born on October 7, 1865, in Jackson County, Alabama. Berry's mother and father moved their family of eight children and three orphaned cousins to Rome, Georgia. Her

In 1926, she established Berry Junior College, which by 1930 had grown into a four-year school, located on 30,000 acres.

father, a veteran of two wars, became a partner in a grocery and cotton brokerage business in Rome. In 1871, he purchased a working farm called Oak Hill. Berry grew up in this home and lived there for her entire life. She never married.

Berry's own education consisted of private tutors and a finishing school in Baltimore, Maryland. She was devoted to her father and accompanied him on horseback to visit poor landowners and tenant farmers. She soon realized that the children did not attend school or church, so she started teaching them Bible stories in a small cabin located near Oak Hill. The classes eventually expanded to include day school activities.

When the attendance outgrew the cabin, Berry built a small school on eighty-three acres of land given to her by her father. Three other nearby locations were also used to accommodate classes. Eventually, classes were held daily and Berry decided that the children needed to live at the schools. In January 1902, she opened the Boys' Industrial School, complete with a dormitory. Later, she incorporated the school and deeded the eighty-three acres to the corporation. The school became known as the Mount Berry School for Boys.

On Thanksgiving Day in 1909, she opened the Martha Berry School for Girls. Both schools offered high school level education. However, only rural students were allowed to attend the schools and students were required to take courses on religious topics, attend chapel three times a week and go to church on Sundays. The students also worked helping to construct and maintain the facilities. Berry believed that a work-program helped encourage responsibility and created a sense of self-worth.

Berry traveled widely raising funds for her schools from such notables as Andrew Carnegie, Henry Ford and President Theodore Roosevelt who held a dinner at the White House to raise money. The schools, showing the need for education of poor people in

rural areas, became the model for vocational, agricultural and mechanical schools throughout Georgia and around the world.

In 1926, she established Berry Junior College, which by 1930 had grown into a four-year school, located on 30,000 acres. Berry personally handed out diplomas to the first graduating class in 1932. The college, like the other schools, maintained Berry's teachings on the

education of the head, the heart and the hands of its students. Her motto was "Not to be ministered unto but to minister."

Martha Berry died in 1942. Eventually, all the schools, except the college, closed. It has been said that Berry was responsible for school programs throughout the South that are grounded in Christian faith. During her life, she received eight honorary doctorates as well as honors from the Georgia General Assembly. Her portrait hangs in the state capitol's Gallery of Distinguished Georgians. The Georgia segment of U.S. Highway 27 is named the Martha Berry Highway.

Berry's gravesite near the Berry College Chapel is marked by the Atlanta Gas Light Company's first posthumous Shining Light Award given to a Georgian who has been an inspiration to the lives of others through service to humanity. ∎

Photo: Ed Jackson

Authur Blank

HOME DEPOT CO-FOUNDER & PHILANTHROPIST . ATLANTA

Arthur Blank turned lemons into lemonade after a 1978 firing and co-founded The Home Depot, the world's largest home-improvement store as well as the fastest-growing retailer in American history.

The Queens, New York, native teamed up with Bernie Marcus—who also was fired from Handy Dan—as well as investment banker Ken Langone and merchandising expert Pat Farrah to raise sufficient capital and scout possible store locations nationally. They envisioned opening warehouse-sized stores for do-it-yourselfers that would stock much more than the average hardware store.

On June 22, 1979, the men opened two Home Depot stores in Atlanta. After a slow start and plenty of fine tuning, the business did quite well; it was listed on NASDAQ in 1981, then the company moved onto the New York Stock Exchange in 1984. Today, there are over 2,250 Home Depot stores throughout the United States, Canada, Mexico and China, earning sales of $70.4 billion as of fiscal 2011.

"Bernie and I founded The Home Depot with a special vision—to create a company that would keep alive the values that were important to us," Blank told Chris Roush, author of *Inside Home Depot*. "Values like respect among all people, excellent customer service and giving back to communities and society."

According to Home Depot's website, their philosophy of customer service—"whatever it takes"—meant cultivating a relationship with customers rather than merely completing a transaction. As Marcus said in the book *Built from Scratch*, "At the end of the day, we're in the people business."

Blank lives in a sprawling Buckhead estate that's a far cry from the one-bedroom apartments that he shared with his parents and brother when growing up in Queens. After graduating from Babson College with an accounting degree, Blank worked at an accounting firm, then for his father's small pharmaceutical company. Daylin bought that business in 1968 and Blank became controller of its discount drug-store unit. He eventually moved over to its Handy Dan division, where the axe fell in 1978.

Fast forward to 2012: Blank owns the National Football League's Atlanta Falcons, which he bought in 2002 after retiring from Home Depot. At that time, the Georgia Dome was about 40 percent empty on game days, so Blank applied his ingenuity to the problem. His solution was to lower ticket prices on about 25,000 seats, acquire additional parking spaces and jazz up the pregame and half-time shows with such entertainers as country singer Travis Tritt.

As a result, the Falcons had its first sold-out season in more than two decades. Blank's reconstruction of the team, coaches and front-office staff also resulted in the Falcons posting four consecutive winning seasons for the first time in franchise history, and in qualifying for the NFC playoffs three of the four seasons!

When he's not busy managing the

According to Home Depot's website, their philosophy of customer service—"whatever it takes"—meant cultivating a relationship with customers rather than merely completing a transaction.

Falcons, Blank is generously giving his money away. The Arthur M. Blank Family Foundation, founded in 1995, has donated more than $250 million to charity while the Atlanta Falcons Youth Foundation has donated more than $17 million to non-profit groups across Georgia.

Blank has been named Georgia's Most Respected CEO twice by *Georgia Trend* magazine as well as National Entrepreneur of the Year by Ernst & Young. As of March 2012, Forbes estimated his wealth at $1.4 billion. ∎

Thomas Watson Brown

PHILANTHROPIST & ATTORNEY . MARIETTA . 1934 - 2007

Tom Watson Brown, a wealthy descendant of an Old Georgia family, was a Harvard-educated attorney who had a thirst for Civil War history and a love for Georgia's educational institutions.

Brown, who died at age 73, often bemoaned the Old South's defeat at Gettysburg. "I am not, nor have I ever been, a member of the Republican Party. I will never forgive Republicans for what they did in 1861," he once said, irate that a GOP candidate had mistakenly referred to him as "my fellow Republican."

Another time, he told the *Marietta Daily Journal* that "One of the great tragedies of modern history was Gettysburg." Though he was a die-hard "son of the South," Brown was awarded the

Brown, who died at age 73, often bemoaned the Old South's defeat at Gettysburg. "I am not, nor have I ever been, a member of the Republican Party.

Martin Luther King Jr. Center's community service award for peace and justice because of his financial contributions to the Atlanta Legal Aid Society.

Born in Washington, D.C., Brown was the son of radio journalist Walter "Red" Brown and great-grandson of U.S. Senator Tom Watson, who was nominated as vice president on the Populist Party ticket with William Jennings Bryan in 1896. His grandfather, J.J. Brown, was the state's Agriculture Commissioner.

Though he was rich and influential, Brown eschewed the limelight. His money came largely from inherited ownership of Spartan Communications, a chain of television stations in medium-sized markets. The stations were sold to Media General in 2000. He also owned a six percent share of the Atlanta Falcons, which were sold to present owner Arthur Blank in 2002.

Brown lived in a large 19th century mansion called Ivy Grove, whose large library overflowed with Civil War history books. He loved to debate current events with friends, many of whom were politicians from both political parties.

"He was a great raconteur and bon vivant," syndicated columnist Bill Shipp told the *Marietta* newspaper after Brown's death. "He told a story like no one I've ever known. His intellect was unmatched."

Brown gave a great deal of money to Mercer University—including *Mercer University Press*—and the University of Georgia. "*Mercer University Press* exists because of Tom Watson Brown," Shipp said. Brown also left his 10,000-volume library to Mercer.

He also donated large sums to finance gubernatorial and congressional debates that were broadcast statewide on Georgia Public Television. Brown's Watson-Brown Foundation, administered by his son Tad, is the largest private scholarship program in Georgia.

Brown served on the boards of the Atlanta Historical Society, the Georgia Historical Society, the Georgia Civil War Commission, the Atlanta Legal Aid Society and the Georgia Legal History Foundation. He also was a Life Trustee of Mercer University. ■

Asa Griggs Candler

BUSINESS TYCOON & PHILANTHROPIST . ATLANTA . 1851 - 1929

Asa Candler's marketing genius was largely responsible for the worldwide growth of Coca-Cola®, which originally was sold as a patent medicine that would cure "nervous afflictions."

Born in Villa Rica in 1851, Candler was one of 11 children of an affluent merchant/planter. Candler apprenticed as a pharmacist before moving to Atlanta, where he built up a prosperous drug business as he and his wife Lucy raised their family.

In 1886, another pharmacist, Dr. John Pemberton, produced a caramel-colored syrup that, when combined with carbonated water, was sold as a five-cent medicinal tonic at Jacob's Pharmacy. Candler bought rights to the formula for $2,300, then set about aggressively marketing it as a soft drink. The beverage, made from an extract of coca leaves and kolanuts, at first contained some cocaine, as the ill effects of that drug were not realized at the time. However, the last traces were removed in 1929.

As a philanthropist, Candler donated a great deal of money and land to the Methodist Church, financing what was to become Emory University.

A canny promoter, Candler began putting the Coca-Cola name on calendars, clocks, fans; even apothecary scales. He distributed thousands of coupons for a complimentary glass of Coke and originated one of the first celebrity endorsements by hiring actress and singer Hilda Clark to promote the beverage. By 1911, Coca-Cola's advertising budget had risen to $1 million.

As the soft drink's fame spread, Coca-Cola opened syrup-making plants in Chicago, Dallas and Los Angeles. While Candler focused on increasing soda-fountain sales, a Vicksburg pharmacist began bottling the drink. Candler wasn't convinced that bottling was the way to go so he sold those rights to two Chattanooga businessmen. They, along with a third partner, went on to develop a worldwide bottling system.

Candler expanded his business interests into banking and real estate. He founded the Central Bank and Trust Company and developed the Druid Hills neighborhood; then built the 17-story Candler Building, then Atlanta's tallest building, to house the bank and Coca-Cola headquarters.

In 1916, when Candler was elected Atlanta's 44th mayor, he turned over control of most of his businesses to his children, Howard, Asa Jr., Walter and Lucy. The family's Coca-Cola investment was sold in 1919 for $25 million to an investor group led by Robert Woodruff.

As a philanthropist, Candler donated a great deal of money and land to the Methodist Church, financing what was to become Emory University. His brother, Methodist Bishop Warren Candler, became the university's first president after it moved to Atlanta from a smaller site in Oxford. Emory's Candler School of Theology is named in their honor.

In 1922, Candler donated more than 50 acres of his Druid Hills property to the city of Atlanta. The land became Candler Park. Candler Field, Atlanta's first airport, also commemorates Chandler's achievements.

Candler died March 12, 1929, and was buried at Westview Cemetery. ■

Photo courtesy of Emory University, Atlanta

Truett Cathy

BUSINESSMAN & PHILANTHROPIST . ATLANTA

"A good name is rather to be chosen than great riches, and loving favor rather than silver and gold." Proverbs 22:1

Truett Cathy grew up in poverty, worked hard to achieve great wealth, yet always hewed to biblical principles as he built the privately held Chick-fil-A® business empire.

Born in Atlanta in 1921, Cathy developed a strong work ethic early in life. His father, an insurance salesman, was devastated by the Great Depression; his mother ran a boarding house to support her seven children. At one point, the family lived in downtown Atlanta's Techwood Homes, the nation's first federally funded housing project, while Cathy delivered the *Atlanta Journal* to help his mother pay the rent.

After graduating from Boys High School (now Grady), Cathy entered the U.S. Army. When his tour of duty ended, Cathy and his brother Ben

Cathy, who has received numerous awards, attributes his business's great success to its corporate mission to "glorify God."

opened the 24-hour Dwarf Grill in Hapeville, a tiny restaurant with 10 counter stools and four tables. First-day sales totaled $58.20.

Ben died in a 1949 plane crash, and Cathy became sole proprietor. By the early 1960s, he was experimenting with a pressure-cooked, boneless chicken breast sandwich and asking customers their opinions. Cathy honed his recipe to include a buttered bun and two dill-pickle slices, then opened the first Chick-fil-A at Greenbriar Shopping Center in 1967.

Over the years, Cathy expanded the menu to include chicken nuggets, waffle fries, hand-spun milkshakes, salads and a breakfast menu featuring Chick-n-Minis™, breakfast burritos and a chicken, egg and cheese bagel. By 2012, the fast-food chain had grown to more than 1,600 franchised restaurants and was exceeding $4 billion in annual sales.

Cathy, who has received numerous awards, attributes his business' great success to its corporate mission to "glorify God." Chick-fil-A

is the only national fast-food chain that closes on Sunday so employees can go to church and spend time with their families.

"I'd like to be remembered as one who kept my priorities in the right order," he has said. "We live in a changing world, but we need to be reminded that the important things have not changed, and the important things will not change if we keep our priorities in proper order."

Cathy's financial success has enabled him to help many others. His WinShape Foundation, founded to help "shape winners," annually awards 20 to 30 youths scholarships to Berry College, while the Chick-fil-A Foundation awards more than $1.9 million in scholarships annually to team members. The WinShape Foundation has opened eight foster-care homes in Georgia, two in Tennessee and one each in Alabama and Brazil. Each home, supervised by two full-time foster parents, provides a positive living environment for up to 12 children.

The WinShape Camps® are two-week summer residential camps at Berry College designed to sharpen young people's character and deepen their Christian faith and relationships. Married and engaged couples benefit from a marriage-enrichment retreat run by Cathy's son and daughter-in-law, Bubba and Cindy, at Berry.

"Nearly every moment of every day we have the opportunity to give something to someone else—our time, our love, our resources," Cathy has said. "I have always found more joy in giving when I did not expect anything in return." ∎

Anne Cox Chambers

MEDIA HEIRESS & PHILANTHROPIST . ATLANTA

Georgia's richest resident, Anne Cox Chambers of Atlanta, inherited a newspaper empire from her father that grew into the $15 billion Cox Enterprises, encompassing television and radio stations, newspapers, cable television and other businesses.

The company was formed in 1898 by former schoolteacher and reporter James M. Cox. When he was 28, Cox bought *The Dayton Evening News*. The success of his newspaper led Cox into public service, and he became Ohio's first three-term governor as well as the 1920 Democratic presidential nominee.

Following the election of the Republican team of Warren Harding and Calvin Coolige, Cox focused on enlarging his business. He started Ohio's first radio station, WHIO, in 1935, then bought *The Atlanta Journal* and WSB-AM. In 1948, WHIO and WSB transitioned to television. Fast-forward more than 50 years and Govenor Cox's daughter Anne is a director of Cox Enterprises while her nephew Jim is chairman of the company.

Born to Gov. Cox and his second wife, Margaretta Blair, on Dec. 1, 1919, Anne attended Miss Porter's School and Finch College, then married Robert William Chambers in 1955. In 2012, she was No. 61 on Forbes' list of the World's Richest Billionaires, with an estimated worth of $12.5 billion.

A Democrat like her father was, Chambers contributed generously to Govenor Jimmy Carter's presidential campaign and was made Ambassador to Belgium after his 1976 election. For her service, Chambers was presented the French Legion of Honor by Belgium's King Baudoin. Chambers also has financially supported the presidential campaigns of John Kerry, Bill Bradley and Barack Obama.

The major recipients of her philanthropy, however, have been cultural organizations. Chambers' work with the High Museum of Art began in 1965, when she helped establish the fund-raising group

"Forward Arts Foundation." She also co-chaired a 1980s fund-raising effort that helped build the museum's Richard Meier complex. In her honor, the High Museum named a wing after Chambers in 2005.

Her support of the arts was recognized in 1994 when President Clinton appointed her to the President's Committee on the Arts and Humanities. In addition, Chambers has contributed to the Atlanta Symphony Orchestra, the Fernbank Museum of Natural History and the Shepherd Center and has served on the boards of Coca-Cola, Bank of the South, the Atlanta Botanical Garden, the Atlanta History Center, the Woodruff Arts Center and Central Atlanta Progress. She was the first woman to sit on the boards of Fulton National Bank and the Atlanta Chamber of Commerce.

A Democrat like her father was, Chambers contributed generously to Gov. Jimmy Carter's presidential campaign and was made Ambassador to Belgium after his 1976 election.

An animal lover, Chambers has seven dogs, five shih tzus and two rescued cocker spaniels. She told *Atlanta Magazine* in 2011 that she avidly reads the "Pet of the Week" column in the *Atlanta Journal-Constitution*, which had once featured her own cocker spaniels, Sam and Missy.

"They were five years old and had never been separated. It was hoped that someone would take both of them," Chambers said. "Well, when I read that . . . I restrained. I didn't call on Sunday. So on Monday afternoon, I gave Becky [her assistant] the article and asked, 'Would you just call and see if they've been adopted?' [Later] Becky came in and… said, 'They're waiting for you!' So I said, 'Come on, Becky, let's go get them!' So we went out to the [Atlanta] Humane Society, and they opened the door into the corridor, and [the dogs] both just came bounding out. They knew!" ∎

Rodney Mims Cook, Jr.

INTERNATIONALLY RENOWNED ARCHITECT . ATLANTA

At the young age of fourteen, Rodney M. Cook initiated a campaign that successfully saved the five-thousand seat Fox Theatre in Atlanta for which he was awarded the National Trust for Historic Preservation Prize. Today, Cook is an international authority on the design and construction of modern classical monuments around the world.

Rodney Mims Cook, Jr. was born in Atlanta, Georgia, on June 30, 1956. His father was a member of the Georgia House of Representatives and a supporter of civil rights. His mother, Bettijo Cook, was responsible for moving and restoring the Tullie-Smith House, an antebellum historic plantation, to the grounds of the Atlanta History Center.

In 1974, Cook served as a White House intern under President Richard Nixon. In 1978, he graduated from Washington and Lee University where he earned a degree which focused on architecture, history and politics. He was influenced by acclaimed classical architect Philip Shutze who had designed three homes for various members of the Cook family. Shutze became a mentor guiding Cook in his architectural education.

Cook established Rodney Mims Cook Interests, a design and development company, in 1982. He founded PolitesCook Architects in 1987 and there designed the Newington Cropsey Museum in New York which houses the largest American collection of Hudson River School paintings. The museum was awarded a New York citation from Governor Mario Cuomo.

Later, with Anton Glikin, a Russian architect and Institute student, Martin Dawe of Atlanta and Dick Reid of England, Cook organized the design and construction of the Prince of Wales Olympic Games monument for the 1996 Atlanta Centennial Games. Cook is a founding trustee of the Prince of Wales' Foundation for Architecture.

Cook founded the National Monuments Foundation in 2003 in order to create destination landmarks of aesthetic as well as historical and national relevance. The Foundation believes that monuments and their surrounding public spaces help to anchor communities, enhance land value and cause people to interact more positively.

The Foundation also directed the design and construction of the

In 2011, the Cook family was honored by the City of Atlanta for their service to the city and the state of Georgia.

classically styled Millennium Gate Museum located inside Atlantic Station in Midtown, Atlanta. The Museum opened in 2008 and is the largest classical monument to be erected in the United States since the Jefferson Memorial. The firm of Rodney Mims Cook is itself located in the Museum.

Cook serves on the board for the Hearst Foundation/Hearst Castle, California, Atlanta Landmarks, the Institute of Classical Architecture and Classical America and The New York Philomusica. He is past president of Animal Health Trust U.S., Newmarket, England. In great demand as a guest lecturer, Cook has been published in *Architectural Digest*, *Time* magazine, *The New York Times*, *The New Yorker*, *Financial Times of London* and *Forbes* to name a few. He is a charter signer of the Congress for the New Urbanism.

In 2011, Cook and co-designer Michael Franck won a commendation prize for the National Civic Art Society Dwight D. Eisenhower Memorial for Washington, D.C. Cook is currently working on a design for a memorial library for Presidents John and John Quincy Adams and their wives to be located in Washington, D.C.

Cook is married to commercial photographer Emily Cook who is responsible for the creation of the largest wildlife sanctuary located in Atlanta. They have two daughters. In 2011, the Cook family was honored by the City of Atlanta for their service to the city and the state of Georgia. ∎

Dr. Leila Denmark

PEDIATRICIAN . PORTAL . 1898 - 2012

Dr. Leila Denmark "lived" for 114 years. She is known as the fourth oldest living person in the world and the oldest practicing physician in the United States, not retiring until the age of 103. She was the only woman in the 1928 graduating class at the Medical College of Georgia and was the third woman to graduate from the college.

Born Leila Alice Daughtery on February 1, 1898, in Portal, Georgia, the third of twelve children, Denmark practiced pediatric medicine in Atlanta for more than seventy years. She was awarded the Fisher Prize in 1935 for co-developing the whooping cough vaccine that has saved thousands of children over the last seven decades.

Denmark began her career as a teacher in schools in Acworth and Claxton, Georgia, after graduating from Tift College in 1922. However, after two years of teaching, Denmark realized that her true calling was in the area of healing. Turned down by Emory University, she convinced the admissions department at the Medical College of the University of Georgia in Augusta to admit her to their medical school. She was the only woman in a class of fifty men.

After graduating in 1928, she married John Eustace Denmark and moved to Atlanta where she volunteered at Grady Hospital. She soon became the first intern and admitted the first patient at what is now known as Children's Healthcare of Atlanta. After her daughter was born in 1930, she opened a private practice at home. Denmark worked out of a small office and never made appointments. She

Five years after she retired, Denmark said that her recipe for a long life wasn't complicated: "You keep on doing what you do best as long as you can.

charged very little for her services and never turned down a referral from the health department. Denmark was very outspoken if she felt a parent was not doing his or her job.

Denmark strived to guide parents and family members in the ways to help a child maintain overall good physical health by teaching proper nutrition and diet, the importance of immunizations and parental guidance and discipline. To this end, she published the book *Every Child Should Have a Chance* (1971) sharing the knowledge gleaned from years of experience. She stressed that how people lived their lives and the choices they made affected their children's lives also.

Denmark was one of the first doctors to assert the harm of exposing children to second-hand smoke and drug use in pregnant women. She is quoted as saying, "No milk after the baby is weaned! No juice, no tea or Cokes. Only water. That cow in the pasture never had a drop of milk after she was weaned and look how strong and healthy she is." Practicing what she preached, she refused cake when celebrating her 100th birthday in 1998, telling the server that she had not consumed food with sugar, other than in fruit, in seventy years.

Denmark's husband passed away in 1990, and she continued practicing medicine until 2001. In 2002, she co-authored a book with Madia Bowman titled *Dr. Denmark Said It: Advice for Mothers from America's*

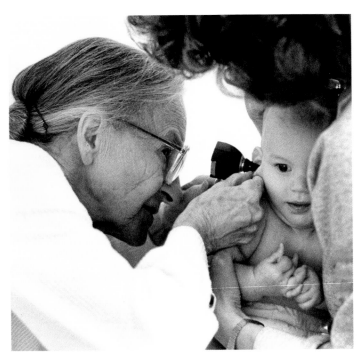

Most Experienced Pediatrician. In 2004 at age 106, she moved to Athens from Alpharetta to live with her only child, Mary Hutcherson, who had two children and two grandchildren. Many patients and friends kept in touch with Denmark until her death on April 1, 2012, at 114.

Denmark's numerous awards include being named Atlanta's Woman of the Year (1953), the Shining Light Award (1989), the Heroes, Saints and Legends Award (2000), three Distinguished Alumni Awards and an Honorary Doctorate from Emory University (2000) where she received a standing ovation.

Five years after she retired, Denmark said that her recipe for a long life wasn't complicated: "You keep on doing what you do best as long as you can. I enjoyed every minute of it for more than 70 years. I'd do exactly the same thing and marry the same man." ∎

Photo by Lynn Johnson

Shirley Franklin

MAYOR OF ATLANTA . ATLANTA

Shirley Franklin ran for political office for the first time in 2001. She was elected and became the first female mayor of Atlanta and the first black woman to be elected mayor of any Southern city. She served as mayor from 2002 to 2010.

Shirley Clarke Franklin was born on May 10, 1945, in Philadelphia, Pennsylvania. She attended an all girls' high school where she learned that she could be anything she wanted to be. Her childhood dream was to be a dancer. Franklin received a B.A. in Sociology in 1968 from Howard University and then a master's degree from the University of Pennsylvania.

Franklin's inaugural ball was unlike others—it was open to the public

In 1972, she married David McCoy Franklin, moved to Atlanta, had three sons and divorced in 1986. She was introduced to politics when her husband campaigned for Maynard Jackson, Atlanta's and the South's first black mayor. She worked for Jackson as the commissioner of cultural affairs. Later, when Andrew Young became mayor, she was appointed city manager—the first woman in the nation to serve in that position in city government.

Franklin was responsible for 8,000 employees and a one-million dollar budget. While in this position, she administered the development of a new city hall, a court building and Atlanta's new airport. In 1990, she was appointed as executive officer for operations and in 1991 helped bring the Olympics to Atlanta.

In 1997, Franklin left government work to start a consulting firm centered on public affairs and strategic planning. She returned to politics when she was appointed to serve on the newly elected governor's transition team. By 2000, she decided to announce her candidacy for mayor.

Franklin's inaugural ball was unlike others—it was open to the public. This openness became a mainstay of her tenure as governor, bringing praise from those who opposed her during the campaign. She was reelected in 2005 with 90 percent of the vote.

Franklin focused her first efforts on overhauling Atlanta's aging sewer system and established the "Clean Water Atlanta" initiative. Two other popular bits of legislation were the creation of Ethics Legislation for public officials and "pothole posse," to repair Atlanta's streets."I get almost as many calls about ethics legislation as I do about potholes. It was important to set a new tone for ethics," said Franklin to *The Atlanta Journal Constitution*.

Over time, Franklin administered a $150 million Quality of Life Bond Program that added new sidewalks, provided for walkways and trails

and improved traffic signals for safety. She also continued with her "open door policy" and held bi-monthly forums for citizens to come and chat with the mayor regarding their concerns.

In the beginning, when she faced an $82 million dollar budget deficit, she cut 50 people from her staff and cut her own salary by $40,000. She used her shrewd business acumen to research the problems. Her successful pro-business policies, which resulted in increased property values and higher real estate taxes, angered segments of the population who argued these decisions helped

push the poor out of Atlanta. She was also criticized for her policies regarding the prohibition of panhandling and feeding of Atlanta's homeless. However, Franklin's administration produced five balanced budgets and a healthy reserve.

Franklin was named 2004 Official of the Year by *Governing* magazine, and in 2005 *Time Magazine* named her one of the five best big-city American mayors. *U.S. News & World Report* included her in their "Best Leaders of 2005" issue. She is also a recipient of the 2005 John F. Kennedy Profile in Courage Award. Franklin currently serves as Treasurer of the Democratic Party of Georgia and serves on the boards of numerous Georgia foundations, nonprofits and government entities. ■

J. B. Fuqua

BUSINESSMAN, POLITICAL LEADER & PHILANTHROPIST . ATLANTA . 1918 - 2006

J.B. Fuqua was a self-made businessman who built a multibillion-dollar Fortune 500 company, became a powerhouse in the Georgia Democratic Party, and donated millions of dollars to charitable causes.

His rags-to-riches story began in Prince Edward County, Virginia, where John Brooks Elam was born on a tobacco farm on June 26,

1918. His mother Ruth died two months after he was born, and Fuqua was reared by his maternal grandparents whose surname he adopted.

Fuqua was a voracious reader who borrowed finance and banking books from Duke University in Durham, North Carolina, via mail. He never attended college, instead pursuing self-education through

books. "I think if I had not had access to those books from Duke and other reading materials, I would certainly have been less successful early on in my business career," he wrote in his 2001 memoir, *Fuqua: How I Made My Fortune Using Other People's Money.*

At age 14, Fuqua listened to a Richmond, Virginia, radio show about Morse code, then ordered a 25-cent booklet entitled, *How to Become an Amateur Radio Operator.* He assembled a ham radio, which along with his knowledge of Morse code, qualified him to become a radio operator in the Merchant Marine. Fuqua later was employed as a temporary engineer at WIS-AM in Columbia, South Carolina, then became chief engineer at the company's Charleston station.

Fuqua was a voracious reader who borrowed finance and banking books from Duke University in Durham, North Carolina, via mail.

In 1940, Fuqua moved to Augusta, Geogia, where he received a $10,000 loan from three businessmen to construct a radio station. Other Augusta businessmen took note of the ambitious young man and became his partners in other businesses, including Royal Crown Bottling, Claussen's Bakeries and WJBF radio and television stations.

Fuqua was on his way to success. In 1965, he bought Natco, a brick and tile maker, followed by Martin Theaters, Georgia Federal and the Snapper Power Equipment Company. As the years passed, Fuqua Industries became a giant corporation worth hundreds of millions of dollars.

Fuqua entered politics in 1957, when he served in the Georgia Legislature. Fuqua ran Carl Sanders' successful gubernatorial campaign in 1962 and, as chairman of the Georgia Democratic Party until 1966, he encouraged peanut farmer Jimmy Carter's early political career.

Fuqua pursued philanthropy in his later years. Grateful to Duke University for lending him books, he donated $10 million in 1980 to establish its Fuqua School of Business. Fuqua became one of Duke's biggest benefactors, eventually contributing close to $40 million. He also gave about $10 million to the Fuqua School (formerly Prince Edward Academy) in Farmville, Virginia, and many millions more to Atlanta's Piedmont Hospital, the Wesley Woods Center of Emory Healthcare and the Atlanta Botanical Garden.

In 1988, Fuqua sold his majority interest in Fuqua Industries, which later became the Actava Group. He died of complications from bronchitis on April 5, 2006, at age 87. ∎

William Berry Hartsfield

ATTORNEY & MAYOR . ATLANTA . 1890 - 1971

William B. Hartsfield, Atlanta's longest-serving mayor, was dubbed the city's "father of aviation" because of his fervent support of air transportation dating back to the 1920s. He is also remembered for steering Atlanta's growth from a big country town into a regional center.

Born in 1890, Hartsfield attended Atlanta public schools but did not graduate from high school or attend college. Instead, in 1915, the 25-year-old began working during the day as a law clerk at Rosser,

Hartsfield didn't run for re-election in 1928, instead returning to his law practice, but his stay in the private sector didn't last long. Hartsfield served as the state legislature's Fulton County representative from 1932-36 before being elected to the first of his six terms (1937-41, 1942-61) as mayor.

As mayor, Hartsfield organized the city's finances and pushed for annexation of the fast-growing suburbs while also making sure that Atlanta's infrastructure could handle such postwar growth. He

As mayor, Hartsfield organized the city's finances and pushed for annexation of the fast-growing suburbs while also making sure that Atlanta's infrastructure could handle such postwar growth.

Slaton, Phillips and Hopkins and educated himself by reading legal books and journals at night. Hartsfield was admitted to the Georgia Bar in 1917 and four years later opened his own law office.

Hartsfield was elected to the Atlanta City Council in 1922. He ran unsuccessfully for the Georgia House of Representatives in 1924, then was re-elected to the City Council in 1925. As chairman of its aviation committee, Hartsfield played a major role in selecting the abandoned, 287-acre Candler Speedway as Atlanta's first landing field.

In 1926, the federal government established airmail routes from New York to San Francisco and New York to Miami. Worried that Birmingham might nudge Atlanta aside for a spot on the north-south line, Hartsfield led a group of prominent businessmen who lobbied the U.S. Assistant Secretary of Commerce successfully for the route.

Night flying was popular by 1927, so Hartsfield made sure that Candler Field had beacon lights to serve pilots 24 hours a day. In 1928, the Atlanta Chamber of Commerce rewarded him for his enthusiastic support of aviation with a certificate of distinguished achievement.

oversaw construction of an expressway system and spearheaded completion of the Buford Dam to ensure that the city had a reliable water supply.

In 1948, Atlanta erected a new airport terminal, a corrugated metal Quonset building that cost only $180,000. By 1957, it was the country's busiest airport, handling more than 2 million passengers daily. Construction began on a new terminal to handle the load that opened in 1961.

After Georgia's white primary was outlawed in 1946, Hartsfield began building biracial coalitions to win his elections. This proved helpful when court-ordered school desegregation took place in Atlanta in 1961. While racial violence was the norm in many other Southern cities, Atlanta's school system was peacefully integrated.

Hartsfield left office in 1962 and died on Feb. 22, 1971. A week later, the Atlanta City Council renamed the airport the William B. Hartsfield International Airport. Today, the 4,700-acre Hartsfield-Jackson Atlanta International Airport is the world's busiest passenger airport. ■

Special Collections Department, Pullen Library, Georgia State University

Samuel Martin Inman

COTTON MERCHANT & PHILANTHROPIST . ATLANTA . 1843 - 1915

Samuel M. Inman was a successful cotton merchant and benevolent civic leader for whom Atlanta's first suburb was named.

Born in Dandridge, Tenn., in 1843, Inman was educated at Maryville College and Princeton University. When the Civil War erupted, the 18-year-old left Princeton and joined the First Tennessee Cavalry to fight for the Confederacy. Inman eventually was commissioned a lieutenant for bravery.

After briefly living in Augusta, he moved to Atlanta and established the S.W. Inman & Son cotton house with his father. The next year, Inman married Jennie Dick of Rome, with whom he had three children. As Atlanta grew, so did Inman's fortune. By 1891, he owned the South's largest cotton business, which employed 500 people and had a branch office in Houston, Texas.

Inman also partnered with civil engineer/businessman Joel Hurt to establish the East Atlanta Land Company through which they would build the residential neighborhood of Inman Park. They formed a second company to invest in streetcars that would serve the new neighborhood, then began investing in banks and insurance. Inman was a director of the

donate $75,000 plus an annual grant to support the school. He also was a board member and generous supporter of Agnes Scott College. Inman was a major backer of the Cotton States and International Exposition of 1895 and chairman of its financial committee. When it became known that the exposition was struggling financially to complete its 100-day run, Inman offered to give half of the $100,000 needed if the other directors would advance the rest of the money, which they did. The exposition helped burnish the city's image and Inman became known in local newspapers as "Atlanta's First Citizen."

Inman's brothers also enjoyed great success. His brother John headed the cotton brokerage firm Inman, Swann & Co. in New York and helped organize the New York Cotton Exchange. John also invested several million dollars in southern railroads, coal and iron mines. Another brother, Hugh, owned the Kimball House hotel.

Inman's wife died in 1890; two years later he married Mildred McPheeters of Raleigh, North Carolina. For many years, he was an elder at First Presbyterian Church.

Even as he built his wealth, the public-spirited Inman gave much of it away. Passionate about education, he helped fund the Georgia School of Technology (which later became the Georgia Institute of Technology)...

Atlanta National Bank, the Lowry National Bank, the Equitable Life Insurance Co. and Southern Railway.

Even as he built his wealth, the public-spirited Inman gave much of it away. Passionate about education, he helped fund the Georgia School of Technology (which later became the Georgia Institute of Technology) and, as an Atlanta alderman, he persuaded the city to

Inman died at age 71 and was buried at Oakland Cemetery. "The death of no citizen has ever been the cause of such a universal and sincere grief," an Atlanta newspaper reported. "Mr. Inman, aside from having been a dynamic factor in the upbuilding of the city, was endowed with qualities which made him the heart's idol of all who came in contact with him." ■

A sketch of Samuel N. Inman from the book by Wallace Putname titled History of Atlanta, Georgia.

Maynard Jackson

MAYOR OF ATLANTA . ATLANTA . 1938 - 2003

When Maynard Jackson moved to Atlanta, Georgia, with his family at age seven, little did he know that one day he would become not only the first black mayor of Atlanta but also the first African American to serve as chief executive of any major Southern city.

Maynard Holbrook Jackson, Jr. was born on March 23, 1938, in Dallas, Texas. One of six children, he was considered to be a member of the "Black aristocracy" as his father was a Baptist minister and his mother was a college teacher with a doctorate in French. His family moved to Atlanta when his father was offered the pastor's position at Friendship Baptist Church.

Considered a child prodigy, Jackson graduated from high school at age fourteen. He enrolled at Morehouse College where he graduated in 1956 at age eighteen with a BA degree in political science

Jackson served two terms and finished many of his public projects, including a new airport, now named in his honor, Hartsfield-Jackson International Airport.

and history. Jackson sold encyclopedias and worked for a brief time at the Ohio State Bureau of Unemployment Compensation. In 1964, he graduated cum laude with a Juris Doctorate degree from North Carolina Central University.

After graduating from law school, Jackson moved back to Atlanta and worked as an attorney for the National Labor Relations Board. He later managed a public interest low-income legal service. Prompted by the death of Martin Luther King, Jr. to enter politics, he filed minutes before the deadline to run against Herman Talmadge for the U.S. Senate seat in 1968.

Jackson lost to Talmadge but garnered a following in Atlanta. In 1969, he ran for vice-mayor of Atlanta and with ninety-nine percent of the African American vote and one-third of the white vote, he swept to victory becoming Atlanta's first African American vice-mayor.

Jackson entered the 1973 mayoral race facing incumbent Sam Massell, the city's first Jewish mayor and a certified liberal. In a runoff, race became a central issue with both candidates appealing to their respective core voters. Jackson won with fifty-nine percent of the vote.

Jackson took office in January, 1974, and brought in outside help to reorganize city departments and to enhance neighborhood and citizen input. However, there was an uproar when he attempted to fire the incumbent white police chief amid charges of racial insensitivity and a growing crime problem. In 1974, Jackson appointed an old

friend and African American activist as public safety commissioner. Much controversy ensued including an outcry of reverse discrimination in hiring and promotion practices. The commissioner was fired after a police exam cheating scandal was revealed.

Jackson served two terms and finished many of his public projects, including a new airport, now named in his honor, Hartsfield-Jackson International Airport. MARTA transit system began its first rail service in 1979. Jackson established a better relationship with Atlanta's business elite even though minority businesses received more than

thirty percent of the city contracts. Barred from a third term by a city charter, he left office and became a bond lawyer working with politically connected African American mayors.

In 1989, Jackson won a third term as mayor promising to work more closely with the business community while at the same time devoting more attention to the problems of the poor. To that end, he formed an organization to assist underachieving students in developing self-esteem and leadership skills. His most popular achievement was securing the 1996 Summer Olympics for Atlanta.

Jackson left public office after his third term due to health issues. He then conducted a $12.3 million bond sale for a city-backed apartment project and opened a restaurant and bar at the airport. As CEO of Jackson Securities, Inc., his firm was named one of the top five black investment companies by *Black Enterprise* magazine.

In 2001, Jackson founded the African American Voters League. In 2003, he was appointed to a top position in the Democratic National Party but died that year at age 65 of cardiac arrest. Jackson left behind three children from his first marriage and a wife and two children from his second. ∎

Lucy Craft Laney

EDUCATOR . MACON . 1854 - 1933

Lucy Craft Laney believed that education was the key to success for black men and women. She devoted her life to this mission and became one of Georgia's most famous female African American educators.

Lucy Craft Laney was born in Macon, Georgia, on April 13, 1854, one of ten children. Her father was a skilled carpenter, a Presbyterian minister and a free man who had purchased his freedom twenty years before Laney's birth. By saving money from odd jobs, he was able to also purchase his wife's freedom.

With a one-way ticket in hand, Laney traveled to Minnesota to the Presbyterian Church Convention where she requested funding for her school's expansion.

At the time, laws prohibited blacks from reading. However, Laney's mother was a maid to Miss Campbell, the slave owner's sister, who took an interest in young Laney and taught her to read at age four. By age twelve, Laney was translating difficult Latin passages.

When the Civil War ended, Lewis High School was founded for black children in Macon. Laney attended the school until she entered Atlanta University (later Clark Atlanta University) at fifteen. With three other students, she was a member of the university's first graduating class in 1873.

After graduation, Laney taught school in Macon, Milledgeville and Savannah before settling in Augusta, Georgia. It was here, with the encouragement of the Christ Presbyterian Church, USA, that Laney opened the first school for blacks with only six students in the basement of an affiliate church. The first graduating class was in 1885 and had outgrown its facilities with 234 students now in attendance.

With a one-way ticket in hand, Laney traveled to Minnesota to the Presbyterian Church Convention where she requested funding for her school's expansion. Turned down by the Convention, but given a ticket home, Laney later received a letter from the president of the Woman's Department of the Presbyterian Church, USA. Having heard Laney speak, Francine H. Haines secured funding in the amount of ten thousand dollars for Laney.

Touched by Haines' kindness, Laney named the new school Haines Normal and Industrial Institute, which was chartered by the state of Georgia in 1886. The school opened on Gwinnett Street, now named Laney-Walker Blvd.

At Haines Normal, students were required to study the classics as well as Latin, algebra, art, music and vocational trades and to participate in sports. The school produced the first black high school foot-

ball team in Georgia. Laney's goal was to develop graduates ready to compete in society. By 1928, the school had grown to encompass an entire city block and had over eight hundred students. The school also served as host to lectures, orchestra concerts and social events.

Laney went on to found the first black kindergarten and the first black nursing school in Augusta, Georgia. One of Laney's protégés, Mary McCleod Bethune, moved to Florida and founded the Bethune-Cookman College for Blacks.

Laney passed away on October 23, 1933, at age 79. Thousands attended her funeral as she was buried on the grounds of the school she so lovingly founded. The school was later named Lucy Craft Laney Comprehensive School.

Laney helped to found Augusta's chapter of the NAACP in 1918. She was active in the National Association of Colored Women and worked to integrate the community work of the YMCA and YWCA. In 1974, she was one of the first African Americans to have a portrait hung in the Georgia state capitol. In 1992, she was posthumously inducted into Georgia Women of Achievement.

In 1991, Laney's former home in Augusta became a museum in her honor. An eternal flame was placed on her gravesite by the Haines Alumnae Association. ■

Photo courtesy Curtis Jackson

John Lewis

CIVIL RIGHTS LEADER & U.S. REPRESENTATIVE . ATLANTA

At an early age, Congressman John Lewis's mother taught him to stay out of trouble, but he has often campaigned on the "good trouble" he has been getting into for the last 50 years. Lewis has been called an American hero for his leadership in the Civil Rights Movement and for his service as Georgia's U.S. Representative for a quarter of a century.

Born near Troy, Alabama, to sharecropper parents in February 1940, Lewis has lived in Georgia much of his adult life. Inspired by Rev. Martin Luther King, Jr., whom he heard on the radio, he chose to be part of the Civil Rights Movement at a young age.

"I believed that America, as a great nation, and we, as a great people, could emerge as a model for the rest of the world," said Lewis. "We could find a way to say to the rest of the world that we're prepared to lay down the burden of race, that we're prepared to create the beloved community and say to our own citizens and the citizens of the world, as Dr. King said, 'We must learn to live together as brothers and sisters or we will perish as fools.'"

He graduated from the American Baptist Theological Seminary in Nashville and earned a bachelor's degree in religion and philosophy from Fisk University. While at Fisk, he organized sit-in demonstrations at segregated lunch counters in Nashville. In 1961, he volunteered for the Freedom Rides to fight segregation at bus terminals across the South.

Risking his life on the Freedom Rides, he was severely beaten by angry mobs and arrested. From 1963 to 1966, Lewis became chairman of the Student Nonviolent Coordinating Committee (SNCC), which organized students to fight for civil rights. By the age of 23, he was one of the Big Six leaders of the Civil Rights Movement and was a keynote speaker at the historic March on Washington in August 1963. The next summer, he coordinated SNCC efforts to organize voter registration drives and community action programs during the Mississippi Freedom Summer. Eight months later, with Hosea Williams, he spearheaded 600 protestors to march across the Edmund Pettus Bridge in Selma, Alabama, on what became known as Bloody Sunday when state troopers attacked the marchers. That day's news coverage helped speed up passage of the Voting Rights Act of 1965.

Lewis left SNCC in 1966 but continued his work for civil rights in critical leadership roles for minority voter registration. In 1977, President Jimmy Carter appointed Lewis to direct the 250,000 volunteers of ACTION.

Lewis has been called an American hero for his leadership in the Civil Rights Movement. . .

In the 1980s he turned to politics and was elected to the Atlanta City Council in 1981, and later was elected as the U.S. Representative for Georgia's Fifth Congressional District in November 1986. In Congress, Lewis is Senior Chief Deputy Whip for the Democratic Party and member of the House Ways & Means Committee.

Lewis is the author of two books, *Across That Bridge: Life Lessons and A Vision for Change* in 2012, and his autobiography, *Walking With The Wind: A Memoir of the Movement* in 1998.

He has honorary degrees from many prestigious universities including Harvard, Brown, Spelman College, Princeton, Duke, Columbia and Georgetown.

Lewis has received numerous awards, including the Medal of Freedom, the highest honor granted to a civilian by President Barack Obama; the Lincoln Medal from the historic Ford's Theatre; the Preservation Hero award given by the National Trust for Historic Preservation; the Martin Luther King, Jr. Non-Violent Peace Prize; the NAACP Spingarn Medal; and the only John F. Kennedy Profile in Courage Award for Lifetime Achievement ever granted by the John F. Kennedy Library Foundation.

Lewis lives in Atlanta and is married to Lillian Miles. They have one son, John Miles.

In 2012 Lewis used his police mug shot from the Civil Rights Movement as part of his congressional primary re-election campaign to show that he was still willing to get into "good trouble" for the people of Georgia. ■

Dr. Crawford W. Long

MEDICAL PIONEER . DANIELSVILLE . 1815 – 1878

Dr. Crawford W. Long, a native of Danielsville, is credited with being the father of painless surgery for his discovery of anesthesia.

The son of a wealthy merchant and planter, Long began attending the University of Georgia in Athens at age 14. His roommate there, Alexander Stephens, later would become Vice President of the Confederate States of America.

After receiving his A.M. degree in 1835, Long studied medicine at Transylvania College in Lexington, Kentucky, before transferring to the University of Pennsylvania Medical College, from which he graduated in 1839. After completing a hospital internship in New York City, Long returned to Georgia and established a medical practice in Jefferson.

Long had attended "ether frolics" during his years in medical school, during which partygoers would sniff sulfuric ether or nitrous oxide for entertainment. He noticed that the participants often bumped into things or fell, yet seemed to feel no pain until the "laughing gas" wore off.

After experimenting with sulfuric ether as an anesthetic, Long performed his first surgery using the gas on March 30, 1842. He removed a tumor from the neck of an etherized young man, James Venable, who later reported that the procedure did not hurt. Long continued to experiment with the surgical use of ether, but did not announce his findings until 1848—two years after a Boston dentist named William Morton had publicly demonstrated the use of ether as an anesthetic.

Long is commemorated by a statue in the U.S. Capitol's crypt, one of two monuments representing Georgia in the National Statuary Hall Collection.

Long presented his written findings, along with letters from former patients, to the Medical College of Georgia in Augusta. By that time, two other men had also claimed to have discovered anesthesia, so Long did not received full credit for the medical advancement during his lifetime.

In 1851, Long and his wife Caroline moved to Athens. During the Civil War, he treated both Union and Confederate soldiers. He died on June 16, 1878, shortly after delivering a baby.

Long is commemorated by a statue in the U.S. Capitol's crypt, one of two monuments representing Georgia in the National Statuary Hall Collection. In 1931, an Atlanta hospital run by Emory University was named in his honor, though the facility's name was changed in 2009. And, since 1957, downtown Jefferson has operated a Crawford W. Long Museum, which features memorabilia and medical equipment from the early days of Long's career.

In addition, Long has been memorialized by a U.S. postage stamp and National Doctor's Day, which was established in Winder on March 30, 1933. ∎

Juliet Gordon Low

FOUNDER, GIRL SCOUTS OF THE USA . SAVANNAH . 1860 – 1927

At age fifty-one, in a time when women felt the restraints of society, Juliette Gordon Low started building what would become the largest voluntary association for women and girls in the United States. She devoted fifteen years and provided the majority of financial support for the Girl Scouts of the United States of America.

"Daisy," as she was known by friends and family, was born on October 31, 1860, in Savannah, Georgia. The family home, where she spent many happy years, was designated an historic landmark in 1965. The second of six children from an upper class family, she attended schools in Savannah, Virginia and New York where she excelled in art. She also wrote poems, sketched and later became a skillful sculptor and painter. Low was a strong swimmer and avid tennis player.

After she graduated and made her debut in society, she traveled extensively in the United States and Europe. She met and married an Englishman named William Mackay Low, the son of a wealthy British merchant, in December 1880. Already suffering from partial hearing loss in one ear, she lost hearing in the other ear when a grain of rice thrown at her wedding lodged in her ear, puncturing the eardrum. This disability would cause Low bouts of depression throughout her life.

The couple bought an estate in England but continued to travel. However, Low returned to Savannah to aid in the war effort when the Spanish American War broke out in February 1898. When the war ended ten months later, she returned to England to an unhappy marriage. Low's husband eventually left her for another woman in 1902 and died in 1905 during divorce proceedings.

In 1911, Low met Robert Baden-Powell, founder of the Boy Scouts. She was soon volunteering with the Girl Guides in Great Britain, the sister organization of the Scouts. After setting up Guides in Scotland and London, she returned to Georgia in 1912 and recruited eighteen girls in Savannah for the first meeting of what would become the Girl Scouts of the USA (GSUSA). By 1925, there were more than 90,000 members in the United States. Single and financially secure, Low was able to devote all her time to building the organization.

Low brought together girls from all economic and ethnic backgrounds, instilling within them self-reliance and resourcefulness. The girls were encouraged to prepare themselves not only for traditional homemaking roles but also professional careers. She provided opportunities for girls to develop themselves mentally, spiritually and physically through outdoor activities and community service projects. Because of her own hearing disability, Low welcomed girls with disabilities.

In 1923 Low was diagnosed with cancer but continued with her busy schedule, traveling back and forth to England. However, on January 17, 1927, she succumbed to the disease and passed away at her home in Savannah at age 67. Her death was mourned by many friends and admirers from all walks of life. Her friends honored her by establishing the Juliette Low World Friendship Fund, which continued her work for girls around the world.

Low brought together girls from all economic and ethnic backgrounds, instilling within them self-reliance and resourcefulness.

Girl Scouts of the USA has grown to over three million members and is the largest educational organization for girls in the world. Since the organization's inception, over 50 million girls have become alumnae.

At Low's request, she was buried in her Girl Scout uniform. A telegram in the pocket from the national officers of GSUSA read: "You are not only the first Girl Scout, you are the best Scout of them all." ∎

A portrait of Juliette Gordon Low (1887, Edward Hughes) located in the National Portrait Gallery in Washington, D.C.

Bernard "Bernie" Marcus

CO-FOUNDER OF HOME DEPOT . ATLANTA

Georgia billionaire Bernie Marcus learned from his mother and father at an early age to give back to those in need.

"We were raised that the glass is always half full and our mother taught us to share our good fortune with others," Marcus said. "In Judaism, tzedakah means to give back. If I can make a difference in this world, I want to pay it back."

His Jewish-Russian immigrant parents, who had moved to Newark, New Jersey, shortly before his birth in 1929, had little money and lived in a poor section of the city.

Working from the age of 13, Marcus built cabinets to pay his way through Rutgers, graduated in 1954 and went to work briefly as a pharmacist. A few years later, he entered retail sales, moved up the corporate ladder, and by the mid-1970s was an executive at Handy Dan Home Improvement Centers, based in Los Angeles with several dozen stores in the West. He met Arthur Blank, Handy Dan's chief financial officer, when both were

> *"In Judaism, tzedakah means to give back. If I can make a difference in this world, I want to pay it back."*

fired from Handy Dan's in April 1978. With the help of an investment banker, they built, from Marcus' plan, a national chain of warehouse-sized home improvement centers called Home Depot.

After a nationwide search, Marcus and Blank set their sights on Atlanta and opened the first two Home Depot stores on June 22, 1979. Within two years, the company went public and became the fastest growing retailer in U.S. history, employing more than 300,000 people in about 2,000 stores throughout the United States, Canada, China and Mexico. Marcus was CEO for 19 years and then chairman of the board.

In the early days of Home Depot, the company gave products and time to help people in need, but never publicized the fact, believing it was simply the right thing to do. The 83-year-old philanthropist retired in 2002 to focus on giving back. He and his wife, Billi, gave Atlanta and the citizens of Georgia an architectural wonder when they donated $250 million to build the Georgia Aquarium. It has more than 8 million gallons of water in its 60 different underwater habitats and is considered the world's largest aquarium.

Through the Billi and Bernie Marcus Foundation, the couple has given millions to health care causes, including $20 million to create

the Marcus Heart Valve Center at the Piedmont Heart Institute. At Emory University, $5 million in foundation money supports the Marcus Society, 15 professorships in pediatrics and the diseases affecting children. In 2008 Marcus started the Marcus Institute for children with disabilities and learning disorders and Autism Speaks in Atlanta. The foundation also provided a state of the art bioterrorism unit at the Center for Disease Control.

In an effort to educate young people, Marcus launched the Job Creators Alliance, a Dallas-based nonprofit of CEOs and entrepreneurs, whose mission is to preserve the U.S. free enterprise system.

"I am concerned that young people think the free-enterprise system is an evil thing and it's not," Marcus said. "All the good that's come in this country, all the things we have and profit from, come out of the free-enterprise system."

He also supports Jewish causes and founded the Israel Democracy Institute, a nonpartisan think tank in Israel dedicated to promoting and defending Israeli democracy.

Marcus and Blank worked with author Bob Andelman to write *Built From Scratch: How a Couple of Regular Guys Grew The Home Depot From Nothing to $30 Billion*, which was published in 1999.

Marcus continues to pay back to those in need just like his parents taught him to do. ∎

Ben Massell

REAL ESTATE DEVELOPER . ATLANTA . 1886 - 1962

Atlanta mayors have described real estate mogul Ben Massell as a "one-man boom" and "the creator of the Atlanta skyline." Massell was a visionary who saw Atlanta's potential in the early 1900s and contributed to its physical rise and development.

Born in Lithuania, Massell was two years old when his father, a wholesale grocer, moved the family to Atlanta. Twenty-five years later, in 1913, he, with his brothers Sam Sr. and Levi, formed the Massell Companies to buy, build and sell real estate. "Atlanta was a growing city and they could see that it was a hot market," said Sam Massell, Jr., Ben's nephew and a former real estate executive himself.

With Ben serving as lead negotiator and Sam Sr. spearheading the marketing, the Massell Companies built most of the three- and four-story apartment buildings in the area now known as Midtown. Of these residential buildings still standing, most can be identified by the Spanish tile parapets lining the fronts. They include The Masselton, a grand structure on Ponce de Leon Avenue that is listed on the National Register of Historic Places.

An immense business success, Ben was also generous with his charitable donations.

Another notable Massell development during that time was the 13-story Henry Grady Hotel, Atlanta's largest hotel when it was built at Peachtree and Cain Streets in 1924. The Great Depression wiped the Massell brothers out, but after World War II Ben resumed his real estate business.

In all, he oversaw construction of approximately 1,000 buildings, including many landmark properties such as the Peachtree-7th, at 500,000 square feet the city's largest office building when built for the General Services Administration in 1952 (now Peachtree Lofts) and the Atlanta Merchandise Mart (now AmericasMart) on Peachtree Street. John Portman was the architect. At one point, Massell was Georgia's largest taxpayer!

"The Merchandise Mart posed an interesting challenge for Ben because another developer was trying to build one out in the country off I-85 North," Sam Jr. recalled. "But Ben and most city leaders felt it should be in the city. So one day Ben got into a taxi cab and rode out to the proposed site so he could tell people how much a cab ride would cost a visitor downtown to get out there." The expense became a selling point that helped win approval for its eventual site.

Decades before Google was invented, the Massell brothers were human databases of real estate information. "All three of them could identify any piece of property in Atlanta and could tell you the size of the lot, who owned it and the last sale price," Sam Jr. said. "They had a wealth of knowledge."

An immense business success, Ben was also generous with his charitable donations. An Atlanta dental clinic that serves the working poor and homeless was named in his honor, as was Brandeis Uni-

versity's Massell Quad. He donated land on 14th Street for a Jewish Home for the Aged and was instrumental in helping raise more than $44 million to fund its causes.

Ben died in 1962, but his real estate legacy lives on. Grandson Steve Selig, his sister Cathy and great-grandson Scott Selig run Selig Enterprises, while Sam Jr. and his son Steve Massell also have been successful in commercial real estate.■

Sam Massell

FORMER MAYOR & CIVIC LEADER . ATLANTA

Sam Massell grew up attending political rallies with his father, but the former Atlanta mayor says the real "credit or blame" for his entry into elected politics actually belongs to a friend who was running for student body president at Druid Hills High School in 1943.

"Charlie Goldstein asked me to help paint his signs. When he got elected, he appointed me Treasurer. I got bit by the political bug right there," Massell recalled.

"Charlie Goldstein asked me to help paint his signs. When he got elected, he appointed me Treasurer. I got bit by the political bug right there," Massell recalled.

Almost 70 years later, Massell has served 22 years in elected offices while also having had successful careers in real estate, tourism and association management. Since 1988, he has been president of the Buckhead Coalition, a nonprofit civic group committed to guiding Buckhead's orderly growth and nurturing its quality of life.

The son of a real-estate-executive-turned-lawyer, Massell attended the University of Georgia and Emory University before receiving a bachelor's business degree from Georgia State, followed by a law degree from Atlanta Law School.

His first job as publications chief for a trade association ended with Massell's firing when he asked for a raise—but only after his boss advised him "to make a real living" by going into real estate, then arranged an interview for him with Allan-Grayson Realty Company. "Real estate was where it 'was at' in Atlanta," Massell said.

He spent the next 20 years as a commercial Realtor® at Allan-Grayson, rising to become a vice president there as well as a charter member of the Atlanta Real Estate Board's Million Dollar Club. Massell was honored three times by the Georgia Association of Real Estate Boards for creating the "Outstanding Transaction of the Year."

He concurrently became involved in civic activities. After serving a two-year term on the city council of Mountain Park, Georgia, where he owned a resort cabin, Massell spent eight years on the Atlanta City Executive Committee, followed by eight years as President (Vice Mayor) of the Atlanta Board of Aldermen (now called the City Council). In 1969, he defeated the Republican Rodney Cook to become the city's first Jewish mayor and, at age 42, its youngest.

"Our administration's greatest achievement probably was winning passage of the one-cent sales tax that financed establishment of the Metropolitan Atlanta Rapid Transit Authority," he said. Massell's four-year term also oversaw development of the city's first enclosed arena, the Omni Coliseum, and increased diversity in city govern-ment, including appointment of the City Council's first female member and the first blacks to serve as department heads.

After his 1973 mayoral defeat by Maynard Jackson, Massell ran a travel agency in Buckhead where he says he "sold dreams and traveled the world." Today, as president of the influential Buckhead Coalition, which consists of 100 CEOs of major companies, Massell is back in public life and still working closely with governments.

While the coalition has had many accomplishments, he is most proud of the fact that it was the first U.S. organization to have defibrillators placed where people work and live, rather than just in ambulances. "The American Heart Association had explained that the instruments could save many lives; but only if used within the first seven minutes following a cardiac arrest, which couldn't be achieved in normal urban traffic on ambulances" he explained.

Life has been good for the former mayor, who in 2012 celebrated his 60th wedding anniversary with wife Doris, their three children and three grandchildren. "I've been very lucky," Massell said.■

Dr. John Stith Pemberton

MEDICAL CHEMIST & COLA INVENTOR . ATLANTA . 1831 – 1888

Dr. John S. Pemberton was a successful medical professional who invented the "delicious, refreshing, exhilarating, invigorating" medicinal tonic that later became known as "the pause that refreshes," Coca-Cola®.

That one soft drink, introduced in 1886 at Jacob's Pharmacy in Atlanta for five cents a glass, has grown into the world's most recognized brand, with customers in more than 200 countries now drinking more than 1.7 billion servings of Coca-Cola brands daily.

Born in Knoxville, Georgia, Pemberton spent his childhood in Rome. He graduated from the Southern Botanico Medical College of Georgia in 1850; he later received a pharmacy degree—accounts vary on which school he attended—and served on Georgia's first pharmacy-licensing board. According to the *Encyclopedia of World Biography*, Pemberton briefly practiced as a "steam doctor," one who uses steam baths and herbs to induce sweating, which it was believed restored people to good health.

In 1855, Pemberton and his wife Anna and son Charles moved to Columbus where he worked as a pharmacist. During the Civil War, he fought with the Confederate Army and was almost killed during an 1865 battle. Various accounts say Pemberton took morphine to ease his pain and eventually became a morphine addict.

After the war, he worked with Dr. Austin Walker in developing botanical home remedies and perfumes. Pemberton also operated a state-of-the-art laboratory for chemical analysis that became the first state-run facility to test crop and soil chemicals, thus helping eliminate the sale of fraudulent substances.

In 1869, Pemberton moved his family to Atlanta where he created and sold French Wine Coca, a drink based on a similar European product. The beverage was a combination of wine and coca extract,

By 1887, he was marketing Coca-Cola with free drink coupons, an ad in The Atlanta Journal, and hand-painted oilcloth signs reading "Drink Coca-Cola" that appeared on store awnings.

which was commonly used at that time to treat digestive problems, soothe nerves and promote sexual drive. The drink sold well, but by 1885, prohibition laws had prompted Pemberton to develop a non-alcoholic version.

At his home on Marietta Street, Pemberton experimented by combining coca leaf and kola nut extracts with assorted essential oils. That concoction, however, tasted too bitter, so he added various amounts of sugar syrup and citric acid until a pleasant taste was achieved.

On May 8, 1886, Pemberton declared that he had perfected the formula. His bookkeeper and co-partner, Frank Robinson, suggested calling the beverage "Coca-Cola" for its alliterative description of the two active ingredients. Robinson, who had excellent penmanship, also designed the now-familiar logo in cursive lettering.

Pemberton took a jug of the syrup to Jacob's Pharmacy where it was mixed at the soda fountain with carbonated water and pronounced "excellent." First-year sales averaged nine drinks a day for a total of $50, which disappointed Pemberton since he had spent $70 on Coca-Cola supplies.

By 1887, he was marketing Coca-Cola with free drink coupons, an ad in *The Atlanta Journal,* and hand-painted oilcloth signs reading "Drink Coca-Cola" that appeared on store awnings.

Pemberton never benefited from the global business colossus that eventually was created from his invention. Ailing from stomach cancer, he gradually sold much of his Coca-Cola interest to other investors while retaining some for his son who would die six years later from a morphine overdose. Just before his death in 1888, Pemberton sold his remaining rights to Asa Candler, a canny businessman who quickly scooped up the additional rights to win complete control of Coca-Cola.

Pemberton died on Aug. 16, 1888, and was buried in Linwood Cemetery in Columbus. ■

John Stith Pemberton, circa 1880.

Richard Peters

CITY PIONEER & BUSINESSMAN . ATLANTA . 1810 – 1889

Residents of Georgia's capital might want to thank Richard Peters for the fact that they're called Atlantans instead of Marthasvillians.

The Pennsylvania native moved to Georgia in 1835 as chief engineer of the Georgia Railroad, which was being extended west from Augusta to the city unofficially called "Terminus." Peters spent between eight and ten years working on the railroad and was named its superintendent when it was completed. By the time Peters moved to what is now Atlanta in 1846, the city had been renamed in honor of Gov. Wilson Lumpkin's daughter, Martha.

Peters, however, saw the town's potential as a transportation center and thought that "Marthasville" was too provincial a name for the great city that he envisioned. A business associate, John Edgar Thomson, suggested the name "Atlanta," a feminine version of Atlantic. Peters concurred and had "Atlanta" printed on company pamphlets that were widely circulated. On December 26, 1845, the state legislature officially changed the city's name.

In the 1850s, Peters founded Atlanta's first steam-powered factory, a flour mill that was powered by burning wood. Peters also bought about 400 acres of timberland—a $2,000 purchase in 1855 that was worth hundreds of thousands of dollars by the 1880s.

In 1871, Peters and George Adair built the city's first streetcar system. The streetcars, drawn by horses, then powered by electricity, provided transportation to a previously remote area being settled by Atlanta's middle class. The streetcars eventually ran along the entire length of real estate that Peters had begun buying in the 1840s, making that property north of downtown much more valuable for residential subdivision. And as Atlanta's economy recovered from the Civil War, wealthy Atlantans began moving to the suburbs (today's West End and Midtown).

In 1884, Peters sold 180 acres to Hanniball Kimball, who intended to build a residential neighborhood called Peters Park. An *Atlanta Constitution* article published on March 30, 1884, said the sale confirmed that Peters was one of the state's richest men.

"That shows what Atlanta will do for those who believe in her future," Peters told the *Constitution*. "I have confidence in this city going squarely to 100,000 inhabitants. Had I invested my $2,000 in stocks that paid 10 percent a year it would have given me less than one-sixth of what the real estate has paid me, and I have had little trouble and no risk with it. I believe in the future of Atlanta stronger now than I ever did."

In 1887, Peters donated four acres to help found the Georgia School of Technology. "I have always felt a lively interest in Atlanta and in everything that promised to advance her growth," he said in an *Atlanta Constitution* article,

In 1871, Peters and George Adair built the city's first streetcar system. The streetcars, drawn by horses, then powered by electricity, provided transportation to a previously remote area being settled by Atlanta's middle class.

which added: "There are few men who envy Mr. Peters' good fortune. He is known and beloved as a man of high character, fine quality and perfect integrity."

After Peters died in 1889, his son Edward became trustee of the Peters estate. Edward later built the Edward C. Peters House (now Ivy Hall), a 2½-story, red brick Victorian mansion that is listed on the National Register of Historic Places. ∎

Photo of Richard Peters taken in 1848.

John C. Portman

INTERNATIONALLY RENOWNED ARCHITECT/DEVELOPER . ATLANTA

John Portman thinks holistically, in terms of how people will interact with his buildings, when he produces the innovative architectural designs that have altered the skyline in more than 60 global cities, including Atlanta.

"Anyone can build a building and put rooms in it," he told *The New York Times* in 2011. "But we should put human beings at the head of our thought process. You want to spark their enthusiasm…Architecture should be a symphony."

Born in Walhalla, South Carolina, Portman grew up in Atlanta and served in the U.S. Navy before graduating from the Georgia Institute of Technology in 1950. Three years later Portman opened his architectural firm and began helping transform downtown Atlanta into the vibrant center it is today.

As the rare architect who also developed his projects, Portman spearheaded the concept of urban mixed-use projects with Peachtree Center. Begun in 1960 with construction of the Atlanta Merchandise Mart (now known as AmericaMart), the development was expanded in subsequent years to include office towers, hotels and retail stores joined by pedestrian sky bridges.

Portman repeated this "city within a city" model with his eight-block Embarcadero Center in San Francisco and the GM Renaissance Center in Detroit, again helping to revive decaying urban neighborhoods and attract suburbanites back to the downtowns. His Hyatt Regency Hotel in Atlanta was the world's first modern atrium hotel. The 22-story structure opened at 265 Peachtree St. in 1967, complete with glass elevators and cascading fountains and topped by the revolving, flying-saucer-like Polaris restaurant.

Other Atlanta hotels followed: the 73-story Westin Peachtree Plaza Hotel was the world's tallest hotel when it was built in 1976; the 1,675-room Marriott Marquis, opened in 1985, contained the world's largest atrium until Burj Al-Arab was built in Dubai. Elsewhere, Portman's notable hotels include the Marriott Marquis in Manhattan's Times

Stephen Cord, Photographer

"But we should put human beings at the head of our thought process. You want to spark their enthusiasm…Architecture should be a symphony."

Square and the Westin Bonaventure in Los Angeles, which has been featured in many movies and television series.

Admirers applauded the "wow" factor and magical sense of arrival that visitors to Portman's hotels experience as they walk through entryways that explode into airy, magnificent atriums. "These knock-your-socks-off spaces were groovy before boutique hotels could claim the term," a *New York Times* article said in 2006. "Within their razzle-dazzle lay the makings of a crowd-pleasing spectacle, one that even attracted tourists who had no intention of spending a night there."

Detractors, however, criticized his designs as lacking integration with their neighborhoods though they usually failed to mention that these buildings generally were constructed in then-seedy, crime-ridden areas with which most people would prefer not to interact.

Portman completed his first international project, the Brussels International TradeMart, in Belgium in 1975 for which the Belgian government later knighted him! His global reputation was burnished with the mixed-use Marina Square (1987) in Singapore, Shanghai Centre (1990) and Yintai Centre (2008), both in China.

Though known for his commercial work, Portman built two houses for his family—Entelechy I in Buckhead and Entelechy II, a concrete beach house on Sea Island that holds his vast art collection.

Portman also expresses his creative energy through painting and sculpting—about 55 of his artworks were exhibited at the High Museum of Art in 2009, along with his design plans, large-scale photographs and architectural models. "Connecting with art, whether viewing a painting, hearing a fine symphony or participating in artistic expression yourself, allows you to get to the core of who you are, which inevitably shapes how you see the world and how you create solutions for the world around you," he told *Forbes* magazine. ■

Jenny Pruitt

REAL ESTATE ENTREPRENEUR & PHILANTHROPIST . ATLANTA

Pruitt (second from left) points to her faith as "the bedrock of my life, and the source of stamina and concentration."

A third generation Atlantan, Jenny Pruitt launched a successful real estate career with the establishment of Jenny Pruitt & Associates in 1988. She led the agency to annual sales totaling over one billion dollars. Soon, six additional offices were established and over 450 employees were added.

When the firm was acquired by HomeServices of America, Pruitt left and co-founded Atlanta Fine Homes in 2007, an exclusive affiliate of Sotheby's International Realty, representing home buyers and sellers as well as developers and builders. With over 200 agents in three Metro Atlanta offices, Pruitt once again demonstrated her entrepreneurial spirit and leadership skills. In 2012, the agency saw an increase of fifty-six percent in sales growth from 2011 and sold more one million dollar properties than anyone else in 2012.

According to Pruitt, Atlanta Fine Homes strives to maintain "unparalleled customer service and to build long-term relationships with customers and clients while empowering their sales associates to achieve success." Pruitt takes this same philosophy of "servant-leadership" into her public service endeavors.

Pruitt serves on the Piedmont Auxiliary, a benefactor to the Children's Healthcare of Atlanta that also helps to build homes with Habitat for Humanity. She is active in Atlanta History Center's Members Guild and the Vinings Historical Society. Pruitt is director of the Buckhead Coalition and founder of the Buckhead Girls Club, which presents grants to associations such as the Atlanta History Center, Shepherd Center and the Margaret Mitchell House. In return for her commitment, club members granted Pruitt the 2002 "Buckhead Woman of the Millennium" Award.

Pruitt currently is the vice-president of the Atlanta Rotary Club and past president of the Atlanta Board of Realtors. She also serves on the board for Chastain Horse Park, the Georgia Cancer Coalition and the Girl Scouts of Northwest Georgia.

In recognition of her integrity and professionalism, the Atlanta Board of REALTORS presented Pruitt with the distinguished E.A. Isakson Award. She received the Georgia Small Business Person of the Year Award and was inducted into Georgia State University's J. Mack Robinson School of Business "Hall of Fame."

Pruitt points to her faith as "the bedrock of my life, and the source of stamina and concentration." To Pruitt it is important to put servant leadership in action both professionally and for the greater community good. ∎

L-R: David Boehmig, president, Jenny Pruitt, CEO, Nancy See, senior vice president and Bill Rawlings, vice president and managing broker north Atlanta office

Herman J. Russell

FOUNDER OF H.J. RUSSELL & CO. . ATLANTA

Herman J. Russell, from Atlanta, proved himself as an entrepreneur early in life and then advanced in the construction business to a lofty level of success. He left his mark on the skyline of Atlanta, including the world-class sports venues, the Georgia Dome, Centennial Olympic Stadium/Turner/Field and Philips Arena.

The organization he founded, H.J. Russell & Company, is one of the largest minority-owned enterprises in the U.S. "What turns me on," Russell says, "is to get to the office every morning, think outside the box, make new deals and particularly to improve the lives of people. Entrepreneurship means the ability to control my own destiny."

At 16, Russell began to control his own destiny, purchasing a small parcel of land on which he built a duplex. Later, he graduated from Tuskegee University and returned to Atlanta to work with his father as a plastering subcontractor. In 1952, he extended his father's business into general contracting and H.J. Russell & Company was born. Seven years later, he formed Paradise Management, Inc., a residential and commercial property management firm.

In the early 1960s, during the civil rights movement, Russell's company began its first major project, an apartment development of 12 units in Atlanta. The company also won a bid to plaster Atlanta Fulton County Stadium. In the late '60s, Russell built HUD housing in the Southeastern U.S.

In the 1970s, Russell built apartments in Atlanta that gave people a sense of community, complete with clubhouses, swimming pools, tennis courts and other amenities. Russell improved the lives of people in these neighborhoods through his leadership and the communities he built.

Russell also became involved in the beverage business, in communications and in part-ownership of the Atlanta Hawks and the Atlanta Flames hockey team. He constructed the Delta Airlines headquarters during the 1970s.

In the 80s, H.J. Russell & Company oversaw residential property developments of more than 4,500 units, built more corporate headquarters—including Coca-Cola—carried out a sizeable project

at Hartsfield Airport and completed other high profile jobs. The company built Atlanta's downtown sports landmarks during the 1990s. However, closest to Russell's heart was the multi-use $300 million Castleberry Hill development in downtown Atlanta.

Herman J. Russell's commitment, through his business, has been to leave the world a better place than he found it.

In 2004, Russell passed the baton of leadership to his sons, Michael Russell, CEO, and Jerome Russell, president. The company now provides development, general construction, program management and property management services. H.J. Russell & Company also has become one of the largest minority-owned real estate firms in the nation.

When he was the chief executive of his company, Russell's intent was to give back to the community. He made a personal investment in revitalizing his company's neighborhood, including construction of The Castleberry Inn/Extended Stay Hotel, Legacy Lofts, Intown Lofts and Paschal's Restaurant.

Russell has earned many awards and honors. He has served on the boards of Citizens Trust Bank, Georgia Power Company, Wachovia Bank, the Georgia Ports Authority and the Atlanta Chamber of Commerce.

Coretta Scott King, widow of the Rev. Dr. Martin Luther King Jr., says Russell is a pioneer. "He has always been a strong supporter and friend and made a very important contribution to the movement. He's a person we can be proud of both as an African-American and businessman."

Mrs. King sees a bright future for H.J. Russell & Company now that it's in the hands of Russell's sons. "I think the next generation will do very well," she says, "because they have grown up in the business in one aspect or another, with good values instilled in them." Herman J. Russell's commitment, through his business, has been to leave the world a better place than he found it. ∎

Photo courtesy of the Tuskegee University, 2012.

Ferrol Sams Jr.

PHYSICIAN & NOVELIST . MACON

Ferrol Sams, a rural medical doctor originally from Fayette County, Georgia, purposed to write his recollections of life in the country between the two world wars so that his descendants would know how things had been in that place and time.

"He clearly and accurately and believably captures the voices of all his characters. His stories capture the times and places of the south over the past six decades."

He wrote down his memories, but, in the process, he accomplished much more. From those recollections, he wrote eight books. He won the Townsend Prize for fiction in 1991 and was inducted into the Georgia Writers Hall of Fame.

Sams was born on September 26, 1922. His parents were Ferrol Sams Sr., school superintendent in Fayette County, and Mildred Matthews. Sams enrolled in Mercer University and, upon graduation, entered Emory University medical school. Sams' medical training was interrupted by World War II, and he served in the Army Medical Corps and saw action in France. After the war, Sams returned to Atlanta to continue his medical studies. In med school, he met Helen Fletcher, whom he married in 1948. Both Sams and his wife earned their medical degrees and they practiced medicine together in Fayette County until retirement in 2006.

Sams and his wife had four children. When they were older, Sams thought it would be good to write down his memories for their benefit. He recalled one of his professors at Mercer University who told his students to write only about things they knew. Sams knew rural Georgia at the time in which he was growing up, so he stuck to this in his writing on behalf of his posterity. Sams' approach proved very successful.

His first book, *Run With The Horsemen*, was published in 1982. Sams was 60 years old and just beginning his second career as a best-selling author.

The protagonist in his first book was a young boy, Porter Osborne Jr., who was apparently modeled after himself. Osborne was a rambunctious and fun-loving boy, growing up in rural Georgia. The story resonated with readers and became a national best seller.

Sams continued practicing medicine and writing and, in 1984, his second novel, *The Whisper of the River*, was published. This story chronicled Osborne's years at a fictional university in Macon, Georgia, where he re-examined some of his beliefs and dealt with profound moral issues.

Sams left his storytelling about Porter Osborne Jr. for a time and wrote a book of short stories and two works of non-fiction. *The Widow's Mite and Other Stories* was published in 1987. Two non-fiction books, *The Passing: Perspectives of Rural America* and *Christmas Gift!* were published in 1988 and 1989 respectively. *Christmas Gift!* was released again in 2010 from Mercer University Press with an audio CD read by the author.

In 1991, the conclusion of Sams' trilogy about Porter Osborne Jr., *When All the World Was Young*, was published. In this story, Osborne was serving overseas as a surgical technician and coming of age. For this book, Sams received the Townsend Prize for fiction. He continued to write: *Epiphany*, published in 1995, *The Passing: Stories*, in 2001 and *Down Town* in 2007.

Sams received an award in 2001 for his dedicated medical service in Fayette County over the span of 50 years. In 2012, he received a lifetime achievement award from the Georgia Writers Association. Thus, in his later years, Sams was recognized for his success in both medicine and writing.

"Sams has produced a solid body of work that resounds with the laughter, tears and joy of southern life," Margaret Walters, executive director of the Georgia Writers Association told *The Atlanta Journal Constitution*. "He clearly and accurately and believably captures the voices of all his characters. His stories capture the times and places of the south over the past six decades." ■

Mary Telfair

PHILANTHROPIST . SAVANNAH . 1791-1875

A prolific reader with strong opinions regarding national and world events, Telfair held strong views that were not encouraged in women in the nineteenth century. She once debated U.S. Supreme Court Justice James Moore Wayne on the merits of renewing the national bank charter. Charles Johnson, Jr. wrote in his biography, *Mary Telfair: The Life and Legacy of a Nineteenth Century Woman* (2002): "Mary Telfair was her own woman, but she affirmed her identity within the framework of good manners, decorum, and taste demanded of women of her station."

A prolific reader with strong opinions regarding national and world events, Telfair held strong views that were not encouraged in women in the nineteenth century.

The family, three brothers and three sisters, was a devoted one. In 1832, when her last surviving brother died, Telfair and her sisters, Sarah and Margaret, took over the supervision of the family's plantation and considerable land holdings. Frequently ill herself, she found comfort in her strong Christian beliefs.

Telfair made her first trip to Europe in 1841. She returned there four more times, captivated by the historical sites and the great paintings in France and Italy. This perhaps inspired her to donate her home in James Square (renamed Telfair Square in 1883), including the books, furniture and works of art, to the Georgia Historical Society upon her death.

Telfair had a vision for a hospital exclusive to women where they could get healthcare in a respectful and compassionate environment. A few days before her death, she placed a provision in her will for the construction of such a hospital. The Telfair Hospital for Females opened in Savannah in 1886. Today, it is a regional leader in the women's healthcare services and includes Telfair Pavilion, The Telfair Birth Place, and The Children's Place. Joined with Candler General Hospital and St. Joseph's Hospital, the Mary Telfair Hospital for Women is a part of the region's largest healthcare provider.

Mary Telfair died at age eighty-four on June 2, 1875. Her home became the Telfair Academy of Arts and Sciences and opened to the public in 1886 as a free art museum. The main facility, now referred to as the Telfair Museum of Art, was declared a National Historic Landmark in 1976. It is the oldest public art museum in the South. A portrait of Mary Telfair hangs in the museum's rotunda. ∎

Standing no more than five feet tall, Mary Telfair was a force with which to be reckoned. Since her inherited wealth freed her from the expectations of marriage, she spent her life in travel and helping others. Telfair was a woman of keen intellect with an independent spirit.

Mary Telfair was a member of the distinguished Telfair family. She was born on January 28, 1791, in Augusta, Georgia, which at that time was the state capital. Her father, Edward Telfair, was a three-term governor; her mother came from a wealthy and prominent Southern family. A child of wealth and privilege, Telfair received her education at private schools in New York and at Newark Academy in New Jersey.

Telfair was as much at home in the drawing rooms of New York and Philadelphia as she was on her plantation in Savannah. She had great personal charm but was critical of other women and had no use for the fashionable "southern belle."

Carl Brandt - Mary Telfair, 1896 - Oil on Canvas 89 3/4 x 64 1/4 in.- Signed and dated lower left, Carl L. Brand 1896
Telfair Museum of Art purchase, 1896.1 - Courtesy of Telfair Museums

Phil Walden

MUSIC IMPRESARIO . MACON . 1940 - 2006

Record executive Phil Walden is remembered as "the father of Southern rock," the bluesy, country-rock sound that was popularized by artists signed to his *Capricorn Records* in the 1970s.

Born in Greenville, South Carolina, on Jan. 11, 1940, Walden grew up in Macon, where he often listened to WIBB-AM's "Night Rider" rhythm-and-blues show. "I had never been exposed to something that raw in my life," he later told biographical writers. "When I heard (Little Richard's) 'Wop bop a lubop a lop bam boom,' I knew I didn't want to sell insurance or used cars. I wanted to be in the music business."

While attending Mercer University, Walden managed Otis Redding, whom he steered to the Memphis label Stax-Volt. Unfortunately, the 26-year-old was killed in a plane crash shortly before his *(Sittin' On) The Dock of the Bay* was released to national acclaim.

Walden also managed Sam and Dave, Al Green and Percy Sledge before he discovered a session guitarist named Duane Allman. After conferring with Atlantic Records chief Jerry Wexler, Walden and his younger brother Alan formed Capricorn Records under Atlantic's auspices and signed the Allman Brothers Band. The band's debut album only sold 33,000 records, but its live double album *At Fillmore East* was a commercial and critical success in 1971.

Walden continued to build his Capricorn empire during the 1970s, signing the Marshall Tucker Band, the Charlie Daniels Band, Elvin Bishop, Delbert McClinton and the Dixie Dregs. He built a recording studio and acquired real estate holdings, a white Rolls Royce, a Picasso painting and other accoutrements of success.

Capricorn's annual barbecue-and-beer picnic became the social event of the year for Southern rockers. Govenor Jimmy Carter even "made the scene" in the early '70s, Walden being an early backer of his successful 1976 presidential campaign.

"I had never been exposed to something that raw in my life," he later told biographical writers. "When I heard (Little Richard's) 'Wop bop a lubop a lop bam boom,' I knew I didn't want to sell insurance or used cars."

In an interview with Country Music Television's *American Revolutions: Southern Rock*, Walden explained the significance of Capricorn records' artists. "For the first time in rock, Southern guys were making the music and living in the South. They were making music in their own environment. This was really an expression of their region, their environment, their culture," he said.

In the late '70s, the economy dipped, disco overtook rock music in popularity, and the Allman Brothers band began a legal fight with Walden over unpaid royalties. Those factors, as well as Walden's drug and alcohol problems, plunged Capricorn Records into bankruptcy in 1980.

Walden moved to Nashville and managed the careers of actors Jim Varney and Billy Bob Thornton before reviving the *Capricorn* label in 1991. Once again, he played star-maker to Widespread Panic, Kenny Chesney and Cake before selling the business in 2000. Even as he fought cancer, Walden and his children, Philip Jr. and Amantha, founded a new record label, Velocette.

Walden died of cancer on April 23, 2006. "He was a brilliantly talented, instinctive music man who lived a wild life," Joe Smith, former president of Warner Bros. Records, told the *Los Angeles Times*. ∎

WATERFRONT SKYLINE *in Savannah, Georgia.*

NORTHERN Georgia

NORTH GEORGIA IS ONE OF THE most scenic parts of a beautiful state. Its charming towns lie in the valleys of the misty Blue Ridge Mountains between rushing rivers. In autumn, the splendor of the blazing foliage rivals any in the country. No wonder the Cherokee, whose native home this land is, called the area The Great Blue Hills of God.

This country is a mecca to those who enjoy hiking, horseback riding, rafting and fishing. Some may simply want to enjoy the beauty of the waterfalls, rivers and gentle old peaks. One of the most spectacular sights is the Tallulah Gorge that runs for 2 miles and is 1000 feet deep. The gorge was cut by the Tallulah River which boasts 6 waterfalls, the largest of which is Hurricane Falls, over 96 feet tall.

Atlanta and its neighboring cities are a huge metropolitan area that offer delights for visitors and residents alike. Once the site of a Creek village named Standing Peachtree, Atlanta is now one of the most culturally diverse cities in the country while losing none of its Southern charm. There is something for everyone.

The city has its own symphony and ballet, opera and theater companies. Touring shows visit the historic Fox Theatre. Art enthusiasts are captivated by the treasures housed in the renowned High Museum of Art, the Museum of Design Atlanta, unique in the southeast, the Atlanta Contemporary Art Center or the Museum of Contemporary Art of Georgia.

The Atlanta Botanic Garden features the Kendeda Canopy Walk that allows guests to view the last urban forest in the area from a height of 40 feet. The Atlanta Aquarium is the largest indoor aquarium in the world. The Fernbank Museum of Natural History and the Atlanta Zoo provide more entertainment.

The Martin Luther King, Jr. National Historic Site, the Atlanta Cyclorama and Civil War Museum, the Margaret Mitchell home and the World of Coca-Cola are all on tap.

Atlanta is home to many educational institutions including the Georgia Institute of Technology, Morehouse, Spelmen and Emory. A visit is not complete without a hot dog at the famous Varsity, the world's largest drive-in restaurant, near the Georgia Tech campus.

There are three professional sport teams, the Braves, the Hawks and the Falcons. For complete relaxation, 6 Flags over Atlanta provides fun and thrills and the famous Stone Mountain Park is nearby. Carved into the side of the huge granite mountain, Jefferson Davis, Stonewall Jackson and Robert E. Lee overlook the fun below.

Whether to a week-end visitor or a life-long resident, Northern Georgia offers friendly people, natural beauty, sporting opportunities and creative inspiration and one of the most thriving metropolitan areas in the country. ▶

Vigorous **ATLANTA** *shows its serene side when reflected in Lake Meer. Photo by Sean Pavone.*

The Watson Mill COVERED BRIDGE, *built in 1885 and 229 feet long,*
spans the South Fork River near Comer, Georgia. Photo by Sean Pavone.

Jefferson Davis, Robert E. Lee and Stonewall Jackson overlook a fireworks display at STONE MOUNTAIN, *Georgia. Photo by Christopher Meder.*

Historic ATHENS *is a thriving modern community in an antique setting. Photo by Sean Pavone.*

Profiles of Distinction

A look at the corporations, businesses and community service organizations that helped make this book possible. These forward-thinking companies and organizations are at the forefront of moving the state into a prosperous future.

Aesthetic Dentistry of Atlanta

Alpharetta Convention and Visitors Bureau

Arnall Golden Gregory, LLP

Ashton Woods Homes

Atlanta Center for Cosmetic Dentistry

Atlanta Dermatology & Laser Surgery

Atlanta Falcons

Atlanta Fine Homes Sotheby's International Realty

Atlanta Gastroenterology Associates

Atlanta Girls' School

Atlanta International School

Barnsley Gardens Resort

Bartow History Museum

Booth Western Art Museum

Brandon Hall School

Brasstown Valley Resort and Spa

Buckhead Coalition

Buckhead Dental Partners

Buckhead Facial Plastic Surgery

Buckhead Plastic Surgery

Campbell-Stone

Cancer Treatment Centers of America

Cartersville-Bartow Convention & Visitors Bureau

Coldwell Banker Residential Brokerage Atlanta

Community & Southern Bank

Cooper Carry

DeKalb Convention & Visitors Bureau

Dermatology Affiliates

Dorsey Alston, Realtors®

Douglasville Convention and Visitors Bureau

Dunson Dental Design

City of Dunwoody

Ellis Hotel

Embassy Suites-Atlanta

Fernbank Museum of Natural History

Georgia Commerce Bank

Georgia Dental Implant Center

Georgia Dept. of Economic Development, Explore Georgia

Georgia State Parks, Dept. of Natural Resources

Georgia's Rome

Goldstein, Garber and Salama LLC

Hartsfield-Jackson Atlanta International Airport

ISIS OB/GYN Alpharetta

Johns Creek

Moore Colson

Oculus Plastic Surgery

Plastikos Plastic and Reconstructive Surgery

Point University

Porter Keadle Moore, LLC

Riverside Military Academy

Rogers & Hardin LLP

Roswell Business Alliance

Roswell Convention & Visitors Bureau

Sandy Springs Hospitality & Tourism

Spa Sydell

Swift, Currie, McGhee & Hiers, LLP

Tellus Science Museum

University of West Georgia

Weissman, Nowack, Curry & Wilco

Wesley Woods

Woodward Academy

LAKE SIDNEY LANIER *is a 59 square mile reservoir created in 1956 that offers recreational facilities to several million visitors a year.*

$\mathcal{A}$esthetic Dentistry of Atlanta
Atlanta Dental Spa

Atlanta Dental Spa provides its patients with dazzling smiles while finding the time to perform a great deal of charitable service. In fact, the practice's entire team thrives on giving back to the community—it's part of their passion for helping people.

CARING, PAMPERING ENVIRONMENT

Atlanta Dental Spa is a comprehensive dental practice that performs general and cosmetic procedures; everything from general cleanings, teeth whitening and porcelain fillings and crowns to complete smile makeovers, porcelain veneers, dental implants and full-mouth reconstructions.

"What if you actually liked going to the dentist?", was the thought behind the practice's establishment. With spa-like offices in Buckhead and Roswell, Atlanta Dental Spa provides a relaxing respite from hectic, modern life. Each patient is offered unprecedented, customized service not usually found in today's fast-paced medical environment. Patients are treated as unique individuals instead of clients to be rushed through a factory-line.

"I get so many compliments on my smile and that makes me smile," said Dolvett Quince, the new trainer on NBC's *The Biggest Loser* and a patient of the practice.

COMMITTED TO EDUCATION, OVERALL HEALTH

Dr. Peter Boulden and Dr. Susan Estep have received fellowships to the Academy of General Dentistry, proving that they have completed 500 hours of approved continuing education and passed a rigorous dentistry exam. They also are two of only three Georgians who are Fellows of the Academy of Comprehensive Esthetics, which evaluates professionals who are committed to clinical excellence, advanced learning and attention to detail.

In addition, Drs. Estep and Boulden are founding members of the American Academy of Oral Systemic Health, whose members strive to provide the highest care as it pertains to total wellness. Since science has confirmed that overall health is linked to the health of a person's gums and mouth, the Atlanta Dental Spa is committed to improving their patients' lives by educating them about this systemic link. The practice provides a number of screenings and services that can potentially identify and/or treat some underlying causes of poor oral health.

CHARITABLE FOUNDATION ESTABLISHED

Drs. Peter Boulden and Susan G. Estep founded Atlanta Dental Spa in 2005. Since its inception, the full-service practice has donated teeth-whitening certificates to charities that have helped them raise thousands of dollars. It also participates

Drs. Susan Estep and Peter Boulden are founders of Atlanta Dental Spa, which provides relaxing, customized service to patients in hopes that they will actually enjoy the experience!

in the American Academy of Cosmetic Dentistry's "Give Back a Smile" program, which offers smile improvements to domestic-abuse victims.

In 2011, Drs. Boulden and Estep founded their Reason to Smile Foundation, then launched a video contest on Facebook to find the person most deserving of a smile makeover. The winner was 50-year-old Carolyn DeFiore, a widow who received $50,000 worth of dental surgery and another $10,000 worth of skin, hair, makeup and wardrobe rejuvenation. "It's just incredible," DeFiore said afterwards. "I can't say 'thank you' enough."

Over the years, Atlanta Dental Spa's team members have raised money for breast-cancer research through Smile Pink, volunteered at the Good Samaritan Health Center and donated oral health gift bags to Cool Girls, Inc. They've run as a team to benefit CURE Childhood Cancer and bowled as a team to benefit the underprivileged.

Each Halloween, the dental practice buys back hundreds of pounds of candy from children that it then sends to U.S. troops overseas via Operation Gratitude. And, when patients refer a new patient to Atlanta Dental Spa, the practice donates $100 to the charity of their choice.

AWARD-WINNING DENTISTS

A native of Marietta, Dr. Boulden is a University of Virginia graduate who received his doctorate in Dental Medicine from the University of Kentucky. His work has received numerous honors, including "Best in Show" and 1st Place for Smile

Makeovers at the 2010 ACE Smile Design Competition held by the Academy of Comprehensive Esthetics. Dr. Boulden also has been voted by his peers to be among "Top Atlanta Dentists" by *Atlanta Magazine* every year since the award's inception.

Dr. Estep graduated with honors from Georgia Tech, then received her doctorate in Dental Medicine from the Medical College of Georgia. She has been voted among America's Top Cosmetic Dentists for five consecutive years as well as one of Atlanta's Top Cosmetic Dentists. Dr. Estep won six medals in the 2010 ACE Smile Design Competition and has been listed in Who's Who of America's Leading Female Professionals for nearly a decade.

Atlanta Dental Spa also benefits from the expertise Drs. Rich Creasman, Dana Brockington and Shannon Creasman, all of whom are graduates of the Medical College of Georgia and Dr. Andrew Currie who graduated from University of Louisville School of Dentistry and who completed a two year residency at Medical College of Georgia.

Drs. Boulden and Estep have assembled a highly skilled team of doctors that encompasses all fields of dentistry. We want our patients to receive complete care in an atmosphere that is relaxing, pampering and patient-centric. We can ensure that happens with our staff of highly expereinced doctors who boast of credentials similar to our own. In addition to delivering advances in general and cosmetic dentistry, we treat implant placements, wisdom teeth removal, cosmetic dentures, root canals and sedation. ∎

Atlanta Dental Spa's state-of-the-art offices are conveniently located in Buckhead and Alpharetta/ Roswell.

Atlanta Dental Spa's sterilization room and operating room.

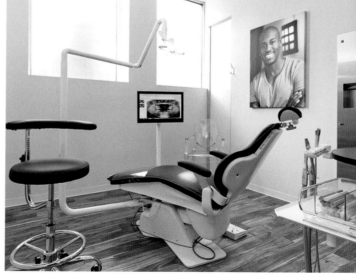

Alpharetta Convention and Visitors Bureau

Big city sophistication and hometown charm provide Alpharetta's over 59,000 residents with a unique quality of life while also making it a superb place for business. In fact, Forbes magazine has ranked the city number one among America's 25 Best Places to Move.

Verizon Wireless Amphitheatre, 12,000 seat state-of-the-art outdoor performance venue.

Walk of Memories, which pays tribute to all Georgia veterans.

"Our city is made up of value-based, no-excuses, get-it-done individuals," Mayor David Belle Isle said. "We are a city of doers, family oriented and community centered. Here, accomplishment, achievement and excellence are still celebrated. Faith is still revered."

Incorporated in 1858, the village in North Fulton County was originally a trading post where white settlers and Cherokee Indians exchanged goods. Today, more than 3,600 businesses —from corporate campuses of global leaders to small, family-owned shops—enjoy the Alpharetta advantage. This energetic city is located about 22 miles north of downtown Atlanta and just minutes further from Hartsfield-Jackson Atlanta International Airport.

GREAT FOOD, LUXURY HOTELS

"In Alpharetta, you can have it all—location, demographics and a proven track record of successful business development and investment opportunities," said Janet Rodgers, President and CEO of the Alpharetta Convention & Visitors Bureau. "The community has a thriving culinary scene, luxury hotel accommodations and endless shopping opportunities. Alpharetta is a true live, work, play and visit community."

World-class shopping can be found at North Point Mall, including one of only two American Girl Boutiques and Bistros in the Southeast. Alpharetta is also home to the Motorcycle Safety Foundation training campus, where private and group lessons are offered in dirt bike, street bike and ATV driving. Sport and nature lovers enjoy more than 750 acres of award-winning parkland as well as the eight-mile Big Creek Greenway for hiking, biking and inline skating which connects to a mountain bike trail, and the Walk of Memories, which pays tribute to U.S. veterans commemorated by nearly 8,000 bricks.

Alpharetta's American Girl Boutique and Bistro

TECHNOLOGY JOBS ABOUND

"We have become the Technology City of the South, hosting more than 900 technology companies and the most technology jobs per capita in the Southeast," Belle Isle said. "We boast the lowest unemployment rate and remain one of only two AAA bond-rated cities in Georgia. We are a small town, yet we rank seventh in total number of jobs within the state."

A new city center development project is underway downtown which will include a new city hall, library and park with planned retail, dining and luxury living spaces. The center is scheduled to open in the summer of 2014.

Enjoy concerts? Alpharetta is home to the state-of-the-art Verizon Wireless Amphitheatre at Encore Park, a 12,000-seat venue that presents today's leading entertainers and the Grammy-winning Atlanta Symphony Orchestra.

AWARD-WINNING CITY

Alpharetta has been honored with numerous awards. It's a Tree City USA; a Certified Green Community, Gold Level; a City of Excellence and a certified City of Ethics. Its family-friendly events, such as the Alpharetta Arts StreetFest and Taste of Alpharetta, have been ranked among the Southeast Tourism Society's Top 20 Events.

"Our people are great, our city is blessed and our future is bright," Belle Isle said. "This is why Alpharetta shines." ∎

Arnall Golden Gregory, LLP

Based in Atlanta with offices in Miami and Washington, D.C., Arnall Golden Gregory (AGG) is a law firm dedicated to helping clients from a broad range of industries turn legal challenges into business opportunities. Living up to the motto, "Not if, but how," AGG attorneys work with public and private companies to optimize business growth.

MORE THAN SIX DECADES OF LOOKING FORWARD

AGG was founded in 1949 in Atlanta by Ellis Arnall, a former Georgia governor and attorney general, Sol Golden and Cleburne Gregory. Often described as the "father of modern Georgia," Arnall made sweeping changes to the state after being elected governor when he was just 35. He created a merit system for state employees, removed the university system from the direct influence of the governor, abolished the poll tax, reformed the state's penal system, lowered the voting age to 18 (making Georgia the first state to do so), and busted the so-called "Northern railroad conspiracy" of discriminatory railroad freight rates, which had hampered the South's industrial development and eliminated the state's all-white primaries. Arnall also paid off a state debt of $36 million and left office with a balanced state budget.

Sol Golden practiced law for 23 years before joining Arnall Golden Gregory and earned a reputation for developing innovative financing techniques for his clients. Cleburne Gregory, described as a "lawyer's lawyer," had been Arnall's right-hand when Arnall served as attorney general.

"AGG has grown from that solid foundation to more than 150 lawyers dedicated to the founders' philosophy of practicing in a collegial environment grounded in strong client relationships and sound business and professional practices," explained AGG Managing Partner Glenn Hendrix. "Many of the client relationships fostered by our founders still thrive today."

THREE GATEWAY CITIES PROVIDE GLOBAL REACH

AGG established a Washington, D.C., office in January 2011 to better meet client regulatory needs. In January 2012, AGG opened its Miami office to serve global logistics, supply chain, healthcare and real estate clients, and expand the firm's international arbitration practice.

GIVING BACK TO ATLANTA

Committed to being a positive force in the community, AGG's attorneys give their time to organizations and pro bono activities. In recent years AGG has received the Philip Heiner Award from the Atlanta Bar Association for its pro bono work, the Philanthropy Award from the *Atlanta Business Chronicle* and the Break the Cycle Award from the Atlanta Volunteer Lawyers Foundation for the free help attorneys provided to domestic violence survivors.

GROWING IN A TOUGH ECONOMY

"We are one of the few large Atlanta firms that managed to grow during the Great Recession," Hendrix said. "AGG attorneys are routinely recognized in *Best Lawyers in America, Georgia Super Lawyers, Chambers Leading Lawyers for Business,* the *Georgia Trend's* 'Legal Elite' and many other lawyer ranking services."

BRIGHT FUTURE BASED ON BUSINESS SENSIBILITY

Hendrix says that AGG is focused on growing in areas in which the firm now holds, or potentially will hold, a leading market position: Bankruptcy, Creditors' Rights and Workout, Corporate, Global Logistics/Transportation, Healthcare/Life Sciences, Intellectual Property/Technology, Litigation, Privacy, Private Wealth and Real Estate.

Underpinning the growth strategy is AGG's "business sensibility:" Listen to the client, become an expert on the client's business and deliver proven results in a cost-effective manner. That's how partnerships that span generations are built. ■

Ellis Arnall, Sol I. Golden and Cleburne Gregory, Jr. founded the firm in 1949. Managing Partner Glenn Hendrix (right) says the firm follows the founders' philosophy of building client relationships through sound business and professional practices.

Photos by Zach Porter

Ashton Woods Homes

Ashton Woods Homes is one of the nation's top builders of exquisitely designed, energy-efficient houses that enhance their owners' quality of life. ■ *"The high standard of living in every Ashton Woods community comes from a combination of award-winning architecture, prime locations, close attention to materials and construction details*

and an unparalleled dedication to homeowner satisfaction," said Greg Huff, division president of Ashton Woods Homes - Atlanta. "We deliver superior houses that provide lasting value and exceed expectations."

QUALITY CRAFTSMANSHIP

Ashton Woods Homes is committed to the time-honored tradition of quality craftsmanship. Energy efficiency, improved airflow and tight, durable construction are an integral aspect of each house. And behind those walls stand nearly two decades of experience, pride in workmanship and a genuine respect for customers.

The PowerHouse Green with Environments for Living (EFL) program dramatically lowers energy costs and can save homeowners an average of 25 to 45 percent on their annual utility bills. Using only LENNOX comfort system products that have earned a Good Housekeeping Seal of Approval, the PowerHouses feature cleaner, more efficient heating, ventilating and air conditioning (HVAC) systems that easily control temperature and humidity levels for a comfortable, healthier environment.

Ashton Woods Homes builds beautifully designed, energy-efficient houses in prime locations around the Atlanta area.

ENERGY STAR STANDARDS EXCEEDED

These single-family houses and townhouses exceed the Environmental Protection Agency's Energy Star™ standards. In fact, Ashton Woods Homes was recognized with a 2012 Energy Star™ Leadership in Housing Award for building houses that collectively will save its customers approximately $424,203 on utility bills annually. These environmental benefits are equivalent to eliminating the emissions from 465 vehicles, not burning 2,812,836 pounds of coal, planting 769 acres of trees or reducing 5,516,537 pounds of carbon dioxide from the atmosphere each year!

More than 20 Ashton Woods Homes communities exist in the Atlanta area and all have great locations. "When we choose locations for our new communities, we only consider those in close proximity to fundamental services that meet the demands of today's lifestyles," Huff said. "Quality school districts, shopping, recreational amenities, arts and entertainment, health facilities, places of worship, highways and public transportation—all are important, and all are factored into our decision-making process."

Some of the Atlanta communities are surrounded by acres of parkland, walking trails and natural green space, while others have an upbeat, urban ambience. Many of them include clubhouses, playgrounds and swimming pools.

SIMPLIFIED BUYING PROCESS

Ashton Woods Homes believes that good service is good business, which is why it makes the home-buying process as

simple as possible. Knowledgeable sales counselors guide buyers each step of the way, while financing is available through Ashton Woods Mortgage for one-stop shopping.

Experienced interior designers at the 12,000 square-foot design studio in Roswell help buyers personalize décor to make the new house uniquely theirs. Many pleasurable hours can be spent choosing paint colors, lighting fixtures, ceiling fans and skylights, flooring, fireplaces, built-ins, plumbing and electrical fixtures…even a dream kitchen!

Service also includes a guided pre-closing orientation and inspection with the sales counselor and builder and a Homeowner's Guide to familiarize the buyer with the new house.

Ashton Woods Homes has developed a 1-5-11 Customer Care Program to ensure total satisfaction. A representative contacts the buyers after the first, fifth and eleventh months in their new house to address any warranty concerns that might arise. The company also offers a comprehensive one-, two- and 10-year warranty that is transferrable if the house is sold.

MANY SATISFIED CUSTOMERS

Not surprisingly, Ashton Woods Homes customers consistently express tremendous satisfaction with their experience.

John and Jan Sandvig, who live at the Villages at Concord Farms in Cumming, wrote Huff to praise their entire Ashton Woods Home team. "We met with our builder, Reagan Anderson, several times while our home was under construction…What always struck us was his quiet, attentive listening and his 'can do' attitude. Reagan always had a positive solution to all of our requests….He made us feel confident that we were getting a superior product."

Kanthi Vinayagasundaram, of Kendrix Park in Alpharetta, lauded the outstanding service delivered by his sales representative. "His professional and courteous attitude, expertise and patience in handling my specific questions were very important to my complete customer satisfaction," he wrote. ∎

Atlanta Center for Cosmetic Dentistry

The Atlanta Center for Cosmetic Dentistry is recognized worldwide as a leader in creating beautiful smiles and it does so in a luxurious, uniquely Southern facility that has clients looking forward to their spa-like visits. ■ *The smell of freshly baked cookies greets patients when they enter the columned, mansion-like building on Roswell Road in the*

Chastain Park area. The upscale reception area looks more like a large comfortable living room than a dental office and includes a refreshment bar, Internet access and a flat-screen television. Aromatherapy and massage therapy also help patients feel more comfortable, as do the "dental concierges" who have been trained in client relations by the Ritz-Carlton Leadership Center.

Dr. Debra Gray King established the Atlanta Center for Cosmetic Dentistry in 1987 and has since changed the lives of thousands of people by improving their smiles and boosting their confidence. To do so, she uses porcelain veneers, cosmetic bonding, whitening and full-mouth reconstruction, creating dramatic results. A pioneer in the art of challenging aesthetic cases such as Instant Orthodontics and Scalpel-less Facelifts, Dr. King also strives to create a comfortable environment for her clients, making them feel more like they are at the spa than a dental office.

As a result, Dr. King has patients travel to see her from around the world and has treated a long list of celebrities. "I didn't like going to the dentist before: the anxiety and the

The upscale reception area makes patients feel as if they're at home. It includes a refreshment bar, internet access and a flat-screen television.

drilling," said Angela Karatassos, a prominent Atlanta philanthropist and model. "Now I cannot imagine going to another dentist. It is a great experience."

DENTAL ZEN

In the treatment areas, patients recline in "Dental Zen chairs," invented by the center, that send soothing sound waves from head to toes. As their dental work is performed, patients are treated to hand, arm and neck massages, warm neck pillows and cozy blankets. Noise-cancelling headphones and flat screen TVs are great to escape into a movie while getting treatment done. "I'm still waiting for a guy to treat me that good," local disc jockey Monte Carlo, who underwent gum surgery, enthused to The Wall Street Journal about her experience.

INDIVIDUALIZED SMILE DESIGNS

The relaxing experience is matched by dental artistry rarely found elsewhere. "We primarily perform Smile Designs," Dr. King said. "A Smile Design requires great skill and knowledge to achieve a natural result. Techniques require precise measure-

ments based upon mouth shape, gum lines, lips and natural shape of the teeth. That's why we devote time to precisely planning a Smile Design before we begin the actual procedure."

Patients receive Smile Designs to fit their age, gender and facial features. Porcelain veneers then are permanently bonded to the front surface of the teeth to improve or restore their position, shape and color. "Many people don't realize that the shape of veneers, combined with occlusal adjustments such as opening the bite, can also have profound impact on the entire face," Dr. King said. "This can result in giving the appearance of a facelift or elimination of wrinkles without any plastic surgery."

INTERNATIONALLY RECOGNIZED EXPERTISE

Dr. King is one of the world's few dentists to limit her practice to full-time cosmetic dentistry and be an Accredited Fellow in the American Academy of Cosmetic Dentistry, which is considered the highest level of competence in cosmetic dentistry. Featured as an expert cosmetic dentist on ABC's "Extreme Makeover," Dr. King is a graduate of the University of Tennessee at Memphis Dental School and post-graduate programs at the Pankey Institute, the Pacific Aesthetic Continuum (PAC-Live) at the University of the Pacific in San Francisco, The Hornbrook Group and the Las Vegas Institute for Advanced Dental Studies. She has lectured extensively at educational seminars around the world and is currently a clinical instructor of full-mouth reconstruction with the Aesthetic Masters program.

She has been featured by *CNN, The Wall Street Journal, Time Magazine, Fox News, CBS, WebMD, Entertainment Tonight, The Doctors, InStyle, Vogue, Glamour, USA Today, Bloomberg* and UK's *The Guardian.* A leading trade publication, *Dental Products Report*, named Dr. King one of the Top 25 Women in Dentistry for 2011. Johnson & Johnson selected Dr. King as a national spokesperson for Listerine for 2010-2011. The Atlanta Center for Cosmetic Dentistry's team includes Drs. Charles C. Cooper Jr., Louisa Berman and Ronald A. Feinman. For more information, visit www.atlantacenterfor-cosmeticdentistry.com. ∎

Dr. Debra Gray King founded the practice in 1987, and has since changed the lives of thousands of patients by improving their smiles and boosting their self-confidence.

It's always a Super Moon over Cartersville's LAKE ALLATOONA *— the oldest U.S. Army Corps of Engineers lake in the nation and one of the most popular. Photograph courtesy Cartersville-Bartow County Convention & Visitors Bureau and Greg Mcary.*

Atlanta Dermatology & Laser Surgery

Atlanta Dermatology & Laser Surgery is a full-service practice that offers state of the art dermatologic and cosmetic procedures. In addition to treating all skin, hair and nail diseases, the practice specializes in cosmetic treatments that make patients look healthier and more youthful.

Dr. Jerry L. Cooper's personal touch has kept many loyal clients coming back to him for more than 40 years. "I take good care of my patients and make them happy," the board-certified doctor said. "I build personal relationships with my patients. I don't run people through."

The staff's customer service is also special. "When you call my office, a real person answers the phone," Dr. Cooper said. "There's no 'push line one' or "push line two" and a recording that continuously loops. I don't think that is good customer service."

MOHS SURGICAL SPECIALIST

On the dermatology side of the practice, Dr. Cooper specializes in Mohs micrographic surgery for removal of skin cancer. Experts say this precision technique offers maximum removal of cancer with minimum damage to surrounding healthy tissue.

Many acne patients can benefit from the latest scientific advances, such as blue light therapy designed to kill acne-causing bacteria, microdermabrasion with and without vitamin C; and photothermolysis laser treatments.

Dr. Cooper also specializes in treating psoriasis, an autoimmune disease characterized by reddish, scaly skin. Light therapy and UVB phototherapy are some of the latest treatments that have proven helpful in alleviating this unsightly skin disorder. "Biologicals are a tremendous advancement in the treatment of psoriasis and can clear most of the very severe cases," he said.

COOLSCULPTING, EXILIS AVAILABLE FOR BODY SCULPTING

The new exciting cosmetic procedures offered by Atlanta Dermatology & Laser Surgery include CoolSculpting®, a non-invasive FDA-approved procedure that eliminates fat cells without damage to neighboring skin; Exilis, a device that uses safe radio waves to heat fat cells, causing them to shrink while at the same time stimulating collagen production; and laser skin resurfacing, which eliminates fine lines and plumps the skin. And, of course, the practice offers Botox®, Radiesse™, Restylane®, Juvederm® and other fillers to help patients maintain a youthful appearance.

Linda Jones, a former Atlanta Falcons cheerleader, has been a patient for more than 30 years. "I would not consider seeing anyone else," she said. "Dr. Cooper is calm, patient and doesn't do anything that isn't necessary, unlike some other doctors."

"My skin is just beautiful," said Jones, who underwent fractional skin resurfacing to remove sun damage. "It's just the difference between night and day."

EXPERT DERMATOLOGICAL CARE

Dr. Cooper graduated from Ohio State University's School of Medicine and served his residency at Henry Ford Hospital in Detroit. Afterwards, he served with the U.S. Army as chief of the dermatology department at Fort Campbell, KY. Dr. Cooper is affiliated with Emory University, Northside Hospital and DeKalb Medical Center. He has been named one of America's Top Physicians in 2003-2005 and Atlanta's Top Doc in 1999, among other awards for his expertise in dermatology.

Dr. Dionne D. Louis, who also is board certified, joined the practice in September 2011. After receiving her bachelor's degree from Spelman College, she earned a doctorate of medicine from the Morehouse School of Medicine. She served a residency in pediatrics at Children's Hospital of Philadelphia and a residency in dermatology at the University of Oklahoma Health Sciences Center. Dr. Louis specializes in pediatric dermatology along with skin cancer, dermatologic surgery, ethnic skin, hair disorders and cosmetic procedures for all racial skin types. ■

VISIT ATLANTA DERMATOLOGY & LASER SURGERY ONLINE: www.atlantadermatologyexperts.com

In 2012, the Atlanta Falcons were flying high, having posted four consecutive winning seasons for the first time in the team's history. They also soar above other National Football League teams in terms of volunteerism and community commitment. ■ *Those two goals are reflected in the Falcons' award-winning "Rise Up!" marketing campaign, begun*

in 2010. "What do Falcons do? They rise up!" Samuel L. Jackson intoned in the first emotionally charged commercial, backed by a gospel choir. "This is our time, Atlanta!"

"The idea is simple," said Falcons president and chief executive officer Rich McKay. "In addition to wanting our fans to help us become the best team in the NFL on the field, we want our fans to Rise Up and volunteer their time and talents throughout the year in an effort to make our great community a better place to live."

PARTNER WITH HANDS ON ATLANTA
The team has partnered with Hands on Atlanta and the City of Atlanta to encourage and organize volunteer opportunities across the city. In May 2012, more than 180 associates from the Atlanta Falcons, Atlanta Falcons Physical Therapy Centers, PGA TOUR Superstores, AMB Group and The Arthur M. Blank Family Foundation—collectively known as the Blank Family of Businesses—participated in a community day of service aiding the City of Refuge, a non-profit agency serving homeless women and children in the inner city.

A month later, nearly 2,500 citizens had committed their time and service after choosing a local volunteer opportunity on the RiseUpAtlanta.com website.

FIGHTING CHILD OBESITY
The Atlanta Falcons are also committed to a fitness initiative to help combat child obesity. The "First Down for Fitness" project, now in its sixth year, challenges students in grades three through seven to participate in physical fitness activities and lead healthy lifestyles. The incentive-based program, in which nearly 50,000 students have participated, rewards participants for being active at least 60 minutes a day, five days a week for three months.

The Atlanta Falcons Youth Foundation has provided more than $18 million in grants to more than 800 non-profit groups, mainly to combat obesity and improve youth fitness.

All 53 players—an NFL record—participate each year with

several Falcons cheerleaders and members of the Atlanta Falcons Women's Association in the NFL's "Hometown Huddle," making surprise appearances at United Way-affiliated schools to deliver new sports equipment and promote physical fitness.

NFL RECORD FOR COMMUNITY WORK
The Falcons perform so much charitable work that it's a wonder they have time to play football! The team also participates in "Dazzle and Dine" to honor breast-cancer survivors, hosts an annual food drive, supports Toys for Tots and conducts Gatorade Junior Training Camps in schools and parks. The players have participated in more than 425 appearances this season, logging more than 3,500 hours around the state.

"We're very proud that our players, in the last four years, have led the league in community appearances," said Jim Smith, Senior Vice President of Sales and Marketing. "Giving back to the Atlanta area is one of our organization's core values." ■

(Top) Former Atlanta Falcons linebacker Coy Wire participates in fitness stations with students at Camp Creek Middle School as a part of the NFL Keep Gym in School program.

(Bottom left) Atlanta Falcons players prepare and serve Thanksgiving meals to the homeless at Crossroads Community Ministries in Atlanta, GA.

(Bottom right) In a continuing effort to tackle youth obesity, Atlanta Falcons players, cheerleaders and students set the Guinness World Record for Largest Virtual Physical Education Class on December 7, 2010 with nearly 2,288 Atlanta area kids. Along with the event at the Georgia Dome, over 5,700 people participated through a live webcast from home, work or school.

Atlanta Fine Homes Sotheby's International Realty

Atlanta Fine Homes Sotheby's International Realty is unique in the Atlanta marketplace as it is the only upper-tier residential brokerage that is owned and managed locally while also having the prestigious global reach of Sotheby's International Realty Affiliates, LLC. In addition, it provides a true entrepreneurial environment in which sales associates can reach their full potential.

"We are passionate in our interactions with clients, associates and employees, as well as in the delivery of our services," said Jenny Pruitt, CEO and Founder. "Not only is the real estate experience of our team unparalleled, but the client's experience in working with our company is second to none."

EXTRAORDINARY MARKETING

The company's exclusive affiliation with Sotheby's International Realty means the agents of Atlanta Fine Homes Sotheby's International Realty can connect qualified buyers and sellers both locally and globally. Marketing efforts include advertisements in *The Wall Street Journal*, *New York Times*, the *International Herald-Tribune*, the *South China Morning Post*, *Financial Times* and the British Broadcasting Company. "We really leave no stone unturned when it comes to uncovering that potential buyer," Pruitt said.

Pruitt, an icon in Atlanta real estate, established Jenny Pruitt & Associates, REALTORS® in 1988 and directed its growth to annual sales of over $1.5 billion, six metropolitan offices and more than 450 agents. The firm eventually was bought by Berkshire Hathaway's subsidiary Home Services of America and Pruitt retired after fulfilling her contract.

Having realized the importance of an Atlanta-based, privately owned residential firm that provides exceptional service and maintains long-term relationships with clients, she and David Boehmig founded Atlanta Fine Homes Sotheby's International Realty in 2007. Five years later, the company has grown to employ 190 agents who use cutting-edge technology to serve their clients.

AGENTS RECEIVE STRONG SUPPORT

"I love working here," Ann Hopkins said. "Not only because of the international brand, but there is such a feeling of support."

Nancy See, Senior Vice President and Managing Broker, concurred. "The agents in the field

love the energy and excitement in this office," she said. "It really is unlike anything I have known before."

Though best known for its high-end properties, Atlanta Fine Homes Sotheby's International Realty provides million-dollar marketing for all price ranges. Its three offices are conveniently located in Intown, Buckhead and North Atlanta.

"We like to say at our company that the global brand + extraordinary agents + distinguished connections = market-leading results," Pruitt said.

ENCOURAGING HOUSING SIGNS

After the downturn in the market, Boehmig is now seeing encouraging signs in the metro Atlanta market. In his winter 2012 update, he noted that, in the most recent quarter, the inventory of available houses for sale was down 27 percent while the number of houses that closed or were under contract rose 17 percent. He attributed the positive signals to low interest rates and properly priced homes. ■

Jenny Pruitt founded Atlanta Fine Homes Sotheby's International Realty to provide exceptional service to qualified buyers and sellers throughout the world for some of Atlanta's highest-end properties.

Atlanta Gastroenterology Associates

Atlanta Gastroenterology Associates (AGA) has been treating patients suffering from digestive and liver diseases for more than 35 years. Ranked as one of the largest gastroenterology practices in the country, Atlanta Gastroenterology has over 30 locations in Atlanta and north Georgia. This gives patients convenient access to the best possible medical care from physicians who are highly skilled at evaluating and treating every type of GI issue—

from common stomach problems to the most complicated gastrointestinal ailments, as well as colon cancer screenings. AGA also operates seven state-of-the-art Endoscopy Centers, where most outpatient procedures are performed.

"Our goal has always been to provide our patients with the most appropriate and cost-effective health care available in locations that are convenient to them," said Dr. Steven J. Morris,

Named as one of Atlanta's 'Top Docs' for the third year in a row, Dr. Norman Elliott was also honored in 2012 for 20 years of service as a team physician for the Atlanta Braves.

Managing Partner. "We are committed to seeing every patient, whether privately insured, on Medicare or Medicaid, or self-pay. In fact," Dr. Morris added, "we have special programs for self-pay patients that make care as affordable as possible. We also have an indigent care program that includes colon cancer screenings since we believe everyone should have such screenings at the appropriate times and intervals."

SPECIAL SERVICES FOR TOTAL PATIENT CARE

Sometimes a patient's digestive issues are symptomatic of a more serious, underlying condition. In addition to general clinical care and preventive screenings, Atlanta Gastroenterology Associates' physicians use a variety of outpatient tests and procedures to more accurately diagnose and treat these conditions and many are performed through one of the practice's specialized centers of care.

Center for Crohn's Disease & Ulcerative Colitis: For patients who suffer from chronic inflammatory bowel disease, this center offers expert diagnosis, on-going evaluation and personalized treatment plans to medically suppress symptoms.

Southeastern Center for Functional GI & Motility Disorders: This center offers evaluation and treatment of patients with various motility disorders, such as difficulty swallowing, GERD, IBS, and delayed gastric emptying.

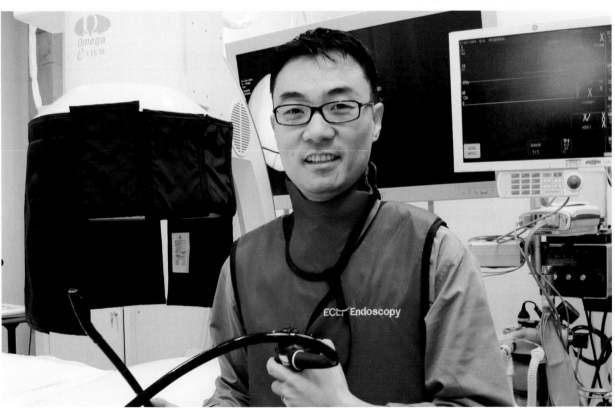

The high-tech equipment used in advanced therapeutic procedures allows Dr. John Suh to uncover hidden GI problems, resulting in more accurate diagnoses and better treatment plans.

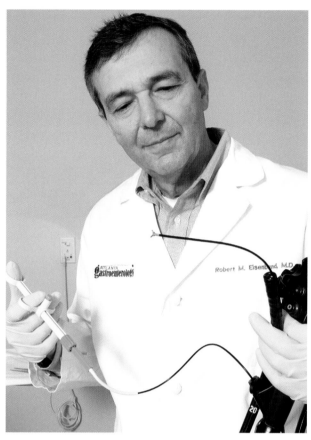

Advanced Center for GI Therapeutics: For patients with pancreatic or biliary disease, Barrett's esophagus and other chronic digestive disorders, specially trained physicians perform advanced endoscopic procedures using the latest tools and technology to make more accurate diagnoses and create comprehensive treatment plans.

The Hemorrhoid Clinic: Non-surgical, pain-free hemorrhoid banding treatments are performed by physicians trained in using the CRH O'Regan Hemorrhoid Removal System.

The Liver Center: Directed by renowned hepatologists, this center offers expert evaluation and treatment for patients with all types of hepatitis and liver disease, as well as liver biopsies and assessment for transplantation.

Center for GI Imaging: For patients who need additional evaluation of the GI tract, the Center offers non-invasive imaging procedures, including CT (computed tomography) scans, CT angiography and CT enterography, as well as abdominal ultrasound services and bone density scans.

Infusion Services: For patients with autoimmune disorders such as Crohn's disease and ulcerative colitis, AGA offers infusion therapy treatment.

Nutrition Counseling: Educational nutrition services and dietary recommendations are provided by a licensed, registered dietitian for patients with chronic GI conditions such as celiac disease, gastroparesis, GERD, IBS, and Crohn's disease.

By providing access to the most comprehensive GI care in Atlanta and Georgia, Atlanta Gastroenterology Associates continues to lead the way in caring for patients. ■

(Top left) Colon cancer is one of the few cancers that, when detected in its early stages, is highly preventable and curable. Here, Dr. Robert Eisenband, prepares to perform a screening colonoscopy, to find and remove any abnormal growths or polyps that may become cancerous.

(Top right) The instruments used in the hemorrhoid banding process are designed to provide gentle, pain-free removal.

(Middle) In addition to her GI practice, Dr. Kavita Kongara serves as Medical Director of AGA's Southeastern Center for Functional GI & Motility Disorders.

Respected by his peers as a leader in innovative practice management, AGA's Managing Partner, Dr. Steven J. Morris, lists among his career achievements being named one of the country's leading gastro-enterologists by Becker's ASC Review and as one of Atlanta's healthcare leaders by *Business to Business* magazine.

Atlanta Girls' School

In August 2000, Atlanta Girls' School opened its doors to roughly 100 students. The school graduated its ninth class in 2012, continuing the great heritage of girls' schools that provide the highest quality college preparatory education. Without the vision and tenacity of its founders, AGS would not be here today providing an all important educational alternative in Atlanta.

Founded in 2000, Atlanta Girls' School (AGS) is an independent college preparatory school. AGS offers a challenging educational program designed to instill strength of character as well as the knowledge and skills its students need as they chart their course to college and in the world. The student body mirrors the diversity of Atlanta with girls from virtually all socio-economic, racial, religious and cultural backgrounds.

CAMPUS AND PROGRAMS

AGS offers a strong academic program where classes are taught using the methodologies most successful for girls' learning. Courses are supplemented by independent study and online offerings suited to each girl's needs. In addition to Honors and AP courses, students in the Upper School have the opportunity to participate in an advanced course strand focused on science, technology, engineering and math. Beginning in the second semester of eighth grade, every student and her family regularly participates in individualized college planning and educational career goal setting.

The Atlanta Girls' School is committed to helping girls and young women develop their fullest potential intellectually, physically, socially, emotionally, and spiritually.

AGS is constantly focused on innovative programs. As one of the first one-to-one lap top schools in the country and an

early user of tablets and hand-held electronic devices for learning, every class integrates technology into its daily routines. In addition, the "Winterim" session provides students with the opportunity to explore nontraditional interests such as backpacking, creative writing, Bob Dylan or the history of Broadway, expanding awareness of the world and helping students identify potential lifetime passions.

AGS has adapted its physical space to help girls learn and thrive. Whether it is the building-wide wireless environment, the Upper School patio where girls work, eat and meet, or the gallery that displays a rotating collection of student and faculty art, AGS's campus space enables students to interact with one another in a way that promotes learning and strong friendships.

BEYOND THE CLASSROOM

AGS's commitment to academic excellence is enhanced by its equal commitment to developing other key aspects of its students. Through the signature Education for the Development of Leadership and Service (EDLS) program, girls learn about themselves, their interaction with others, their role in a community and how to serve and transform the world around them. The program builds to internships in the eleventh and twelfth grades where girls work in one or more settings that range from clinics, laboratories and libraries to nonprofits in the arts, human services and the environment.

AGS uses its "extra-classroom" experiences in athletics, arts, clubs and foreign travel in a deliberate manner. Over eighty-five percent of the student body participates in athletics, and all students participate in the fine arts. Students in both Middle School and Upper School are encouraged to participate actively in clubs meaningful to them. All Upper School students are required to take at least one foreign trip focusing on global community service or science, cultural literary, history or language skills.

PORTRAIT OF AN AGS GRADUATE

"Having graduated from AGS in 2009, I continue to appreciate the skills gained and the lessons I learned during my time there. I developed confidence as a student, leader, and an athlete. I learned the value of maintaining a supportive sisterhood and created lasting memories. Atlanta Girls' School is truly a special place, and I will forever be grateful for all that I gained as an AGS student," says Terranicia Holmes (AGS '09, Bowdoin College '13). ■

Atlanta International School

Today, education must prepare students to succeed in a globally connected and interdependent world. Since 1985, Atlanta International School has been providing students with the tools, knowledge and skills to thrive and be competitive through its challenging academic program and activities.

Located in Buckhead, Atlanta International School (AIS) is an independent, non-profit, secular school and one of a handful of schools in the United States which offers the International Baccalaureate (IB) program in grades 3K through twelve.

The campus features the Adair Art, Science and Design building, extensive media commons, performing arts center, campus-wide Wi-Fi, playgrounds, an athletic complex, a state of the art turf athletic field and the new Early Learning Center which opened in August 2012. The Upper School is listed in the National Register of Historic Places. The picturesque campus has been the site of a number of major motion pictures and commercials.

More than one thousand students attend AIS. The student body is made up of approximately fifty percent American and fifty percent international students, with more than 95 nationalities represented in the entire community of faculty, staff, students and parents. All faculty members are IB-trained and most are multilingual with advanced degrees. Many have taught at leading schools around the world. All language teachers are native speakers of the languages they teach.

LEADING-EDGE CURRICULUM
In the Early Learning Center, 3K and 4K students participate in a full-immersion program in Spanish, French or German. In the Primary School, a dual-immersion program of English plus Spanish, French or German is offered to students in grades 5K-5. All students in grades 3K-5 participate in the IB Primary Years Program (IB-PYP). Students then progress to the IB Middle Years Programme (IB-MYP) where emphasis is placed on developing life skills and critical thinking abilities.

Students in grades eleven and twelve participate in the IB Diploma Programme (IB-DP), an academically challenging curriculum that calls for students to pass certain benchmarks to receive the coveted diploma, including an extended essay, a service learning requirement and internationally standardized examinations.

AIS is located in the heart of Buckhead's historic Garden Hills neighborhood.

BEYOND THE CLASSROOM
Students participating in Atlanta International School's athletics program truly embody the ideals of the scholar-athlete. Students may participate in a wide array of sports such as volleyball, soccer, basketball, Ultimate, swimming, cross-country, golf and tennis—to name a few.

The award-winning theater program stages several productions each year and has received multiple Shuler Hensley Awards for Excellence in High School Musical Theater. The Department of Music serves the needs of over 700 students.

COMMITMENT TO EXCELLENCE
"With 100 percent of the eleventh and twelfth grade students enrolled in the IB-DP, AIS is one of only a few schools that can claim full participation in a program that will pave the way for entrance into the finest universities worldwide," said Headmaster Kevin Glass.

AIS students have received awards, scholarships and honors on the local, state, national and international level. Each graduating class typically receives more than $4 million in scholarship offers per year, not including Georgia's HOPE scholarship monies.

"AIS will continue to accept the challenge and commitment to develop each student's potential, providing the necessary skills and the intellectual and cultural confidence to succeed in a globally connected world," emphasized Glass. ■

(Left) Over 1,000 students in grades 3k–12 are enrolled at AIS, 50% of which are Americans and 50% international.

(Right) The Visconti di Modrone Media Commons at AIS boasts 36,000 books, 58,000 e-books and 50 periodicals in five different languages.

TURNER FIELD *in Atlanta, built in 1997, has become*
a landmark as the "Home of the Atlanta Braves."
Photo by Eugene Buchko/Shutterstock.com.

Barnsley Gardens Resort

Leave city life and everyday stress behind and head to Barnsley Gardens Resort where 3,300 expansive acres encourage visitors to get outside and play like they did when they were young. ■ *Outdoor enthusiasts will enjoy the resort's plethora of exciting activities. An award-winning golf course features challenging play and stunning vistas.*

Miles of trails that wind through the property are perfect for hiking, biking and horseback riding. Tennis courts and lawn games like croquet and bocce ball are a fun way to strike up friendly competition.

UNPARALLELED DIVERSIONS

Guests who want to have a more relaxed vacation will enjoy a visit to the award-winning Spa at Barnsley Gardens Resort. This European-style spa features 10 treatment rooms, a variety of massages, facials, wraps and skin treatments and lounges, saunas, steam rooms and a whirlpool. The resort's Grecian-style pool, located adjacent to the spa, is the perfect place to lounge

Barnlsey Gardens Resort offers a variety of activities, including horseback riding, paintball, team-building opportunities and so much more. A charming boutique resort with cozy accommodations in a 19th century style pedestrian village with tree-lined sidewalks.

while catching some rays and enjoying an ice-cold beverage.

Springbank Plantation, the Southeast's premier hunting preserve, is the place to learn how or to improve clay shooting skills; the 12-station course boasts a diverse layout of shots. In the fall, Springbank hosts full- and half-day quail, pheasant and turkey hunts. Expert guides and hunting dogs accompany guests on this exciting adventure.

WORLD CLASS ACCOMMODATIONS

Guests of Barnsley Gardens Resort are housed in English country-style, multi-bedroom cottages that feature living rooms and beautiful porches with stunning views of the grounds and gardens. Fire pits that dot the property are a favorite place for guests to gather and toast S'mores, as they did when they were younger.

Barnsley Gardens Resort is also home to acres of stunning gardens filled with hundreds of beautiful blooms and is a delightful place to stroll on a sunny afternoon. A favorite destination is the Boxwood Parterre, located in front of the historic manor house ruins.

After a day of fun, guests may dine at one of the three on-property restaurants. The Woodlands Grill is a casual dining establishment that features breakfast, lunch and dinner. Menu items range from soups, salads and sandwiches to steak and fish entrées, and meals can be enjoyed on the large patio that overlooks the golf course. The Rice House is a fine dining restaurant and the ideal place to enjoy a number of chef-prepared specialties. In the winter, special Wine Dinners are hosted here. For a more casual experience, The Beer Garden is the place for guests to stop in for a cold brew and casual fare while listening to live music and watching the sunset. The Beer Garden hosts "Yappy Hours" when guests are encouraged to bring their dogs. The entire facility is pet friendly.

ACCOLADES: 2010, 2011 & 2012 Conde Nast Gold List World's Best Places To Stay. 2010 & 2011 Conde Nast #14 of the Top 100 Resort Spas in the U.S. 2010 Silver Medalist Golf Course by Golf Digest. 2009, 2010 & 2011 Conde Nast Best in World Reader's Choice. 2008 GGCOA Course of the Year Travel + Leisure, 500 World's Best Hotels. ■

Bartow History Museum

Since 1987, Bartow History Museum has preserved for future generations the history of Bartow County through exhibits, programs and outreach activities. In December 2010, the Museum moved into the newly restored 1869 Bartow County Courthouse, occupying both floors of the historic structure. Through the exhibits, archives, programming and gift shop, the museum provides a look into the lifestyles and culture of years past, spanning more than 200 years of history.

Located in downtown Cartersville, Georgia, Bartow History Museum welcomes thousands of visitors annually.

Divided into six galleries, the permanent exhibits of the museum include "A Sense of Place," "Bartow Beginnings," "The Coming War," "People at Work," "Community Makers" and "Toward New Horizons." Regular programming includes a wide range of educational opportunities for school children, lunchtime and evening lecture series, special events, tours and more.

A STEP BACK IN TIME

Bartow History Museum focuses on the settlement and development of Bartow County from the early 19th century when Cherokee Indians inhabited the area. Visitors gain insight into early European settler life, the agriculture, iron and textile industries and notable figures.

In the Interactive Gallery, visitors can experience first-hand the hardships of a Civil War soldier, touch the belongings of early pioneer and Cherokee families, work a shift in a textile mill, shop at a general store and listen to the stories of Bartow County history makers in an authentic 1940's telephone booth.

The Museum Gift Shop offers visitors a variety of books, jewelry, locally made pottery, clothing, prints, chenille and much more. Book selections on topics such as local history, Native Americans, the Civil War and World War II are available.

A FUN WAY TO LEARN HISTORY

The Museum offers students many avenues for learning about the culture and history of Bartow County through field trips, traveling trunks, camps, home school days and Scout workshops. Through a mix of fun and challenging activities, students can not only learn history but also improve their research skills.

Students experience hands-on activities for learning map skills, take slate and quill pen writing lessons in the one-room schoolhouse, examine the lives of the Cherokee Indians by handling artifacts, viewing a blowgun demonstration or playing Cherokee games.

Student groups experience what life was like on a farm over 100 years ago by hand washing clothes and churning butter. Students also explore the lives of men, women and children during the Civil War and World War II eras.

MORE THAN A MUSEUM

The Museum maintains an archives and research library with an extensive collection of historic documents, photographs, genealogical files, newspapers and books.

In the archives, historians, students, and others can access primary and secondary resource materials. General information is available on antiques and collectibles. Information can be found on famous Bartow County residents, area churches, historic sites, businesses and the Civil War. Research requests are accepted by telephone, mail and email.

Bartow History Museum preserves an important part of local and state history. The museum stands as a testament to the perseverance of the early founders of the area and continues in its mission to educate the community and visitors about the county's unique heritage.

"As our motto says at the Bartow History Museum, we are 'opening a door to the past' for our visitors, both local and those from out of town. Whether it is through one of our exhibits or programs, we preserve our past and make it available to the public," says Trey Gaines, museum director. ■

Through its archives, resource materials, and exhibits, Bartow History Museum gives visitors a glimpse into the early history, culture, and people of Bartow County.

*B*ooth Western Art Museum

Located in historic Cartersville, the Booth Western Art Museum is Georgia's second largest art museum and the only museum of its kind in the Southeast. The public is invited to come and "See America's Story" and explore the American West in the 120,000 square feet of exhibition space. The museum features the largest permanent exhibition of Western art in America.

(Top) The North Entrance to the Booth Western Art Museum, an Affiliate of the Smithsonian Institution.

(Bottom) The Mythic West Gallery provides a contemporary vision of the West.

The Booth Western Art Museum opened in August 2003 and in 2006 was named an Affiliate of the Smithsonian Institution. Its permanent galleries include the American West Gallery, the Cowboy Gallery, the Faces of the West, Heading West, the Modern West, Sagebrush Ranch, the James and Carolyn Millar Presidential Gallery, War is Hell and a two-story Sculpture Court. Three temporary galleries showcase ten to twelve stimulating exhibitions each year.

"The Booth Museum provides an opportunity unique in the Southeast to understand the lure of the West through the eyes of artists. Our permanent collection focuses on living artists, giving us the opportunity to bring them to the Museum for events where visitors can interact with them directly. We invite everyone to experience the West through a visit to the Booth," says Seth Hopkins, Executive Director.

WILD, WILD WEST

The American West Gallery is the starting point in experiencing the westward expansion of America and reflecting on the roots of Western art, history and culture. Visitors may view more than 100 paintings and sculptures by famous western artists portraying the settlers, Native American tribes and the grandeur of the old west.

The Cowboy Gallery is a fitting reminder of the romance and reality of the American Cowboy. The gallery showcases the cowboy at work, rest and play in more than 35 paintings and sculptures.

In the Faces of the West Gallery, visitors will encounter the images of legends such as Doc Holliday and Geronimo along with portrayals of everyday folks, including Native Americans, African Americans and women.

Art in the Heading West Gallery reflects the experiences of those who journeyed west: fur trappers, mountain men and pioneer families in search of a new opportunity. The Native Hands Gallery houses more than 200 artifacts and Native American objects.

VISITOR FAVORITES

The Presidential Gallery is a visitor favorite. The collection includes a one-page original, signed letter from each President along with portraits and memorabilia. These letters provide visitors with insight into the thoughts of these famous men.

A favorite among children is Sagebrush Ranch, a real working ranch with a farmhouse, barn, bunkhouse and corral. Aspiring cowpokes and cowgirls can dress in Western gear, sit in the saddle of a life-size horse or take a ride through the desert in a stagecoach. Thirty interactive stations provide non-stop learning and fun.

Another timeless favorite is the War is Hell Gallery with paintings of Civil War battles hung in chronological order. The paintings and sculpture displayed depict the heroism, glory and tragedy of the war that pitted brother against brother.

THE MODERN WEST

Visitors will see the non-traditional side of the west in the Modern West Gallery, where art depicts the stylistic changes in western art over the last fifty years. The Mythic West takes a look at how the west was sold to generations fascinated by the tall tales and larger than life figures popularized by the movies and magazines. This gallery includes a display of large vintage movie posters and paintings and sculptures of the movie stars

who portrayed Western heroes on the silver screen.

A signature feature of the museum is a two-story Sculpture Court with both contemporary and traditional sculptures. The focal point is the awe-inspiring Eagle Catcher which expands two stories, surrounded by a floating staircase.

NOT JUST A BUILDING

At Booth Western Art Museum things don't just hang on the wall—things happen. Through artist and scholar lectures, book signings, annual events, school programs and exhibition openings, visitors experience America's heritage in a personal way. The annual October Southeastern Cowboy Festival & Symposium features Native American dancing, gunfight reenactments, a Western marketplace and more. The Southeastern Cowboy Gathering in March highlights western music, cowboy poetry and chuck wagon cooking. The Civil War Comes Alive! event, held in April, highlights the life of soldiers on both sides of the war.

The award winning film *The American West* plays continuously in the Orientation Theatre. Snacks and light lunches are available in the Café and books and art prints are sold in the Museum Store. A ballroom is available for special event rental and the reference library is available to the public by appointment.

A visit to the Booth Western Art Museum is a visit to "See America's Story"—the land, the people, the struggles, the dreams and the legends. A visit to the Booth Museum is a chance to view the spirit of America captured in the works of two hundred of the finest artists in the country. ∎

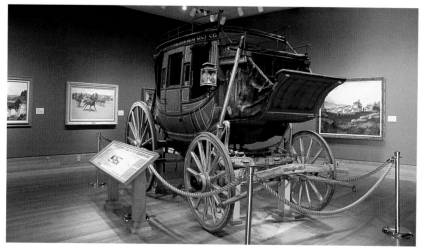

The paintings in the War Is Hell Gallery are hung in chronological order to help visitors understand the battles as they occurred.

Concord Coach Number 84, the "Cadillac" of Western vehicles.

Begin the journey by exploring the classic western vision in the American West Gallery.

The Carolyn & James Millar Presidential Gallery has in its collection a one-page, signed letter from each President.

Brandon Hall School

Brandon Hall School is a coeducational, college preparatory day and boarding school that provides personalized instruction for students in Georgia and around the world, turning their potential into reality. ■ "We believe that all students can become successful learners. There are no preset limits to what they can achieve," said Dr. John L. Singleton, President and Headmaster. "We celebrate the idea that learning, creativity and innovation are at the heart of education."

CELEBRATING MORE THAN 50 YEARS

Brandon Hall School was founded in 1959 as a tutorial proprietary school by Theodore Hecht and evolved into a nonprofit, nondenominational college preparatory school. Founded on the late Morris Brandon summer home estate, the entire school initially was housed in a great stone mansion now known as the Great Hall. Enrollment grew, additional facilities were built and the school's programs expanded.

Today, Brandon Hall is metro Atlanta's only traditional, college-prep boarding and day school for grades 6-12. Residential life staff and Directors provide supervised evening study, while coordinating weekend activities that add to the excitement of boarding school life.

DELIVERING A WORLD-CLASS ACADEMIC CURRICULM

The beautiful 27-acre campus, situated along the Chattahoochee River in Sandy Springs, offers a secure suburban environment for boarders and is also accessible to Atlanta's numerous cultural and entertainment offerings. In addition, team-centered sports and extracurricular activities are offered to help produce a well-rounded individual. The college preparatory curriculum includes multisensory instruction, supervised study, daily homework evaluation and applied study skills.

Brandon Hall is proud to be an Apple Education School. Each middle school student has an iPad with which the child can access the Internet's vast resources while also learning the technological skills needed to thrive in today's world. Core advanced classes in math and/or foreign language are offered for students who have reached the requisite levels of achievement. The upper school's curriculum also emphasizes Apple technology and rigorous core and elective courses. More than 25 Advanced Placement and Honors classes are available.

EDUCATING FOR THE 21ST CENTURY GLOBAL SOCIETY

Global studies are at the heart of Brandon Hall's curriculum. Each year, a specific country's culture and history is interwoven into the academic disciplines, with studies culminating in a trip to the country. "We try to teach our children that there's a larger world out there," Singleton said. "With today's global society, students need to be able to understand a variety of cultures and how they co-exist." Brandon Hall's emphasis on global education provides students with opportunities to travel abroad and interact with classrooms around the world.

The faculty is multinational, as is about 20 percent of the

Headmaster and President, Dr. John L. Singleton.

Faculty members welcome the opportunity to provide individualized instruction.

The Great Hall invites everyone to enter Brandon Hall.

student body, representing 13 countries. For those who do not use English as their primary language, Brandon Hall offers an English as a Second Language program, (ESL). "We literally are a global family, offering a unique world-class education," Singleton said.

The school's 27 wooded acres on the Chattahoochee River abound with natural beauty.

SALUTING AN ACCOMPLISHED FACULTY

Brandon Hall is a non-sectarian school focusing on the individual learner in small group classes. A 4:1 student-teacher ratio and an average class size of six help ensure learning success, as do experienced instructors who are passionate about providing a research-based education.

"Having small classes enables me to watch every student in the class and make sure that they're where they're supposed to be," said Kevin Langley, who has taught history at Brandon Hall since 1984. "Some students get lost in a big class. Here, no one sits in the back row," Singleton said.

More than 70 percent of Brandon Hall's faculty and administration hold advanced degrees. "All of our teachers are versed in multi-sensory instruction, so they can present educational materials in the manner best suited for each student," Singleton said.

CELEBRATING THE BRANDON HALL FAMILY

Brandon Hall's goal of providing a "living" education incorporates a vibrant campus and social life as well as exciting and challenging academics, while fostering a family style atmosphere.

"There's a great deal of satisfaction at Brandon Hall because I can see each day a light bulb go on and someone has learned something. Something good has happened," Langley, a long-tenured faculty member, stated.

Parents also are impressed with the school's track record. "Brandon Hall is the best-kept private school secret in the Atlanta area," said Dr. Claudia Signal-Leon, whose children, Taeler and Tyler, are students. "The whole experience is one of nurturing, of caring. It's one-on-one. You won't find that your child is just a number here. He's part of a family."

When Georgia's on your mind, think of Brandon Hall School. The college preparatory school overlooking the majestic Chattahoochee River is proudly molding the 21st century learner. ■

Our diverse student body hails from over 13 countries.

Brasstown Valley Resort and Spa
Lake Blackshear Resort and Golf Club

For vacations with family, business conferences, weddings or romantic getaways, Brasstown Valley Resort and Spa and Lake Blackshear Resort and Golf Club have everything to make the event perfect. ■ *Offering all the modern amenities in a rustic, relaxing environment, these resorts treat visitors with personalized service and attention. For years,*

(Top) 503 acre mountain resort. 134 rooms (traditional, cabins, suites) Offering exceptional dining, golf, spa, trail rides and much more.

(Bottom left) Open for breakfast, lunch and dinner. The menus feature a variety of local and regional offerings.

(Bottom right) The Equani Spa offers a true sanctuary from the stress of the urban life.

they've welcomed guests with world-class service and Southern hospitality, and all proceeds from their operation are reinvested in Georgia. Both are owned by the Georgia Department of Natural Resources and help raise funds to protect and promote the state's stunning array of forests, mountains, lakes and wildlife.

THE BEAUTY OF THE MOUNTAINS
Located in Young Harris, Georgia, in the Blue Ridge Mountains, the Brasstown Valley Resort and Spa features a spectacular lodge with 102 rooms and suites with fireplaces and mountain-view balconies. Log cottages provide cozy seclusion with grand parlors, fireplaces, kitchenettes and hillside verandas.

Year-round activities include hiking, kayaking and canoeing, white-water rafting, horseback riding, tennis, fishing and golf on a course recently named by *Golf Styles* magazine as one of the "Must Play Public Golf Courses" in the nation. In addition, the Equani Spa is a relaxing retreat where visitors can pamper themselves in ultimate comfort and relaxation.

"Some think of us as a land-based cruise ship," says Charles Burton, general manager of Brasstown Valley Resort and Spa. "First-class service is something we take very seriously. Many of our employees are local residents and take great pride in making sure their guests have a positive experience and become repeat customers for many years to come."

All of Brasstown Valley Resorts' amenities, plus top-rated restaurants and meeting facilities, are within walking distance. After a full day of fun and discovery, guests can sit back in rocking chairs on the front porch and experience cool, quiet north Georgia evenings and pure mountain serenity.

THE ALLURE OF THE LAKE
Cordele, Georgia, is home to one of the state's most spectacular bodies of water, the 8,500-acre Lake Blackshear, the centerpiece of Lake Blackshear Resort and Golf Club.

A convenient two-hour drive from Atlanta, Lake Blackshear Resort and Golf Club is located in the middle of Georgia Veteran's Memorial State Park. Established as a memorial to U.S. veterans, the park features a museum with aircraft, armored vehicles, uniforms, weapons, medals and memorabilia dating back to the Revolutionary War.

"The state park is one of many highlights that make our resort experience a popular destination year-round," says Bob Johnson, general manager of Lake Blackshear Resort. "Our visitors can discover the area by land or lake and take advantage of all the activities we have to offer in a quiet, relaxing setting."

Lake Blackshear's accommodations are a mix of rustic charm and contemporary comfort. Visitors can choose from 14 guest rooms within the lodge, 64 private villas and 10 lakeside cabins, all with incredible lakeside views, comfortable furnishings, high-speed Internet and cable television. The resort also offers meeting and conference facilities with full AV support.

The lake provides year-round entertainment with boating, fishing and swimming. For golf lovers, Lake Blackshear boasts an 18-hole championship golf course designed by Denis Griffiths and rated four stars by *Golf Digest*. Hunters will be impressed by the variety of hunting facilities and game— quail, turkey and deer—as well as year-round skeet shooting. Guided hunts are also available.

The resort's mix of restaurants includes upscale and casual dining options. Full banquet and event-planning services ensure that weddings, family reunions and parties are memorable successes. ■

Buckhead Facial Plastic Surgery

A personalized approach. Combined with her board certifications in otolaryngology and facial plastic surgery, Dr. Theresa M. Jarmuz conveys a fresh and progressive approach by offering a combination of surgical, nonsurgical, and laser treatments delivering natural, beautiful results.

Entering her field as a female surgeon, Dr. Jarmuz employs a first-hand perspective. "When I start to notice aging symptoms in my appearance, I don't jump to a facelift; I employ multiple means to prevent one," she says. "I uphold this same philosophy for all of my patients." In order to do so, Dr. Jarmuz may recommend Sculptra™, ReFirme™—a painless, FDA-cleared skin-tightening procedure—and Botox®. The stylish surgeon's sincere candor, friendly disposition, sophisticated office, and compassionate approach complement her attractive appearance and instill a sense of confidence in her patients. Her impressive credentials and vast experience further relay a sense of credibility.

LASER-ENHANCED NECKLIFTS

As part of Dr. Jamuz's commitment to effective, progressive methods, the experienced surgeon has developed a procedure that involves a combination of laser therapies with a one-hour necklift procedure to yield firmer, more youthful results. I'm conservative and believe in employing the least invasive treatments possible to garner effective results. I find that my patients appreciate my personalized, ethical approach. Their contentment is very important to me." Moreover, Dr. Jarmuz feels that such treatments can successfully help turn back the hands of time. The conception of the laser-enhanced necklift was developed for male patients desiring facelift-type results with minimal incisions and downtime. "When patients undergo a combination of laser technologies with necklift surgery, they benefit from significant tightening around the jawline. minimal downtime and a hidden, one-inch incision under the chin. Patients can go to work the next day while achieving results that approach that of a facelift." Although initially used by Dr. Jarmuz to treat men, Dr. Jarmuz's female patients find the procedure postpones their need for more extensive procedures. "We've had very positive feedback with the results we've achieved."

EMPHASIS ON PREVENTION

Having performed hundreds of facelifts, Dr. Jarmuz only recommends surgery when she feels a patient needs it and "wants it for the right reasons." When deemed appropriate, Dr. Jarmuz says that advances in technologies and tehniques have made facelift surgeries less invasive and painful than they used to be decades ago, making them more popular, too. Dr. Jarmuz values modern ideals of beauty and believes people should not feel guilty for wanting to improve their appearnce. With a full-service practice that caters to a host of aesthetic concerns, Dr. Jarmuz offers numerous procedures to restore patients' self-images and help them look like younger versions of themselves, without distortion. "Surgery should be subtle and practically undetectable. I've had patients come up to me after treatment saying, 'My friends noticed I looked better, but couldn't pinpoint the change.' Such a response continues to motivate me."

WARMTH AND DISCRETION

No matter what procedure a patient is seeking, Dr. Jarmuz and her skilled, experienced staff treat all patients with compassion and an understanding of the discretion involved in this life

changing event. Patients are provided with the best in follow-up care and monitoring as the clinic's goal is to make sure the experience is positive, special and successful.

"In the workplace, at home and in social situations, a person's appearance can influence how they feel about themselves. Through extensive education and experience, at Buckhead Facial Plastic Surgery, we have developed an understanding of the aging process and its effects, both physically and emotionally. The tools we use are more affordable than ever and our first line of defense is an emphasis on 'prevention.' We work with patients to produce not just outer, but inner, confidence," says Dr. Jarmuz. ■

Jezebel magazine named Dr. Jarmuz Best Facial Surgeon in their "Best of Atlanta" section (April 2012).

Old and new merge in DOWNTOWN *Atlanta.*
Photo by Chris Calhoun

The OLYMPIC TORCH *commemorates the*
1996 Summer Olympics held in Atlanta.
Photo by Sean Pavone.

The FLATIRON BUILDING *on Peachtree Street in*
downtown Atlanta was completed five years
before its better known New York City counterpart.
Photo by Joel Shawn.

The Buckhead community in North Atlanta is one of the South's most vibrant and affluent neighborhoods—a wonderful place to visit, play, work and live. "When you look at the sustainability of the amenities we offer, who else can compete?" asks Sam Massell, former Atlanta mayor and founding president of this nonprofit civic group. "Buckhead is the address of choice!"

Today's gleaming skyscrapers, upscale shopping malls, dense traffic and lush residential settings are a far cry from what Henry Irby found when he bought 203 acres in what is now Buckhead's center in 1838. The South Carolina native built a tavern and grocery near the intersection of Peachtree Road, Roswell Road and Paces Ferry, where Triangle Park now sits.

The area, originally called Irbyville, was a community gathering place that became known as Buckhead after the head of a buck was mounted upon a nearby post.

LENOX SQUARE BUILT IN 1959

In 1952, Buckhead was annexed by the City of Atlanta. Seven years later, the largest shopping mall in the Southeast was built, Lenox Square. Anchored by Rich's and Davison's, the mall kept up with the times, eventually expanding and adding an enclosure, food court and covered parking and opening hotel and office space.

Buckhead ladies could always count on The Regency Room at Rich's when they needed a dress for a special occasion, but after Phipps Plaza opened across the street in 1969, they had no need to fly to Manhattan to shop. After all, Saks Fifth Avenue and Lord & Taylor, plus a bevy of designer boutiques, were now at their disposal. And, when Neiman Marcus opened at Lenox Square in the early 1970s, many flights to Texas must also have been cancelled!

Today, the Buckhead district has 1,400 retail outlets, which conduct about $1.5 billion in annual sales. Of those sales, 40 percent are by visitors from 100 miles away or further, making Buckhead a strong regional tourist attraction.

ELEGANT NEIGHBORHOODS

Of course, Buckhead's 78,686 residents also take advantage

(Top) Buckhead Coalition President and former Atlanta Mayor, Sam Massell.

(Bottom left) The Cathedral of St. Philip (nation's largest Episcopal congregation), one of 34 Buckhead houses of worship.

(Bottom right) The "Swan House" by famed architect Phillip Trammell Shutze.

of the shopping opportunities. Its elegant, tree-lined neighborhoods have been the address of choice for both Old and Nouveau Atlanta since after World War I, when rich Atlantans built mansions in what was formerly a rural vacation spot. Renowned architects, such as Philip Trammell Shutze and Neel Reid, designed many of the palatial residences, built on large, wooded lots. (One Shutze creation, the Swan House at 3099 Andrews Drive, is open to the public.)

The winding streets of exquisite classical mansions are always a treat for sightseers to behold, but they become even more beautiful in the springtime, when a profusion of pink and white dogwood and azalea blooms accent the manicured lawns.

SKYSCRAPERS ALSO ABOUND

In addition, Buckhead is home to many corporate offices. With zoning height restrictions lifted by the Atlanta City Council, Tower Place, a 30-story office building, became its first skyscraper in 1973. Today, towering buildings line Peachtree Road and the district has just over 23 million square feet of office space.

Though Buckhead's commercial real estate market was hit hard by the recession that began in 2008, it has started to bounce back, Massell said. "We predicted this. I said luxury markets like Buckhead would be the last to feel the economic downtrend and would be the first to recover…. It's almost shocking how much construction we have underway."

STRONG COMMUNITY LEADERSHIP

Why has Buckhead weathered this fiscal storm so well? Massell credits the community's leadership, 40 neighborhood associations, 33 religious congregations, 17 parent-teacher associations and 5 service clubs, that have worked together to nurture the quality of life and help coordinate orderly growth.

The community's booming growth during the last 20 years has, at times, brought some undesirable challenges, such as traffic congestion, crime and noise from the business district's nightclubs. The Buckhead Coalition responded by petitioning the city council to enforce existing laws, Massell said. "Our

(Top) Part of Buckhead's booming skyline.

(Bottom left) An interior scene at Phipps Plaza.

(Bottom right) A popular sculpture in Charlie Loudermilk Park.

crime stats are lower than any other part of the city," he added, noting that crime in Buckhead declined 13 percent between 2010 and 2011.

The Community Improvement District was created in 1999 to help fund infrastructure and landscaping improvements. The quasi-governmental entity raises more than $5 million annually in self taxation to finance such projects.

"However, unlike many governmental entities," Massell explains, "the Buckhead Coalition isn't structured to provide grant funds or tax incentives to attract commerce and industry … but we know how to nurture an image and its atmosphere to attract the cream of the crop. I've only been in Buckhead about 60 years, but I'm a native Atlantan, and I know what competitors offer and how we can upgrade the amenities." ■

Buckhead Dental Partners

Healthy, white teeth, pink gums and a great smile are what Buckhead Dental Partners strives to provide its clients. The Atlanta practice offers quality dental care in a state of the art facility, performing everything from simple cleanings to root canals, cosmetic procedures and extractions.

"Our patients' comfort is our top priority," said Dr. Jeff Ballard. "We're experienced in using oral conscious sedation for any patients who need a little extra help. We also take the time to explain each procedure and dispel any apprehensions a patient might have." In addition, patients may listen to their iPods during their appointments.

An emphasis on patient education sets Buckhead Dental Partners apart from other dental practices. "We teach our patients how to take better care of their teeth so they hopefully only need to see us for regular cleanings," Dr. Ballard said. "And the value of teaching good oral health habits to children cannot be underestimated."

TREATMENT FOR YOUNG PATIENTS

The American Academy of Pediatric Dentistry and the American Dental Association recommend that a child's first dental examination be performed when he or she is 12 months to 15 months old. At Buckhead Dental Partners, preventive dentistry for children includes cleaning to remove plaque and bacteria that cause tooth decay, full mouth X-rays every three to five years to find any cavities not seen visually, sealants, fluoride treatment, fillings and extractions.

Cosmetic procedures are available for teenagers and adults who want to be happier about the appearance of their teeth. Whitening, bonding, veneers and even dentures are some solutions that Buckhead Dental Partners can provide.

DENTAL IMPLANTS OFFERED

Dental implants are performed when one or more permanent teeth are lost because of decay, gum disease or trauma. These implants consist of two parts: a screw—usually titanium—that is placed in the jawbone, and a false tooth placed on the screw. Most people are good candidates for implants as long as there is enough bone to support them and the clients have no underlying disease that might deteriorate the bone.

Bridges are another solution when one or more teeth are lost. A dental bridge usually consists of three connected crowns, with the middle crown replacing a lost tooth and the adjacent crowns used to keep the new tooth properly anchored.

PLASTIC GUARDS HELPFUL

The practice can provide relief for those who awake with a sore jaw or aching teeth. "Grinders," those who grind their teeth in sleep, need a custom-fit bite guard to lessen the tooth damage done during sleep. Mouth guards also can be made for athletes who need to protect their jaws and teeth during games.

Dr. Ballard graduated in 1998 from the Medical College of Georgia, where he was the second youngest person in his class. He is a member of the American Dental Association, the American Academy of Implant Dentistry, the Georgia Dental Association, the Academy of General Dentistry and the American Academy of Cosmetic Dentistry. ∎

Dr. Jeff Ballard educates his patients about good dental practices so that regular cleanings, hopefully, will be the only procedure they need.

VISIT BUCKHEAD DENTAL PARTNERS ONLINE: www.buckheaddentalpartners.com

Buckhead Plastic Surgery
Exceptional Results for Exceptional People

Board Certified Plastic Surgeon, Dr. Alan Larsen, serves as the Medical Director of Buckhead Plastic Surgery. Dr. Larsen completed medical school at the University of Nevada, a general surgery program and residency at the University of Jacksonville and a plastic surgery residency at prestigious Wake Forest University.

PRECISION RESULTS EXPERIENCE

For over 15 years, Dr. Larsen has had the pleasure of helping restore the youth and beauty of many Atlantans, as well as patients throughout the country. He is passionate about helping patients achieve their goals to improve their body and self image. Dr. Larsen is known for his caring, individual approach with patients, his artistry, and his meticulous attention to detail.

Dr. Larsen holds double board certification, both in Plastic Surgery and in General Surgery. This extensive background and training provides patients with the knowledge and judgment they should demand from a plastic surgeon. Dr. Larsen was the first plastic surgeon in Atlanta to perform and perfect the Belt Lipectomy and ThoracoBrachioMastopexy. This has led to him being known for and receiving one patient referral after another, for the incredible results of his Mommy Make-Overs and Body Lifts. Face Lifts, Mommy Make-Overs and Body Lifts are some of Dr. Larsen's most gratifying surgical procedures. Dr. Larsen states, "The determination and gratefulness these patients portray once we have obtained their goal of facial rejuvenation and a sexy and youthful body shape, more accurately representing how they feel, continuously reiterates my love and passion for plastic surgery. We love to hear patients state how we have helped them regain their self-confidence and self-esteem."

The most popular Mommy Make-Over and Body Lift procedures include some combination of breast augmentation to restore size and shape; breast lifts to give the breast a youthful, perky appearance; tummy tucks and belt lipectomies to provide a slimming silhouette; liposculpture to reshape hips and thighs; and buttock enhancement via fat transfer. Each surgery is tailored to the individual and patients are amazed by their body transformation.

HAPPY CLIENT TESTIMONIALS

"Four years after Mommy Makeover surgery by Dr. Larsen and still looking great and confident. His work stands the test of time. You're the best, Dr. Larsen. Money well spent." Marsha, Kennesaw, GA.

"At the consultation, I remember being both excited and nervous," said Nancy of Marietta, Ga. "Dr. Larsen spent a lot of time with me on the best choice for breast enlargement. Now my clothes fit better, I'm not self-conscious. I love my body!" Nancy, Marietta, GA.

"Love Dr. Larsen—the man is a genius with a scalpel and an all-around great guy. My "before and after" pictures still take my breath away!" Samantha, Ormond Beach, FL. ■

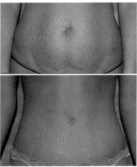
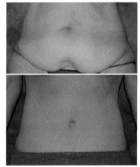

Tummy Tuck/Lipo   Belt Lipectomy

Campbell-Stone

Respect, excellence, care and compassion for the elderly are found at Campbell-Stone, which offers "retirement living as it should be" at two convenient Atlanta locations. ▪ "Our mission is to provide retirement living with an emphasis on value, services and quality amenities," Executive Director Cliff Pepper said. "We consider ourselves to be the best value in town and probably the state."

Founded in 1964 by the Christian Church (Disciples of Christ) in Georgia, Campbell-Stone is a non-profit, mission-driven corporation. Its Buckhead and Sandy Springs locations serve nearly 600 residents, most of whom qualify for a federal rental subsidy.

INDEPENDENT, ASSISTED-LIVING OPTIONS

Independent living is provided at both communities, while the Sandy Springs location includes 22 apartments for assisted living. All residents enjoy safe, comfortable environments that include 24-hour security.

Amenities include dining facilities, transportation services, libraries, beauty salons and barber shops, fitness rooms, computer centers and Chaplain Ministries. Cultural programs, day trips and planned activities offer residents even more opportunities for enhanced wellness and a sense of connectedness and socialization.

Wellness and Enrichment staff members provide personal and educational development programs, health and wellness screenings, emergency assistance and help residents to coordinate public benefits. Service Coordinators facilitate such regular programs as meditation, yoga and tai chi classes; poetry low-vision groups and computer training.

Campbell-Stone's assisted living program is one of the few in Georgia to offer financial subsidies. The staff works with residents and their families to develop a care plan tailored to each individual's needs.

Campbell-Stone's Buckhead and Sandy Springs locations serve nearly 600 residents. Campbell-Stone's exceptional services—including on-site rehabilitation services, help with personal care, medication administration, housekeeping and emergency-call response–deliver peace of mind for family members who know their loved one is well cared for.

"HIDDEN" DIAMOND

"Campbell-Stone is a diamond hidden under all the beautiful trees in fabulous Atlanta," resident Gloria Waddell said. "The community is nestled amidst some of the most beautiful homes, world-renowned shopping, and cuisines that would satisfy anyone's tastes and budget. I have lived in some great places in Atlanta, and this is one of them. What's not to like?"

Staff members are committed to supporting each person's social, psychological, physical and spiritual needs. In fact, five Campbell-Stone employees have won the LeadingAge Georgia Award of Honor for exemplary service and commitment to quality, while two other employees have won LeadingAge Georgia Distinguished Service and Caring Heart awards.

At Campbell-Stone, residents enjoy the pleasures and privacy of retirement living in a safe, comfortable and compassionate environment. The community offers remarkable value in providing exceptional services, robust resources and prestigious locations in Sandy Springs and Buckhead. ▪

VISIT CAMPBELL-STONE ONLINE: www.campbellstone.org

Cartersville-Bartow Convention & Visitors Bureau

Whether seeking historic sites, amazing museums or true southern hospitality, the Cartersville-Bartow CVB promises visitors that they will find a destination of choice in Cartersville and Bartow County conveniently located only 45 minutes north of Atlanta and 85 miles south of Chattanooga in the Appalachian foothills.

"Though Cartersville is centrally located within a few hours' drive of popular travel destinations, the area itself boasts many amazing attractions," says Ellen Archer, Cartersville-Bartow CVB executive director.

VIBRANT COUNTY, SMALL-TOWN CHARM

Bartow County is a patchwork of small towns, each named after early settlers or their Native American predecessors. It seems everything has meaning in this vibrant county. Cartersville's written history dates to the 16th century when the De Soto Expedition encountered the present-day Etowah Indian Mounds State Historic Site, the most intact Mississippian Mound Builder Site in the Southeastern United States.

Historians also relish this area for the dramatic Civil War events that unfolded here. Bartow County was at the heart of the "The Great Locomotive Chase," one of the war's most daring espionage attempts. Other noted events are the Battle of Allatoona Pass and Georgia's last surrender of Confederate troops at Kingston.

Modern advertising history was made in Cartersville when the first wall sign for Coca-Cola was painted at Young Brothers Pharmacy in 1894. Visitors flocked to Cartersville's square while traveling the Dixie Highway. Find more revelations at the Bartow History Museum and in historic Cassville.

Adairsville was the first Georgia town to be listed in its entirety on the National Register of Historic Places and is a must-see for lovers of history, antiques and great food. Nearby, the conflict between North and South changed the course of history for Barnsley Gardens at Woodlands, Godfrey Barnsley's antebellum estate. Today the manor house ruins and historic gardens are the centerpiece of Barnsley Gardens Resort, consistently designated as one of the *World's Best Places to Stay* by *Condé Nast* readers.

ATTRACTIONS FOUND NOWHERE ELSE

Not one, but two, Smithsonian Affiliate Museums await visitors in Cartersville. The Tellus Science Museum is a hands-on source for "everything that is science." The Booth Western Art Museum features America's largest permanent exhibition of Western Art and is the Southeast's only museum of its kind.

The jewel of Cartersville's Historic District, beautifully restored Rose Lawn, was the home of Victorian evangelist Samuel Porter Jones. Tours reveal Jones' legacy and connection to Nashville's Ryman Auditorium.

A welcome respite is Red Top Mountain State Park. The sparkling waters of Lake Allatoona make this a natural retreat with more than 1,000 secluded campsites, magnificent hiking trails, picnic shelters, cottages and more.

KICKING BACK AND MOVING FORWARD

The Euharlee Covered Bridge, built in 1886 and listed on the National Register of Historic Places, takes visitors back to the days of "horseless carriages."

Coming to Emerson is LakePoint Sporting Community and Town Center, slated to be the most comprehensive youth sports tournament destination in the world, thereby moving Bartow County forward with visits for future generations.

"A visit to Cartersville will leave visitors better read on the South's most interesting pages of history. Begin at the Visitor Information Center inside the Clarence Brown Conference Center, the region's host to successful meetings and memorable events. Here you will find that Bartow County provides the simple pleasures of small-town living with rich cultural experiences that rival larger cities," says Archer.

Whether musing at the Grand Theater, enjoying a concert or relaxing lakeside, Cartersville welcomes all to kick back and move forward in its daily celebration of Georgia living. ∎

(Top) Bartow County is home to the Atlanta Steeplechase, a spring ritual that is known as "The Best Lawn Party in Georgia!"

(Inset) These famous burial effigies unearthed at Etowah Indian Mounds are two of the largest anciently carved stone sculptures ever discovered in North America.

(Bottom) Historic Downtown Cartersville

Cancer Treatment Centers of America
at Southeastern Regional Medical Center

Cancer Treatment Centers of America® (CTCA) at Southeastern Regional Medical Center opened in Newnan, Georgia, in August, 2012, to bring more state-of-the-art treatment options—and more hope—to patients fighting complex and advanced-stage cancer.

The metro Atlanta location joins CTCA® regional destination hospitals in Chicago, Philadelphia, Phoenix and Tulsa to provide fully integrated and personalized cancer care, delivered by a multidisciplinary care team focused on quality care, efficiency and absolute service excellence.

"At CTCA, patients are at the center of all that we do," says Kane Dawson, president and chief executive officer of CTCA at Southeastern Regional Medical Center. "We deliver innovative and compassionate care that empowers patients and focuses on the whole person to meet their individual needs."

In addition to providing high quality, comprehensive cancer care, Southeastern will provide a major boost to the local economy. Recognized by former Georgia Governor Sonny Perdue as one of the "State of Georgia's Top 10 Economic Development Projects," the hospital is expected to generate 500 new jobs and $500 million in economic activity over the first five years of operation.

CHANGING THE FACE OF CANCER CARE

Cancer Treatment Centers of America was founded in 1988 by Richard J Stephenson. Stephenson was disappointed with the impersonal and insensitive care his mother, Mary Brown Stephenson, received. When she lost her battle with cancer in 1982, Stephenson set out to change the face of cancer care. Stephenson's commitment to creating a truly patient-centered cancer treatment experience has been the organization's guiding principle ever since.

CTCA promises that the treatment, quality of life and service needs of every patient will be at the center of the hearts, minds and actions of its staff every day. At CTCA, patients find accomplished physicians who are experienced in caring for individuals living with advanced and complex cancer, along with experienced nutritionists, naturopathic doctors, chiropractors, mind-body therapists, spiritual counselors and other clinicians who provide integrative care and support.

Collectively, physicians and staff work to address the individual needs of patients, as if each patient was his or her own mother or loved one. They ask themselves: "If my mother had cancer, how would I want her to be treated?" That simple question has evolved into the CTCA Mother Standard® of care—a unique, vibrant approach that delivers a complete, quality treatment experience based on what cancer patients and their families value most.

TREATING THE WHOLE PERSON

Patients and their families travel hundreds of miles to access the unique care model found at CTCA hospitals, Patient Empowered Care®, that places patients at the center of their own care, encouraging and enabling them to take an active role in treatment decision making.

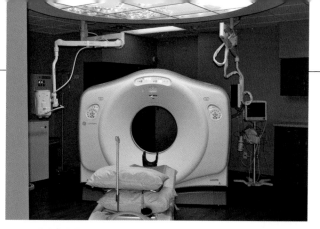

(Top left)
CT Scan with skylight ceiling.

(Top right)
Dr. George Daneker and Kane Dawson with TomoTherapy® machine.

(Bottom left)
Guest accommodations.

(Bottom right)
Nursing staff in Surgery Department.

This innovative model combines leading clinical treatments and technologies with scientifically supported complementary therapies to help manage side effects and improve quality of life. All these services are delivered under one roof by a dedicated, multidisciplinary team of oncology care providers who personalize treatment plans based on the individual needs of each patient.

"My doctors and team at Cancer Treatment Centers of America gave me a plan that was right for me," said prostate cancer patient George Drennan of Canton, Georgia.

To support its commitment to provide clear information that helps patients and their families make informed treatment decisions, CTCA posts its length of life, quality of life, speed of care and patient experience data on its website.

PERSONALIZED TREATMENTS AND TECHNOLOGY

Using an integrated, patient-centered approach, CTCA combines advanced treatments and technologies with an array of complementary medical therapies. Oncologists work as a team with nutritionists, naturopathic doctors, mind-body therapists, rehabilitation therapists and spiritual support staff to treat the whole person. This means patients and caregivers enjoy the convenience of tests, treatments and supportive therapies all under one roof.

For CTCA Chief of Staff, Chief of Surgery and Surgical Oncologist Dr. George Daneker, it's an exclusive focus on cancer that sets CTCA apart. "At CTCA, we understand the urgency of bringing more options, more powerful and innovative therapies—and more hope—to patients and their families today. We're a team focused on bringing cancer treatment back to the needs of patients," he says.

METRO ATLANTA HOSPITAL SERVES PATIENTS IN SOUTHEAST

Located about 25 miles southwest of Hartsfield-Jackson Atlanta International Airport, CTCA is a 226,000-square-foot, fully digital hospital focused exclusively on treating cancer.

Among the new hospital's features are 25 private inpatient treatment rooms, large surgical suites, specialized treatment suites for endoscopy and bronchoscopy, state-of-the-art radiation and therapy departments, rehabilitation and physical therapy, concierge services, a dining room, chapel and onsite guest accommodations. Advanced medical technologies include magnetic resonance imaging (MRI), positron emission tomography-computed tomography (PET-CT), Varian TrueBeam™, TomoTherapy®, Calypso®, TheraSphere, digital imaging, interventional angiography and more.

Outside the hospital is a swan pond visible from many guest rooms, with a peninsula and gazebo for relaxation. The outdoor patio area adjacent to the dining room has a koi pond and gazebo garden. Two rooftop terraces overlook the beautiful grounds and adjacent woods and fountains greet passersby at the main and outpatient entrances. Also available are 12 full-service RV parking spots for guests who prefer to travel by RV, bus or camper.

AVAILABLE AROUND THE CLOCK

Medical decisions are among the most important decisions patients and their families make in life. CTCA believes patients and their families should never have to wait to begin their journey toward finding the right treatment option. Oncology Information Specialists are available to discuss treatment options 24 hours a day, 365 days a year at 888-831-4493 or online at cancercenter.com.

For more information on Cancer Treatment Centers of America at Southeastern Regional Medical Center in Newnan, Georgia, please visit cancercenter.com/southeastern or call 855-848-5766 toll-free. ■

The Pavilion at Lake Meer in historic Piedmont Park,
189 acres of parkland just northeast of Downtown Atlanta.
Photo by Sean Pavone.

Coldwell Banker Residential Brokerage Atlanta

Serving the Atlanta area for more than 50 years, Coldwell Banker® has more than a dozen offices and close to 1,000 real estate professionals dedicated to helping people move to and around the Atlanta Metro. As a top real estate company, Coldwell Banker Residential Brokerage knows how to move Atlanta.

iStockphoto/Thinkstock

Let our specialists bring you home to the lifestyle of your dreams.

Atlanta offers an attractive selection of housing options, from affordable family homes to multimillion-dollar estates, and plenty in between.

EARTH SHAKING BEGINNINGS

Following San Francisco's devastating earthquake in 1906, Colbert Coldwell, a young real estate sales professional, witnessed many a sales associate acquiring property from vulnerable sellers that was immediately sold at high profits. He recognized a need for an honest and knowledgeable real estate company and opened his new firm. Arthur Banker was one of his early sales associates and the two soon recognized common shared values.

Well into its second century, Coldwell Banker continues to offer clients a level of services which both Coldwell and Banker would be proud to have associated with their names.

SOLID ON CUSTOMER SERVICE

"Coldwell Banker was founded on a commitment to profes-

sionalism and customer service that continues to be the core of our business today," said Tina Tyler, Director of Relocation Services for Coldwell Banker Residential Brokerage in Atlanta. "We are a full-service real estate company that is part of a large and successful network. Backed by the resources and capital of a leading global real estate services company, we've partnered with experts in every facet of the real estate transaction to meet the changing needs of our customers.

"We offer 'one stop shopping' with our partners: Coldwell Banker Home Loans, Regency Title Services, NRT Insurance, Inc., Coldwell Banker Home Protection Plan and Coldwell Banker's Concierge Services."

COMMITTED TO ATLANTA

In a committed belief to helping the communities they serve, the Coldwell Banker's Residential Brokerage CARES foundation is dedicated to improving the quality of life for families and individuals in Atlanta and surrounding areas. "We have more than 1000 sales professionals and employees who generously contribute a portion of each closing or paycheck to the Foundation that is matched dollar-for-dollar by the company," Tyler explained. "Our goal is to help those in need across the greater Atlanta area."

MOVING TO METRO ATLANTA?

The Relocation and Corporate Services Division of Coldwell Banker Residential Brokerage provides a full array of managed move and employee programs. "Whether a company is considering moving their headquarters to metro Atlanta or an individual chooses to move for a fresh start, we provide personalized services to streamline the relocation process and ease the stress," said Tyler. The company provides a single point of contact to orchestrate the services that lead to a smooth move. Services include assisting with the home sale anywhere in the world, home purchase, temporary housing, household goods shipping and more, based on the client's needs. "As part of a national network of top-performing real estate brokers, we can assist in selling a client's existing home, whether it is across town or around the globe," Tyler explained.

CONCIERGE SERVICES TAKES SERVICE TO THE NEXT LEVEL

"Coldwell Banker Concierge® Service is our complimentary program created to help buyers and sellers find the products and services they need before, during and after their move. It's a single resource center for all our client's home-related needs," Tyler said. "It's one more way we're moving into our second century of helping people relocate." ■

(©iStockphoto.com/EricV

Community & Southern Bank

Community & Southern Bank understands what drives customers, recognizing that inside every small business is a big one trying to make its mark, and behind every savings deposit is hope for a better future. CSB has created a true financial partner to offer a wide-range of solutions—and they do so with excellence, integrity and innovative thinking.

CSB Corporate Headquarters, Riverwood Parkway, Atlanta

Patrick M. Frawley
Chief Executive Officer

BIG BANK IDEAS WITH SMALL BANK FEEL

Founded by a team of experienced bankers in 2010, CSB was established to offer something unique to the people of Georgia by combining community-based banking expertise with enhanced services to create an environment that encourages both growth and prosperity. The bank has successfully brought a sense of community to financial services.

CSB offers a full range of financial products and services including personal and corporate lending options, wealth management, online banking, checking, mobile banking, savings, alternative financial services, treasury management solutions and more. With branches throughout Metropolitan Atlanta and the surrounding suburbs, CSB's mission is to proactively respond to customer needs by providing convenient options while displaying integrity in each and every business decision.

CSB's corporate culture is built around five core values: making a difference, developing innovative solutions, serving with passion, acting with urgency and delivering a professional and positive customer experience. Everything at CSB is built on these values, from opening a checking account to mobile banking capabilities—or facilitating a multi-million dollar corporate loan.

ENABLING SMALL BUSINESSES TO DRIVE THE ECONOMY

Market conditions can change quickly, and new competitors can consistently evolve. For a small business to succeed, it needs the ability to act—not simply react—which requires a bank partner with the same forward-thinking capabilities. CSB is that bank, enabling achievement and developing customer-centric solutions.

CSB knows and understands its customers and their business needs. As a local financial expert in the communities it serves, CSB is able to make faster, more informed decisions to enhance operations and improve returns.

To ensure small businesses experience fewer bumps along the road to success, CSB offers a variety of transaction accounts, lending and financial programs to help businesses thrive. From real estate and equipment purchases to acquisitions, expansions, accounts receivable and inventory financing—solutions are scalable, flexible and affordable. And when a small business customer grows larger, CSB is there to help foster that growth.

A COMMITMENT TO THE COMMUNITY

Many people believe that a bank is just a bank—regardless of its name. However, CSB is a true financial partner and understands the special circumstances of each customer. CSB brings an unparalleled sense of personal service to its operations.

Everyone desires a secure future. CSB provides the banking products and strategic financial expertise to help customers reach their full potential. CSB keeps it simple, enabling customers to move forward, reach higher and achieve financial goals through utilization of realistic plans tailored to fit individual circumstances. CSB provides its customers with excellence, integrity and innovative thinking, always working diligently for the betterment of the communities, businesses and individuals throughout the communities it serves. ∎

Cooper Carry

Cooper Carry provides architecture, planning, landscape architecture, interior design and environmental graphic design services. Founded in 1960, the firm specializes in the design of mixed-use, corporate, office, hospitality, residential, retail, education, science + technology, transit and government projects. It has designed projects in 45 states and globally in the Caribbean, Middle East, Asia, Africa and Central America.

(Top left) 10 Terminus Place, Atlanta, GA. A 19-story condominium in the heart of Buckhead.

(Bottom left) Residence hall at Berry College, Mount Berry, Georgia. Awarded 2010 Amerian School & University Educational Interiors Showcase, Silver Citation. LEED-NC Gold Certified.

(Bottom right) Southern Polytechnic State University, Architecture Studio, Marietta, Georgia. Recipient of AIA Georgia 2011 Merit Design Award; Gold Award, 2011 Brick in Architecture Awards; 2010 Craftsmanship Award of Excellence, Masonry Association of Georgia.

THE CENTER FOR CONNECTIVE ARCHITECTURE

Engaging a fundamental design philosophy centered around the concept that environments should connect people to people and people to place, the firm practices "connective architecture." Cooper Carry's designers understand the local market and the specific cultural and physical contexts in which the building will serve those who interact with it while conceiving memorable spaces, inside and out. Listening to the client and gaining a deep understanding of the market and site before commencing design, Cooper Carry balances passionate creativity with client service. The firm expands vision and adds value to every project and its community.

SUSTAINABILITY

Sustainability is a key attribute of each design. The firm considers environmental friendliness and the options for composing buildings and landscapes in ways that maximize solar orientation as well as many other factors that affect environmental performance. Commitment to environmentally responsible design is demonstrated by comprehensive, in-house education programs that support LEED® (Leadership in Energy and Environmental Design) accreditation of team members to enhance their command of sustainable design techniques. The firm designs each project to meet the stringent energy efficiency guidelines established by the U.S. Green Building Council.

A BROAD REACH

Notable projects in Georgia include Underground Atlanta, 10 Terminus Place, NSI's headquarters, Bloomingdale's, at Lenox Square, the Georgia Health Sciences University Cancer Research Center (formerly the Medical College of Georgia) and many buildings for state and private schools and universities. The firm recently completed projects for the National Aeronautics and Space Administration (NASA), the Federal Bureau of Investigation (FBI), the Centers for Disease Control Prevention (CDC) and the Navy.

Over 80 percent of Cooper Carry's portfolio is new work from existing clients, a testament to high-quality design, consistent service and bottom-line results. Cooper Carry has received more than two dozen awards including many from the American Institute of Architects and the American Society of Landscape Architects. This Georgia-grown design firm reaches far beyond the borders of the state; through its locations across the United States, the firm applies its philosophy of connective architecture to every project it touches. ■

VISIT COOPER CARRY ONLINE: www.coopercarry.com

DeKalb Convention & Visitors Bureau

DeKalb County, just east of downtown Atlanta, is home to the world's largest lasershow, projected on the side of Stone Mountain, as well as being a smorgasbord of international culture. ■ *Georgia's top tourist attraction is here, Stone Mountain Park, which also features the world's largest relief carving, that of Confederate Generals Robert E. Lee,*

Stonewall Jackson and President of the Confederacy, Jefferson Davis and their horses. Visitors may either hike or take a Swiss cable car to the top of the mountain to see the carving and an awesome view of the Atlanta skyline.

FAMILY-FRIENDLY FUN

The 3,200-acre Stone Mountain Park offers a variety of recreational activities, including golfing on two championship courses. Sky Hike™ is a family adventure course consisting of a quarter-mile of suspended bridges, climbing nets and ropes. More fun awaits at the Camp Highland Outpost, which includes a low ropes course, zip lines and rock walls. The Great Barn offers trampoline floors, interactive games and super slides.

The park's newest attraction, Geyser Towers, features sporadic water eruptions that cool off visitors on hot summer days. Visitors also may take a 40-minute tour of Stone Mountain Park, on water and land, via Ride the Ducks™, an amphibious open-air vehicle fashioned after vehicles used during World War II.

Love attending festivals? Stone Mountain Park hosts a bevy of annual celebrations, including the Yellow Daisy Festival, the Scottish Highland Games, the Indian Festival & Pow Wow and the Country Living Fair.

WOLRD-CLASS MUSEUMS

Georgia's third largest county also boasts a number of world-class museums. Bronze dinosaurs greet visitors at the entrance of the Fernbank Museum of Natural History, which contains reproductions of the world's largest dinosaurs, ancient fossils, an IMAX® theater and a NatureQuest that offers children hands-on activities. The Michael C. Carlos Museum of Emory University maintains the Southeast's largest collection of

ancient art, with more than 16,000 objects showcasing cultures from around the world.

DeKalb County has become an international oasis, home to about 700,000 people who speak more than 64 languages. This diversity is reflected in the number of international stores, groceries and restaurants found throughout the county.

AWARD-WINNING RESTAURANTS

Speaking of cuisine, the city of Decatur has been named "One of the Top 10 Tastiest Towns in the Southeast" by *Southern Living* magazine and its Cakes & Ale restaurant has been named among "The Hot 10: America's Best New Restaurants" by *Bon Appétit* magazine. So, by all means, dine out in DeKalb!

Decatur, six miles east of Atlanta, is the county seat and a small town with an artsy vibe and many eclectic stores, boutiques and art galleries. Eddie's Attic in Decatur is the place to be in the evening—it's where such artists as the Indigo Girls and Sugarland got their start.

Film stars also can be seen occasionally in DeKalb County, which is a "camera ready" county. In fact, Agnes Scott College, Druid Hills High School and Shamrock Middle School have appeared in scenes from *The Blind Side, Driving Miss Daisy* and *Remember the Titans* while Stone Mountain Park and Avondale Estates appeared in *The Three Stooges* and *The Odd Life of Timothy Green*, respectively.

DeKalb County Cities and Communities include Avondale Estates, Atlanta in DeKalb, Beacon Heights, Brookhaven, Chamblee, Clarkston, Decatur, Doraville, Druid Hills, Dunwoody, Ellenwood, Lithonia, Lynwood Park, Oakhurst, Pine Lake, Scottdale, Shermantown, Stone Mountain, Toco Hill and Tucker. ■

Lasershow Spectacular in Mountainvision at Stone Mountain Park. Courtesy of Stone Mountain Park

$\mathcal{D}$ermatology Affiliates

The six board-certified dermatologists at Dermatology Affiliates help their patients achieve healthy, beautiful skin by artistic application of the latest medical, cosmetic and surgical knowledge. ■ *Founded by Rutledge Forney, MD in 2004, the Atlanta practice treats various skin, nail and hair conditions, including acne, psoriasis and eczema, while also offering cosmetic, laser and aesthetic services to help rejuvenate skin.*

Dermatologist Affiliates' board-certified doctors help combat sun damage as well as the effects of aging.

PREVENT SUN DAMAGE

"We believe that prevention is as important as diagnosis and treatment, so we also take the time to educate our patients about how to prevent skin cancer and minimize signs of aging," Dr. Forney said, noting that brown spots and wrinkles are her clients' biggest cosmetic complaint. "Years don't destroy the skin, sun does. We cannot remove sun damage, but we can slow it down and make it less obvious by using chemical peels, lasers and scientifically based products."

A variety of sun hats adorn her office, attesting to the 12 weeks Dr. Forney spent as a medical student studying skin cancer in Melbourne, Australia, and at the Centers for Disease Control and Prevention in Atlanta.

Dermatology Affiliates' arsenal of sun-damage fighters include Fraxel® Restore and Dualwave, the first fractionated, nonablative laser that targets brown spots and improves skin texture; Gentlewaves®, a flashing, yellow light that supports collagen production; IPL, or intense pulsed light, a multiple wavelength light device that treats brown spots and redness and VBeam® Perfecta, a pulsed dye laser designed to treat individual red lines, bumps or areas of redness as well as individual brown spots.

LASER USE EVOLVING RAPIDLY

"The technology has improved by leaps and bounds over the last 15 years driven by demand from the aging Baby Boomers," Dr. Forney said. "We have an Exilis to help with skin tightening. We have always offered IPL, hair laser and vascular laser treatments for red spots and facial veins. We continue to hope for a great laser for superficial leg veins, but sclerotherapy is still the gold standard."

Dermatology Affiliates also offers Botox®, Radiesse™, Restylane®, Dysport® and Juvederm® to help patients maintain a younger, relaxed appearance. With three convenient locations in midtown Atlanta, Buckhead and East Cobb, a Dermatology Affiliates office is convenient for most Atlantans.

A graduate of Duke University, Dr. Forney graduated cum laude from the Emory University School of Medicine. She then served an internship in internal medicine at Duke, followed by a dermatology residency at the University of California, San Francisco, where she served as Chief Resident.

AWARD-WINNING DERMATOLOGISTS

An industry leader, Dr. Forney was selected by her peers as one of Atlanta's Top Doctors in 2010, 2011 and 2012, and received

the President's Award for Service from the Medical Association of Atlanta in 2006. She is a former Chairman of the Board and President of the Medical Association of Atlanta as well as past President of the Atlanta Dermatological Association. She is Vice Chair of the Medical Association of Georgia. She is board certified by the American Board of Dermatology.

Dermatology Affiliates also benefits from the expertise of Drs. Jennifer Burger, Cynthia Abbott, Sumayah Taliaferro, Corinne Erickson and Mark Chastain, all of whom are certified by the American Board of Dermatology.

Dr. Burger graduated cum laude from Agnes Scott College, then from Emory University School of Medicine. The Albany, Georgia, native served an internship in internal medicine and pediatrics at Emory University Hospital, then a dermatology residency at the University of Michigan.

Dr. Abbott graduated magna cum laude from Kentucky Wesleyan College, then received a master's degree in medical art illustration from Medical College of Georgia. After graduating from the University of Louisville School of Medicine, she served an internship in pediatrics at Kosair Children's Hospital and a dermatology residency at Ohio State University. Dr. Abbott won a Patients Choice Award in 2008, 2009, 2010 and 2011.

Dr. Taliaferro graduated with honors from Brown University, then from its medical school. She served an internal medicine residency at Yale Primary Care Internal Medicine and did a dermatology residency at Howard University. Dr. Taliaferro received the Patients Choice Award in 2011.

A Stanford University graduate, Dr. Erickson graduated from University of Rochester Medical School. She served an internship in internal medicine and a dermatology residency at the University of Maryland, Baltimore.

EXPERT IN MOHS SURGERY

Dr. Chastain, a native of Columbus, Georgia, specializes in Mohs micrographic surgery as well as advanced reconstructive techniques, melanoma excision and routine skin surgery. He graduated Phi Beta Kappa from Emory University, then from Tulane University School of Medicine. Dr. Chastain served an internship in internal medicine and a dermatology residency at Tulane, followed by a fellowship in Mohs surgery with Dr. Gary Monheit in Birmingham, Alabama. He serves on the medical staff of Wellstar Kennestone Hospital and Piedmont Hospital. He also is a diplomate of the American Board of Dermatology and a fellow of the American College of Mohs Surgery. ■

For more than 65 years, generations of Atlantans have trusted Dorsey Alston, Realtors and its commitment to bring together the highest quality client service and the area's most comprehensive market knowledge. The company's agents are legendary for uncovering hidden gems from the city of Atlanta to Roswell, Marietta or Sandy Springs and all the diverse neighborhoods in between, and guiding buyers and sellers with integrity and professionalism from start to finish.

Separating Dorsey Alston from competitors is its attention to personalized service. In addition to being a family business, Dorsey Alston is one of the oldest privately held companies in Atlanta. Their experience in the Atlanta-area real estate market is broad and deep, and they treat clients as individuals with specific needs, tastes and requirements.

These qualities culminate to support Dorsey Alston's claim to be: "Atlanta's First Family of Real Estate."

"The fact that we are a family-owned business and not a big corporation gives us the latitude and flexibility we need to focus on people who come to us for assistance," says Michael M. Rogers, president and CEO of Dorsey Alston, Realtors. "Looking for a home is a personal experience, and corporate policies and procedures only complicate the process. We are driven to provide the highest level of customer service and our hands-on executive structure allows us to do so, which is important in this business."

NO SUBSTITUTE FOR EXPERIENCE

Boasting a proud history, Dorsey Alston, Realtors was founded in 1947 by Atlantans Roy Dorsey and Robert Alston. They sold the business to Rogers' father in the 1980s, and Michael Rogers became chairman in 2000. At that time, the team consisted of 27 agents. Today, the firm features 180 agents. As the top-performing real estate company in Buckhead, it enjoys active partnerships with more than 1,600 luxury real estate firms and 120,000 dedicated sales associates throughout the United States and around the world.

"In the last three years we have sold more homes in our market than any other office," Rogers says. "I think people immediately sense our commitment to our client's best interest through every level of our organization. Our goal is to help them with one of the most important financial decisions they will ever make: where to live and raise their families."

One of Dorsey Alston's greatest assets is market knowledge. On average, Dorsey Alston agents have more than 14 years of experience, and the agency employs two of the area's longest-tenured brokers, Spalding White and Jim Ware. Such depth is crucial in a market as competitive and complex as Atlanta, where school districts, city and county taxes, neighborhood trends and location are all factors in making successful real estate decisions.

"In guiding buyers and sellers, there is no substitute for experience," Rogers says. "Our agents and brokers have proven experience and know-how to serve the needs and priorities of our clients. Furthermore, our track record shows that we deliver on our commitments."

A SPECIAL HOMETOWN ATTACHMENT

Rogers is the third Atlanta native to own and run Dorsey Alston, Realtors. He lives in Buckhead with his wife, a veterinarian, and their three children.

Rogers graduated from The Westminster Schools in Atlanta before receiving his bachelor's degree in economics from the University of Virginia and his MBA from the Stanford Graduate School of Business. He holds a broker's license with the Georgia Real Estate Commission, and he is a member of the Atlanta Board of Realtors.

"We love Atlanta, and we cannot imagine living anywhere else," Rogers says. "I think our attachment to Atlanta is why Dorsey Alston has experienced so much success and longevity in this market. This is our home, and we are excited about sharing it with others." ∎

Michael M.Rogers, president and CEO of Dorsey Alston Realtors®.

Dorsey Alston Realtors® new facility in the heart of Buckhead.

VISIT DORSEY ALSTON REALTORS® ONLINE: www.dorseyalston.com

Douglasville Convention and Visitors Bureau

Just a few miles west of downtown Atlanta, Douglasville is a vibrant community, full of life and charm, with many treasures. ■ *From the heart of Douglasville's historic downtown, featuring O'Neal Plaza with its cheerful brick fountain, visitors can stroll down Broad Street and delight in the friendly merchants' offerings.*

Close by is a tremendous selection of dining choices, from quick and casual to formal and elegant. And, depending on the season, Douglasville offers various civic, cultural and sporting events.

MANY FESTIVALS DOWNTOWN

Downtown Douglasville, a designated Main Street City, hosts many festivals including The Taste of Douglasville, Main Street Farmer's Market, dance and talent competitions, the annual Juneteenth Celebration, spring, summer and fall concerts, the sanctioned Moonlight 5k run, a Chili Cook-off, the West GA Quad Bike Ride, the July 4th celebration and Christmas parades.

With over 1,800 sleeping rooms, more than 200 restaurants and the largest indoor shopping mall west of Atlanta, located in a city of over 30,000 residents and covering 21 square miles, Douglasville can accommodate the needs of almost any group. Conveniently located along Interstate 20, Douglasville is less than 10 miles from Six Flags theme park and only a few minutes more from Hartsfield-Jackson International and Charlie Brown airports. Douglasville is always a good choice for an overnight stay while visiting the metro Atlanta area.

NEW CONFERENCE CENTER

Nestled in historic downtown Douglasville, the new Downtown Conference Center is uniquely equipped to offer whatever is needed to stage a spectacular event. The conference center, which features exquisite architecture and beautiful landscaping, includes a 7,672-square-foot ballroom that can be divided into five separate rooms, a business center, a fully equipped kitchen, bride and groom dressing rooms, two pre-function areas and a 150-seat auditorium. The unique blend of elegance and technologicly-savvy rooms makes the new Douglasville Conference Center the perfect choice for weddings, social and corporate events.

HISTORY OF DOUGLASVILLE

Located at a natural rise in the topography, Douglasville was originally known as Skint Chestnut. The name derived from a large tree, used by Native Americans as a landmark, which was stripped of its bark so as to be more conspicuous.

The Town of Douglasville was established by the Georgia General Assembly on February 25, 1875. An election was held on the first Saturday in March 1875, and a mayor, treasurer, records (secretary) and marshal were chosen. Thus began the official history of Douglasville, today one of the most attractive, historic parts of the Atlanta metro area. ■

(Top right) The Heart of Downtown Douglasville.

(Bottom left) Annual Charity Bike Ride held in Douglasville.

(Bottom right) One of the many yearly events held Downtown.

The famous red clay of Georgia is evident at
ARABIA MOUNTAIN *in DeKalb County.*
Photo by Sean Pavone.

$\mathcal{D}$unson Dental Design

Making people smile is no laughing matter at Dunson Dental Design. The Atlanta-based practice is all business when it comes to providing superior oral health services. Begun in 1996 by Bernee Dunson, D.D.S., the dental design office is conveniently located in Midtown to serve patients in the Atlanta Metropolitan area and throughout Georgia.

Dr. Bernee Dunson, recognized nationally and internationally for his achievements in oral implantology/ implant denistry, chose to return to Georgia and help the people of his home state.

Dunson Dental Design, which offers free consultations, provides general, restorative and cosmetic services that can give patients a brighter, more beautiful set of teeth in just a few visits. Procedures include crown and bridge, porcelain veneers, metal free restorations, tooth-colored fillings, teeth whitening and more. Dr. Dunson is also a recognized expert in implant dentistry, offering custom designed treatment plans for patients to regain their smiles with natural-looking teeth.

Every day, Dr. Dunson and his team are focused on fulfilling

their mission—to provide the finest blend of science and art while yielding the highest quality care.

"Our patients have the confidence that they're being treated with the safest and most innovative procedures available in dentistry, and they also appreciate our friendly, personalized service," says Dr. Dunson. "We strive to make the entire experience special for everyone who comes to us and we pride ourselves on having satisfied customers with beautiful smiles."

IMPROVING TOTAL HEALTH AND WELL-BEING

Many people who have problems with their teeth risk losing more than just their smiles. They may also experience difficulties with eating and speaking. Even if their problems are strictly cosmetic in nature, such as chipped, discolored or missing teeth, these imperfections can burden them with feelings of self-consciousness.

Whatever category the dental issue falls into, it can have a significant daily impact on an individual's quality of life and self-image. All of that can change for the better with a visit to Dunson Dental Design.

Included in the restorative procedures is implant dentistry, an excellent option for anyone missing one or more natural teeth. Unlike removable bridges and dentures, dental implants are fixed solidly and permanently into the jaw. They do not become loose or ill-fitting over time, and because they replicate the foundational structure of a tooth when restored, they look and feel just like natural teeth.

Dr. Dunson takes great care in determining the placement of implants and in tailoring the design of crowns, bridges and dentures. Implants blend seamlessly and comfortably with the unique shape of each individual's mouth.

For patients who experience anxiety during dental visits, Dunson Dental Design offers conscious sedation dentistry to put them at ease. Dr. Dunson uses advanced methods in local anesthesia along with sedation dentistry (sleep dentistry) so that patients enjoy a more comfortable and relaxing experience during their treatment.

"Although the anxiety feeling isn't uncommon, it should never keep you from seeking the dental care you need to look and feel your very best," says Dr. Dunson. "This is in keeping with our efforts to create a safe and comfortable environment for all of our patients, no matter what procedures are being performed."

A CONTINUOUS QUEST FOR EXCELLENCE

Dr. Dunson has outstanding educational qualifications and continues to participate in extensive training around the country. However, when deciding where to establish his professional practice, his desire was to return to Georgia and help the people of his home state.

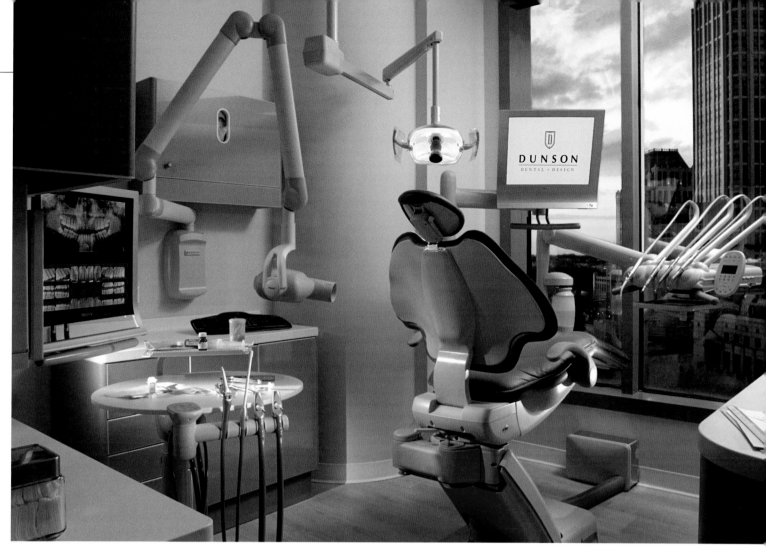

A native of Albany, Geogia, Dr. Dunson holds a biology degree from Morehouse College and a Doctorate in Dental Surgery from the University of Southern California. He attended Columbia University's general dentistry residency program at Harlem Hospital in New York and completed the oral implantology residency program at Loma Linda University in California.

Dr. Dunson also has an IV and oral conscious sedation certificate from Miami Valley Medical College in Dayton, Ohio, making him one of the select few restorative dentists in Georgia certified and licensed to do IV sedation.

In 2008, Dr. Dunson was one of nine dentists nationwide to be honored as a Diplomate of the American Board of Oral Implantology/Implant Dentistry. The following year he was one of 11 members to gain the distinction of Fellow of the American Academy of Implant Dentistry, the highest credential distinction bestowed by the first professional dental implant organization.

Dr. Dunson remains actively engaged in the latest developments in his discipline. He regularly lectures for national and international organizations and conferences on the advances in implant dentistry. In 2009, he launched the Atlanta Academy of Reconstructive Dentistry. Dentists travel from all over the world to learn, from Dr. Dunson, how to effectively place and restore dental implants.

"A lot has changed since the early days of dentistry," notes Dr. Dunson. "We are a modern facility where patients are treated with the best equipment, materials and procedures in the industry. Perhaps the only old-fashioned thing about us is the care we give our patients, and we are constantly looking for ways to improve." ∎

Dunson Dental Design is a modern facility where patients are treated with the best equipment, materials and procedures in the industry.

Dunwoody has the family-friendly feel of a small town, complete with good public schools, beautiful neighborhoods and a low crime rate. Its location just minutes away from downtown Atlanta lends it the cosmopolitan appeal of a big city. Small town charm combined with cosmopolitan opportunities make it a great place to live, work and play.

Just a few miles north of Atlanta in DeKalb County, Dunwoody is easily accessible via Interstate 285, Georgia 400 and three Metropolitan Atlanta Rapid Transit Authority (MARTA) stations. Perimeter Center, the metro Atlanta's largest contiguous business district, is located partly in Dunwoody, which is home to the North American headquarters of InterContinental Hotels Group.

The Dunwoody Village is the heart of the community and home to several shops, restaurants, and other locally-owned businesses.

GREAT SHOPPING, LONG HISTORY

Dunwoody's five upscale hotels are conveniently located in Perimeter Center and within walking distance of Perimeter Mall, the South's second-largest shopping center with over 200 specialty stores. Shopping also abounds at the charming boutiques in Dunwoody Village, which is distinguished by its Colonial Williamsburg architecture.

Although Dunwoody is one of Georgia's newest cities, incorporated in 2008, its history stretches back almost 200 years. The area originally was inhabited in the early 1800s by the Cherokees, who were drawn by its proximity to the Chattahoochee River and a robust trading center. They were followed by white settlers, who arrived around 1820.

PURSUING ECONOMIC DEVELOPMENT

Today, the city's location, its educated workforce, efficient transportation access to all parts of metro Atlanta and diverse real estate options are the incentives for many businesses and their employees to relocate to Dunwoody. The city works in partnership with the Dunwoody Convention and Visitors Bureau, the Dunwoody Chamber of Commerce and other stakeholders to pursue economic development and produce wealth for its businesses and residents while also expanding its tax base.

Dunwoody's economic development plan particularly targets these business segments: national and regional headquarters, foreign direct investment/operations of international firms, technology, business services, small businesses and destination services, such as hotels, retail and upscale restaurants.

WONDERFUL PLACE TO LIVE

The city has 46,000 residents, of which 40 percent hold bachelor's degrees and 20 percent hold advanced degrees. Dunwoody residents have access to six major parks, an eight-mile bicycle trail, a nature center, a weekly green market and a police force that has one officer for every 847 people.

The Dunwoody Village is the heart of the community and home to several shops, restaurants, and other locally-owned businesses.

The Dunwoody Farmhouse is an historic landmark in the Dunwoody Village. Today it operates as a special events facility for weddings and parties.

DeKalb County public schools are another advantage to living in Dunwoody. Their students most recently outperformed the state average on two new subject areas of the state-mandated End-of-Course Tests, topping the state average on algebra and geometry by 15 percentage points. Dunwoody also is home to a campus of Georgia Perimeter College, which is part of the University System of Georgia. The college focuses on serving non-traditional and international students; many of them take evening and online classes.

ARTS, FESTIVALS EMBRACED

Dunwoody residents who love the arts often attend plays at Stage Door Players. They also enjoy taking art classes and attending gallery showings at the Spruill Center for the Arts and Spruill Gallery, which Creative Loafing has been recognized as one of the area's best galleries for emerging artists.

Dunwoody's community groups host festivals that give neighbors the chance to have fun and socialize. The Dunwoody Art Festival, held annually on Mother's Day weekend, transforms Dunwoody Village into a vast art show, complete with live music, food, children's activities and more. The inaugural show was such a hit that it was named "Best New Event of 2010" by the Southeast Festivals and Event Association.

BUTTERFLIES, LEMONADE & 4TH OF JULY

Beautiful butterflies are the focus of Dunwoody Nature Center's annual Butterfly Festival each August. Games, crafts, live music and food are offered, but the real stars of the festival are hundreds of awe-inspiring butterflies enclosed in a tent.

Lemonade Days is a five-day festival in April that offers carnival rides, carnival food, live entertainment and a petting zoo. Sponsored by the Dunwoody Preservation Trust, the event raises money to help preserve and maintain the city's historic properties and provides education about Dunwoody's past. Proceeds from the 2012 festival benefited the Donaldson-Bannister House, a two-story house built in the 1870s.

Dunwoody is also home to Georgia's largest Fourth of July parade. Begun in 1976, the annual parade features a multitude of marching bands, floats, clowns, animals and local celebrities and attracts more than 32,000 spectators. ■

Brook Run is one of Dunwoody's premier parks located off Peeler Road and North Peachtree Road. The park is comprised of over 100 acres featuring a playground, Dog Park, Skate Park, Community Garden, trails and multi-use fields.

Dunwoody is home to the largest 4th of July parade in Georgia, held annually the morning of July 4.

Ellis Hotel

Modern, luxurious accommodations, exceptional service and an eco-friendly environment greet visitors at the historic Ellis Hotel in the heart of downtown Atlanta. ■ *Listed on the National Register of Historic Places, the award-winning hotel celebrates its 100th anniversary in 2013. Its age, however, is belied by a $27 million facelift that, in 2007, transformed the building into one of Atlanta's most exquisite boutique hotels.*

The 15-story hotel, located at 176 Peachtree Street, indulges its guests with 127 lushly appointed rooms. The hotel offers 114 guest rooms, 12 premium doubles with two double beds

and a living area with sofa bed and one large premium suite with a king-sized bed, private parlor and wet bar.

LUXURIOUS BED AND BATHROOMS

Each sophisticated guest room includes pillow-top mattresses, choice of feather or foam pillows, an iPod docking station, a 32-inch LCD television with premium cable stations and an executive work area. Luxury also unfolds in the bathrooms, which feature natural limestone floors, granite countertops, Kohler rain-shower heads and Gilchrist & Soames amenities.

Guests may enjoy a complimentary wine tasting in the evening, complimentary Wi-Fi access, a 24-hour business center and a fitness center. Hungry visitors also will enjoy the hotel's sustainable, organic (whenever possible), farm-to-table Terrace restaurant, which trades with approximately 27 local farmers, producers, artisans and fishermen.

ROMANTIC GETAWAY

For those planning a romantic getaway, the hotel offers a Romantic Package, which includes the Deluxe King Room, a bottle of house champagne, chocolate-covered strawberries and a romantic rose petal turndown service. The package also provides valet parking with 24-hour access, a 1 PM late checkout and breakfast in bed.

On the other hand, business travelers will appreciate the hotel's modern full-service business center, business support services and brand new meeting space that can accommodate up to 80 people for dinner, 40 people in a classroom and 125 people at a reception.

The Ellis Hotel's Women's Only Floor has won a place in Better Business Travel's Top 13 Business Hotels around the World. This floor features a secured entry and upgraded amenities, such as curling and straightening irons.

CLOSE TO DOWNTOWN ATTRACTIONS

The Ellis Hotel is within convenient walking distance of restaurants, local athletic arenas, corporations and such attractions as the Georgia Aquarium, Coca-Cola Museum, Centennial Park, the Margaret Mitchell House and the Georgia World Congress Center. It's only 10 miles from Hartsfield-Jackson Atlanta International Airport, which is an 18-minute MARTA ride from the Peachtree Center Street Station.

A well-trained, friendly staff makes sure that each guest's stay is everything he or she expected, and more. For additional pampering, the concierge can even arrange for licensed and bonded Spa Services to provide hot stone, Swedish or deep tissue massages, manicures, pedicures and wax services in the privacy of the guest's room.

While working to exceed guest expectations, the hotel's staff also demonstrates a commitment to the environment by using sustainable practices in waste minimization, reuse and recycling, energy efficiency, conservation and management, management of fresh water resources, waste water management, hazardous substance management and environmentally sensitive purchasing decisions.

ENVIRONMENTAL AWARDS

In fact, the Ellis Hotel is one of only two hotels in Georgia that have received the Green Seal™ Environmental Standard for Silver Lodging Properties. The hotel continually earns the Division 1 Outstanding Good Earthkeeping Award from the Georgia Hotel and Lodging Association. It also has earned the national American Hotel & Lodging Association's 2011 Good Earthkeeping Award.

The eco-responsible practices acknowledged by those awards include timed light systems installed in maintenance and housekeeping closets to save energy, landscaping that does not require watering and use of paper products that contain at least 30 percent post-consumer recycled content or tree-free fiber. In addition, the kitchen recycles oils through the Refuel Biodiesel Company, while linens and towels are washed every three days unless a guest requests otherwise.

TOP-RANKED HOTEL

Accolades have poured in from many satisfied guests: Expedia travelers have ranked the Ellis Hotel #1 in Atlanta and among the world's best hotels on the Expedia Insiders' Select™ list. TripAdvisor members have rated the Ellis Hotel the #2 business hotel in Atlanta and among the Top 10 Hotels in Atlanta.

In addition, the hotel has won the Atlanta Regional Commission's Exceptional Merit Award for Historic Preservation, Atlanta's Downtown Design Excellence Award and Urban Design Commission Award for Historic Preservation.

When it comes down to it, the Ellis Hotel considers its greatest award to be well-satisfied guests who become repeat customers. That is, after all, why it strives to provide world-class service and luxurious accommodations that meet—or exceed—their needs. ■

The historic Ellis Hotel is one of downtown Atlanta's hippest boutique hotels and just a short walk away from many tourist attractions and local athletic arenas. The award-winning hotel's classical façade belies its modern, comfortable rooms, full-service business center and farm-to-table Terrace restaurant.

Embassy Suites-Atlanta

Leisure and business travelers visiting Atlanta have happily found their "home away from home" at Embassy Suites Perimeter Center. The upscale, all-suite hotel is conveniently located in the North Atlanta suburb of Dunwoody, close to a number of corporate offices, including prominent Fortune 500 companies, as well as three access points to a MARTA public transit train station.

This Embassy Suites is steps from Perimeter Mall, the new Perimeter Place Shopping Center and, since it is close to Interstates I-85 and I-75, the I-285 Atlanta By-Pass and Georgia 400, is also just a few minutes from the legendary shopping at Lenox Square and Phipps Plaza. Downtown Atlanta can be reached in about 15 minutes, so visitors who want to see the Georgia Aquarium, the Georgia Dome or Turner Field, for example, can do so easily while based at a secure high-end hotel.

Embassy Suites Perimeter Center in Dunwoody is conveniently located near several Fortune 500 companies, and also has facilities to host corporate meetings.

CONVENIENT, SAFE LOCATION
"This hotel, located in one of Georgia's most affluent and newest cities, has many natural advantages over other metro Atlanta hotels, such as tremendous access to all parts of Atlanta, free parking at the hotel and the safety of our exclusive location," said Brad Sturgeon, the hotel's general manager.

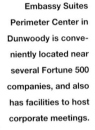

Embassy Suites features spacious two-room suites overlooking a sky-lit tropical atrium. Guests may choose from a king-sized or two queen-sized beds, both featuring luxurious Sweet Dreams® bedding

custom designed by Serta. A plush-top mattress and patented innersprings provide comfort as well as extra support for the lower back.

The living area consists of a sofa bed, work-style desk, chairs, microwave, coffee maker and a wet bar with refrigerator. Both rooms have 32-inch LCD high-definition televisions and high-speed wireless Internet access.

BUSINESS CENTER AVAILABLE 24/7
Business travelers find their work is made a little easier by the Embassy Business Link™ centers, which offer 24-hour-a-day access and mobile printing capability through PrinterOn®. In addition, Embassy Suites' eFolio tool provides online check-out and makes travel-expense reporting easier by providing access to hotel receipts online.

Guests seeking recreation will be delighted to find a bright and spacious indoor swimming pool and sun deck, whirlpool and 24-hour fitness center.

HOME-COOKED BREAKFASTS
Delicious cooked-to-order breakfasts, which include custom-

made omelets, meats, potatoes and pancakes, are complimentary for Embassy Suites guests, as are traditional continental breakfast items such as pastries, cereals and fruit. In the evening, a Manager's Reception offers house wine, select draft beers, non-alcoholic drinks and light snacks. A casual restaurant is available on site to satisfy hungry visitors, who also may choose among more than 30 eateries within a three-mile radius.

Embassy Suites Perimeter Center has meeting rooms, banquet facilities and catering services to serve corporate meetings, family reunions, weddings and other special groups. Its attentive staff can help coordinate all details, even down to the seating chart and room décor.

The hotel is 25 miles from Hartsfield-Jackson International Airport and seven miles from the DeKalb-Peachtree Airport. Complimentary shuttle service is provided within a three-mile radius, including to businesses, shops and the Sandy Springs MARTA station.

HIGHEST GUEST SATISFACTION AWARD

Founded in 1983, Embassy Suites pioneered the all-suite hotel and is the nation's largest brand of such value-added lodging. Numerous accolades attest to its success in serving visitors. This past year, for example, Embassy Suites Hotels won the J.D. Power and Associates Award for Highest Guest Satisfaction in the Upper Upscale Hotel Chains category; this was the company's ninth such award in 12 years!

In 2012, *Parents Magazine* named Embassy Suites among the "10 Best Hotel Chains for Families," saying, "You've got to love the layout. It's the only chain in our survey where all the accommodations are two-room suites with a door that separates the master bedroom (your digs) from the living area with a pull-out couch (the kids' space)."

TripAdvisor echoed that recommendation recently when it deemed Embassy Suites the "most family-friendly hotel brand."

And once a family has enjoyed its Embassy Suites experience, the adults might want to add a free iPhone, iPad or Android app that lets them browse and book reservations at more than 200 Embassy Suites nationwide. ■

Leisure and business travelers alike enjoy the delicious, cooked-to-order breakfasts and Manager's Reception held daily on the main floor. The spacious two-room suites feature specially made bedding by Serta, two 32-inch flat-screen televisions, a work area and sofa bed.

Taste the Coke side of life

Coca-Cola is a trademark known and loved worldwide. In Memphis, Tennessee, "THE WORLD OF COKE" showcases miles of Coca-Cola memorabilia along an abandoned railway track.

Fernbank Museum of Natural History

Science comes to life at Fernbank Museum of Natural History in Atlanta, where visitors can roam among bronze dinosaurs, explore Georgia ecosystems and walk on sea-fossil floors, then enjoy martinis and watch a five-story IMAX® movie. ■ *"Fernbank Museum inspires life-long learning of natural history through immersive programming and*

unmatched experiences to encourage a greater appreciation of our planet and its inhabitants," said Fernbank's President and CEO, Susan Neugent. "It's exciting to see visitors enthralled with fossils, dinosaurs and the many other fascinating creatures that used to roam the Earth. It's also rewarding when they connect natural history to modern world cultures, nature, live animals and how science continues to unlock many of the world's mysteries."

The museum draws its inspiration from the adjacent 65-acre Fernbank Forest, the country's largest old-growth urban Piedmont forest. These woods surrounded the Druid Hills home of Emily Harrison, who named the area Fernbank after the ferns she found along the forest's creek banks. Emily helped organize Fernbank, Inc. in 1938 to purchase and preserve the forest, which is owned and managed by Fernbank Museum of Natural History.

DINOSAURS AND MORE!

Fernbank Museum, which opened in 1992, has continued to grow and expand its programs. Today, a family of bronze dinosaurs greets visitors at the entrance plaza, signaling the wonders that wait inside. As visitors encounter the Giants of the Mesozoic exhibit, families come face-to-face with the world's largest dinosaurs, including the 123-foot-long, plant-eating Argentinosaurus and the 47-foot-long, carnivorous Giganotosaurus beneath flying pterosaurs.

The award-winning exhibition Fernbank NatureQuest offers children more than 100 hands-on activities as they explore a waterfall, river, swamp, estuary, ocean, forest, rock wall, cave and archaeology excavation to learn about nature and habitats.

Other permanent exhibits include A Walk Through Time in

Georgia, which tells the story of Georgia's natural history and the Earth's development; Sensing Nature, which reveals how our senses combine to interpret everyday events like the weather; and Reflections of Culture, which features beautiful jewelry, clothing, and other objects of cultural expressions.

SEA FOSSILS AMID STAR GALLERY

As visitors wander through the museum, they tread upon more than 40,000 limestone tiles that hold sea fossils over 100 million years old. Other highlights include ancient artifacts from St. Catherines Island, objects connected to Hernando de Soto's expedition through the state, a Naturalist Center, a Native American dugout canoe, and Star Gallery.

Martinis & IMAX® is a popular Friday evening attraction for adults, complete with live music, dancing, cocktails, great cuisine and IMAX® movies. The third Friday of each month is Salsa Night.

A RARE ACCREDITATION

Fernbank Museum of Natural History has been accredited by the American Association of Museums, a distinction awarded to fewer than five percent of museums nationwide.

Now one of the most visited museums in the Southeast, Fernbank celebrated its 20th anniversary in 2012. Explore the Museum's special programs at fernbankmuseum.org. ■

(Bottom left) The world's largest dinosaurs are featured in Giants of the Mesozoic.

(Bottom right) Young visitors can explore a variety of habitats that feature live animals and hands-on activities in Fernbank NatureQuest. Photo by Boris

(Top right) Visitors explore the Coast and Barrier Islands diorama in A Walk Through Time in Georgia. Photo by Daemon Baizan

Georgia Commerce Bank

Georgia Commerce Bank delivers on its motto "Your Success is our Business" by offering quality products and personalized service. A community bank dedicated to meeting every customer's needs, Georgia Commerce provides the full range of banking and lending services at branches throughout the metro Atlanta area.

SOLID LEADERSHIP

With over 60 years of combined banking experience, Chairman and CEO Mark Tipton and President Rodney Hall established Georgia Commerce Bank in 2003 to provide an alternative to impersonal and less flexible larger banks. Weathering the savings and loan crisis in Texas in the late 1980s, Tipton and Hall both learned the importance of diversification and teamwork.

The Board of Directors supporting Tipton and Hall is comprised of local business owners, entrepreneurs, corporate executives and long-time banking professionals with extensive knowledge of the Atlanta market. This combination of leadership, knowledge and dedication resulted in GCB showing its first profitable quarter less than a year after opening.

FOCUS ON RELATIONSHIPS

Georgia Commerce Bank is a locally owned and managed independent community bank where clients are on a first name basis with the branch employees and where the Chairman of the Board means it when he says, "Call me if you need anything."

Georgia Commerce specializes in lending to privately-held owner-operated companies and the professional/executive market. The bank offers the complete spectrum of commercial and personal banking services. For business clients, Georgia Commerce offers credit card processing, remote deposit capture, commercial real-estate, SBA and working capital loans. Individuals can take advantage of the bank's online banking, interest checking, private banking and wealth management services. Residential and commercial mortgages are also available at competitive interest rates. More information about the services and products offered is available on the bank's website: www.gacommercebank.com.

COMMUNITY INVOLVEMENT

Georgia Commerce is passionate about supporting local community causes. CEO and Chairman Mark Tipton is an active volunteer, fundraiser and board member for Big Brothers Big Sisters of Metro Atlanta and United Way of Atlanta. President Rodney Hall is Chairman of the Board of Directors of the Bobby Dodd Institute which supports disadvantaged and disabled people in pursuit of economic self-sufficiency. The bank is also a sponsor of Captain Planet and Skyland Trail.

Branch managers and commercial lenders are active in local Rotary and Kiwanis Clubs as well as the business associations of Buckhead, Marietta, Woodstock, Cumming, Acworth and Peachtree Corners. Companywide, GCB supports and participates in various Multiple Sclerosis fund-raising events,

Big Brothers Big Sisters Bowl-a-thons and Susan G. Komen three-day walks.

In support of all the bank's families and friends, the Georgia Commerce banner flies proudly at school ballparks, gymnasiums and soccer fields throughout the metro Atlanta area.

GROWTH AND EXPANSION

The original "world headquarters" branch on Cumberland Boulevard opened in 2003 with eleven employees. In 2006,

a second branch opened in Marietta across from Kennestone Hospital. In 2011, Georgia Commerce opened branches in Buckhead, Cumming, Woodstock and Acworth. The Peachtree Corners branch opened Fall 2012.

As the bank continues to grow, the four key factors that distinguish Georgia Commerce Bank from the rest of the pack remain the same: Experienced Staff, Individual Solutions, Local Decisions, Personal Relationships and "Can Do" Leadership.

With every branch opened, Georgia Commerce Bank remains committed to excellence in customer service, the individual focus of community banking and to the motto: "Your Success is our Business." ∎

Chairman & CEO Mark Tipton (left) and President Rodney Hall established Georgia Commerce Bank as an alternative to impersonal and less flexible larger banks.

Explore Georgia
Georgia Department of Economic Development

Looking for a vacation with a fresh new twist? From its energetic and lively cities to the gorgeous barrier islands and breathtaking mountain scenery, Georgia provides a contemporary and modern feel with the heritage and hospitality of the old South.

DISCOVER DIVERSE LOCATIONS

Within the city limits of Atlanta see the world's largest aquarium, follow in the footsteps of Martin Luther King, Jr., taste many flavors at the World of Coca-Cola or stroll through art collections from around the world.

Georgia's coast stretches approximately 100 miles between the Savannah and St. Marys rivers. Nature lovers can wander along isolated beaches where wild horses gallop in the surf, paddle the tranquil waters of a saltwater marsh or stroll cobblestone streets in historic Savannah. The Golden Isles along Georgia's coast have been a vacation destination since the late 1700's.

In the North Georgia mountains, visitors can enjoy eco-adventures including zip line tours, fly fishing excursions and whitewater rafting. North Georgia also is home to more than 30 wineries. Enjoy wine tastings at the vineyards, festivals, the Georgia Wine Trail and other special events in this region.

FAMILY FUN

Georgia has plenty of options for the entire family. Children will enjoy playing at Imagine It!, The Children's Museum of Atlanta or seeing the stars at the Tellus Science Museum in Cartersville. Spend the day exploring an interactive neighborhood at Interactive Neighborhood for Kids, Inc. (INK) in Gainesville. Or take a ride on the Sam Shortline Excursion Train through southwest Georgia in vintage 1949 train cars.

Georgia offers something for every shopper. Atlanta, one of the country's top ten retail markets, has such spectacular shopping venues as Lenox Square and Phipps Plaza, as well as small boutiques in neighborhoods like Buckhead and Virginia-Highland. Great discounts are found at several outlet centers

Georgia's mountains, beaches and rivers offer outdoors enthusiasts a variety of sporting choices.

around the state. Atlanta has five outlet centers within a one-hour drive. Stroll through the attractive outdoor village setting of the North Georgia Premium Outlets in Dawsonville or visit the Tanger Outlet Centers in Commerce and Locust Grove.

GEORGIA'S CIVIL WAR

From Chickamauga, the second-bloodiest battle of the Civil War, to Andersonville, the notorious prison camp, Georgia has a wealth of battlefields, cemeteries, arsenals, museums, mansions and stories. The Civil War's impact on Georgia was greater than any other event in the state's history with some 11,000 Georgians killed and more than 100,000 total casualties. The Blue and Gray Trail, which extends from Chattanooga to Atlanta, highlights some of the preserved land and battle sites. Georgia is commemorating the 150th Anniversary of the Civil War through 2015 with special events and activities across the state.

DRIVING TRAILS

The most memorable and widely recognized American film was written in Atlanta and can still be experienced in Georgia today. The Gone With the Wind Trail offers visitors access to the history and legacy behind the Pulitzer Prize-winning novel while also exploring the complex life of Margaret Mitchell. The trail travels from Marietta through Atlanta to Jonesboro.

Georgia's Antebellum Trail is a 100-mile trek through seven communities that escaped burning during Gen. William T. Sherman's march through Georgia. Stately, pillared manors line the streets of such historic communities as Madison, Washington and Eatonton. Visit Milledgeville and tour the Old Governor's Mansion or observe Athens' famous double-barreled cannon before seeing "the town that time forgot," Old Clinton.

A unique combination of sites can be found along the Chieftains Trail throughout the Northwest corner. This 200-mile driving trail highlights the extensive Native American history and heritage of what the Cherokee called "The Enchanted Land."

OUTDOOR ADVENTURES

Waterfalls and lakes, wetlands and mountains are just some of the beautiful environments within Georgia's state parks. Enjoy camping, hiking, fishing, boating, geocaching, birding, photography and more. Georgia's State Historic Sites include presidential homes, ancient Indian mounds, battlefields, plantations and a gold museum. The daring can even canoe with alligators on the Okefenokee Swamp at Stephen C. Foster State Park. The swamp is one of the oldest and most well preserved freshwater areas in America.

Visitors have many options in terms of accommodations—everything from luxury resorts and upscale hotels to comfortable, family-friendly motels and historic bed-and-breakfasts.

For a week-long family vacation or a weekend getaway, Georgia is the place where the most inspiring, entertaining and unforgettable vacation memories await. Visit *www.Explore Georgia.org* to plan a trip! ∎

Georgia is the ideal place to visit wineries, shop and visit Civil War battlefields. The 5,200-acre Chicka-mauga Battlefield (pictured below) in Walker County was the scene of the last major Confederate victory.

The Georgia Dental Implant Center and Gentle Dental Care specializes in advanced prosthodontics which focuses on restoring teeth to their optimum function and appearance, then in helping patients maintain their healthy smiles. Founded by Dr. Steve Hahn in 2007, it is one of the few U.S. practices to offer the wide range of advanced

prosthodontics and implant surgery as well as routine dental care. With offices in Acworth and midtown Atlanta, the Georgia Dental Implant Center is conveniently located for most North Georgia residents.

People often lose teeth because of decay, disease, injury or wear from grinding. "Tooth loss results in unwanted changes to a person's facial appearance while also having a detrimental effect on the jaw structure, bite alignment and a patient's overall health," Hahn said. "By using dental implants, we can improve a patient's quality of life as well as self-esteem by eliminating the missing or defective teeth."

IMPLANTS PROTECT HEALTH
Dental implants are devices, usually made of titanium, that replace tooth roots and are used to support restorations resembling a tooth or group of teeth, such as crowns or

Drs. Steve Hahn and Jason Kim specialize in advanced prosthodontics as well as dental implants.

bridges. They are the only tooth-replacement solution that can protect a patient's dental health by simulating a natural tooth and its root structure.

Dental implants have several benefits over dentures. Implants provide a chewing efficiency similar to natural teeth, while use of dentures results in a 75 percent decline of efficiency. Dentures also eventually wear down the bone supporting them, resulting in an improper fit.

The All-on-4 procedure, invented in the 1990s, often is used on eligible patients who cannot undergo the rigors of bone graft surgery, yet want the benefits of a full implant. This procedure provides four implants and a full set of new replacement teeth in a few appointments, so it also is less time consuming and less costly than alternative treatments.

DR. STEVE HAHN
Prosthetic dentistry requires several years of additional training beyond dental school. Hahn received his academic training in dentistry at Boston University and earned a certificate in Advanced Education in general dentistry from Columbia University's College of Dental Medicine. He completed an additional specialty residency, receiving a Master of Science degree in advanced prosthodontics from Columbia, followed by an Implant Fellowship with a surgery focus at New York University's College of Dentistry. During this time, Hahn also taught at Columbia. Dr. Hahn has been certified by the Institute for Advanced Laser Dentistry as one of a handful of dentists in the Atlanta area able to perform LANAP® Periodontal Laser surgery.

Hahn also is a member of the American College of Prosthodontists, the International Congress of Oral Implantation, the Academy of Osseointegration, New York and New Jersey dental associations and the American Dental Association. He is board eligible for the American Board of Prosthodontics, belongs to the Omicron Kappa Upsilon Honor Society and serves as an advisor for Columbia University's Korean American Dental Student Association.

DR. JASON KIM
Dr. Jason Kim, who has been a dentist since 1994, also works at the Acworth office. Kim attended the State University of New York at Buffalo where he received his Doctor of Dental Surgery degree. He also served in the U.S. Navy, including a posting at the Naval Dental Center at Miramar "Top Gun" in San Diego. Kim performs root canals, restorations, crown and bridge, bonding, veneers and extractions. He also makes an annual mission trip to Haiti to help the less fortunate. Kim, who enjoys golfing and all sports, is married and has two beautiful daughters.

Drs. Steve Hahn, Jason Kim and their staff are experienced, caring professionals who maintain the highest levels of accreditation and pursue continuing education to stay abreast of the latest dentistry trends. Their offices in Acworth and midtown Atlanta are equipped with cutting edge technology.

DR. AMY MANDALIA

The Midtown Atlanta office includes Dr. Amy Mandalia, an experienced, board-certified dentist focusing on cosmetic dentistry. Born and raised in Pennsylvania, she completed an undergraduate dual-degree with honors at New York University in 2002, then obtained her dental degree from the New York University College of Dentistry. She has also received extensive cosmetic training under the mentorship of her father, Dr. Vinod Mandalia, an accomplished dentist in Feasterville, Pennsylvania.

Dr. Mandalia performs all disciplines of dentistry including aesthetic, restorative, endodontic, periodontic, pedodontic, implant and oral surgery. She is a member of the American Dental Association, Georgia Dental Association and the Academy of General Dentistry. She is certified in Invisalign® and Lumineers®. ■

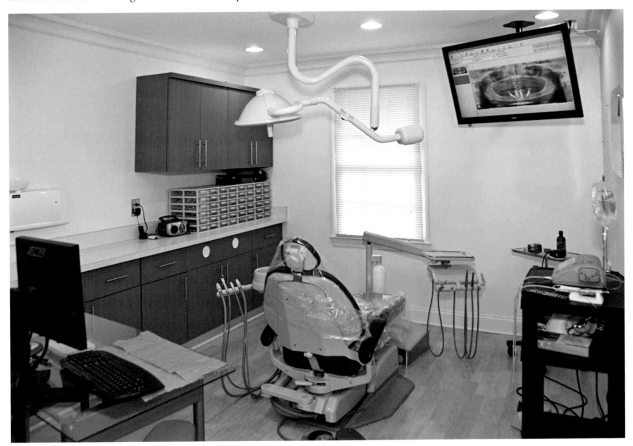

Georgia State Parks
Department of Natural Resources

From the top of Amicalola Falls in Dawsonville down to the Okefenokee Swamp, Georgia is one of the country's most naturally diverse states. And how better to experience the Peach State's natural beauty than by staying at a state park and waking up to the sunrise?

Georgia's state parks offer a multitude of accommodations to satisfy every preference and budget. Many people prefer to stay in rustic cabins, which are available at nearly 30 state parks. Most of these one-, two- and three-bedroom cottages are on hillsides or beside lakes, offering outstanding views. All are fully equipped with stoves, refrigerators, kitchen and dining utensils, towels, bed linens and blankets as well as heating and air conditioning. Many cabins include screened porches or decks, wood-burning fireplaces or stoves and televisions.

LODGES WITH SCENIC VIEWS

(Top right) Guests at Smithgall Woods State Park near Helen can sleep tight right next to Dukes Creek.

Four hotel-style lodges also are available which can host group meetings. Those in Amicalola Falls and Unicoi have excellent views of the North Georgia mountains and the George T. Bagby and Little Ocmulgee lodges in South Georgia feature golf courses and lakes.

GLAMPING AND CAMPING

(Bottom left) The Lodge at Amicalola Falls State Park is located a short hike from the Southeast's tallest waterfall.

If camping is your preference, Georgia's state parks offer more than 2,700 campsites, with rates averaging around $23-$28 per night. Most parks have laundry facilities and sell camping supplies. There are RV pull-through sites with modern comfort station, and primitive back-packing sites. The Fort Mountain and Unicoi parks even offer covered platforms where visitors can roll out their sleeping bags.

(Bottom right) Several of Georgia's State Parks have lakeside camping, such as Seminole State Park near Bainbridge.

Yet others prefer staying in a yurt. These canvas-and-wood tents—available at Red Top Mountain, High Falls and Fort Yargo state parks—have comfortable furniture to sleep six people, electrical outlets, large windows and locking doors. With a grill, picnic table and water spigot outside, all visitors need to bring are linens or sleeping bags, a cooler, food, cooking utensils and their friends or family!

Georgia's parks offer a variety of recreational activities, including geocaching, disc golf and boating. Eight state parks have golf courses, several of which have been praised by *Golf Digest*. Love to hike, fish, kayak, canoe, bike or bird watch? There's a state park for those activities, too. More than 90 wildlife management areas are open to hunting, some also include archery and firearm ranges.

OUTDOOR EXERCISE 'TONS OF FUN'

Outdoor recreation is a cornerstone of the Georgia State Parks' Tons of Fun fitness challenge, which encourages Georgians to exercise. "When exercise is fun, people tend to stick with it much longer," Parks Director Becky Kelley said. "Exercise doesn't have to be a chore—it's literally a walk in the park." ■

Georgia's Rome

The founders of Rome, Georgia, discovered distinct parallels between their new city and its namesake across the Atlantic. Today, the history, grandeur and beauty of Georgia's Rome make it a top Southern tourist destination, with plenty of modern touches to appeal to new generations of visitors and adventure-seekers.

Located in the center of the Atlanta-Birmingham-Chattanooga triangle, Rome is a convenient drive for a weekend getaway or an action-packed family vacation.

There are many ways to discover Rome—through its mix of fascinating museums, on miles of hiking and biking trails, or strolling through the historic Between the Rivers District downtown, filled with restaurants, boutiques and some of the finest antique stores around. Even Rome's historic Myrtle Hill Cemetery is an irresistible tourist stop.

"Visitors to Rome are always enchanted by the diversity of activities here and the natural beauty of our city," says City of Rome Mayor Evie McNiece. "The surrounding hills, mountains and rivers have shaped Rome's character, and our many landmarks and museums tell the remarkable story of one of America's most historic cities."

ROMAN HISTORY: AN ALL-AMERICAN JOURNEY

As one of the few towns that saw continuous action during all the years of the Civil War, Rome is a must-see destination for history buffs. Myrtle Hill Cemetery includes more than 300 graves of Civil War soldiers and key military figures and is the final resting place of First Lady Ellen Axson Wilson, wife of President Woodrow Wilson.

Now, tourists can experience Myrtle Hill Cemetery with a smart phone app. Launched in 2012, the first-of-its-kind app guides visitors through over 65 notable cemetery sights while providing context for the history observed there. Visit www. MyrtleHill.mobi to experience the free tour.

The history of Rome and Floyd County unfold in three unique museums, each providing a compelling perspective of the city's past. At Chieftain's Museum, a National Trail of Tears certified historic site, visitors are introduced to Major Ridge, a Cherokee leader who played a pivotal role in Native American and United States history.

Another historic stop is Oak Hill and the Martha Berry Museum, the Greek revival home of Martha Berry, founder of Berry College and a legacy among strong, powerful Georgia women. The Rome Area History Museum in the heart of historic downtown enables visitors to walk through time, from the Native Americans and early settlers to the Civil War and the development of Rome's culture, lifestyle and industries.

ALL TRAILS LEAD TO ROME

Cyclists and hikers will fall in love with the Heritage Trail, a 10 mile network of paved, riverside promenades leading past many of the area's most celebrated landmarks. Others will love the Jackson Hill Mountain Biking Trail, a 1.4-mile loop located less than a mile from downtown Rome, providing a wilderness trail experience in the center of the city.

In the nearby village of Cave Spring, families flock every summer to the giant, spring-fed swimming pool near the town square. After a refreshing plunge, visitors can enjoy a meal at one of the square's many restaurants and overnight at charming bed and breakfast inns.

Baseball fans may catch the Rome Braves in action and see the future stars of major league baseball playing today. The class-AAA affiliate of the Atlanta Braves plays home games at State Mutual Field two miles from the heart of downtown and located on the Heritage Trail system. The Braves Miracle Field opened in 2012 and is a specialized field of latex-free rubber that allows children with disabilities to play baseball.

Golfers come from far and wide to play at Stonebridge Golf Course. Set in the foothills of the Appalachian Mountains, Stonebridge backs up to the 26,000 acres that comprise Berry College, the world's largest college campus and a protected wildlife area offering breathtaking views of the mountains and countryside.

"Everyone who visits Rome leaves with something great to say," says McNeice. "Our many amenities make it the perfect destination for conventions, board meetings, staff retreats, reunions, weddings and sports tournaments. We urge folks to come experience what makes Georgia's Rome an American classic." ∎

Civil War history is found on all seven hills of Georgia's Rome. With three forts and nearly a dozen hospitals, Rome was an important city to the Confederacy and was the first city burned in Sherman's March to the Sea. Photo by Greg McCary.

Rome's historic campus of Berry College, the world's largest college campus at 26,000 acres. The campus offers numerous public trail systems and opportunities for fun outdoors. The college also supports a world class museum and antebellum home: Oak Hill & the Martha Berry Museum. Photo by Jason Blalock.

Aptly named the BLUE RIDGE MOUNTAINS, this section
of the mighty Appalachian Chain is located in North Georgia.
Photo by Dave Allen.

Goldstein, Garber and Salama LLC

Goldstein, Garber and Salama LLC is a comprehensive, world-renowned dental practice that offers virtually all specialties in one Atlanta office. With three dual-certified dentists/lecturers, three other specialists and an in-house dental laboratory, this one-stop shop focuses on providing the best possible results for each patient.

"Solutions in oral care often require the expertise of multiple specialties," Dr. Ronald Goldstein said. "For this reason our staff is made up of talented, multi-specialized dentists including periodontists, prosthodontists, orthodontists and oral surgeons who work together to expedite first-class results."

EXPERT ON COSMETIC DENTISTRY

A main focus of the practice is cosmetic dentistry. Goldstein literally wrote the book on cosmetic dentistry, authoring the first textbook about the subject in 1976, *Esthetics in Dentistry*, which is now in its third edition. He also has written for consumers; his *Change Your Smile* (now in its fourth edition) educates readers about the various procedures that can improve their teeth as well as how to maintain their perfected smile. That book, translated into 10 languages, has been read by millions of people worldwide.

"Your smile reveals your self-image," said Goldstein, a native Atlantan. "If you don't like your smile, you tend to look down, cover it…psychologically and subconsciously it can be a real problem for a lot of people. Conversely, if you love your smile, you can be fat or thin, short or tall and you can still look great. People love a great smile."

Goldstein, Garber and Salama perform everything from teeth whitening and bleaching to dental bonding, cosmetic contouring and porcelain veneers. A trial smile is even possible! One version is a snap-on smile; others can consist of tooth-colored composite resin materials temporarily bonded to the teeth or laboratory-constructed temporary restorations that give the look of the final restorations. This ensures that the patient will like his or her dental outcome before proceeding with the final treatment.

BRACES, INVISALIGN IMPROVE TEETH

Orthodontic treatment is another way Goldstein, Garber and Salama can dramatically improve a patient's appearance. Translucent braces can properly align the teeth, as can Invisalign. Instead of wires and brackets, Invisalign uses custom-made "invisable" plastic aligners to straighten teeth. Conditions typically treated with Invisalign include spaced teeth, overly crowded teeth, crossbite, underbite and overbite.

Drs. Goldstein, Garber and Salama are well-known for their clinical expertise in dental implants, which provide a foundation for replacement teeth that look, feel and function like natural teeth. "You can walk in with a set of dentures in the morning—provided there's enough bone—and we can place the fixtures and you can walk out that afternoon with teeth," Dr. David Garber said.

SOLUTION FOR SLEEP APNEA

The practice also can help alleviate such wellness problems as obstructive sleep apnea, which is characterized by abnormal pauses in breathing or periods of very low breathing during sleep. This disorder is caused by a blocked or narrowed airway during sleep, usually due to relaxed throat muscles, the tongue or tonsils, the shape of head or neck or being overweight. Dr.

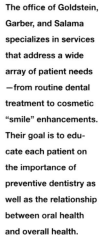

The office of Goldstein, Garber, and Salama specializes in services that address a wide array of patient needs —from routine dental treatment to cosmetic "smile" enhancements. Their goal is to educate each patient on the importance of preventive dentistry as well as the relationship between oral health and overall health.

Maurice Salama custom fits such patients for a dental appliance designed to keep the airway open and help prevent apneas; this treatment does not involve drugs or surgery.

During the last decade, scientists have discovered a link between chronic periodontal infections and heart disease, diabetes, stroke and some cancers. That's why Goldstein, Garber and Salama offer three salivary diagnostic tests. One test identifies and measures certain bacteria that can cause gingivitis and periodontitis, while another test can determine if a patient is at increased risk genetically for severe gum tissue infections. A third test can tell if a patient carries the HPV virus; all three tests also help determine the appropriate treatment regimen for the patient.

STEM-CELL BANKING OFFERED

Another innovative service is stem-cell banking: a patient's stem-cell-rich dental pulp is collected when he or she has an orthodontic or wisdom tooth extraction, then sent to a lab to be cryogenically preserved, stored and monitored. This is done in the hope that scientists will discover how to use the stem cells to help prevent diseases or regenerate muscle.

These cutting-edge procedures weren't even a gleam in their inventors' eyes in 1929, when Goldstein, Garber and Salama was founded by Goldstein's father, Dr. Irving H. Goldstein.

The senior Goldstein was later joined by his brother, Marvin, who became a leading orthodontist, and his cousin Dr. Theodore Levitas, who became a renowned children's dentist.

Their tradition of preventive and minimally invasive dentistry remains the basis for patient care today. "Our goal is simple: to preserve your natural teeth for life and maintain overall oral health at the highest level," Goldstein said.

During the initial visit, new patients are screened for periodontal disease, malocclusion, TMJ dysfunction (a main cause of headaches), oral cancer and tooth decay. A full-mouth set of minimal exposure digital X-rays is included as well as a "video exam" of the entire mouth using a small intra-oral camera. A special light also helps diagnose possible decayed lesions. All of this information is used to create a comprehensive treatment plan.

THEIR PATIENTS SAY IT BEST

The dental practice has had many satisfied patients over the years. "There are simply no people any better at what they do than these guys, anywhere on earth—and that is straight from the patient's mouth," said Don Smith, a television producer. "The Goldstein Garber Group is one of the most competent and service-oriented organizations I have ever dealt with," said Richard Marriott, chairman of the board of Host Hotels and

Continued on next page

Goldstein, Graber and Salama continued

Resorts. "Their work is the best and they treat you like both an honored guest and a member of the family. They truly excel."

Goldstein, Garber and Salama are such experts that they spend a great deal of time training dental groups from around the world. They teach courses on dental implants, restorative and cosmetic dentistry and periodontics, helping dentists become more proficient at bonding, porcelain veneers, all-ceramic crowns and bridges and other procedures.

the story of Goldstein's illustrious career: he has received 36 awards, honorary degrees, citations and honors and belonged to 42 dental societies and academies, serving as president or chairman for eight of them.

Goldstein is a featured columnist for *Southern Seasons Magazine* and is on *New Beauty* magazine's Editorial Advisory Board. He has produced more than 70 consumer-oriented programs about dentistry for the popular television show *P.M. Magazine*.

The doctors at Goldstein, Garber, and Salama are world-renowned clinicians, university teachers and masters in their individual specialties. Their practice offers the latest in dental technologies, state-of-the-art facilities and a wellness approach directed towards customized treatment of each patient's specific needs.

DR. RONALD E. GOLDSTEIN

Goldstein, widely considered the father of modern cosmetic dentistry, specializes in smile makeovers, porcelain veneers, cosmetic contouring, all-ceramic crowns, dental bonding, teeth whitening, laser therapy for periodontal disease, trial smile and microabrasion. "The most rewarding part of my work is seeing the looks on the patients' faces after they see their new smiles," he said.

A University of Michigan graduate, Goldstein received his dental degree from Emory University School of Dentistry. He is a clinical professor at Georgia Health Sciences University and an adjunct clinical professor at Boston University and the University of Texas. He also has presented continuing education courses at more than 20 universities and lectured at more than 600 dental meetings worldwide. Numbers also tell

DR. DAVID GARBER

Garber specializes in porcelain veneers, cosmetic contouring, all-ceramic crowns and bridges, dental bonding, fixed dentures, teeth whitening, laser therapy for periodontal disease and microabrasion.

Born in Johannesburg, South Africa, Garber graduated from the University of the Witwatersrand, South Africa, and received his dentistry degree from the University of Pennsylvania School of Dentistry. He graduated with post-doctoral training in both periodontics and fixed prosthodontics. Garber is a clinical professor in the Department of Periodontics at the Georgia Health Sciences University School of Dentistry and also serves as a visiting professor in Louisiana State University's prosthodontics department. He lectures extensively 40 to 50 times annually throughout the United States, Europe, South America and Asia.

DR. MAURICE SALAMA

Salama is a native of Egypt who grew up in Brooklyn, N.Y. His expertise includes orthodontics, Invisalign, dental implants, periodontal surgery and laser-assisted periodontal surgery. A graduate of State University of New York, he received his dental degree from the University of Pennsylvania. Salama is on the faculties of the University of Pennsylvania and the Georgia Health Sciences University School of Dentistry as a clinical assistant professor of periodontics. Salama has published 20 articles and won two

teaching awards. Also a sought-after lecturer, Salama has served as the dental expert for Fox (WAGA) TV in Atlanta, and serves as the Scientific Chairman of *Dentalxp.com*, the worldwide leader in online dental education.

OTHER TEAM MEMBERS

Goldstein, Garber and Salama also benefit from the expertise of Drs. Maha El-Sayed, Abtin Shahriari, Wendy AuClair Clark, Henry Salama and Nadia Esfandiari. In addition, five world-class technicians, who work in the in-house dental lab, are available to meet with patients to evaluate their facial shapes and skin tones and to discuss expectations before creating the most precise aesthetic result possible.

"Providing my patients with a beautiful and healthy smile is the most rewarding part of my job," Dr. Esfandiari said. "It brings me much joy and happiness." ■

Hartsfield-Jackson Atlanta International Airport

Hartsfield-Jackson Atlanta International Airport is the world's busiest airport, serving more than 92 million passengers per year. It is an economic powerhouse for the city and state. According to its latest economic impact study, the airport contributes an estimated $32.6 billion per year in direct business revenue to the metro Atlanta economy. It is also the state's largest employer, providing more than 58,000 jobs.

STARTED AS A RACETRACK

An old, abandoned automobile racetrack was the beginning of what is now Hartsfield-Jackson. On April 16, 1925, Atlanta Mayor Walter A. Sims signed a five-year lease on 287 acres and committed the city to developing it as an airfield. In 1929, the city of Atlanta bought the land and changed the name to Atlanta Municipal Airport. By 1942, the airport was the busiest in the country in terms of flight operations.

William B. Hartsfield, who had served six terms as mayor and was considered by many to have turned Atlanta into an aviation powerhouse, died in 1971. On February 28 that year, which would have been Hartsfield's 81st birthday, the airport's name was changed to William B. Hartsfield Atlanta Airport. By 1999, it was the world's busiest airport in passenger volume, having served 73.5 million passengers the previous year.

The Atlanta City Council changed the airport's name to Hartsfield-Jackson Atlanta International Airport in 2003 to honor the late Mayor Maynard H. Jackson Jr. He was the city's first African-American mayor and ushered in major changes to the airport during his tenure, including construction of the world's largest terminal complex and a 9,000-foot fourth parallel runway.

LOCATION. LOCATION. LOCATION.

Hartsfield-Jackson not only is within a two-hour flight of 80 percent of the U.S. population but also connects travelers to downtown Atlanta within 10 minutes and to many of the area suburbs within 20 minutes.

The domestic terminal has connections to three trains: The Plane Train, which takes passengers to all seven concourses; the ATL SkyTrain, which has a stop at the Georgia International Convention Center and takes passengers on a scenic, five-minute trip to the airport's off-site rental car center; and a Metropolitan Atlanta Rapid Transit Authority (MARTA) rail station.

CIVIC PARTNERS

Hartsfield-Jackson leaders and employees are dedicated to giving back to the community.

"Many of our executives work closely with area chambers of commerce and other civic organizations. Several of them have positions on the chambers' boards of directors," said Myrna White, Hartsfield-Jackson director of Marketing and Stakeholder Engagement. "Dedicated to youth development, we are engaged in the Partners in Education program conducted by public schools in the area. We invite students into our airport world, introducing them to different careers in aviation and offering them mentoring opportunities. Most students are familiar with the work of pilots and air traffic controllers; we expose them to other potential careers in aviation, such as finance and engineering. As the largest employer in the state, the airport offers a vast array of occupational choices."

Departing passengers and their family and friends can watch aircraft activity through the sweeping windows of the international terminal's ticketing hall.

FOUR-FOOTED PASSENGERS

To better accommodate passengers traveling with pets and guide dogs, Hartsfield-Jackson opened an off-leash, fenced dog park—complete with grass, landscaping, benches, artwork and biodegradable waste bags—in 2009. In 2011, gravel pathways were added to the park for the human visitors, and in 2012 the natural grass was replaced with ecologically friendly, durable artificial turf.

NEW INTERNATIONAL TERMINAL GOES GREEN

On May 16, 2012, Hartsfield-Jackson opened the Maynard H. Jackson Jr. International Terminal. Construction of the 1.2 million-square-foot facility began in 2008; its planning, design and construction created about 3,000 jobs. The international terminal's Concourse F has 12 gates, which combine with the 28 gates on Concourse E to form a 40-gate international travel complex. The airport serves nearly 70 international destinations in more than 45 countries.

Some of the benefits of the international terminal are the elimination of the baggage recheck process for Atlanta-bound passengers; separate facilities, such as security checkpoint and baggage handling systems, for international travelers; separate levels for arrivals and departures; and more than 3,500 covered parking spaces.

The facility also reflects the airport's emphasis on and commitment to environmental responsibility. The international terminal completed the checklist to receive LEED (Leadership in Energy and Environmental Design) certification from the U.S. Green Building Council and was set to receive confirmation by the end of 2012.

"Sustainability in our growth and maintenance is a top priority at Hartsfield-Jackson," White said. "Our Asset Management and Sustainability division works closely with the Mayor's Office of Sustainability to ensure that our initiatives are in step with Mayor Kasim Reed's sustainability initiatives and goal of becoming one of the nation's top-tier sustainable cities and the world's greenest airport. We are creating a new master plan to govern the development projects for the next 20 years at Hartsfield-Jackson. Exercising environmental responsibility is a key part of our organizational mission, and it will be a component of every project the airport undertakes." ∎

(Top) Passengers can be dropped off at the departures curb of the international terminal, which operates almost as an entirely separate airport, with its own security checkpoint, baggage handling systems and other functions.

(Middle) The ATL SkyTrain takes passengers on a short, scenic ride from the domestic terminal to the rental car center.

(Bottom) The airport's domestic terminal features the scenic Atrium, which connects the north and south sides of the terminal and serves as a meeting point and landmark.

ISIS OB/GYN & Midwife Services

At ISIS OB/GYN & Midwife Services in North Metro Atlanta, clients receive the highest standard of care through a comprehensive range of gynecological and obstetric services to women of all ages. The staff proudly maintains a relaxed, boutique environment and understand that a patient's time is valuable, doing everything possible to keep wait times to a minimum.

PARTNERS IN YOUR CARE

ISIS physicians spend time with women to understand their needs and offer well researched health solutions tailored to each individual. Everyone from adolescents to post menopausal women receives the same excellent care in order to meet their changing health needs.

Patients are given detailed and comprehensive physical exams. The medical team has in-depth knowledge and experience with nonsurgical and surgical treatment. An added convenience for patients is the ability to perform minor out-patient procedures on site.

Hughan R. H. Frederick, MD, FACOG; Kim Storey, CNM.

A Midwife Program is available for those who are exploring alternative childbearing techniques, including water births. While the midwives at ISIS are among the few water birth experts in Atlanta, they are also specialists in facilitating natural labor, often without the use of an epidural or other drugs.

CUTTING EDGE TECHNOLOGY

ISIS manages routine and most "high risk" pregnancies. They offer the latest in ultrasonographic screening, including a non-invasive option for prospective parents concerned with genetic disorders.

The convenience of diagnostic ultrasound is available in the OB suite and uses sound waves to create a picture of the baby in the womb. With a 3D/4D ultrasound, expectant parents can see movements of their unborn baby from a yawn to a cry to an outstretched hand.

ISIS goes beyond conventional laparoscopy with the robotic da Vinci System, a less invasive method for hysterectomies, removal of ovarian cysts and fibroids, endometriosis and pelvic diseases. This innovative technology provides patients with a faster recovery time, a reduction in scarring, a shorter hospital stay and reduced expenses.

ACCESSIBILITY IS THE KEY

Established in 2007 by Dr. Hughan Frederick, ISIS has grown to be one of the most sought-after women's care practices serving the North Metro Atlanta area. "Our clients appreciate their ability to reach me or another practitioner 24 hours a day, 365 days a year," says Dr. Frederick. "We take pride in being accessible to people during their time of concern whether it is over the phone or in any one of our metro Atlanta locations." ∎

Moore Colson

As one of Atlanta's largest accounting and consulting firms, Moore Colson has more than 30 years of experience working with closely-held businesses, private equity groups and their portfolio companies, and publicly traded businesses.

"We build long-term relationships to fully understand our clients' needs, enabling us to provide unique solutions to maximize profits, lower taxes and create financial security," managing partner Bob Kiser said.

Its 70 employees, including 15 partners, provide tax, assurance, management consulting, estate and financial planning, lender advisory services, IT audit consulting, and corporate accounting services. They serve clients throughout the Southeast in various industries, including manufacturing, wholesale/distribution, transportation, construction, real estate, technology, healthcare, staffing, hospitality, retail, professional services and high net-worth individuals.

PARTNERSHIP BENEFITS CLIENTS

As a true partnership—rather than a traditional CPA "book of business" model—Moore Colson matches clients with employees who have the most appropriate skill sets for a particular project. "This sets us apart from much of the competition because we can freely bring our resources to bear in the most collaborative and efficient manner possible to meet our clients' needs," founding partner Greg Colson said.

Moore Colson is also an independent member of PrimeGlobal, one of the largest associations of independent accounting firms and advisors in the world. PrimeGlobal provides Moore Colson with the opportunity to work with other independent member firms to gain access to additional expertise and service clients across the United States and around the globe.

The firm's excellent work has fueled consistent growth and drawn media plaudits. Moore Colson has been named one of Atlanta's Top 20 Accounting Firms by the Atlanta Business Chronicle and one of the Top 25 CPA Firms in America by *Inside Public Accounting*, a trade magazine.

TOP WORKPLACE IN ATLANTA

In addition, Moore Colson has been selected as one of Atlanta's Top Workplaces by the *Atlanta Journal-Constitution* for two consecutive years. "Our people are our most valuable resource," Kiser said. "We make a concerted effort to provide work-life balance for everyone, including having a popular summer-hours program. Moore Colson also offers an exceptional compensation/benefits package and invests in employee enrichment through training, technology and mentorship."

Community involvement, along with client satisfaction, is paramount. "Many of our partners and associates are board members, volunteers and sponsors of such local non-profit organizations as The Center for Family Resources, Eagle Ranch, Trinity Community Ministries and MUST Ministries," Colson said. "Our 'Volunteer Moore Colson' program is an integral part of our firm's culture that encourages and provides opportunities for all employees to volunteer and be involved in giving back to the community." ∎

Moore Colson's employees provide tax, assurance, management consulting, estate and financial planning, lender advisory services, IT audit consulting, and corporate accounting services to clients throughout the Southeast.

BAPS Shri Swaminarayan **MANDIR**, *a Hindu place of worship, was established in 1907 and serves spiritual needs throughout North America. Photo by MISHELLA.*

Johns Creek is a thriving city located 30 miles north of Atlanta in northeastern Fulton County. It is the 10th largest municipality in Georgia and offers residents and travelers a wide array of cultural arts, stunning outdoor activities and a quality of life second to none in the Southeast. "Our city was incorporated in 2006 and we have a wealth of

amenities to offer visitors, businesses and residents," explained Heather Blanchard of the Johns Creek Convention & Visitors Bureau (JCCVB).

"Johns Creek has been named one of the nation's best places for suburbanites by Coldwell Banker, Real Estate LLC and Onboard Informatics" said Beverly Miller, City Council-member and Mayor Pro Tem. "We are listed as the #1 place in Georgia for suburbanites to dwell. It's a great place to call home—whether it's for your family or your business."

Named one of the best cities to live in the American Southeast by *Business Journals*, Johns Creek is often described as a beautiful, clean and safe community. Johns Creek is only 30 to 40 minutes from downtown Atlanta and close to the

Photo by Bob Maynard

Johns Creek provides 13.5 miles of Chattahoochee River waterways and more than 52,000 yards of golf. It is also home to the Atlanta Athletic Club—the home club of golf champion Bobby Jones and host of more than 10 major championships, including the U.S. Open Championship, three PGA Championships, the U.S. Women's Open and the 2014 U.S. Amateur.

mountains and lakes of North Georgia. "We like to say we are 'The right distance from everything,'" said Phil McCarn, JCCVB's chairman.

OUTDOOR RECREATION

Johns Creek takes advantage of its 13.5 miles of waterways along the Chattahoochee River and is proud to offer residents and visitors access to America's first National Water Trail, a designation by the National Park Service. As Johns Creek's largest border, the waterway is enjoyed by kayakers, anglers, tubers, canoers and rafters.

Johns Creek also plays host to youth and amateur sports including the Southeastern Lacrosse Conference Championship, the largest collegiate club tournament in the United States. Home to four city parks, a network of multi-use trails, a world-class dog park and more than 52,000 yards of golf, Johns Creek is invested in recreational activities for people of all ages. Their six golf facilities collectively host numerous tournaments annually. Johns Creek has also been the host of several major golf tournaments. The Atlanta Athletic Club (AAC) is the home club of the world's most famous amateur golfer Bobby Jones. "We hosted the PGA Championship in 2011 and were one of only five courses in the country to host a third PGA Championship," said Atlanta Athletic Club General Manager Chris Borders. "We are very proud of our two 18-hole championship venues."

Off the course, Johns Creek has a 46 acre preserve featuring a circa 1850 village. Visitors to Autrey Mill Nature Preserve and Heritage Center, can enjoy guided walks on two miles of mulched hiking trails, explore a Native American village with a large collection of Southeastern Indian artifacts and view animal exhibits featuring live amphibians and reptiles.

CULTURAL ARTS ALLIANCE IN JOHNS CREEK

For a city of 76,000, Johns Creek has a tremendous art scene. Bringing the arts to the forefront, the Cultural Arts Alliance at

Johns Creek is a group of organizations working together to promote cultural arts in the area.

The alliance is directed by six founding committee organizations, including Autrey Mill Preserve and Heritage Center, Johns Creek Arts Center, which features a gallery and hosts numerous juried art shows each year and offers an array of art classes, camps and workshops; Johns Creek Symphony Orchestra, a nonprofit performing arts organization which is an all-professional ensemble of 45 musicians; Performing Arts North, a collection of three theater companies located in the Dancing Goat Theatre; The Chopin Society of Atlanta, an organization dedicated to promoting Frederick Chopin's music; and the North Atlanta Dance Theatre, the performing wing of the two-tiered organization presents two feature-length professional performances annually and provides pre-professional opportunities to the most dedicated North Atlanta Dance Academy students.

The city celebrates the arts each fall with the popular Johns Creek Arts Festival. Visitors and neighbors alike enjoy a dazzling artist market with imaginative and unique artisans, live music, continuous entertainment, a Kidz Zone and a not to be missed Food Pavilion.

DINING IN JOHNS CREEK

One of the city's more noteworthy characteristics is their dining. Eating in Johns Creek can be an epicurean's dream. Foodies can travel the globe and sample fine dining options and cuisine ranging from Italian to Greek or Mexican to Indian.

Johns Creek can satisfy a variety of cravings, from pizza to steak or dim sum. Culinary tourists and residents can experience farm-to-table cuisine, engage in the community garden, or visit the local farmer's market for organic and sustainable foods and produce.

JOHNS CREEK MEANS BUSINESS

"The quality of life in Johns Creek is what attracts businesses and homeowners to the city," explained Miller. "With award winning schools, quality healthcare, and easy access to amenities, Johns Creek is a place families want to call home. We strive to maintain a culture that balances a friendly, safe, residential community with a healthy business climate."

With bustling retail centers throughout the city and Johns Creek Technology Park, a mixed-use property offering space options for office and retail in addition to world-class medical

Nature's beauty, diversity of dining options and professional arts all thrive in Johns Creek. Truly a great place to visit, call home or conduct business.

facilities, the city lives up to its reputation as a thriving live, work, play community.

"We have managed to attract and retain large businesses while creating an environment where small businesses can thrive," said Craig McCoy, CEO of Emory Johns Creek Hospital and President of the Johns Creek Economic Development Corporation. "Enhancing the business environment— whether the business is home-based or a large corporation—is not only good for that business, it's good for everyone who visits, conducts business or decides to relocate here. Johns Creek is truly a jewel of the Southeast." ■

When savvy Atlantans need facial rejuvenation or repair, they often turn to Oculus Plastic Surgery and its medispa which go "beyond excellence" to help clients become more beautiful. ⁿ Dr. Harvey "Chip" Cole, III is an internationally recognized surgeon who is board certified in four specialties: OculoFacial Plastic Surgery, cosmetic surgery, ophthalmic surgery, and laser surgery.

"We specialize in procedures to rejuvenate facial features, reconstruct facial defects and diminish signs of aging," he said. "A surgical approach should restore and refresh a person's own natural beauty."

BOARD CERTIFIED IN FOUR SPECIALITIES

Dr. Cole, who has performed over 18,000 surgeries, is quadruple board-certified in OculoFacial Plastic Surgery, cosmetic surgery, ophthalmic surgery, and laser surgery. He has been named, by his peers, in *Harper's Bazaar* as one of the country's Top 10 cosmetic eye surgeons and included in *Town and Country's* Directory of Top Cosmetic Surgeons.

Dr. Cole has pioneered new techniques, such as the Eye-Light™ Blepharoplasty that uses lasers and endoscopes to repair and rejuvenate the upper and lower eyelid and cheek region. The EyeLight™ Process starts by endoscopically stabilizing the eyebrow to restore proper distance between the brow and eyelashes. The laser is then used to reduce the upper and lower eyelid's wrinkling and laxity. The fatty cushions are repositioned from behind the eyelid with a laser that is then used around the eyes to resurface fine lines and crow's feet. Unlike traditional surgery, this procedure involves no visible incisions

Dr. Harvey "Chip" Cole III is an internationally recognized surgeon who is board certified in four specialties: ophthalmology, cosmetic surgery, ophthalmic plastic and reconstructive surgery, and laser surgery.

or stitches to remove and achieves natural-looking results.

"I always say a millimeter is the difference between success or failure around the eye, where an inch is the difference between success and failure on the face. So it's a very precise procedure," Dr. Cole explains.

PERFORMS MEDICAL, COSMETIC SURGERIES

What are the benefits of Dr. Cole's quadruple board certifications? "If someone has a tear gland that's out of position during surgery, I'll go ahead and repair it while I'm there because I also understand the functional aspects of all the anatomy from having a background in ophthalmology. If someone has a lid that is drooping more than the other lid, general plastic surgeons are not going to be able to repair that muscle or fix that lid while they're doing the cosmetic surgery."

When he's not busy with his practice, Dr. Cole is working to help improve the skills of other physicians. As one of the nation's leading BOTOX® instructors, he travels around the country teaching the precise administration techniques that ensure optimal cosmetic results. Dr. Cole also instructs other doctors in surgical and non-surgical laser procedures.

Computer imaging during the initial consultation helps

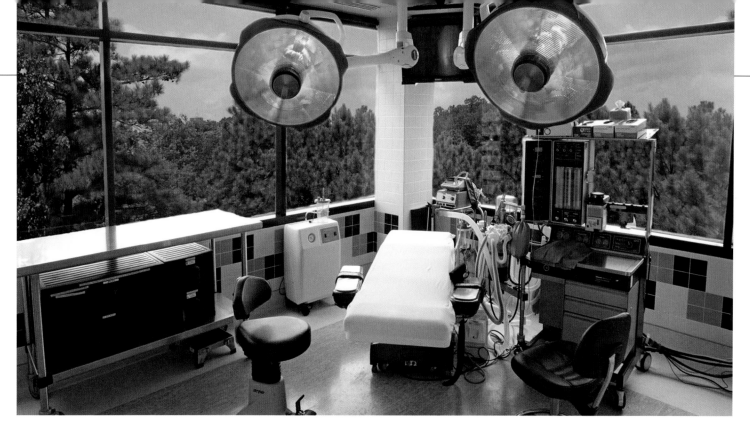

patients envision the results and feel more confident about their choice to undergo surgery. "Every patient is unique and every surgeon has a surgical style all his own," Dr. Cole said. "It is important that your goals align well with my style. With that said, my style is natural and meant to enhance and complement your features, not to recreate you all together or to make you look unlike yourself. Most of my patients say afterwards that they look even better than the computer imaging they received!"

ACCREDITED SURGERY CENTER

The Specialty Surgery Center was founded by Dr. Cole to provide patients a safe, comfortable environment for their surgical procedures. It uses only board-certified anesthesiologists and is accredited by the Joint Commission on Accreditation of Healthcare Organizations. That accreditation means that patients are in the same sterile environment, protected by the same stringent standards and treated with the same world-class technologies and expert skills as found in a first-rate hospital.

Dr. Cole is also the medical director of the Oculus Skin Care Centre, which was developed to instruct clients about proper skin care. Its experienced staff performs facials, chemical peels, laser treatments, neuromuscular/deep tissue massages and nutritional counseling. A state of the art VISIA® digital skin analysis performed by a licensed medical esthetician lets clients see their skin's condition and is an excellent way to measure the improvement of their skin regimens.

"Our goal is to set ourselves apart from the traditional 'day spa' by combining medical aesthetics with a therapeutic touch," Dr. Cole said.

HONORS GRADUATE OF TULANE

A summa cum laude graduate of Tulane University School of Medicine, Dr. Cole interned at the Ochsner Clinic in New Orleans, then served residencies at Tulane University Medical Center and a fellowship at Vanderbilt University Medical Center. He has taught at Emory University School of Medicine as well as the VA Medical Center in Atlanta.

Dr. Cole has been named by *Harper's Bazaar* as one of the country's Top 10 cosmetic eye surgeons and included in *Town and Country's* Directory of Top Cosmetic Surgeons.

"It is really nice to go home each day feeling like I have truly made a difference in the way that someone feels about themselves, that I have improved the functionality of their body face or resolved an ailment that has brought a patient chronic pain for many years," Dr. Cole said. ■

Plastikos Plastic and Reconstructive Surgery in Atlanta performs a broad variety of plastic and reconstructive surgical procedures, incorporating state of the art medical technology with holistic and integrative medicine. ■ Drs. Susan Kolb and Julian Gordon, both of whom are board certified in plastic surgery, specialize in silicone and saline breast

Drs. Susan Kolb and Julian Gordon specialize in silicone and saline breast implants, with an emphasis on serving women who have had complications from breast implants.

implants. Dr. Kolb, in fact, has made it her mission to successfully treat women who have had complications from breast implants. She has written a book entitled *The Naked Truth About Breast Implants* (www.thenakedtruthaboutbreastimplants.com).

"This is personal for me because in the 1990s I had a leaking silicone implant that made me very ill," she said. "I had to develop treatment protocols for a disease that medicine said didn't exist. These protocols have helped thousands of women, and my medical clinic has become an international center for women recovering from breast implant disease and related systemic immune disorders."

HOLISTIC, SPIRITUAL MEDICINE INCORPORATED

To recover from her illness, Dr. Kolb had to expand her concept of medicine beyond conventional science and learn about holistic and spiritual practices and traditional Chinese medicine. She found functional medicine the only way to successfully deal with the chemical toxins that leaked into the body from defective implants. Toxins also were spread into her body when her doctors did not entirely remove the scar capsule around the implant—a complication that Dr. Kolb finds in most of her patients.

"The toxic effects of these substances include chemical and silicone toxicity, which manifests in symptoms such as joint pain and muscle aches," she said. "Many of my patients also have symptoms of biotoxicity from mold and yeast overgrowth due to an immune deficiency common in any patient with defective silicone or saline implants."

PROTOCOLS HELP HEAL IMPLANT PATIENTS

"Detoxification protocols help the body eliminate chemical toxins and biotoxins and include measures to support and

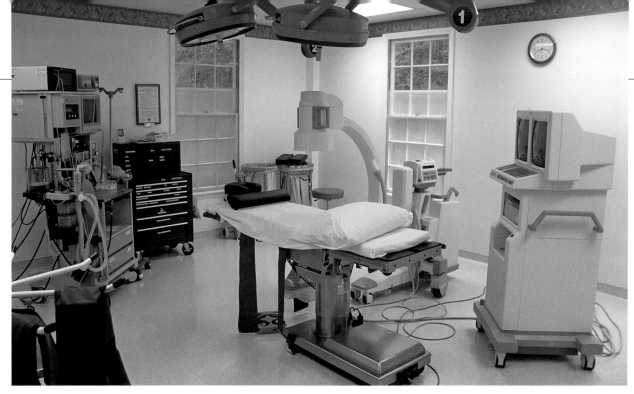

Plastikos Plastic and Reconstructive Surgery incorporates state of the art medical technology with holistic and integrative medicine.

restore functioning to the immune and endocrine systems," said Dr. Kolb, a founding diplomat of the American Board of Holistic Medicine. "Detoxification alone, however, will not help patients regain their health if they do not also have surgery to remove the entire scar capsule and abnormal nodules and lymph nodes."

Drs. Kolb and Gordon also are experts in breast augmentation, reconstruction, lifts and reduction (even for men). In addition, Dr. Kolb performs labiaplasty or labia reduction. "Many women have oversized or asymmetrical inner and outer lips to the vagina, which can be functionally or psychologically troubling," she explained. "Now those women can have surgery to aesthetically reshape the labia and clitoral hood with a safe outpatient surgical procedure that requires minimal recovery time."

NON-SURGICAL TREATMENTS AVAILABLE

Founded in 1995, Plastikos Plastic and Reconstructive Surgery is committed to providing for each patient's total well-being. As part of that commitment, its MedSpa offers a full array of non-surgical treatments including the Perfector (facial aging), the Ion Magnum (contour problems) and Lipomassage (cellulite). Chemical peels, facials, injectables and fillers, massage, microdermabrasion and permanent makeup are also available.

Plastikos also is affiliated with Millennium Healthcare, an integrated healthcare center with board-certified physicians in family medicine and chiropractic.

Dr. Kolb graduated from Johns Hopkins University and received her medical degree from Washington University School of Medicine. She completed her post-graduate education in plastic surgery and general surgery at Wilford Hall Medical Center, then served as an Air Force surgeon before founding her own practice in 1990.

She is a member of the American Society of Plastic and Reconstructive Surgeons and the American Holistic Medical Association and is a Fellow of the American College of Surgeons. Dr. Kolb has been certified by the American Board of Plastic Surgery since 1985 and is a founding diplomat of the American Board of Holistic Medicine (2000).

HOSTS RADIO PROGRAM

She hosts a weekly radio program, Temple of Health, every Saturday from noon to 1 p.m. on www.bbsradio.com. Archived radio programs are available on www.plastikos.com. Dr. Kolb also has written *The Naked Truth about Breast Implants: From Harm to Healing* and contributed to two anthologies: *Goddess Shift: Women Leading for a Change* and *Optimism!-Cultivating the Magic Quality that Can Extend Your Lifespan, Boost Your Energy, and Make You Happy Now*. She is also a contributor to the book *Plastic Surgery Tales: A Look Behind the Face of the Specialty*, by Dr. Robert N. Cooper.

A graduate of Amherst College, Dr. Gordon received his medical degree from New York Medical College. He completed his general surgery training at Saint Vincent's Medical Center in New York City, then finished plastic-surgery training at the University of Medicine and Dentistry in New Jersey where he also was chief resident. Dr. Gordon served a one-year fellowship in breast and microsurgery at Memorial Sloan Kettering Cancer Center in Manhattan. He has been certified by the American Board of Plastic Surgery since 2005.

Dr. Gordon, who has been in private practice since 2002, has published articles and book chapters on liposuction and breast surgery and regularly attends plastic-surgery symposiums. ∎

Point University

Point University has spent more than 70 years preparing students for Christ-centered service and leadership in an academically challenging, spiritually vibrant and internationally engaged environment. ▪ *Judge T.O. Hathcock founded the private school, then known as Atlanta Christian College, in East Point, Georgia, in 1937.*

He and his wife, Nora wanted to educate ministers, missionaries and other church-related workers. Over the years, the University's curriculum was broadened to include the humanities, fine arts, early education, business, math and science, with biblical studies remaining at its academic core.

GROWING CAMPUS MOVES

Today, the four-year Christian liberal arts university offers traditional and adult programs, awards associate and bachelor degrees and has more than 1,200 students. Point University, in fact, has been so successful in fulfilling its mission that its student body has outgrown the original campus, prompting a move to a larger site.

In fall 2012, the main campus was moved to West Point, Ga., about an hour from Atlanta, near the Georgia-Alabama border. During Phase I, students are housed in a nearby apartment community and have access to a 54,000-square-foot sports complex right next door. Phase II of the move calls for student housing to be constructed in West Point's walkable downtown.

"We've been searching for nearly four years for a place that would give us the ability to grow in every aspect of campus

life—from enrollment to constructing additional dorms and athletic facilities—and the thriving community of West Point and the Greater Valley Area had everything we were looking for," said Point University President Dean Collins.

TRADITIONAL, ADULT PROGRAMS OFFERED

Accredited by the Commission on Colleges of the Southern Association of Colleges and Schools, Point University's program for traditional students has 26 full-time faculty and a 1:22 teacher-student ratio.

"Our goal is to develop the total student spiritually, intellectually, socially, physically and professionally," Collins said. "Point University equips students to be points of influence in culture and the workplace."

In addition, Nearly 700 adult learners are on track to earn or complete degrees through the Access program at an off-campus site in East Point and at locations in Peachtree City, Savannah and West Point. The Peachtree City location also offers a dual-credit enrollment program for high school students.

SUCCESSFUL GRADUATE THANKS GOD

One shining example of a graduate who intends to apply her Christ-centered education to her career is Jamie Grace Harper. In 2012, the singer-songwriter graduated from Point University and was named Best New Artist of the Year at the Dove Awards shortly after being nominated for a Grammy Award for Best Contemporary Christian Music Song.

"I'm so thankful for the influence Point University has had on my life, my faith and my career," said Harper, 20. "It's a special place and I'll always cherish the way I was challenged there. Point University played a part in equipping me to be a leader in ministry and the world of Christian music. My Point University education will forever be a part of who I am." ▪

Point University has been so successful at educating students for Christ-centered service that it outgrew its original campus and had to move to a larger one in West Point, Ga.

VISIT POINT UNIVERSITY ONLINE: www.point.edu

Porter Keadle Moore, LLC

Founded in 1977, Porter Keadle Moore, LLC (PKM) has grown into one of the most respected accounting and advisory firms in the country. Once known as a community banking firm, PKM has grown to represent leading corporations in the financial, insurance, technology, biological science and government service arenas.

AN "ALWAYS ACCRETIVE" EXPERIENCE

PKM has a fresh approach. The firm strives to provide a sense of reassurance and peace of mind to clients by going above and beyond the expected to understand their business challenges, not just their accounting issues.

"Here, we believe the success of our clients' businesses should be our number one focus, not just completing the accounting work we're given," noted Managing Partner Phil Moore. "The firm's DNA is built around continually seeking to provide our clients with the most holistic and growth-driven financial solutions. We never just 'check the box'."

Through substantive relationships cultivated over years of working together, clients of PKM receive an exceptional service experience based on the firm's passionate approach to the success of each and every client. PKM associates pride themselves on being the most responsive professionals in the industry and are dedicated to treating their clients' businesses as if they were their own.

THAT STRATEGY HAS PAID OFF

"PKM offers us the knowledge and expertise we need, but takes it a step further," remarked Joan Herbig, Chief Executive Officer of ControlScan, Inc. in Alpharetta. "They make us feel like a top priority, regardless of our size," she said. "They have a genuine interest in the success of our business and are both responsive and sensitive to our needs. They understand the constraints under which we operate and compete and have proven themselves to be an integral part of our team, rather than merely a service provider."

EMPLOYEES ARE THE GREATEST ASSETS

At PKM, the company works hard to keep their employees happy, devising fun and innovative ways to keep them engaged in the business and the profession. PKM is continually ranked on *Accounting Today's* list of the nation's "Best Accounting Firms to Work For" and has even been named by the American Psychological Association as one of the nation's most "Psychologically Healthy Workplaces"—the only accounting firm ever to receive that honor.

"We are not a firm of cold, hard numbers or floors of accountants," Moore added. "We are a firm of people. Great people. People who are not only co-workers, but friends. So we treat them as such."

It makes sense from a business perspective and morally. Happy employees inevitably lead to happy clients.

"It ultimately boils down to: 'Can you work with them? Can they be responsive?'" said Ann Lawson, Chief Financial Officer of Nicolet National Bank in Green Bay, Wisconsin. "That's what I like about PKM; they offer large-firm services with community flair." ■

Managing partner Phil Moore in the PKM lobby.

Nighttime Atlanta skyline overlooking the Peachtree Center.

The FLAIR SCULPTURE *in the Georgia International Plaza was created by Richard MacDonald and donated by him to commemorate the 1996 Summer Olympic Games. Photo by Sean Pavone.*

The Centennial OLYMPIC PARK *in Atlanta was built for the 1996 games and continues to be a welcome leisure spot in the busy city. Photo by Sean Pavone.*

The FOUNTAIN OF RINGS *that delights visitors to Centennial Park is the world's largest interactive fountain. Photo by L. Kragt Bakker.*

Riverside Military Academy

As one of the nation's top military college preparatory schools, Riverside Military Academy has been preparing young men to become responsible, successful adults for more than 100 years. ■ *"The military process at RMA is not an end in itself; it is simply the means to an end," said Dr. James H. Benson, Col., USMC (retired), president. "The result is an*

educated young man who has experienced the challenges of the military model of education and who is completely prepared for the rigors of college and life."

PERSONALIZED INSTRUCTION

The Gainesville school, about 45 minutes north of Atlanta, teaches approximately 420 boarding and day students in grades 7-12 how to excel individually and as a group. With a student-teacher ratio of 14:1, Riverside offers personalized academic and leadership instruction that helps its cadets blossom and paves the way for their college success.

Each cadet's day is filled with rigorous academics, military activities, athletics and social activities and is structured to provide discipline and accountability. The cadets learn to manage their time wisely and avoid procrastination. A daily two-hour study hall is mandatory each Sunday through Thursday evening.

Recognizing the differences between the way boys and girls learn, Riverside has tailored its academic program to appeal to the male learning style. Classes are 45 minutes long, rather than the 90 minutes in many schools, and "hands on" lessons are incorporated so boys can "do" as well as sit and listen. The single-sex classrooms also offer fewer distractions.

Riverside teaches cadets discipline and helps them to become confident, poised young men.

UNDERACHIEVERS OFTEN BLOOM

"During their first 30 days, cadets go through our Recruit On Campus (ROC) cycle, an orientation where they must learn to wear the uniform, march, prepare their rooms, learn the requisite social skills and understand our patriotic expectations," Benson told *Education Executive Magazine*. "In many cases, kids who have been perennial underachievers experience a dramatic change in their personas after they come here."

Parents of Riverside cadets are quick to concur. "Our son is already more confident, disciplined and respectful of others," said Libby Quanstrom of Marietta, whose son Will is in the ninth grade. "He began his homework this past weekend without prompting from parents and without complaining! We can only anticipate what the future holds for him."

IMPRESSIVE FACILITIES

Founded in 1907, Riverside has a beautiful 206-acre campus that underwent an extensive renovation that was completed in 2004. New facilities include a residential complex, classrooms, a fine and performing arts center, a gymnasium, a library, a weight-training room, an indoor rifle range and lighted athletic fields.

The academy boasts an impressive college acceptance rate, with most graduates pursuing higher education. Upon graduation, a Riverside cadet is completely prepared for the rigors of college. He is poised, polite, and confident in any social environment. Riverside cadets stand tall, offer a firm handshake, respect authority, and display a level of confidence that parents may not have observed previously. For more information about Riverside Military Academy call 1-800-462-2338. ■

Rogers & Hardin, though smaller than many of its peers, is considered one of Atlanta's "major" law firms. An unwavering commitment to professional excellence has enabled it to maintain a level and quality of practice equal to that of much larger firms.

IT BEGAN WITH EIGHT

Rogers & Hardin was founded in 1976 by a group of eight lawyers who had practiced in large Atlanta and New York firms, who had an unwavering commitment to excellence and who shared a common philosophy about the delivery of legal services. From its inception, the firm has enjoyed a special reputation for its ability to advise and represent clients in connection with complex business transactions and commercial disputes.

In the first year of its existence, the firm was involved in two high-profile matters. "The first was the Midfield Terminal case," explains Richard Sinkfield, a partner with the firm. "We represented Delta and the other major airlines operating in Atlanta and were on the same side as the city, which was seeking to construct a new, expanded airport terminal to handle Atlanta's growing needs. When the suit was filed attacking key aspects of the planned terminal, the challenge to the firm was to find a way to resolve the suit in 60 days; otherwise, the terminal could not be built. This seemed insurmountable. It was resolved in 45 days. At about the same time, the firm's corporate lawyers, in the politically-charged North American Acceptance Corporation matter, were handling one of the country's first tender offers for the debt securities of a company in bankruptcy reorganization."

These high-profile cases helped forge the firm's sterling reputation and permitted it to be selective about the matters it accepts and the lawyers that it recruits.

A SIMPLE RECIPE FOR SUCCESS

"Our commitment to hiring the best people is at the root of our success," explains partner Jack Hardin. It may sound simple, but it is a basic tenet of the firm's philosophy.

"We place great emphasis on academic achievement and professional excellence and the practical, business-oriented delivery of services, recognizing that sophisticated users of legal services choose experienced and qualified lawyers, not law firms. Our commitment to these principles led us to reject the fast-growth, high-leverage law firm model before it became fashionable to do so and to create a firm distinguished by its reputation for excellence and uniform quality, a thriving and interesting practice and the accomplishments and diverse social, economic, cultural and personal backgrounds of its lawyers."

COMMITTED TO ATLANTA

Rogers & Hardin is committed to community service. "Our commitment to diversity in every aspect is reflected in the many ways the firm's lawyers are involved with the community," Sinkfield explains. "Almost everyone here dedicates a portion of his or her time to efforts aimed at improving our community in areas about which they are passionate." Collectively, the firm is active in United Way and in legal services to the indigent. Individually, the firm's lawyers provide hundreds of hours of service every year to dozens of charities.

LOOKING FORWARD

"We are dedicated to maintaining our reputation for excellence and continuing to enjoy our sophisticated and challenging practice. We believe that hiring the best people permits us to achieve those objectives," Hardin says.

Named "Georgia Firm of the Year - 2012" by Benchmark Litigation, Rogers & Hardin looks forward to keeping its clients and employees happy, and continuing to receive awards in the process. ∎

"Our commitment to hiring the best people is at the root of our success. It may sound simple, but it is a basic tenet of the firm's philosophy."

Roswell Convention & Visitors Bureau

Historic Roswell, Georgia's eighth largest city, boasts parks, nature retreats, good public schools, good neighbors and a low crime rate, all of which make it enticing for families, businesses and tourists. ■ *"Roswell offers a quality of life unmatched by many cities," said Kenneth Davis, president of the Roswell Convention & Visitors Bureau, the governing*

body for the City of Roswell tourism program and the Roswell Business Alliance economic development program. "We have a quality education system and natural, historic treasures coupled with a thriving arts and cultural environment. Businesses considering relocating to Roswell will find a city government with a AAA Bond Rating that's focused on initiatives to help businesses be successful."

Historic Roswell has been chosen twice by *Atlanta* magazine as the metro area's best place to live.

MANY HISTORIC ATTRACTIONS
Conveniently located 20 miles north of Atlanta, the city lies along the northern banks of the Chattahoochee River in an area that the Cherokee Indians called "Enchanted Land." In 1828, a gold rush in North Georgia brought Roswell King to the area, where he discovered lush forests and the waters of Vickery Creek. Ten years later, he started construction of a water powered cotton mill, which was incorporated as The Roswell Manufacturing Company. Union forces burned that mill and others in 1864 during the Civil War.

Today, visitors to the city's Old Mill Park can view the ruins of a mill that was built in 1853. Three historic mansions from the Civil War era, Bulloch Hall, Barrington Hall and Smith Plantation, also attract many visitors. In fact, 122 acres of the city's Historic District are listed on the National Register of Historic Places.

FABULOUS NATURE CENTER
Nature lovers flock to the Chattahoochee Nature Center, the oldest and largest private, non-profit natural science learning center in the Southeast. The center features 27 species of native wildlife, 127 acres of native plants and gardens as well as a Gold LEED-certified Discovery Center that interprets the Chattahoochee River watershed. In the summer, locals also enjoy "shooting the Hooch," rafting down the Chattahoochee River.

The city's location along the Georgia 400 corridor provides easy access to the North Georgia mountains and is also convenient to downtown Atlanta. Roswell is about 30 miles from Hartsfield-Jackson Atlanta International Airport and close to several regional commercial airports.

BEST PLACE TO LIVE AWARDS
This city of 88,346 residents has won so many accolades that it's difficult to count: Roswell has been chosen twice by *Atlanta* magazine as the metro area's best place to live, named by Frommer's as one of the top three U.S. cities to raise a family, ranked by City Crime Rankings as the 18th safest U.S. city, named by *Black Enterprise* magazine as the sixth best U.S. place to retire, named by the Arbor Day Foundation as a Tree City USA for 20 years in a row, recognized nationally as the first Bicycle Friendly Community in Georgia and that's not even mentioning the park system's numerous awards!

Some of the same factors that make Roswell such a great place to live also make the city attractive for businesses. A well-educated population (65 percent of residents have an associate's degree or higher) with good incomes ($117,000 is the average household income), pleasant weather and a low crime rate all encourage business.

Roswell has about 5,000 businesses. Its largest employers are Kimberly Clark, the Fulton County School System and Verizon Wireless, but many small businesses also call Roswell

home. Historic downtown, for example, is lined with art galleries, antique stores, trendy boutiques and popular restaurants. Canton Street recently was named a "Great Street" by the Georgia Planning Association because of its great dining and shopping offerings and special events like Alive After 5.

OPPORTUNITY ZONE JOB TAX CREDITS
Roswell encourages economic development with its Opportunity Zone Job Tax Credit Program, which offers the highest, most user-friendly job tax credit in Georgia. Among the program's advantages: each designated zone is eligible for the maximum state job tax credit of $3,500 per net new employee for five years starting the year of the hire.

There are no restrictions on the type of jobs created. Only two or more net new jobs need to be created in any one year to be eligible (other programs require 10), and there is no upper limit on eligible jobs. Lastly, if the company's state income tax liability is insufficient to absorb all of the credits, the balance may be taken by retaining employee withholding taxes that would otherwise be paid to the state.

The Roswell Business Alliance works with the city to encourage development of new businesses while also bolstering existing businesses. "A dynamic business community adds to the quality of life for Roswell residents and attracts visitors," Davis said. ■

Roswell offers plenty of outdoor activities, such as rafting down the Chattahoochee River. The city also is a shopper's paradise, complete with sidewalk cafes, trendy boutiques and a modern Town Center Mall.

$\mathscr{S}$andy Springs Hospitality & Tourism

The city of Sandy Springs is only seven years old, yet the northern Atlanta suburb has been ranked among CNN/ Money Magazine's Best Places to Live and one of Forbes' Top 25 Towns to Live Well. ■ *The affluent suburb is rich in amenities that provide a high quality of life for its residents: a low crime rate, more than 20 miles of beautiful*

shoreline along the Chattahoochee River, 11 lovely parks and two public high schools recognized by the College Board as "AP Honor Schools" because of their Advanced Placement programming and test results.

Tourists also have discovered Sandy Springs' convenient location and hospitable people.

"Sandy Springs combines high-rise modern office towers with the most beautiful wooded neighborhoods in the entire metro area," Mayor Eva Galambos said. "And it is easy to reach our community. Sandy Springs is at the intersection of the two busiest limited-access highways in Atlanta, Interstate 285 and Ga. 400. Additionally, the Metropolitan Atlanta Rapid Transit Authority has three rail stations here and the airport is a 45-minute MARTA ride away."

FIRST NEW CITY IN 50 YEARS

Georgia's sixth largest city was formed Dec. 1, 2005, after a 30-year fight against annexation by the City of Atlanta. Sandy Springs was the first new city in Georgia in 50 years, and its successful incorporation served as the model for Johns Creek, Milton, Chattahoochee Hills and Dunwoody to become cities.

After the city was formed, Sandy Springs' mayor and city council approved a plan to contract out government services, with the exception of public safety and city manager administration, to private vendors in order to reduce costs and improve service for taxpayers. The City has a 24-hour staffed Call Center offering residents, businesses and visitors a one-number connection to the city. This innovative partnership between city government and private enterprise has permitted the city to

All work and no play makes for dull lives, so Sandy Springs residents can enjoy golfing as well as kayaking in the Chattahoochee River.

devote 15 to 20% of its annual budget to capital improvement on roads, parks and sidewalks, as well as develop a state-of-the-art traffic management system.

"We have regular visitors from all over the United States, as well as other countries, who inquire about our unique outsourcing method," Galambos said. "We are delighted to share the results of greater efficiencies at lower costs to our taxpayers."

EXCELLENT MEDICAL CARE

Sandy Springs provides world-class medical care at three hospitals: Saint Joseph's Hospital, Northside Hospital and Children's Healthcare of Atlanta at Scottish Rite. The city received a 2011 American Heart Association "Mission Award" for its forward-thinking approach on educating citizens about cardiopulmonary resuscitation (CPR) and has been named a Heart Safe Community by the International Association of Fire Chiefs.

Tourists particularly enjoy the convenience of Sandy Springs' prime location. It takes less than 20 minutes to get to the Georgia Aquarium, CNN Center, High Museum of Art, World of Coca-Cola®, Martin Luther King Jr. National Historic Site and Centennial Olympic Park.

ANNE FRANK EXHIBIT

After visitors partake of Atlanta's cultural and artistic offerings, Sandy Springs still has plenty for them to experience—and for free! The "Anne Frank in the World" museum exhibit in Parkside Shopping Center tells the story of the young Jewish girl's experience during the Holocaust. Rare film footage and approximately 600 photographs detail her days of freedom in the 1930s, Anne's hiding with her family in Amsterdam and her eventual death in the Bergen-Belson concentration camp in 1945.

Outdoor lovers can enjoy kayaking, rafting and fly-fishing in the Chattahoochee River, which is the country's first National Water Trail. Morgan Falls Overlook Park offers breathtaking views of the river and park amenities designed for perfect group outings.

Hungry? Foodies will be enthralled by the city's culinary choices. The city boasts authentic foods for all tastes, including Mediterranean, Japanese, Italian, and French.

The moderate climate in Sandy Springs means outdoor enthusiasts can partake of their favorite activities for much of the year. Free admission is offered at the "Anne Frank in the World' exhibit, which tells the story about a young Jewish girl's experience during the Holocaust.

Heading north on "Hospitality Highway" takes motorists to Georgia's mountains, wineries and the North Georgia Premium Outlets in Dawsonville, which include Saks Fifth Avenue's Off Fifth, Coach, Burberry and other sought-after brands.

CAMERA-READY CITY

Sandy Springs also welcomes filmmakers, who have made good use of its modern office buildings, genteel Southern homes, exquisite views of the Chattahoochee River and busy street scenes. *Driving Miss Daisy, Remember the Titans* and *Warm Springs* are just a few of the movies that have been filmed in part here. ∎

$\mathscr{S}$hepherd Center

As the nation's largest spinal cord and brain injury rehabilitation hospital, Shepherd Center is dedicated to helping people rebuild their lives with hope, dignity and independence. ▪ Founded in 1975 as a private, not-for-profit hospital, the Atlanta-based facility is ranked by U.S. News & World Report among the top 10 rehabilitation hospitals

in the nation. Shepherd Center provides a full continuum of services from acute care to inpatient rehabilitation, to outpatient and lifelong wellness programs.

Shepherd Center also specializes in the research and treatment of multiple sclerosis and other neuromuscular problems and operates one of the country's leading pain-management institutes. All of the hospital's rehabilitation programs focus on a successful return of patients to their homes, schools and communities.

"Patients at Shepherd Center get more than just medical care; they get an experience that brings healing and hope," says Gary Ulicny, Ph.D., CEO and president of Shepherd Center. "We understand that patients are going through more than just recovery from an injury; they are learning a new way of life."

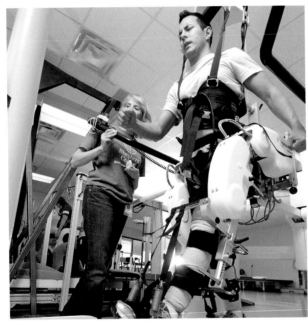

Patient Joe Mendes on the Lokomat® Nanos.

Patient Molly Welch in therapy.

A FAMILY APPROACH TO PATIENT CARE

At Shepherd Center, patients find a nurturing environment that facilitates their return to independent living, and this commitment extends to their families. Families of patients who live outside the Atlanta metropolitan area receive a complimentary apartment for the first 30 days of a patient's stay.

Of significance are comprehensive training sessions designed to help patients and their families learn as much as possible about the injury or illness. The process provides for ongoing medical care after the patient's return home and leads to support and understanding through which patients can take full advantage of the rehabilitation process and are less likely to require re-hospitalization.

Other unique offerings include therapeutic recreation, community outings, pastoral care, assistive technology, back-to-school programs, peer support, vocational counseling and return-to-work programs.

Shepherd Center offers 24 departments and services, many of which are funded by charitable contributions from public and private donors, including annual employee donations of more than $110,000 to help patients and their families. Many volunteers also donate time at the hospital by helping with tasks such as feeding patients breakfast or bringing them mail.

"We see patient care as a team effort in which everyone plays a critical role in a patient's rehabilitation and recovery," Dr. Ulicny says. "We work with each person to draw up a blueprint for rehabilitation and help patients and their families obtain the care they need."

PUBLIC PERFORMANCE RATINGS

The level of specialization provided by Shepherd Center leads to a decisive advantage in patient care and recovery. When it comes to functional improvements, patients are more independent and have better outcomes than the national average, and the center's return-to-home and return-to-work rates are among the best in the nation.

Nothing speaks more to the success of Shepherd Center than feedback provided by patients. Shepherd Center believes that people should have as much accurate information as possible to make informed decisions about their healthcare. That's why the center publicly posts and reports its ratings on a range of quality standards and benchmarks. Included is an online "outcomes scorecard" so patients can easily access outcome data, as well as the results of patient satisfaction scores.

"At Shepherd Center, our strategy from the start has involved bringing as many services as possible into a single facility to better accommodate our patients and their families," says Dr. Ulicny. "We're proud of the level of excellence we have achieved and we are very excited about the future." ▪

Swift, Currie, McGhee & Hiers, LLP

Swift, Currie, McGhee & Hiers, LLP, is one of the largest law firms in Georgia dedicated solely to the area of civil litigation. With more than 85 attorneys, it has the resources and abilities to tackle the most complex legal problems while at the same time providing its corporate clients with individualized, cost-effective service.

"We're adept at finding creative solutions to complicated problems," Managing Partner Steve Schatz said. "Our trial lawyers are known for their diligence, efficiency, teamwork and strategic thinking. Through our extensive network of international law firms, we're also able to appear and try cases in state, federal and administrative courts throughout the United States and to provide international representation in certain matters."

SPECIALIZES IN CIVIL LITIGATION AND WORKERS' COMPENSATION

Swift Currie has the largest workers' compensation department in Georgia, and its attorneys are well connected with the Georgia Workers' Compensation Board. In fact, Swift Currie partners James B. Hiers, Jr., and Robert R. Potter wrote *Georgia Workers' Compensation Law and Practice*, which is used by general practitioners as well as workers' compensation specialists.

Swift Currie also has a lobbying department for the insurance industry which has been successful in persuading the state to embrace tort reform and changes in trial evidence. Its civil litigation department handles a vast array of litigation including commercial, automobile, real estate, trucking, aviation, construction, environmental, product liability, employment and discrimination, insurance and bad faith, subrogation, general liability, and intellectual property cases.

SERVING THE COMMUNITY

"Besides providing our clients with the best legal services possible, Swift Currie believes it's important to help serve our community," Schatz said. "That's why we partner with such organizations as the Atlanta Food Bank, Service Juris and Families First to help make a positive difference in other people's lives."

Since its founding in 1949, the firm has been committed to providing a relaxed, supportive environment so its attorneys and staff function at an optimal level. "We've always prided ourselves on having a culture in which we treat each other very well, almost like a family, so that people feel respected and appreciated," Schatz said. "That also applies to the professional and collegial manner in which we treat judges, opposing counsel and, of course, our clients."

ONE OF THE 'BEST PLACES TO WORK'

Indeed, Swift Currie was named as one of the *Atlanta Business Chronicle's* Best Places to Work in 2011. "We continue to strive to make the firm one of the best places to have a long and fulfilling career," Schatz said.

Swift Currie has also been listed among *Fortune* magazine's Top Ranked Law Firms, which is compiled from data provided by LexisNexis Martindale-Hubbell. This honor is bestowed upon U.S. law firms of 21 or more attorneys, where at least one out of three lawyers was chosen by their peers as performing at the highest level of professional excellence. ■

(Top) Swift Currie lobby entrance.

(Bottom left) Employees and clients collected 4,474 pounds of food during the firm's food drive, equating to 3,441 meals for the Atlanta Food Bank.

(Bottom right) Firm home office, Midtown Atlanta.

Spa Sydell

In 1982, Spa Sydell opened in the Buckhead neighborhood of Atlanta with a vision to promote the spa concept based on providing Atlantans with the perfect escape from the daily pressures of life. ■ *More than 30 years later, Spa Sydell is one of Georgia's most recognized and preferred day spas, with a continuing commitment to deliver personalized attention and superior service to each and every customer.*

Since 1982, the company has grown to include spas in six metro Atlanta locations, including Alpharetta, Buckhead Plaza, Peachtree Parkway, Brookwood Plaza, Park Place and Roswell Corners.

Today, Spa Sydell is finding new ways to thrive via the guidance of Reina Bermudez, who became chief executive officer in 2011 after directing the company's financial affairs for several years. Notably, Spa Sydell is expanding its suite of services and bringing many of the world's most innovative and advanced spa treatments to Atlanta. And with a focus on health and

fitness, Spa Sydell is the ultimate destination for massage therapy, reflexology, skin care and other services that enhance wellness and well-being.

"At Spa Sydell, we are committed to providing guests with the highest quality of services and products in the most convenient way," says Bermudez. "Our partnership with Intraceuticals and the introduction of advanced injection techniques exemplifies our dedication to health, wellness and results as we continue to expand our business and spa offerings."

UNPARALLELED PROFESSIONALISM AND SERVICE

Spa Sydell's excellence begins with its staff of dedicated professionals. Each technician is licensed and trained to perform services at a level far above industry standards. Their mission is not merely to meet expectations, but to create a superior level of spa appreciation and enjoyment. Employees are the reason Spa Sydell was voted No. 1 for facials and sunless tanning in Best of Atlanta 2011.

Each Spa Sydell location offers an exclusive list of more than 75 treatments with unique services customized to fit guests' every need. Customers can also enjoy several signature services found only at Spa Sydell, including the Signature Facial, which

Spa Sydell creates a welcoming environment in the lobby of each spa location.

Spa Sydell's signature line of skin care and beauty products are available for guests to browse through in the lobby of the spa's Midtown location.

offers a unique combination of precious ingredients for revitalization and moisturizing, and a Mineral Mud Body Wrap that refines the skin's texture and tone.

Spa Sydell visitors also enjoy manicures, pedicures, airbrush tanning and waxes, along with an impressive menu of specially tailored packages for luxurious spa days, including gentlemen's services, couples and bridal parties. An assortment of microdermabrasions and peels are also available to guests, in addition to several express services that are ideal for busy spa-goers.

Ambiance is an essential element in any spa experience, and Spa Sydell creates the perfect atmosphere for relaxation and enjoyment. Soft music, the muted sound of running water and soothing fragrances enhance the services performed by caring experts. Cell phones and other electronics do not exist during the time guests are at Spa Sydell; even conversation is muted and limited to guests' needs.

TAKING HEALTH AND WELLNESS TO THE NEXT LEVEL

Health and wellness are fields that have expanded beyond the medical profession. They are no longer looked upon as just the absence of disease but also the presence of well-being, which includes a sense of balance in body and mind.

Spa Sydell is a leader in the field of complementary medicine, boasting a staff of carefully selected professionals who are licensed by the State of Georgia to provide massage therapy, skin care, reflexology, nutritional advice and a regimen of proper home care with products designed and specifically recommended for each individual.

In recent years, spa treatments have incorporated several new and innovative technologies to obtain desired results. The spa's Sydell Luxe suite of services includes advanced injection treatments such as Botox®, Juvéderm® XC and RADIESSE®, and, most recently, the celebrity-praised Intraceuticals 02 treatment.

Spa Sydell's health and wellness services are designed to meet a wide range of personal needs. For example, the Athletic Performance Massage Series provides passive stretching by an expert massage therapist to support relaxation, flexibility and improved range of motion. Arthrissage addresses the unique needs of individuals with acute and chronic arthritis by providing relaxation, improved range of motion and relief of pain and stiffness.

For those who wish to slow the appearance of aging and restore a feeling of youthful vitality, Spa Sydell offers individually designed skin-care regimens. All products used in Spa Sydell's treatments have been formulated and tested by a panel of senior massage therapists and aestheticians for safety and effectiveness.

BOOK YOUR NEXT EVENT AT SPA SYDELL

In addition to offering phenomenal individual services, Spa Sydell caters to groups. Spa Sydell offers a luxurious departure from the norm for all types of special occasions, including bridal parties, private spa parties and even corporate events and conventions.

And for a touch of glamour and romance, Spa Sydell recently joined with Alimena Limousine to create incredible Atlanta spa and limo packages.

For those looking for unique gift ideas, Spa Sydell gift certificates are perfect, regardless of the occasion. Birthdays, anniversaries, corporate gifts and even get-well wishes are much more memorable when combined with the Spa Sydell experience.

"Every service performed and every product applied is selected specifically for each customer," says Bermudez. "In spite of the size and scope of Spa Sydell, all of our clients receive highly individualized and personal attention to their needs and goals. Not only do we help heal and restore your skin and body, we do a lot to restore caring service to your world." ■

Spa Sydell's relaxing massage rooms create a tranquil and peaceful environment ideal for guests receiving therapeutic treatments.

Spa Sydell's signature Big Burgundy Gift Certificate is the perfect gift to share with friends, family and coworkers.

Spa Sydell offers an acclaimed selection of enticing spa products from their signature Sydell skin care line.

The Relaxation Room at Spa Sydell Midtown provides a comforting haven for guests to unwind before their treatments.

A rare glimpse of the Aurora Borealis is pictured near
the GEORGIA GUIDESTONES, *sometimes called*
"America's Stonehenge," in Elbert County.
Photo by Sean Pavone.

मानव और प्रकृति के बीच संतुलन
तक सीमित रखें
मानव और प्रकृति के संतुलन
बनाए रखें
प्रजनन प्रक्रिया को बुद्धिमता
से निर्देशित करें
योग्यता और विविधता के
सुधार के साथ

एक नई भाषा
मानवता को उन्नति
द्वारा एकजुट करें

विवेक का धर्म हो
भावना, आस्था और परम्परा
एवं अन्य गतिविधियों पर

जनता एवं राष्ट्रों की
समुचित कानून एवं न्याय
अधिकृत अदालतों द्वारा
रक्षा करें

निराधार शासन करते हुए
बाह्य विवादों का विश्व
न्यायालय के
माध्यम द्वारा समाधान करें
लघु कानूनों एवं बेकार अफसरों
का परित्याग करें

व्यक्तिगत अधिकारों को
सामाजिक कर्तव्यों के साथ
संतुलित करें

सत्य, सौंदर्य एवं प्रेम का मूल्यवान
करें
असीम के साथ समन्वय का
सृजन करते हुए

ऐसा कुछ न करें जो धरती के
लिए संघातक रोग बन जाए
प्रकृति मानव-सीमा से उन्मुक्त
हो।

प्रकृति मानव-सीमा से
उन्मुक्त हो।

Tellus Science Museum

Tellus Science Museum is a world-class, 120,000 square foot museum located in Cartersville, Georgia. Since opening its doors to the public on January 12, 2009, Tellus has become an exciting destination point. A visit to Tellus opens minds and ignites a passion for science in young and old alike.

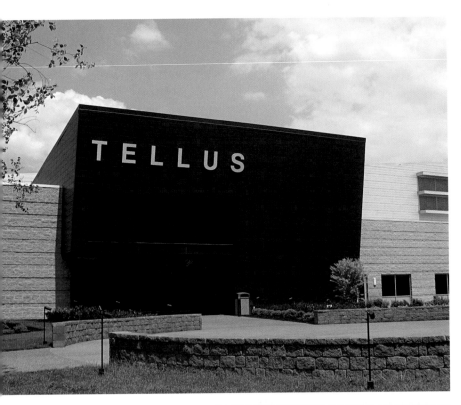

Tellus Science Museum began with the Weinman Mineral Museum in 1983 and was originally operated by the city of Cartersville as a tourist destination. Later, the museum became part of what is now Georgia Museums, a nonprofit public charity. The focus was education and the museum soon expanded into the state-of-the-art science facility it is today.

TELLUS GALLERIES

The museum features four main galleries that offer interactive and engaging activities for visitors of all ages.

The Weinman Mineral Gallery hosts a variety of gems, gold and some of Georgia's most prized minerals. Visitors can guess how many pennies can be made from a seven-foot high copper bolder, learn how minerals are cut and made into gems, explore the earth's crust and learn about the study of the motion of the Earth's lithosphere.

The Fossil Gallery offers a walk through history past millions of years of reptiles, giant mammals and dinosaurs that dominated the land, the sea and the air before becoming extinct.

The Science in Motion Gallery propels visitors through 100 years of changes in transportation technology featuring electric, steam and gasoline powered cars and vintage vehicles on display. A portion of the gallery is dedicated to space exploration with replicas of Sputnik and the Apollo I capsule.

The Collins Family "My Big Backyard" Gallery is the most interactive of the four galleries where the world of science becomes every child's playground. Young visitors can play with light, rainbows, mirrors and more in the greenhouse. They can delight in the sound experiments in the shed or experience the properties of magnets and electricity in the garage. The interactive garden and the walk-in tree makes exploring science fun and engaging for children of all ages.

MUSEUM FAVORITES

The Fossil Dig and Gem Panning areas are favorites among museum visitors. Young and old paleontologists alike can grab a brush and wipe away the sand to uncover fossils of all shapes and sizes, whether shark teeth or snail shells. There are several

(Top) Tellus Science Museum is 120,000 sq. feet and features four unique galleries.

(Right) The Weinman Mineral Gallery exhibits amazing specimens from all over Georgia, the country and the world.

(Left) This replica steam engine in the Science In Motion Gallery is one of many examples of how transportation has changed.

larger areas where visitors can dig and uncover larger dinosaur bone recreations.

Next, visitors can grab a pan and sift for gems and stones buried in the sand. The area features a working water wheel in addition to plenty of gems for visitors to find and take home.

MORE SCIENCE, MORE LEARNING

It is time to take a seat, lean back and prepare for an incredible ride in the Tellus planetarium. The digital projector takes visitors through the solar system to the edge of the galaxy and beyond with shows running every 45 minutes.

The Solar House is designed to be self-sufficient and show how energy can be used to make homes energy efficient and "green." The house has thirty-nine solar panels and a water capture and reclamation system.

The Tellus observatory gives visitors a view of the night sky through a twenty inch telescope. It also houses a seismograph used to detect earthquakes all over the world.

The Tellus café offers a respite where visitors may relax and enjoy a wide variety of meals, snacks and drinks. The Tellus store provides memorabilia of the museum that includes unique jewelry, educational books, rock specimens, T-shirts and much more.

FAMILY FRIENDLY DESTINATION

"Family Science Night" in February, April and November offers hours of entertainment for families. "Night at the Museum" in August features more than forty big names in science such as Galileo, the Wright Brothers, and characters from Star Wars and Star Trek. There is even a costume contest for kids.

The Tellus lecture series presents talented speakers on various ideas related to science. The Lunch and Learn sessions are a pleasurable way to spend the lunch hour while exploring interesting topics. The annual June "RockFest" event is a two-day celebration of the earth and all its wonderful treasures. The weekend, filled with door prizes, jewelry and mineral and fossil vendors, rock bingo and food and beverages, provides fun for the whole family.

Science Saturdays invites visitors to explore such experiments as a miniature exploding volcano, prisms, hands-on activities and interesting programs showing in the Theater. The Summer Passport Programs provide an outlet for students to stretch their science skills in the labs. This program also includes a tour of all four of the galleries.

Last but not least, Tellus Science Museum offers a unique setting for weddings, receptions and business meetings. A visit to Tellus Science Museum, when shared with friends and family, provides amazing memories of the wonders of science. ∎

Children of all ages will enjoy experimenting with light, sound and electricity in the Collins Family My Big Backyard.

This replica of the Wright Brothers Flyer anchors the Science In Motion Gallery.

The Bell-47 helicopter is one of the centerpieces in the Science In Motion Gallery.

Visitors to the Fossil Gallery can walk among fearsome dinosaurs like the Tyrannosaurs rex and the Appalachiosaurus.

University of West Georgia

Just west of Atlanta, a spirited University lies nestled among the rolling hills and tranquil lakes of Carrollton. Across campus and around town, you'll hear the hum of intellectual exploration, the laughter of camaraderie, and—of course—the howl of the Wolves. At the University of West Georgia, we see things differently. We respect our roots but we're

not bound by tradition. We blaze our own trails rather than follow the crowd. And we're making history, not simply studying it. This is the land of opportunity and discovery. If you ask us, the stars shine just a little brighter here—in the sky and among us.

We're committed to academic excellence and a vibrant campus life. Our respected, experienced faculty can supply you with the up-to-date knowledge and cutting edge skills required to excel in today's marketplace, while our academic and personal resource centers provide a support network designed to give you the best possible chance of success. You can also have a full campus experience while pursuing your studies. Student events, clubs, and recreational opportunities abound.

Explore our 645-acre campus. Cheer a Wolves athletic team to victory. Grab a coffee break at Starbucks. Take in a theatre production, an art exhibit, or a lecture on any number of topics—all without leaving campus. And don't forget to check out our ever-expanding facilities. From our athletics complex and University Stadium to brand-new residential housing to current building projects for art and nursing students, UWG is

committed to ensuring that our facilities support your growth.

We're growing our graduate programs, too. In addition to master's degrees in a variety of disciplines, we now offer four doctoral programs: a Ph.D. in Psychology and Ed.D. degrees in Nursing Education, School Improvement, and Professional Counseling and Supervision. Need the flexibility of an online education? We can do that, too. And our Newnan and Douglasville centers continue to increase their offerings. You can now complete all core undergraduate work in Newnan, along with undergraduate and graduate work in business, nursing, and education. High school students can take advantage of joint enrollment in Newnan, as well.

We're also committed to telling the UWG story. And we have a lot to tell. We've got students performing biomedical research, outranking private university debate teams, studying trees to evaluate historical sites, and submitting winning tee shirt designs for the Peachtree Road Race. We've got cheerleaders winning national competitions…over and over again. UWG students are studying overseas, developing local outreach programs, and building robots. Our faculty and staff

Our Campus Center is home to ballrooms, a track, cardio and weight equipment, basketball courts, fitness classes, the rock-climbing wall, and the game room.

The Lighting of the Flame is a cherished tradition marking the beginning of each new academic year.

are doing some pretty amazing things too. They're visiting far-flung reaches of the world to give lectures, provide medical services, and educate the less fortunate. They're publishing books, advising small businesses, and excavating archaeological sites. And don't get us started on our alumni. They're newscasters, authors, international business leaders and teachers of the year. They're entrepreneurs, critical care nurses, and everything in between. They're truly reaching the stars—as Hollywood makeup artists and NASA project engineers.

Then there's UWG itself. We're one of the top producers of both nurses and educators in the state. Our Richard's College of Business is AACSB accredited—and one of a small percentage of schools with separate accreditation for accounting. Our new School of the Arts breaks down traditional boundaries by celebrating and incorporating creativity in all its forms. We're the official home of Georgia's Political Heritage Program, the center for eCore education in the state, and we have the only fully functioning forensic anthropology lab in the area. Our Honors College offers academic high achievers an opportunity to shine through advanced coursework and special research opportunities. And the Advanced Academy of Georgia at UWG is one of the few programs nationwide that allows high school juniors and seniors a chance to earn concurrent high school and college credit in a fully residential setting.

Everywhere you look, UWG is blazing trails to new possibilities for scholarly achievement, creative expression, and service to humanity. We invite leaders, life-changers, seekers, creators, visionaries, investigators, and game-changers to join the more than 11,600 students enrolled at UWG. With 106 mind-blowing majors, more than 150 student organizations, and countless research and internship opportunities, you can mix and match to create your right-fit college experience. Seems there's no doubt about it: amazing things really do happen when you Go West.

UWG ONLINE

Credibility. Affordable Quality. Convenience. That's what sets our online programs apart.

Sure, you can Go West from anywhere. You can attend class whenever and wherever is convenient for you. But you can also be confident that you're earning a valuable degree from a respected university. UWG is a public, SACS accredited, brick and mortar institution and we have a history of academic excellence. In fact, we've been educating students since 1906. Our diverse student population is spread across the country and internationally and we're committed to helping you succeed. Our respected, experienced faculty can supply you with the up-to-date knowledge and cutting edge skills required to excel in your chosen field.

Whether you're fresh out of high school, an adult learner, military personnel, or a veteran, we have online options that can help you achieve your dreams. We even offer opportunities for high school students interested in joint- or dual-enrollment. Depending on the program, you can earn your degree

(continued on next page)

The recently renovated Irvine Sullivan Ingram Library provides engaging study space, extensive research resources, and professional staff dedicated to helping students find what they need.

UWG undergraduates have unusual opportunities for research in a variety of fields – as well as the chance to present their findings at regional and national conferences.

online, face-to-face, or in a hybrid setting. You'll be taught by experienced, well-credentialed experts and you can expect low student-teacher ratios.

Earn the undergraduate degree you've always wanted… or complete one you've already started. Investigate the RN-BSN program. Get your MBA. Or earn a master's in nursing, music teacher education, school media, or applied computer science. In just a few semesters, you can prove your passion for special education, library media, or instructional technology with an Ed.S. degree that sets you apart from the crowd or advance

your healthcare career with a post-master's certificate in nursing education or health systems leadership. You can even get your Ed.D. in nursing education or school improvement online. And we're always evaluating new options and looking for new programs to meet your needs.

Come find out why *Princeton Review* calls UWG a Best Southeastern College and "one of the best overall bargains—based on cost and financial aid—among the most academically outstanding colleges in the nation."

You can truly Go West from almost anywhere. And

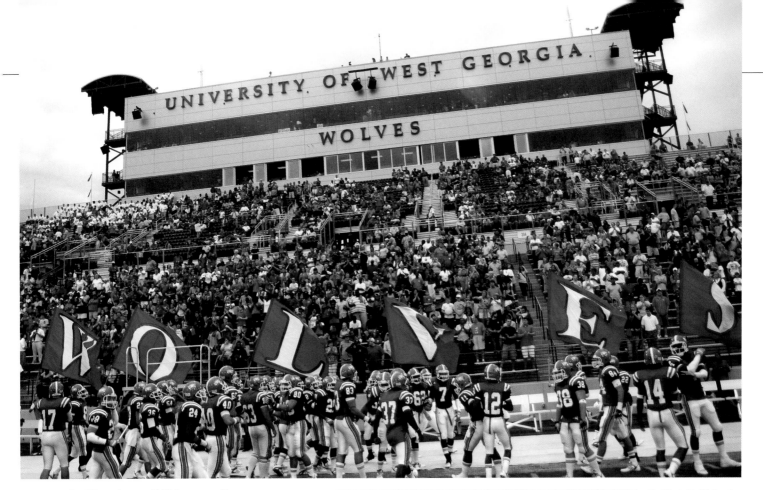

once you Go West, the possibilities are endless.

Go West. Go Wolves!

WHAT IS A WOLF?

A wolf is a student-athlete, someone who takes pride in donning a UWG uniform and charging onto the field or court with passion and commitment. It is someone who believes that every player has a strength and a purpose. Someone who understands that the best strategists take advantage of every individual's assets to create a powerful, united team.

A wolf is a UWG student, someone who takes pride in our school, marks our games on the calendar and looks forward to them all week. It is someone who surges into the stands to cheer with elation at every successful play and every hard-fought victory. It is someone whose faith in the team remains unshaken even when the going is tough.

A wolf is a faculty or staff member, a dedicated professional who takes pride in working at a university that is academically strong, diverse in perspective and allows students to combine activities and classes into a unique, personalized college experience. It is someone who sees the value of balancing rigorous study and individual development.

A wolf is an alumnae or alumnus, a person who takes pride in being part of the UWG family long after graduation. It is someone who revels in the excitement of a homecoming game, in a long line of colorful floats proclaiming UWG spirit, the sound of drums rippling through the stadium and the scent of tailgate hamburgers mingling with the first hint of fall air.

A wolf is a community member, someone who takes pride in sharing Carroll County with UWG. It is someone who loads up the entire family on game day and heads over to show the kids how their future college plays the game. It is someone who adopts the young men and women at UWG as their own, supporting their studies, their athletics and their growth.

A wolf is a leader, a fierce individualist with hopes and dreams and ideas. But a wolf also values the pack, understands that there is strength in numbers and realizes that the most awesome achievements are those shared with others. A wolf is someone who can join a group, become part of a common movement and work for a larger goal, all without losing that ever-important sense of individuality and self-purpose that makes a wolf a wolf.

The girl to your left with a UWG tattoo on her cheek is a wolf. The season ticketholder to your right is a wolf. There is a wolf sitting in every seat, playing every position, tuning every instrument, selling every shirt, preparing every cheer and snapping every picture.

Together we are a pack. Together we are Wolves. Together we are unstoppable. ■

Wesley Woods

Wesley Woods' roots trace back to 1954, when visionary leaders of the North Georgia Conference of the United Methodist Church and Emory University collaborated to create the original community adjacent to the Emory Campus. Since that time, Wesley Woods has grown and now operates nine retirement communities throughout North Georgia.

Wesley Woods Senior Living remains affiliated with Emory Healthcare and the North Georgia Conference of the United Methodist Church.

The Wesley Woods continuum of care approach is comprehensive, holistic and above all compassionate. Aging is addressed in its physical, mental, emotional, social and spiritual dimensions. The communities serve all races, faiths and income levels. "As a not-for-profit provider, we put people first, not the bottom line," said Kenneth Weber, President and CEO of Wesley Woods.

SENIORS GAIN HOPE AT WESLEY WOODS

Its roots are in creating community, and Wesley Woods is a pioneer in making the retirement experience healthy and fulfilling for residents of all income levels, races and faiths. Asbury Harris Epworth Towers, in Southwest Atlanta; Branan Towers, in East Atlanta; Branan Lodge, located in Blairsville; Lanier Gardens, located in Athens and adjacent to Talmage Terrace, all provide rental subsidy programs to seniors throughout North Georgia. St. John Towers, the largest Wesley Woods community, located in Augusta, provides apartment homes offering some rental subsidy and apartment homes licensed as personal care programs to provide assistance with activities of daily living. Wesley Mountain Village, located in Blairsville adjacent to Branan Lodge, offers owner-occupied cottage homes.

"Aging often is characterized by things that are lost: the loss of independence, the decline of health and mobility, the failing of memory," Watson said. "When older adults become part

of the Wesley Woods community, they receive help in coping with those losses. They also gain hope from all that is found at Wesley Woods…dedicated professionals who specialize in geriatric services…an organizational culture committed to helping people age with grace…safe, affordable, independent and assisted living options…new friends and new experiences."

WESLEY WOODS OF NEWNAN

Adults 62 years and older also might enjoy living at Wesley Woods Newnan, located about 25 miles southwest of Hartsfield-Jackson International Airport. The beautiful 52-acre community offers assisted living, independent living and memory support options; residences include one- and two-bedroom apartments as well as cottages.

All residents enjoy two or three meals daily, scheduled courtesy chauffeured transportation, weekly housekeeping, weekly flat laundry service including changing of bed linen and various activities, programs and trips. The community also includes a 200-seat auditorium, a billiards room, bistro and fitness center.

"We have a lot to offer at Wesley Woods, which makes it very easy to convince people to make it their home," said Beth Lever, marketing director.

Residents with Alzheimer's and dementia live comfortably in a secured wing that is staffed by certified nursing assistants. Also available is a 23-bed skilled nursing facility staffed by a licensed practical nurse 24/7, a registered nurse five days a week and certified nursing assistants.

"Our employees think this is not just a job, but a mission," said Steve Threlkeld, assistant administrator.

Springtime at Wesley Woods of Newnan.

Let Wesley Woods become a part of your family.

Wesley Woods residents enjoy frequent get-togethers, including parties to cheer on the Georgia Bulldogs.

CONTINUING CARE IN ATHENS

One of Wesley Woods' continuing care retirement communities is Talmage Terrace in Athens. With residences for independent living and assisted-living apartments, it's perfect for senior citizens who want to live independently, yet be secure in the knowledge that they have access to on-site assisted living if it is ever needed.

Talmage Terrace offers excellent estate protection through a range of entry fee options and predictable monthly fees. If your loved one needs a little help managing medications or preparing meals, for example, the retirement community has a licensed personal care center where trained staff create a care plan based on your individual needs.

Situated in a quiet, tree-lined neighborhood, Talmage Terrace is within walking distance of a shopping center and convenient to the University of Georgia where many residents enjoy attending college courses there as well as concerts and plays. Athens has been ranked by *Kiplinger's Personal Finance* and *TopRetirement.com* as being among the top places to retire.

FOUNDATION GIFTS FUND CARE, RESEARCH

As a non-profit organization, Wesley Woods relies on generous donations to fund its foundation. The Foundation of Wesley Woods provides millions of dollars a year for charitable care, vital research in geriatric medicine and capital support for its retirement communities.

"Almost 40 percent of our rental residents live below the poverty level, and 75 percent need assistance from the foundation or HUD rent subsidies," Mike Watson, President and CEO of the Foundation of Wesley Woods said. "It's through the gifts of caring donors that we are able to ensure that our most vulnerable seniors can age in a place of safety and security." ∎

Love where you live.

Woodward Academy

Woodward Academy is one of the largest college-preparatory schools in the nation. Since 1900, Woodward Academy has graduated more than 10,000 young men and women who have gone on to achieve greatness in all walks of life. Woodward provides students with an innovative, challenging and well-rounded educational experience.

Celebrating more than 112 years of academic excellence, Woodward Academy was founded in 1900 as Georgia Military Academy, a military boarding school for boys. In 1964, the school opened its doors to girls and, after discontinuing its military program, was renamed Woodward Academy in 1967 for its founder, Colonel John Woodward. More than 2,700 students from more than twenty metro Atlanta counties attend Woodward Academy and represent a wide range of talents, interests and backgrounds.

ACADEMIC EXCELLENCE

Woodward Academy and its families share the belief that an excellent education is the most valuable gift a child can receive. Strong academic programs and a wide range of extracurricular activities make it possible for students to develop into well-rounded young men and women.

Woodward is divided into five different schools, serving students from pre-kindergarten to grade twelve. The Primary and Lower Schools set the pace for lifelong learning. Both curriculums include instruction in language arts, reading, math, social studies and foreign languages. Students explore the areas of music, the arts, physical education and technology.

The Middle School incorporates work at the academic, college-preparatory and honors levels. Students participate in a wide variety of clubs, athletic activities and field trips.

The Upper School offers a challenging college-preparatory curriculum with advanced placement and honors classes. Students can choose from a broad range of electives and extracurricular activities.

STATE OF THE ART FACILITIES

The Main Campus of Woodward Academy is located on 90 acres near downtown Atlanta. The Academy offers a transportation system which serves more than 1,000 students daily. On any given day, 400 students ride Atlanta's public transit system, MARTA, to and from school.

The Main Campus combines the traditions of the Academy with state-of-the-art facilities. Math and science classes are housed in the new 43,000-square-foot facility that includes a lab dedicated to independent research. The 15,000-square-foot library houses 20,000 volumes, 50 desktop computers and seats 200 students.

The athletic complex boasts three gymnasiums, a lively student center and campus store, an eight-lane swimming pool, an eight-lane track, a 5,000-seat stadium and baseball, softball and tennis complexes.

Both the Primary and Lower Schools are housed in self-

Aerial view of Woodward Academy's Main Campus. The campus encompasses 90 acres and is nestled in a historic neighborhood near downtown Atlanta.

Woodward's seventh president, F. Stuart Gulley, Ph.D., enjoys some downtime with middle school students.

contained facilities with their own cafeterias, gymnasiums and libraries. The Woodward North campus, located in Johns Creek, prepares students for the college-preparatory programs in the Middle and Upper Schools.

TECHNOLOGY, THE ARTS, ENRICHMENT

Technology enhances instruction throughout the Academy. Students are taught to become proficient on computers at an early age. Each of the five schools maintains an on-site computer laboratory. In addition, the Upper School operates a four-bay lab with more than 100 computers. SMART-Boards give students and teachers interactive capabilities as they work through math problems, diagram a sentence or perform online research.

The Richardson Fine Arts Center, which houses the performing and visual arts programs for the Middle and Upper Schools, provides students with an understanding of the arts and a way to express their creative ideas. Students can choose from courses in dance, theater, choral music, broadcasting, band or orchestra. The fine arts center has a 400-seat theatre, classroom space for photography, ceramics and painting, an exhibition gallery, a television studio and ample space for choral, band and orchestra courses.

FOSTERING STUDENT SUCCESS

Woodward Academy teachers work every day, at every step, to ensure that each student reaches his or her fullest potential. College counselors work diligently to pair students with their best-fit college. Students collaborate both in and out of the classroom to solve problems, create masterpieces and win with honor on the athletic fields. Every day, more than 575 faculty and staff members dedicate themselves to the success of Woodward students.

A BRIGHT FUTURE AHEAD

Typically, 100 percent of Woodward Academy graduates are accepted to four-year colleges and universities, attend 100 colleges across the nation and the globe, earn upwards of $14 million in merit scholarship awards and contribute more than 5,000 hours to community service projects.

Woodward Academy provides a learning environment where a student's individual talents are nurtured and challenged to reach the most complete definition of success. Because of this, Woodward graduates surpass commonly held definitions of success and arrive confidently at their own self-defined markers of achievement and satisfaction. ■

Weissman, Nowack, Curry & Wilco

Whether for a closing of a simple single-family home or a complex half billion dollar mixed-use development, Weissman, Nowack, Curry & Wilco is the law firm to trust when it comes to real estate in Atlanta. With more than 60 lawyers focusing on every aspect of real estate investment, development and lending, the 21-year-old firm is a key provider of real estate legal services throughout the Southeast.

The firm's clients include real estate developers, institutional landowners, real estate brokers, mortgage lenders, home builders, title insurance companies, buyers and sellers and homeowner and condominium associations. Its attorneys assist clients in every aspect of their real estate transactions, from the zoning and entitlement stage through the acquisition or disposition of their properties.

About half of the attorneys at Weissman, Nowack, Curry & Wilco are involved in real estate, mortgage and general litigation, representing agents, brokers, appraisers, banks and lenders. Litigation expertise also includes general commercial litigation, alternative dispute resolution, title insurance defense, insurance coverage claims and corporate and government transactions. "People don't always realize the depth of our services," said Leigh Wilco, head of the firm's litigation practice. "With over 20 attorneys, our litigation practice group provides large-firm legal experience in a boutique atmosphere."

Pictured from left to right are George E. Nowack, Jr., Seth Weissman and Leigh Wilco.

CLIENTS COME FIRST

The approach to practicing law at Weissman, Nowack, Curry & Wilco reflects their core belief—that clients come first. The attorneys work hard and use their broad expertise to help clients achieve their goals. Billing at lower rates than bigger firms, they create true value for clients without sacrificing quality.

As a legal pioneer of the new urbanism and complex vertical mixed-use developments, the firm has drafted numerous documents for developers of innovative real estate developments that dot the Atlanta skyline. Its lawyers also have drafted many real estate statutes that are in effect in Georgia today and, in addition, serve as general counsel to the Georgia Association of Realtors® and the Greater Atlanta Home Builders Association.

ACADEMY EDUCATES CLIENTS

Weissman, Nowack, Curry & Wilco's emphasis on education also differentiates it from competitors. "Through our WNCW Academy, we proactively educate clients to keep them on the cutting edge of industry changes, legal requirements and trends that affect their industries," founding partner George E. Nowack, Jr. said.

In addition, Weissman strives to educate with his authoritative books *The Red Book on Real Estate Contracts in Georgia* and *Secrets Of Winning The Real Estate Negotiation Game*, both co-authored by attorney Ned Blumenthal, and a soon-to-be-published book on zoning and land-use law in Georgia.

COMMITTED TO COMMUNITY SERVICE

"Community service is important to us because the firm wants to be a good corporate citizen and show appreciation for its success," said Wilco, who sits on the board of directors of the Georgia Legal Services Program.

After more than two decades, Weissman, Nowack, Curry & Wilco still maintains its original focus of providing a client-focused law firm with excellent customer service and devotion to meeting its clients' changing needs and fostering a workplace environment where open doors and open minds thrive. ∎

*Golden globe of Georgia—*CAPITAL DOME *in Atlanta, against a cloudy blue sky. Photo by Steven Frame.*

CENTRAL

Georgia

CENTRAL GEORGIA, WAS a place of rolling hills and dense forests of hickory and oak when the Cherokee and Creek roamed the land. Nearly 300 years have brought many changes. Much of the old forest is gone, although the area remains heavily wooded and the Chattahoochee-Oconee National Forest provides nearly 900,00 acres of wilderness and wildlife.

This is the area of Georgia that Sherman passed through on his infamous March to the Sea and there is much for history buffs to see and study. Although the general burned everything in his path, the devastated counties rose from the ashes to a spectacular rebirth.

Columbus lies in the western part of the state, near the Alabama border and adjacent to Fort Benning, known as the Home of the Infantry. The U. S. army post, established in 1918, is home to 120,00 military personnel and their families and continues to expand.

The city of Columbus is also thriving and growing. The National Civil War Naval Museum and the National Infantry Museum attract visitors as does the Coca-Cola Space Science Center, a part of Columbus University and located on the beautiful Chattahoochee Riverwalk, a 15 mile linear park that runs through the city.

Visitors to the area are also drawn to Warm Springs, home of Franklin D. Roosevelt's Little White House, where the president found comfort during the trying years of World War II.

More centrally located in the state is Macon, founded in the early 1800s as Fort Benjamin Harris on historic Native American lands and renamed "Macon" in 1823. The largest African American museum in Georgia is located here, the Tubman African American Museum. Macon is home to Wesleyan College, the first chartered women's college in the world. Visitors also enjoy Sidney Lanier's cottage and the Georgia Children's Museum.

A scant thirty miles from Macon is the historic town of Milledgeville, known as the "Antebellum Capital of Georgia." Visitors to this jewel of a small city are treated to views of historic architecture and vivid reminders of the Civil War.

In central Georgia, one is never far from a place of interest or entertainment. Natural beauty combines with history and 21st century progress to make the area a perfect place for a visit or a permanent home. ▶

Where Civil War battles were once fiercely fought, Georgia's famous **PEACH TREES** *now bloom. Photo by David Kocherhans*

Even Justine Leonard can sometimes use a bit of advice!
AUGUSTA MASTERS OF GOLF, *2006.*

The splendid **MORGAN COUNTY COURTHOUSE**, *completed in 1905, well deserves its place on the National Register of Historic Places. Photo by Sean Pavone.*

The **SACRED HEART CULTURAL CENTER** *Sacred Heart Cultural Center in Augusta is a former Catholic church now home to various cultural activities and events. Opened in 1900, the interior of the cultural center features many fine European embellishments, including 94 stained glass windows.*

THE GEORGIA STATE FAIR, *a Macon tradition since 1851,*
features fun and food for every taste.

Timber remains an important part of the
CENTRAL GEORGIA *economy and adds*
natural beauty to the landscape.

Wildlife is plentiful at LAKE TOBESOFTBEE *in Bibb County. Photo by Steven Frame.*

This footpath in CENTERVILLE *invites a stroll to enjoy the peace of early morning. Photo by dotshock.*

"Come visit me!" at the Wild Animal Park in STATESBORO, *Pine Mountain, Georgia. Photo by Gigi Phillips.*

Profiles of Distinction

A look at the corporations, businesses and community service organizations that helped make this book possible. These forward-thinking companies and organizations are at the forefront of moving the state into a prosperous future.

Clayton State University

Columbus State University

The Hughston Clinic

Mercer University

Milledgeville Convention & Visitors Bureau

Peachtree City Convention and Visitors Bureau

Peachtree Planning Corporation

The Ritz-Carlton Lodge, Reynolds Plantation

Tanner Health System

Stratford Academy

The Vein Guys

A majestic BUCK AND HIS HERD *roam though a foggy woodland.*
Photo by Matt Gibson.

Clayton State University is located 15 miles from downtown Atlanta in a beautiful lakeside setting that is complemented by its proximity to a major, vibrant metropolitan hub. Additional instructional sites provide outreach to neighboring communities and online classes extend educational alternatives.

With 6,900 students, Clayton State embraces the rich cultural and socio-economic diversity of the greater Atlanta region through its faculty, its multiethnic and multigenerational student population, its successful alumni and the wide variety of clubs and organizational activities for students.

The university offers eight master's degree programs and 40 baccalaureate degree majors. A highly regarded faculty with academic, clinical, performance and business-world expertise in their fields leads the Clayton State classroom experience. Clayton State fosters learning and excellence through integrated academic instruction encompassing a technological classroom environment, internships and student research.

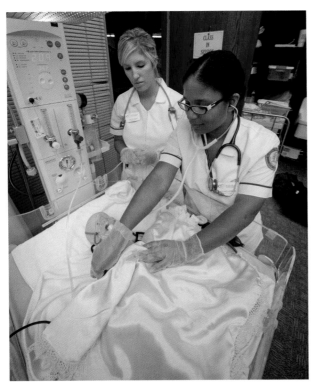

Student nurses gain valuable practical experience in the School of Nursing's state of the art Simulation Lab.

STRATEGICALLY POSITIONED

NCR CEO Bill Nuti has cited Clayton State University's supply chain management degree program and identified its proximity as a significant factor in NCR's relocation to Georgia. Just minutes from the world's busiest airport, Hartsfield-Jackson Atlanta International, Clayton State is ideally situated to assist companies seeking supply chain and logistics training and consultation. Recognizing this need, the College of Business has established a Center for Supply Chain Management.

Addressing critical healthcare issues, Clayton State graduates more minority nurses than any other nursing school in Georgia. The university's nursing graduates consistently have one of the highest overall National Council Licensure Examination/State Board pass rates—99.5 percent.

Clayton State University is the only university in the United States adjacent to both state and national archive facilities, the Georgia Archives and the National Archives in Atlanta. This proximity is invaluable for both undergraduate students and the Master of Archival Studies degree program, which exposes students to state of the art preservation techniques, digital archives creation and electronic records access.

CAMPUS LIFE ENHANCED

Recently constructed buildings and property acquisitions have dramatically changed and enhanced Clayton State's academic

Dr. Thomas J. Hynes, Jr., President of Clayton State University, welcomes entering freshmen at the New Student Convocation in Spivey Hall.

and campus life. The LAB Building provides laboratory space for sciences and psychology as well as classrooms. A new facility houses the College of Business, which is accredited by the Association to Advance Collegiate Schools of Business. The 62,000-square-foot Student Activities Center contains a state of the art fitness center, game room, student organization office space and a ballroom.

Laker Hall, a 451-bed student housing structure completed in 2008, was Georgia's first gigaplex residence hall with gigabit Ethernet for every hardwired connection and 100 percent wireless Ethernet. A national pioneer in ubiquitous mobile computing, Clayton State in 1998 became the nation's third public "notebook university."

Student housing options were expanded in the summer of 2011 with the addition of the Clayton Station apartments, which increased the main campus to 192 acres. Another recent purchase on Trammell Road, Clayton State-East, provides newly renovated space for numerous university departmental offices as well as additional academic and Continuing Education classroom space.

A CULTURAL TREASURE

Clayton State's Spivey Hall is considered to be the finest small performance facility in the southeastern United States and has a national reputation for excellence as a classical and jazz music venue. Spivey Hall annually presents more than 400 events, including one of the nation's foremost secondary education outreach programs. The hall's annual concert series offers world-class musicians performing timeless music in an acoustically perfect setting.

The equally famous Spivey Hall Children's Choir attracts aspiring young choral singers from 18 metro Atlanta counties, providing an exemplary choral music education to its singers since 1994. Comprised of both male and female singers ages 10 through 18, this treble choir program consists of three choirs that perform and tour throughout the world.

CHAMPIONSHIP WOMEN'S BASKETBALL TEAM

The university's athletics program features 12 sports and competes in NCAA Division II in the Peach Belt Athletic Conference. The Clayton State Lakers 2010/11 women's basketball team won the NCAA Division II National Championship in March 2011. Between 2007 and 2012, 22 Clayton State athletes were recognized as All-Americans, led by women's basketball first team All-American Tanisha Woodard.

As characterized by Dr. Thomas J. Hynes, Jr., President, "Clayton State is a transformational place. We activate learning in a way that empowers students to achieve everything they know, and we know, they're capable of achieving. I couldn't be more proud of this community and the experience we provide."

Clayton State is an empowering, diverse, engaging, supportive university—a place where dreams are made real for students, alumni, faculty and staff. ■

The Clayton State campus offers natural beauty—192 wooded acres with lakes, ponds, and wildlife—in close proximity to Atlanta.

Housing options include Georgia's first gigaplex residence hall as well as 4 BR/4BA apartments within walking distance.

NCAA Division II National Champions, Women's Basketball Team 2011

Columbus State University

Students from diverse backgrounds and from homes throughout Georgia are making Columbus State University their first choice—and for good reason. CSU provides students with relevant, in-demand degrees and a deeply personal educational environment not available at larger universities.

(Top) A Steinway concert grand piano sits on the stage of Columbus State University's Legacy Hall in Columbus' RiverCenter for the Performing Arts. CSU's Schwob School of Music's piano inventory, more than 60 pianos in all, is comprised exclusively of models made by Steinway.

(Bottom left) One of Columbus State University's state-of-the-art classrooms found on both campuses.

(Bottom right) Students, faculty, and staff enjoy the RiverPark campus' close proximity to the scenic Columbus Riverwalk, with miles of biking, walking, and running trails.

Just 100 miles southwest of Atlanta, Columbus State offers an array of degree programs and a doctorate in education, many of which are available completely online. With an 18:1 student-faculty ratio, its professors offer individualized instruction in and out of the classroom. As part of the University System of Georgia, Columbus State offers nationally and internationally accredited programs in such fields as art, business, music, nursing, teacher education and theater.

"Coming from a small town in southwest Georgia I heard about CSU through one of my good friends," said communication sophomore Jordan King. "I was accepted into the Servant Leadership program and I knew that CSU was right for me. Within my first week of classes I knew I was going to be just fine. All of my teachers were so welcoming and they really helped me adjust to CSU easily and quickly."

TRENDY, URBAN RIVERPARK CAMPUS

Besides its main campus, CSU has a beautiful RiverPark campus along the banks of the Chattahoochee, in historic Uptown Columbus. The campus includes stages for students in CSU's nationally recognized Department of Theater, the Corn Center for the Visual Arts featuring the work of visiting artists and CSU art students, the internationally renowned Schwob School of Music and the RiverCenter for the Performing Arts.

"When I started looking for a school at which to spend my college career, I asked around in my community of Griffin, Georgia," said music education sophomore Thomas Adams. "Everyone I asked immediately said 'Columbus State.' They knew the community of students this school nurtures and they wanted the best for me. As far as I am concerned, and it has been confirmed by the last two years, the Schwob School of Music is the best college for music in Georgia."

Apartment and loft student living, a new dining hall, bookstore, convenience shop and shuttle service to the main campus serve this downtown campus community, which soon will be adjacent to the world's longest urban whitewater experience. A multi-million dollar project to breach two dams will create opportunities for whitewater rafting and other water activities while also reclaiming the natural habitat of many aquatic species, making the area an angler's paradise.

This trendy, urban environment is enhanced by weekly outdoor concerts during warm months, an open-air farmer's market spring through fall, running, rollerblading and bicycling along the Riverwalk and opportunities to unwind in neighborhood restaurants and coffee shops.

Three nearby university outreach centers—the Oxbow Meadows Environmental Learning Center, Coca-Cola Space Science Center and the Carson McCullers Center for Writers

and Musicians—offer more learning opportunities for the entire community.

FROM HUMBLE BEGINNINGS COMES GROWTH

Columbus State's growth came from its roots as Columbus College, founded in 1958. Housed in a former hosiery mill, the junior college moved to its current main location in 1963, signaling a long period of expansion. In 1965, CSU became a four-year institution; the first four-year class graduated in 1970. In ensuing years, a range of master's, specialist and doctoral degrees were added. Community support, always strong from the start, helped supplement state funding to provide modern facilities and state-of-the-art equipment.

Today, Columbus State offers more than 70 programs in a mix of traditional and online formats. Students also may enhance their traditional learning through internships, clinical experiences, cooperative education, field research and international studies with senior professors and in collaboration with various businesses, civic, arts and governmental partners.

FULFILLING ITS PROMISE

"Columbus State University has always maintained a promise to the residents of Columbus," said President Tim Mescon. "From its very beginning, CSU promised to be a transformational force for Columbus' people and economy. We continue fulfilling that promise today as we graduate highly qualified professionals into a global workforce and provide a $236 million per year boost to the local economy."

Other university efforts also enhance the community and the university experience. Examples include hosting speakers such as former secretary of state Condoleezza Rice and former president George Bush at the annual Jim Blanchard Leadership Forum and establishing an interactive learning center and gallery downtown for acclaimed painter and Columbus native Bo Bartlett.

"Most importantly, our faculty and staff at Columbus State

share a passion to ensure our students' success on every level," Mescon said. "While we continue to grow and enhance our programs and add world-class facilities, we never lose sight of the promise that founded Columbus State University." ■

(Top left) The Thomas Y. Whitley Clock Tower, built in 1991, soars over Columbus State University's main campus as a center of activity for the campus community.

(Top right) Located on the Chattahoochee River, Columbus State University's RiverPark campus is an iconic fixture of Columbus' river skyline.

(Bottom) The university's new $26 million, 106,000-square-foot Student Recreation Center houses a fitness area, aquatic center, two basketball courts, workout area, two aerobic rooms, free weight area, running track, multi-purpose court, two racquetball courts, indoor soccer, volleyball, climbing wall and bouldering area.
© Hastings+Chivetta Architects, Inc. / Fentress Photography

Jack C. Hughston, MD, a pioneer in sports medicine, established The Hughston Clinic in Columbus in 1949. His private practice has since grown into nine clinics across Georgia and Alabama with 21 physicians, a hospital, an outpatient surgical center and a nonprofit research and education foundation.

Hughston graduated from Auburn University and received his medical degree from Louisiana State University. "Dr. Hughston was an amazing individual," said Jacqueline Decell, executive director of the Georgia Sports Hall of Fame, into which Dr. Hughston was posthumously inducted in 2006. "He truly changed the care of athletes."

THE SIDELINE COVERAGE CONCEPT
While working with crippled children during the 1940s, Dr. Hughston became interested in caring for young athletes, and, in 1951, his association with Auburn football coach Ralph "Shug" Jordan led to his becoming the Auburn Tigers' team physician. Thus, a career in sports medicine was born. Hughston's professional relationship with Auburn's head athletic trainer, Kenny Howard, helped form the affiliation between the National Athletic Trainers' Association and the American Medical Association, which, in turn, led to the eventual certification and recognition of athletic trainers as allied health care providers.

Because of his sideline observations of injuries to young athletes, Hughston helped institute the rules making it mandatory for high school football players to use a protective mouthpiece and to eliminate the practice of crack-back blocking.

SHARED MEDICAL KNOWLEDGE
Dr. Hughston fervently believed in sharing his medical knowledge and that being a successful educator was as important as being a physician. To that end, he partnered with Tulane University Medical School to start the first residency program in orthopaedic sports medicine. He founded The Hughston Foundation for research and education and established the first and longest continuing postdoctoral fellowship training

Over 50 years, one ground-breaking medical practice in Columbus, Ga., has morphed into nine clinics, a hospital, surgical center and nonprofit research and education foundation.

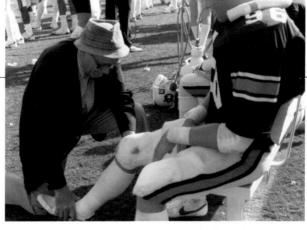

program in orthopaedic and primary care sports medicine in the world. More than 120 orthopaedic residents, 400 sports medicine fellows and 50 primary care fellows have trained at Hughston.

Dr. Hughston was a founding member of the American Orthopaedic Society for Sports Medicine. He was the first editor of its scientific journal, the *American Journal of Sports Medicine*, which publishes articles on current medical research and surgical techniques in the field of sports medicine. The legacy of Jack Hughston's educational philosophy can be traced through the many scientific publications produced by Hughston's medical professionals. Their many peer-reviewed medical journal articles, medical textbooks and numerous textbook chapters, scientific presentations at national and international meetings and free quarterly patient education newsletter continue Hughston's educational mission.

MORE THAN A CLINIC

The Hughston Clinic offers specialized spine, hand, joint, sports medicine and trauma care. This care is supported by Hughston Diagnostics, which provides ultrahigh-resolution imaging through a 1.5 Tesla GE MRI machine; Hughston Health, a state of the art exercise and training facility; and Hughston Rehabilitation, an advanced physical therapy and rehabilitation facility.

Today, the Jack Hughston Memorial Hospital in Phenix City is ranked by HealthGrades, the nation's leading independent healthcare ratings organization, as best in the Georgia-Alabama region in patient outcomes for overall orthopaedic services in 2012. The advanced acute-care hospital also received the organization's Outstanding Patient Experience Award™ for four consecutive years (2009-2012), ranking it among the top 5

percent of hospitals nationally for patient experience (2009-2012). The hospital, with 70 private patient rooms and six operating suites, is among the nation's 100 best hospitals for specialty care in joint replacement and orthopaedic surgery.

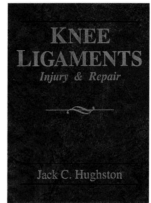

"If there is ever a time that a patient needs to be comfortable and cared for, it is after surgery," said Dr. John I. Waldrop, president of The Hughston Clinic. "Our patients are treated as if they are in a five-star hotel rather than in a hospital. Our patient-satisfaction ranking proves that point."

MANY SATISFIED PATIENTS

Satisfied patients have praise for The Hughston Clinic. Deb Duke of Columbus, Georgia, had severe arthritic pain in both knees before she had bilateral knee replacement. "It got to the point where I couldn't do any of the things that I enjoy and want to do," she said. "I can do everything now. I can go in stores and browse and really shop. I can play with my grandkids, and I'm able to ride [motorcycles] and spend quality time with my husband. I've got my smile back because my face is not etched with pain."

Dabne Adams of Phenix City, Alabama, couldn't hunt or fish because of a rotator cuff tear. "Having the surgery was a life-changing experience," he said. "Now I go hunting and fishing and can play with the kids. I'm grateful because it changed my life." ∎

Dr. Jack Hughston pioneered the practice of sports medicine and was passionate about sharing his knowledge with others.

Central Georgia's AUTUMN BEAUTY *is unrivaled.*
Photo by Eric Gevaert.

Mercer University

Since Mercer University's beginning in 1833, every accomplishment, every breakthrough, every idea—great or small—has been fueled by an unwavering determination to make a difference. From a comprehensive set of educational options and groundbreaking research to award-winning service initiatives and an educational

environment that embraces intellectual and religious freedom, the Mercer experience is transforming and empowering communities throughout the world.

At the heart of Mercer's success is a forward-thinking mission, which integrates five defining components of student life and personal development: liberal learning, professional knowledge, discovery, service to humankind and community.

"Generations of young men and women have gone on from Mercer to become leaders of great deeds and influence," says William D. Underwood, president of Mercer. "Central to the

(Top) Among the colleges and schools on Mercer's Cecil B. Day Campus in Atlanta is the nationally recognized Georgia Baptist College of Nursing.

(Bottom left) The R. Kirby Godsey Administration Building, signature landmark on the Macon Campus, was built in 1874.

(Bottom right) Students gather in front of the University Center on the Macon Campus.

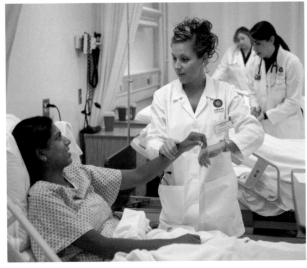

lives of those individuals is an education that uniquely prepares students to lead virtuous, meaningful and responsible lives and encourages a thoughtful examination of ethical and moral choices."

Today, Mercer comprises three major campuses in Macon, Atlanta and Savannah, plus the recent addition of a site in Columbus for third- and fourth-year medical students, and four Regional Academic Centers in suburban Atlanta and in Eastman. In addition, the university operates the Mercer Engineering Research Center in Warner Robins.

AN INTIMATE, STUDENT-FOCUSED CULTURE

With an ideal size of just over 8,300 undergraduate, graduate and professional students, Mercer is one of the nation's few universities that successfully combines the intimate environment and personal attention of a small liberal arts college with the academic resources of a major research university.

Faculty members, whose credentials are from some of the world's finest academic institutions, are distinguished for both teaching and research. More than 90 percent hold doctorates or the highest attainable degrees in their respective fields.

Mercer also offers undergraduate and graduate programs in business, education, engineering, liberal arts, music and nursing, as well as professional programs in medicine, law, pharmacy and health sciences and theology.

The university has achieved state and national recognition for maintaining high levels of academic excellence. The Georgia

Baptist College of Nursing, operated by Mercer, is nationally known for bridging undergraduate classroom learning with clinical experience. The Tift College of Education is the largest private preparer of teachers in Georgia. The Walter F. George School of Law is one of the oldest law schools in the South, with a legal writing program ranked the best in the nation by *U.S. News & World Report* for two consecutive years. Mercer's School of Engineering is one of the three best engineering schools in the Southeast for non-doctoral programs, according to *U.S. News & World Report*.

The College of Liberal Arts is the oldest of the university's academic units and remains the cornerstone of Mercer's educational programs. Mercer also operates a College of Pharmacy and Health Sciences, the Eugene W. Stetson School of Business and Economics, the James and Carolyn McAfee School of Theology, the College of Continuing and Professional Studies and the Townsend School of Music.

LEARNING, COMPASSION AND ACTION

Recognizing that a college education is much more than receiving a degree, Mercer provides students with numerous opportunities to interact directly with communities to apply their skills and learning to real-world challenges.

Mercer's School of Medicine, which accepts only Georgia residents for admission to its M.D. program, has a unique focus among medical schools for its commitment to meet the health care needs of medically underserved areas. In 1982, Mercer developed a program specifically for preparing doctors for service in rural areas. As a result, a higher percentage of Mercer physicians practice in the state. The School of Engineering also has a strong community-based foundation. When Robins Air Force Base expressed a need for engineering graduates, Mercer partnered with the base to launch an engineering curriculum and began admitting students in 1985.

Mercer's global outreach is reflected in Mercer On Mission, a unique blend of study abroad and service learning that provides life-changing experiences for students through academic instruction, cultural immersion, meaningful service and spiritual reflection. Working with in-country partners, Mercer students and faculty have distributed mosquito nets to villages in Africa, taught orphans in Guatemala, delivered medical care in Thailand and fit amputees in Vietnam with low-cost prosthetic legs. In 2009, Mercer on Mission's Vietnam project was one of only

four "commitments" by universities around the country to be recognized by President Bill Clinton as part of the Clinton Global Initiative University program.

Mercer's presence has made an impact throughout Georgia by helping to prepare generations of young men and women for positions of civic, political and professional leadership. Alumni include renowned physicians, attorneys, preachers, athletes, scientists, business leaders and Pulitzer Prize-winning journalists and authors, as well as 12 governors, four U.S. senators and a U.S. attorney general.

MERCER MEANS MORE!

Beyond the classroom, Mercer offers more than 115 student organizations that offer year-round opportunities for involvement, leadership, entertainment, and fitness and sports activities. The University's Division I athletic program features 16 intercollegiate sports, including baseball, basketball, cross country, golf, lacrosse, sand volleyball, soccer, softball, tennis and volleyball. In August 2013, the Bears will return to competition in intercollegiate football, ending a 70-year hiatus. To prepare for the occasion, Mercer is building a state of the art football and lacrosse complex on campus that promises to be one of the South's finest sports facilities.

"Our students can enjoy all of the exciting dimensions of college life in an enriching environment that promotes academic, social and spiritual development," says Underwood. "We invite potential students and their families to our campuses to experience first-hand the many qualities that make Mercer University a formative step in life's continuing journey." ∎

(Top left) Hawkins Arena in the University Center is home to Mercer's volleyball and men's and women's basketball programs.

(Top right) The Cecil B. Day Campus in Atlanta is home to the McAfee School of Theology, Georgia Baptist College of Nursing, and College of Pharmacy and Health Sciences. Academic programs in the Tift College of Education, the Eugene W. Stetson School of Business and Economics and the College of Continuing and Professional Studies are also offered on the Atlanta campus.

(Bottom) Mercer On Mission was awarded The Clinton Global Initiative Award for its efforts to help amputees in Vietnam and other developing nations.

Milledgeville, Georgia's Antebellum Capitol

In a state filled with historic treasures, Milledgeville, Georgia, truly stands out. Known as the "Antebellum Capital of Georgia," Milledgeville brims with stunningly preserved and historically significant buildings and homes, not to mention natural wonders and recreational activities for the whole family.

Milledgeville is one of seven cities on Georgia's Antebellum Trail, with a wealth of well preserved architecture enhanced by noteworthy Greek Revival, Victorian and Classic Revival homes.

Milledgeville is also home to Georgia College and State University, which operates a Natural Science Museum and organizes concerts, plays, art exhibits and cultural events for the entire community's enjoyment and enrichment.

"Whether visitors are history buffs, sightseers, shoppers, students or vacationers, Milledgeville is the perfect destination, with many activities to keep our guests thoroughly charmed, entertained and even spellbound," says Jane Sowell, executive director of the Milledgeville Convention and Visitors Bureau.

A GEM ON GEORGIA'S ANTEBELLUM TRAIL

The story of Milledgeville's founding provides clues to its enduring allure. The city was established in 1803 by the state legislature and named for then-governor John Milledge. Local tradition holds that a group of legislative commissioners

charged with locating the site of the new town came upon a large oak by a spring. Their leader, John Clarke, sampled the spring water, mixed it with some whiskey, thrust his cane into the ground and announced, "This is it!"

Milledgeville's central location and access to the Oconee River fueled the city's early growth and success. Milledgeville and Washington D.C. share a point of distinction as the only cities in the United States designed to be capital cities.

Milledgeville served as Georgia's second capital from 1803 to 1868. Built in 1807, the Old Capitol Building is considered the first example of Gothic architecture in a U.S. public building and today serves as a popular history museum.

The Old Governor's Mansion was home to Georgia's governors for three decades and was occupied by General Sherman during his March to the Sea. Known as one of the best examples of Greek Revival architecture in Georgia, the mansion recently opened its doors to the public after the completion of a three-year, $10 million restoration.

Milledgeville's Trolley Tour, which operates Monday-Saturday, is the best way to take in the town's landmark historic district, including haunted historic sites and fascinating museums.

CLEAN WATER, NATURAL BEAUTY, LITERARY GIANTS!

Milledgeville's many natural attractions make the area a year-round destination for boating, fishing, skiing, hiking and enjoying the great outdoors. Along the Oconee River, a spacious greenway offers walking trails, bicycle trails, fishing stations and spots just to relax and listen to the sounds of the river passing by.

Meanwhile, Lake Sinclair, declared the "Cleanest Lake in the State," boasts more than 500 miles of shoreline and a number of marinas, campgrounds, picnic areas and unsupervised beaches.

Hiking trails guide visitors through Bartram Forest, where they'll see diverse wildlife, natural wetlands and an erosion ravine with soil deposited by ancient shallow seas that covered Georgia 100 million years ago. Lockerly Arboretum is another one of Milledgeville's unique public attractions, featuring 47 acres of native and exotic flowers, shrubs and trees.

Milledgeville is proud of its claim to fame as the home of Flannery O'Connor, one of the South's most acclaimed writers. O'Connor wrote many of her novels and short stories at the local Andalusia Farm, and an extensive collection of her manuscripts and books are on display at her alma mater, Georgia College and State University.

"In many ways, the story of Milledgeville is the story of our state, our nation and the South," says Sowell. "Visitors are always amazed by the wide range of interests offers, and our goal is to preserve the beauty and uniqueness of Milledgeville for generations to come." ∎

(Top) Sherman slept here! The Old Governor's Mansion, c.1839, is a National Historic Landmark and operating house museum.

(Inset) The Antebellum Inn, c. 1890, is a historic bed & breakfast featuring beautiful Greek Revival portico.

(Bottom) This c.1824 home was originally designed in Classic Revival style and only had four columns. Was rebuilt in 1890 in Neo-classical style and is now on the National Register of Historic Homes.

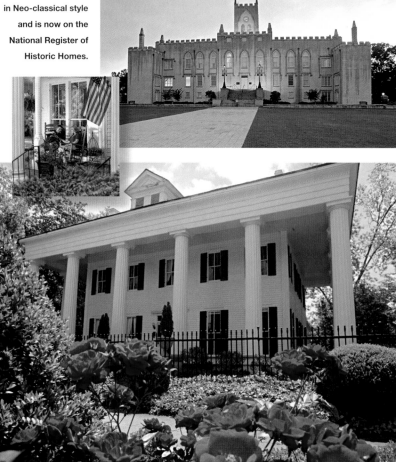

The Vein Guys is a collection of four vein centers that has become one of the largest and most respected vein practices in the country. All doctors are Board Certified Surgeons and, to date, have collectively performed more than 13,000 treatments. The Vein Guys combine their medical sub expertise with the latest technology to provide minimally invasive treatments for vein disease.

The entire staff at each of the Vein Guys locations is dedicated not only to improving their patient's legs by treating their vein disease but also to the overall quality of each individual's lifestyle.

DR. STEVEN ROTH

Fellowship trained and Board Certified in Vascular Surgery, Dr. Roth's training in the diagnosis and treatment of vascular diseases included all parts of the human body.

After receiving his M.D at Eastern Virginia Medical School in Norfolk, he received an appointment to the Vascular Surgery Fellowship training program at the University of South Florida in Tampa. During this time, he learned of minimally invasive procedures and how they could revolutionize the treatment of vein disease.

"When I saw the new technology, I realized that this could truly make a difference in people's lives," Roth explained. "People with venous reflux disease experience throbbing, aching, cramping, heaviness and swelling in their legs. They may also experience fatigue and tiredness. Thirty million people are affected by vein disease and many may not have any visible symptoms. The difference treatment can make in their lives is immeasurable. Today's treatments can have a person up and active the same day."

Roth focused on the treatment of vein disease in the legs and opened his own vein care center in 2004. The first location in Augusta was soon complemented by centers in Nashville, Tennessee, Raleigh, North Carolina, and Atlanta.

NEW TECHNOLOGY PROVIDES INSTANT RELIEF

"Earlier treatments of vein disease in the legs consisted of surgically stripping the veins from the leg. The recovery time was lengthy and frequently the patient didn't experience relief," Roth explained. "Today, a 15-minute procedure will provide a patient a significant level of immediate relief. They can leave the office within 20 minutes of the procedure and immediately get back to their lives."

GROWING INVOLVES SUSTAINING THE HIGHEST STANDARDS OF PATIENT CARE

The Vein Guys adhere to the highest standards of quality and professionalism. "At each of our locations, we have an accredited vascular laboratory. We provide state of the art vein treatments and compassionate care," Roth said.

The continued growth of the Vein Guys is the result of a lesson Roth learned in the Army Reserve. "We'd go in and take our best staff and set up operations. Our existing staff would train any new members and we'd be operating a successful OR within days or even hours. Hiring the best and training by the best is what creates a good center.

That's how I'm going to enlarge this practice. I'm going into each new market with a commitment to train new staff by utilizing professionals I know give their best to patients. Word of mouth referrals from patients and their stories are our best testimonials. When someone feels better they are more active and enabling our patients to live a more productive life means we've done our job." ∎

The entire staff at each of the Vein Guys locations is dedicated not only to improving their patient's lives by treating their vein disease but also to the overall quality of each individual's lifestyle.

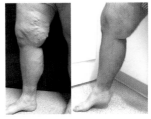

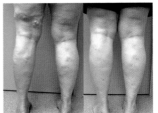

Peachtree City Convention and Visitors Bureau

Peachtree City, the golf cart capital of the world, is an award winning master planned community that BusinessWeek magazine has called Georgia's Best Affordable Suburb. ▪ *"We're a family-friendly community because of our low crime rate and excellent schools, and Peachtree City also is an excellent site for business meetings," said Nancy Price,*

executive director of the Peachtree City Convention and Visitors Bureau. "Our city is less than a half hour away from the world's busiest airport, yet lacks Atlanta's distractions and traffic challenges. We also have a regional airport that can accommodate small planes. It's easy to get down to business here."

GOLF COURSES, LAKES, PARKS

Conveniently located 26 miles south of Atlanta, the city of 34,364 residents offers resort-style living with three golf courses, two lakes, an award-winning tennis center and indoor and outdoor aquatics center. The Fayette County city also has numerous parks, baseball and soccer fields and a BMX track.

Two conference centers and five hotels with 834 rooms total are available to serve business visitors as well as tourists. Peachtree City also has a 2,500 seat outdoor amphitheater—The Fred—that hosts national and touring acts all summer.

Peachtree City is a planned community with 90 miles of golf-cart and multi-use paths. It offers resort-style living with three golf courses, two lakes and an award-winning tennis center.

HOP ON A GOLF CART!

Peachtree City, chartered in 1959, was developed as five villages, each with its own recreational facilities, shopping areas and elementary schools. Residents traverse the city by way of a 90-mile wooded network of golf-cart and multi-use paths. In fact, more than 9,000 households own a golf cart and use them for extra transportation, while several businesses have specially designed golf-cart parking spaces. The Peachtree City Police Department even uses golf carts to patrol along the paths.

Peachtree City's national reputation as a great place to live is evidenced by a multitude of honors: *Family Circle* magazine named it among the Top 10 Cities for Families in 2011 and *CNN/Money Magazine* has twice named it among the Top 10 Best Places to Live in the U.S.

SITE OF TV, MOVIE MAKING

Television and moviemakers also are enamored with Peachtree City. Lifetime's *Drop Dead Diva* show is taped in the city and the movies *Sweet Home Alabama* and *Joyful Noise* were partially filmed there.

"Georgia's tax credit has been a big help in attracting film crews to our area," Price said. "We like to think of ourselves as the Hollywood of the South."

The Peachtree City Convention and Visitors Bureau, established in 2010, helps develop tourism and promote the city's economic development. Its success in doing so earned the CVB a Bronze Level Benchmark of Excellence from the Georgia Association of Convention and Visitors Bureaus in 2011.

The Peachtree City CVB operates the Visitors Center at 201 McIntosh Trail, which shares space with the Frederick Brown Jr. Amphitheater's box office. ▪

VISIT PEACHTREE CITY CVB ONLINE: www.visitpeachtreecity.com

Peachtree Planning Corporation

Helping thousands of individuals and businesses plan for and reach their dreams, Peachtree Planning Corporation has built a 25-year, stellar reputation as one of Georgia's leading financial services firms. The concept of serving clients by providing a proven financial-planning process and using products that best fit the client's individual needs was relatively new when Bob Mathis founded the Atlanta-headquartered company in 1987.

Today, Peachtree Planning has grown from a four-advisor firm in 1987 to approximately 100 financial advisors in more than 20 offices throughout the Southeast. Its successful model is also serving clients through Peachtree Planning of Tennessee, LLC based in Nashville, Tennessee, and Southeastern Financial Group, LLC based in Birmingham, Alabama.

HELPING PEOPLE, MAKING MONEY

"Help some people, make some money and have some fun" remains the firm's mission. "The way we live our lives can have a positive effect on others," Mathis explained. "If we spend our time trying to help people live well and attain their dreams, then our own dreams are realized as well."

His vision has proven true, with about 95 percent of Peachtree Planning's clients and financial advisors coming from referrals. Those advisors are managing more than $2.4 billion in client assets.

THE LIVING BALANCE SHEET®

All fiscal decisions are interrelated. What looks like a smart move in one area might have negative implications elsewhere, which is why clients need to have an organized, integrated view of their finances. Peachtree Planning provides this via The Living Balance Sheet®, a personal, secure website that lets clients plan, manage and track their various financial assets and liabilities and see where they are meeting their goals.

PROTECT, ORGANIZE AND FOCUS ON WHAT MATTERS MOST

The Peachtree Planning process begins with a commitment to ensure that the client's most important assets are protected against the many risks that can endanger financial success. Each asset is organized for easy analysis and understanding. Finally, financial plans are individually designed to meet each client's specific needs, goals and appetite for risk.

FORBES' TOP 10 WEALTH MANAGER

Peachtree Planning has built a positive environment in which its advisors are truly connected to their work, clients and colleagues. Not surprisingly, the firm has earned many accolades, including listing on *Forbes'* Top 10 Wealth Managers, the *Atlanta Journal-Constitution's* No. 1 Top Small Business Workplace, one of the *Atlanta Business Chronicle's* Best Workplaces, and the *Daily Report's* Best Financial Advisory & Investment Regional Firm.

"We have an inclusive corporate culture, so virtually everyone feels a vested interest in helping the company grow," Mathis said. "Our people feel good at the end of the day about what they're doing." ∎

The firm's partners are (top row, from left) Bob Mathis, David Fosgate, Brad Stonecipher, (bottom row, from left) Andy Meehan, John Hill, Keith Dykes, Al Robertson and Corky Dawes.

"Help some people, make some money and have some fun" is the mission of Peachtree Planning Corporation, which has approximately 100 financial advisors in more than 20 offices throughout the Southeast.

The *R*itz-Carlton Lodge, Reynolds Plantation

Overlooking the sparkling waters of Lake Oconee, The Ritz-Carlton Lodge, Reynolds Plantation, in Greensboro, Georgia, is unlike any of its counterparts. ■ While it is undoubtedly true to The Ritz-Carlton name—concierge services, a 24-hour business center, a world-class spa, indoor and outdoor pools and three fine dining restaurants—its rustic setting gives The Lodge a unique and inviting Southern twist that keeps guests coming back year after year.

Located 75 miles from Atlanta and the world's busiest airport, The Lodge affords guests all the comforts of modern living while surrounded by the radiant beauty and peaceful seclusion of the Georgia countryside.

The Ritz-Carlton Lodge offers avid golfers 99 holes of golf and invites guests to relax in the heart of nature.

'LINGER LONGER'

Hiking, fishing, golfing, sightseeing. The Ritz-Carlton Lodge offers a host of family friendly activities and nearby towns are filled with antebellum home tours and historic landmarks. Visitors soon discover why the founders called the land "Linger Longer."

"We find that many of our guests grew up on a lake, and with so many activities that bring people outside to enjoy the water, staying here reminds them of their childhood. Georgia has four distinct seasons, each with its own unique beauty and recreational opportunities. We take advantage of that seasonal diversity to give our guests the full Ritz-Carlton Lodge experience" says Ralph Vick, General Manager.

Each summer, The Lodge offers a complimentary Sunday night concert series and fireworks show. During the day, guests can sign up for the wakeboarding school on Lake Oconee, and at night they can huddle under the stars and enjoy s'mores around The Lodge campfire. In winter, an ice-skating rink is open daily for the enjoyment of guests.

RUSTIC, ROOMY AND LUXURIOUS

Guests of The Ritz-Carlton Lodge may choose from a number of accommodations, each offering its own distinct amenities and updated continuously to provide the finest in style and comfort.

More than 250 fully appointed guest rooms, suites and cottages are available with picturesque views from private terraces. Guests seeking more spacious accommodation can choose the 892 square-foot Executive Suite or the 2,392 square-foot Ritz-Carlton Suite. Six lakeside cottages feature either two or three bedrooms, a living room, a butler's pantry, a wood-burning fireplace and a homey porch with scenic views.

The pinnacle of lakeside luxury is the Presidential House, a three-story manse featuring four master bedroom suites and a first-floor great room that opens to a private, heated outdoor pool overlooking the shores of Lake Oconee.

Guests of lakeside cottages and the Presidential House can enjoy an exclusive Ritz-Carlton Lodge service—the BBQ Butler. The BBQ Butler prepares the ultimate made-to-order cookout while providing instruction on the fine art of grilling, smoking and barbecuing. The BBQ Butler assists guests in the selection of meats as well as complementary woods, specialty sauces and sides, designed to make any group's meal a highlight.

WORLD-CLASS GOLF AND TAYLORMADE LAB

Golfers at The Ritz-Carlton Lodge experience a new caliber of the game—five signature courses designed by world-renowned architects Rees Jones, Jack Nicklaus, Tom Fazio and Bob Cupp. Top 100 instructor Charlie King is available for lessons at the Reynolds Golf Academy.

Serious golfers will appreciate the TaylorMade™ Performance Lab, one of only eight such facilities in the world. Club fittings meet 21st century technology with TaylorMade's revolutionary MATT System, which analyzes golf swings using multiple high-speed video cameras.

"The Ritz-Carlton Lodge provides many activities that make it the perfect getaway, whether guests are traveling with families, as couples or for business events. When it comes to maximizing your enjoyment of Georgia's Lake Country, The Ritz-Carlton Lodge, Reynolds Plantation, is built to please." says Ralph Vick, General Manager. ■

Tanner Health System

In the years following World War II, communities outgrew the small country clinics that had been treating local families for decades. With initial funds provided by local grocer and businessman C.M. Tanner and donations from the community, Tanner Memorial Hospital opened in 1949 in Carrollton, Georgia.

Today, Tanner Health System offers four hospitals and a medical staff of more than 300 physicians representing 34 medical specialties, all focused on its mission to improve the health of the communities Tanner serves.

"Tanner's legacy is one of neighbors caring for neighbors," says Loy Howard, who has served as Tanner's president and chief executive officer since 1994. "Our patients aren't just people who are sick; they're members of our church congregations, the parents of our children's classmates. That's why the staff at Tanner is committed to getting every detail of a patient's care right. We want to ensure the best possible outcome and the best opportunity for people to return to a healthy life."

EVER GROWING QUALITY SERVICES

Setting Tanner Health System apart is its continuum of care that rivals any healthcare provider in the state of Georgia. Of significance is that it provides some of the most advanced technology available in the medical industry to treat two of the most devastating health threats facing patients: cardiovascular disease and cancer.

The state-of-the-art Tanner Heart and Vascular Center, opened in 2008, provides a single location for diagnosis, treatment and recovery. Meanwhile, Tanner Cancer Care brings together diagnostics, surgery, radiation therapy, medical oncology, radiology and more to provide an advanced, seamless, integrated approach to treating cancer.

In addition, Tanner offers two regional maternity centers, in Carrollton and Villa Rica, as well as community-based home health and hospice services, occupational health, pain management, surgical services and sleep medicine in two regional sleep centers.

Tanner's commitment to exceptional care has not gone unnoticed. In 2012, research firm Thomson Reuters recognized Tanner as one of the 15 top health systems in the nation, and Tanner Medical Center/Carrollton has been ranked No. 1 in Georgia for overall orthopedic services by HealthGrades for three consecutive years, from 2010 to 2012. Individual Tanner medical facilities have received

much acclaim for quality care and patient satisfaction as well.

BUILT FOR THE FUTURE OF HEALTH CARE

In 2012, Tanner opened a new 40-bed emergency department and an expanded surgical services unit at Tanner Medical Center/Carrollton. It's the latest project in a decade-long commitment to developing the infrastructure to meet the region's growing needs and to ensure that Tanner is prepared to continue serving the many generations of west Georgia residents to come.

Healthcare has become a cornerstone of west Georgia's economy, due largely to the continued growth of the non-profit Tanner Health System. A 2010 report from the Georgia Hospital Association indicated that Tanner contributed almost $662.3 million to the region's economy and created more than 5,300 full-time jobs.

Ensuring that every member of the community has access to care, Tanner contributes more than $63 million to indigent and charity care, as well as almost $4 million to improve the health of the communities Tanner serves.

"At Tanner, we understand that our success as a health system depends on earning the trust of the communities we serve," says Howard. "Every time someone turns to us for care, we see that as an opportunity to exceed expectations and earn their continued support. We know we're not just caring for patients, we're caring for our neighbors." ■

(Top) Tanner Medical Center/Carrollton is the largest of Tanner's four hospitals, serving as a major tertiary care center with advanced cancer, heart, orthopedic, maternity and other services.

(Bottom left) Serving the bustling community of Villa Rica and Carroll, Douglas and Paulding counties, Tanner Medical Center/Villa Rica offers a full continuum of care.

(Bottom middle) Higgins General Hospital in Bremen has been named one of the Nation's Top 100 Critical Access Hospitals by the National Rural Health Association.

(Bottom right) Willowbrooke at Tanner is the first new, inpatient behavioral health facility built in Georgia in at least 20 years, and offers 52 beds to serve adults, children and adolescents.

Stratford Academy is middle Georgia's only non-sectarian and oldest college preparatory school, one that guides children to become independent learners and teaches them how to think rather than what to think. Located in Macon, the school provides an academically challenging, yet nurturing, environment for students in pre-school through 12th grade.

"One of our slogans is 'Excellence Never Rests,' and we demonstrate this belief in all we do," said Dr. Robert E. Veto, Head of School. "From our academic program to our arts offerings, our extracurricular activities and our athletic program, we strive for excellence in everything we do."

PREPARATION FOR COLLEGE

Stratford was founded in 1960 by a group of Macon parents who wanted to insure that their children were prepared properly for the rigors of higher education. The school, then located in the antebellum Overlook Mansion, opened its doors to 117 students and 17 faculty members.

More than a half century later, Stratford Academy has graduated over 3,400 young people. Today, its community includes over 960 students and more than 100 faculty members and staff.

Now located on more than 70 acres in northwest Bibb County, Stratford Academy consists of four divisions: Preschool, Lower School, Middle School and Upper School. Its

Stratford Academy in Macon provides an academically challenging environment to more than 960 students in pre-school through 12th grade. Fine arts activities help students discover where their strengths lie.

contemporary complex includes a 17,500-square-foot library that features modern computer labs as well as a new science center where students experience the joy of discovery in state-of-the-art labs, prep rooms, an 80-seat fully wired lecture hall and classrooms.

NEW SCIENCE CENTER

"This is Middle Georgia's newest and most advanced science center," Veto said. "Technology and science careers are the foundation for our society's economic future and Stratford is preparing its students for later success."

A child's Stratford years are full of exploration, growth and development. Small classes help ensure personalized academic instruction, while fine arts and athletic activities help broaden each student's experience and help them discover where their strengths lie. "We strive to help students find their gifts and talents, overcome personal challenges and become stronger, self-reliant individuals," Veto said.

Stratford also is a compassionate community that emphasizes service to others. All of "the Stratford family" is involved in charitable work—preschoolers might collect canned goods for the Middle Georgia Food Bank while the Lower School collects coats for Mulberry Outreach, Middle School students support Jay's Hope "Hats 4 Hope" and the Upper School raises cancer awareness and collects funds for the American Cancer Society.

COMMUNITY SERVICE REQUIRED

Community service is a graduation requirement; since 1989, Stratford students have performed nearly 130,000 community service hours on projects that have helped them develop a sense of responsibility and build character and leadership skills.

"In addition to its academic excellence, Stratford's require-

ment of community service is a meaningful way to be involved in helping others," said Sharon Walker, mother of two students. "It has exposed my children, Charlie and Suzanne, to people in need, and it has taught them the necessity of helping others."

School officials are proud of what Stratford students have accomplished. More than 80 percent have received Advanced Placement Scholar designation by demonstrating college-level achievement, compared to the state average of 55 percent. In the 11 years that the Georgia Independent School Association has awarded the Athletic Excellence Award, Stratford has won the honor four times and been a runner-up the remaining times.

PRODUCING SUCCESSFUL STUDENTS

An environment that commands excellence, fosters integrity and community, promotes freedom and demands responsibility is an environment that builds successful students. "Students here are taught early to be independent thinkers and to develop critical learning and time-management skills," Veto said. "That's why they go on to do so well in college."

The results speak for themselves: Stratford students enrolled in the University of Georgia system retain their HOPE scholarships at a rate of 89 percent, compared to the state average of 35 percent. The graduating Class of 2012 was awarded more than $3 million in scholarships (excluding HOPE) and accepted at such prestigious colleges as Vanderbilt, Duke, Emory, Washington & Lee, The Citadel, Williams and Harvard.

"We believe that our graduates leave for college better prepared than the vast majority of their peers from other schools, particularly in the areas of writing and critical thinking," Veto said. "It's great to be a Stratford Eagle." ∎

Athletic activities help Stratford students learn the value of teamwork and accomplishing goals while also boosting their self esteem.

SOUTHERN
Georgia

THE CROWN OF THE GEORGIA COAST is Savannah, known as the Hostess City of the South. This graceful small city of less than 140,000 was the colonial capital of the state. Founded and designed in 1733 by James Oglethorpe who planned its defining feature, the squares around which many of the most beautiful homes, churches, museums and notable landmarks are located. Visitors enjoy touring the historic sites and unique architecture of the area, often during a carriage ride. The city has a rich history. Its Telfair Academy of Arts and Sciences is one of the oldest public museums in the South and the First African Baptist Church is one of the oldest congregations in the country. Even ghost tours are on offer, through the mysterious cemeteries made famous by the book and film *Midnight in the Garden of Good and Evil*. River tours show visitors extensive rice fields and antebellum plantations while dolphin tours allow visitors up close and personal encounters with these delightful creatures. The city is full of art galleries, antique shops and charming boutiques to tempt visitors. Speaking of temptation, the restaurants, many located in charming old homes, offer a range of fare from local creole and southern dishes to the exotic.

The Georgia coast extends 193 miles from Savannah to St. Marys. The coast is famous for its beaches and barrier islands and is a favorite vacation spot. Saltwater fishing, scuba diving and kayaking are among the many aquatic adventures on offer here and the area is lined with famous golf courses. Wildlife abounds, especially visible at the Cumberland Island National Seashore whose beaches are protected wildlife areas.

The Low Country region is home to the Gullah, or Geechee, peoples. These descendants of slaves have preserved much of their African heritage, although the years have brought changes. They have also enriched our country's cuisine with their spicy dishes.

The Okefenokee Swamp, called "the trembling land" by Native Americans, at 700 square miles is the largest blackwater swamp in North America and is located near Waycross, Georgia. The 438,000 acre area is protected by the Okefenokee National Wildlife Refuge and the Okefenokee Wilderness. About 400,000 people visit the swamp each year to marvel at its giant cypress tress and the dark marshes below. There are four parks in the swamp that offer camping, fishing and guided wildlife tours as well as water tours that allow access to the swamp's prairie areas.

Coastal Georgia offers fine dining on the secluded patios of old Savannah homes, journeys through mysterious shaded swampland where alligators lurk beneath the dark waters and sunny beaches and warm salt water perfect for enjoying the sea air and swimming. It is not a place to miss. ▶

*Low tide at **OSSABAW ISLAND,** one of Geogia's largest barrier islands just south of Savannah. Photo by Clay S. Turner.*

A covered pier on TYBEE ISLAND *is an invitation to relax and enjoy the view. Photo by Jack Schiffer.*

The lighthouse on COCKSPUR ISLAND *that marks the South Channel of the Savannah River has stood since 1854. Photo by Paul Brennan.*

Savannah is known for it gracious and welcoming squares,
the "JEWELS" OF THE CITY.

The palatial ARMSTRONG HOUSE, *at the mouth of Forsyth Park in*
Savannah, was constructed c. 1919 and designed by Henrick Wallin.

Danger lucks in the OKEFENOKEE SWAMP, *the natural habitat of the American alligator. Photo by Brian Lasenby.*

Legend holds that the ancestors of the CUMBERLAND ISLAND
horses arrived in the 1500s with the Spanish conquistadors.
Photo by Paula Stephens.

The rising spires of the **CATHEDRAL OF ST. JOHN THE BAPTIST** *were completed in 1896. French Catholic émigrés from Haiti established the first altars for this congregation in 1799. Photo by Cindy Haggerty.*

The Savannah **WESLEY MONUMENTAL** *United Methodist Church, facing Calhoun Square, was dedicated on May 30, 1890. Photo by Travel Bug.*

Profiles of Distinction

A look at the corporations, businesses and community service organizations that helped make this book possible. These forward-thinking companies and organizations are at the forefront of moving the state into a prosperous future.

Albany Convention & Visitors Bureau

Armstrong Atlantic State University

Savannah Country Day School

Memorial University Medical Center

Savannah State University

Tybee Island Tourism Council

Stately **LIVE OAKS** *are a hauntingly beautiful part of the South Georgia landscape.*
Photo by Stacy Funderburke.

Albany Convention & Visitors Bureau

Albany sits at the center of Southwest Georgia, a storied region closely tied to America's early Native American culture, the antebellum age of the Old South and the timeless sports of fishing and hunting. Albany sits on a Floridian Aquifer, an ocean of fresh water that feeds the area's rivers and creeks and fuels its economy.

"Outdoor adventure, the arts, shopping, dining and the friendliest folks anywhere, Albany has it all! With so much to see and do, you'll want to visit us again and again," says Rashelle Beasley, Albany Convention and Visitors Bureau Manager.

HISTORY UNVEILED

The first inhabitants of the area now known as Albany were the Creek Indians who called their home along the riverbank Thronateeska, "the place where flint is picked up." Fittingly,

the river that flows through Albany is called the Flint. Nelson Tift founded the city in 1836, hoping that the settlement would prosper as a trade center like Albany, New York.

Albany grew to incorporate several plantations during the mid 1800s and saw no battles during the Civil War that would interfere with the plantations' production. Rather, the large plantations provided cotton and desperately needed food for the Confederacy.

Albany eventually turned to the rails for transportation, becoming a rail center by the turn of the 20th century after finding that low water and sandbars in the Flint River made steamboat navigation unreliable. Union Station, which united the seven railroads that offered as many as 55 trains daily, is now home of the Thronateeska Heritage Center.

Currently located in Thronateeska Heritage Plaza, on the last brick street in Albany, remains one of the oldest train depots in the State of Georgia. The History Museum is housed in the 1912 Train Station and features multiple exhibits about Albany throughout the year. In 2008, a new high definition, surround-sound full dome Planetarium, the first in the world of its kind, opened along with a new Science Museum.

DIVERSE ATTRACTIONS

Mingle with the meerkats in the "wild." Listen to Ray Charles, a native Albanian, play in the Plaza. Divine climate conditions in the new weather center. Get an eyeful of the universe and come face to face with creatures of the deep. Albany has adventure that is out of this world and right up everyone's alley.

"Albany's diverse appeal gives visitors the opportunity to enjoy not only historic landmarks but also recreational and cultural attractions," says Beasley.

In 1961, crowds gathered at Mount Zion Baptist Church to hear Dr. Martin Luther King, Jr, and other civil rights leaders inspire listeners to challenge the systematic oppression of African Americans. Old Mount Zion, built in 1906, is now the most important artifact in the new Albany Civil Rights Institute's collection. Since Albany Civil Rights Institute's opening

(Top) The Historic Bridge House, now home to the Albany Welcome Center and Albany Convention & Visitors Bureau, was built in circa 1858 by freed slave Horace King.

(Middle) Thanks to the mild year around climate and access to the Flint River, Albany has become a hot bed for outdoor sports. Specifically fishing for shoal bass.

(Bottom left) Along with a new Science Museum, Thronateeska welcomed the first in the world of its kind, a new high definition, surround sound, full dome Planetarium in 2008.

(Bottom right) Since the Albany Civil Right Institute opened in 2008, visitors have learned about the long Southwest Georgia Movement that stretches back to slavery and reaches right up to today.

In the center of Ray Charles Plaza sits a life-size bronze sculpture of the pioneering soul musician.

A special predator calls the Flint RiverQuarium home—Moonshine, an albino alligator.

in 2008, visitors have learned about the long Southwest Georgia Movement that stretches back to slavery and reaches right up to today. While visiting the Albany Civil Rights Institute visitors can hear the power of music in the movement and see what happened to ordinary people in extraordinary times.

Chehaw Park, nature's playground, provides nearly 700 acres of fun, including a 100 acre, AZA-accredited zoo, Chehaw Wild Animal Park. Noted naturalist and Albany native Jim Fowler of TV's Wild Kingdom originally laid out the park which features natural exhibits with native and exotic animals. Young children can head for one of the state's largest play parks, visit the petting zoo, take an African Veldt Safari ride or ride the miniature train. Camping, hiking, disc golf and BMX bike racing are also available inside the park.

In downtown Albany, visitors will find a six-acre park spread out along the Flint River. Riverfront Park has a beautiful lawn for family picnics and gatherings. Also included is a play fountain, pavilion areas, a 1.5 mile Greenways Trail System with a three-mile Riverwalk, the Horace King Overlook, the Albany Welcome Center located in the Historic Bridge House and Turtle Grove Play Park. This safe community-built park features seven irresistible areas for children ages one to fourteen with shaded benches for adults to relax.

Holding court in the center of the Ray Charles Plaza that runs along the Flint River is a life-size sculpture of the pioneering soul musician, seated at a Baby Grand piano that rests on a rotating pedestal. Born in Albany, Charles' beloved melodies play at timed intervals while water flows over the pedestal and spills into a reflecting pool at its base. Grab a piano key bench and enjoy the "concert."

The Flint RiverQuarium follows the Flint River's amazing journey from north Georgia to the Gulf of Mexico and the 175,000 gallon Blue Hole is one of the few open-air aquariums in the world. Get a unique look at Southwest Georgia's mysterious underwater world with more than 100 species of fish, alligators, turtles and other aquatic animals. Then visit the Cypress Pond Aviary, home to more than 30 types of birds indigenous to the Flint River watershed. Next door is the Adventure Center which houses changing exhibitions and the Imagination Theater, the area's only large screen format theater.

The Albany Museum of Art has six galleries and hosts

numerous exhibitions throughout the year showcasing works from their permanent collection as well as temporary exhibitions from nationally and internationally recognized artists.

"We are fortunate to be able to offer a diversity of attractions that speak to a cross section of travelers as well as gourmet food and top notch accommodations. Once you visit, you will want to come back," says Beasley.■

The Friends of Chehaw Conservation Society and National Bicycle League worked together to build a BMX Racing Track for motocross enthusiast at Chehaw Park.

Mingle with the Meerkats at Chehaw Wild Animal Park, AZA accredited zoo, at Chehaw Park.

Rail was a leading way to transport agricultural goods to and from Albany. Today you can still see trains using trestles across the Flint River.

Armstrong Atlantic State University

Founded by the city of Savannah in 1935, Armstrong is a dynamic public university with more than 7,400 students from across Georgia, the U.S. and 69 countries. Its location, just 15 minutes from historic downtown Savannah and 25 miles from Tybee Island beach, makes this beautiful, 268-acre arboretum campus a popular destination for students who seek a unique college environment that brims with learning and career opportunities.

Armstrong is teaching-centered and student-focused, providing diverse learning experiences and professional programs grounded in the liberal arts. The university offers more than 100 undergraduate and graduate academic programs in its College of Education, College of Liberal Arts, College of Science and Technology, and the College of Health Professions, one of the leading undergraduate health professions education centers in Georgia. The university also offers a Doctorate of Physical Therapy.

Armstrong has nearly 30,000 alumni who serve as leaders in their professions and their communities across Georgia and the globe.

DEEP ROOTS IN SAVANNAH

Armstrong has been rooted in the Savannah community since its founding. As the university has grown, so too has its deep connection to the history and the coastal environment. Students in every discipline and extracurricular program can expand their horizons through engagement with the community that enriches the quality of life in our area. The biannual university-wide Treasure Savannah days of service, outreach opportunities with local schools and organizations, real-life sea turtle nest rescues, and charity medical assessments are just a few examples of the opportunities Armstrong students have to take advantage of the rich culture around them.

LEARNING THAT FITS DIFFERENT LIFESTYLES

Armstrong also provides options outside of Savannah. The university's Liberty Center location in Hinesville, Ga., offers academic programs for residents of Liberty County and the surrounding areas, including Fort Stewart military personnel, veterans and military families. Students can also advance their education and career on their own terms while balancing work, family, or military obligations with Armstrong Online, which brings courses taught by world-class faculty through online and blended certificate and degree programs.

DIVERSE POPULATION AND EXPERIENCES

Armstrong offers diversity in both its student population and experiences. Its Latino student success programs have received national recognition, and with proximity to two military bases, Armstrong has earned designation as a military-friendly institution. The variety and depth of academic programming, a stellar honors program, countless study abroad opportunities, and myriad campus clubs and organizations provide the same kind of opportunities found at larger schools. Yet, Armstrong students enjoy small class sizes where they learn from talented and dedicated professors who serve as mentors and partners in research, while providing connections that lead to internships and career opportunities.

Armstrong Pirates athletic teams excel in Division II Peach Belt play. The men's and women's tennis teams have 10 national championships between them, and recently the Pirates won conference championships in tennis, baseball, women's golf, soccer, softball, and volleyball, all in the same year. Intramurals and club teams such as ultimate frisbee are popular on campus.

COMMITMENT TO STUDENT SUCCESS

"Armstrong has a foundational commitment to student success, and we are dedicated to preparing graduates not just for careers, but for thoughtful, civically engaged lives," says Linda Bleicken, Armstrong president since 2009. "That has been our focus since the doors opened in 1935 and must remain our purpose today, tomorrow, and far into the future." ■

Original Armstrong site, 1935

Savannah Country Day School

As Savannah's preeminent college preparatory school, Savannah Country Day School strives to cultivate a lifelong passion for learning in its students while encouraging them to serve others with a compassionate spirit. Its goal is to produce youth who are well prepared for college and for the global world that lies beyond.

The private, coeducational preK-12 school has a gifted, dedicated faculty who engage students in the excitement of learning while also challenging them to meet high expectations. Its curriculum of rigorous academics, combined with instruction in the fine arts and athletics, is intended to foster well-rounded students who will meet their future with confidence, imagination and integrity.

BALANCED STUDENT LIFE

"While Country Day's unparalleled academic reputation is easy to quantify and well-earned, what is especially notable is the balance that we strive for in student life," said Dr. Steve Kolman, head of the Upper School. "Football players are honors students who also perform in our theatrical productions. We want—and need—students who are anxious to excel in all aspects of their lives at Country Day and are willing and eager to explore all of our offerings within the context of our demanding liberal arts setting."

Savannah Country Day School's origins go back to 1905, when Nina Anderson Pape founded the Pape School to "educate the whole child," mind, body and spirit. The founders of Savannah Country Day School acquired the Pape School's assets, including its faculty, facilities, curriculum and most students, in 1955 and continued its tradition of academic excellence.

Today, the school's beautiful, 65-acre campus includes two libraries, a fine arts center, three gymnasiums, organic vegetable and butterfly gardens, a cross-country trail and several athletic fields. In addition to a myriad of fine and performing arts offerings, about 86 percent of Middle and Upper School students participate in at least one of 19 sports offerings.

ENVIRONMENTALLY FRIENDLY

SCDS is also proud of its commitment to environmental sustainability. In 2011, the National Wildlife Federation named SCDS as the nation's first Green Flag Eco-School, applauding its "green" management of facilities and integration of environmental instruction into the curricula. In 2012, it was one of only 12 independent schools to be recognized as a Green Ribbon School by the U.S. Department of Education.

Savannah Country Day's small classes make possible personalized instruction by the faculty, 64 percent of whom hold master's degrees and 4 percent of whom have doctoral degrees.

The success of this warm, supportive atmosphere is apparent in each graduating class. In 2012, the graduates received over $2 million in scholarships (excluding Hope Scholarships) and were accepted into such higher educational institutions as Harvard, Yale, Vanderbilt, Duke, Rollins, Washington and Lee, Georgia, Virginia and North Carolina-Chapel Hill.

TRULY UNIQUE SCHOOL

"Savannah Country Day School is truly unique compared to other schools in the region," said Allison Hersh, whose two children attend the school. "With its emphasis on academic excellence, character development, athletics and community service, SCDS strives to educate the whole child at every stage of development." ∎

(Top) Students enjoy an array of rich elective offerings.

(Bottom) Extra-curricular offerings enhance the Country Day school experience.

Memorial University Medical Center

Memorial Hospital in Savannah, Georgia, opened its doors as a 300-bed hospital in 1955. It was named "Memorial" in honor of the men and women of Chatham County, Georgia, who died fighting for our country. Today, it has grown into Memorial University Medical Center (MUMC), an award-winning 530-bed academic medical center that serves 35 counties spanning southeast Georgia and southern South Carolina.

The approximately 650 physicians and 5,000 Team Members at MUMC pride themselves on providing the region's most advanced care. Their mission is: With compassion, we heal, teach, and discover. Here are just a few of the high-level services provided by MUMC.

CANCER CARE AND RESEARCH

The Curtis and Elizabeth Anderson Cancer Institute (ACI) at MUMC provides a wide breadth of treatment and support for all types of cancer. The ACI features the region's only children's cancer care, the area's first gynecologic oncology services, and a practice dedicated exclusively to breast care. The ACI is also

(Top) Memorial University Medical Center has 21 state-of-the-art operating rooms. Our surgical services include minimally invasive and robotic surgery suites.

(Bottom) Memorial University Medical Center is the largest healthcare provider in southeast Georgia. Many of the services it provides are not available anywhere else in the region.

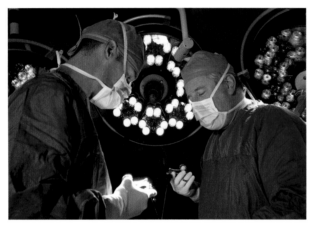

involved in a leading-edge cancer research program. Scientists in on-site laboratories study the molecular genetics of cancer. They work closely with physicians to conduct laboratory research that can be applied to patient care within five years. This is also known as "bench-to-bedside" research.

CARDIOVASCULAR CARE

Memorial pioneered open-heart surgery in southeast Georgia in 1967. Today, it continues to provide leading-edge care through its Heart & Vascular Institute. The facility offers cardiovascular inpatient services, surgical suites, imaging services, a catheterization lab, and an angiography suite.

CHILDREN'S CARE

The Children's Hospital at MUMC is the only children's hospital in southeast Georgia. The facility opened its doors in 1992 and cares for approximately 25,000 children every year. Services include pediatric critical care, surgical care, and emergency care. The Children's Hospital houses the region's only Level III neonatal intensive care nursery to care for the most critically ill or premature infants.

JOINT REPLACEMENT SURGERY

Memorial Bone & Joint specializes in hip, knee, and shoulder replacement. Orthopedic surgeons at Memorial offer bilateral hip and knee options and anterior approach hip replacement.

PHYSICAL REHABILITATION

The Rehabilitation Institute at MUMC provides both inpatient and outpatient physical rehabilitation services for children and adults. The 50-bed facility features specialized rehabilitation programs for people recovering from stroke, brain injury, and limb amputation. The Rehabilitation Institute also offers a children's program with physical therapy, occupational therapy, and speech/language services.

SPINE SURGERY

Memorial Spine is a center of excellence for spine surgery and the treatment of spine conditions at MUMC. Experienced neurosurgeons and therapists offer both surgical and non-surgical options for a variety of spine conditions. Memorial Spine participates in clinical studies to find newer, better ways to care for people with spine conditions.

STROKE SERVICES

At MUMC, a team of neurologists, emergency-trained physicians, and specially trained nurses are always available to quickly evaluate and treat patients experiencing stroke symptoms. Memorial's neurologists were the first in the state to launch a telestroke program. Using real-time audio and video platforms, the neurologists can assess stroke patients in rural Georgia, where stroke specialists are not readily available.

SURGICAL CARE

Surgeons at MUMC perform more than 20,000 procedures every year. Memorial was the first facility in the region to offer single-incision laparoscopic gallbladder and spleen removal, the first to offer anterior approach hip replacement surgery, and the first to establish a weight-loss surgery program. Memorial is proud to offer minimally invasive and robotic surgery services that feature the da Vinci Si Surgical System.

TRAUMA SERVICES

As the region's only Level 1 trauma center, MUMC provides the highest level of emergency care as established by the American College of Surgeons. To maintain Level 1 status, MUMC has designated trauma surgeons, a highly trained trauma team, a trauma operating room, three trauma treatment rooms, and intensive care units available around the clock.

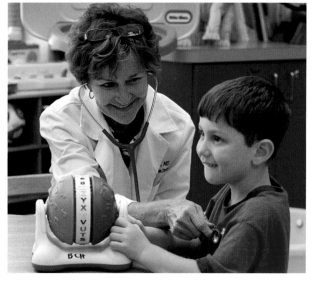

WOMEN'S SERVICES

Memorial was the first facility in the region equipped to handle high-risk pregnancies and deliveries, including the birth of multiples, preemies, babies with serious birth defects, and babies or mothers with serious medical conditions. In addition, MUMC provides gynecologic oncology, robotic surgery for gynecologic malignancies, and high-level mammography and breast cancer treatment services for women.

MEDICAL EDUCATION

The campus of MUMC also serves as the Savannah campus of Mercer University School of Medicine, a four-year medical school. In addition, MUMC offers six physician residency programs, a nursing residency, and a pharmacy practice residency. It is part of MUMC's core mission to educate and train the healthcare providers of tomorrow.

Memorial takes great pride in providing high-level care for every member of the community. The medical center has received local, state, and national accolades for its quality care, commitment to safety, and operational efficiency. The men and women at MUMC are never content with "business as usual." Their goal is to create a new standard for healthcare that will not only serve current patients, but also change the future of medicine. ∎

(Top) The William and Iffath Hoskins Center for Biomedical Research houses high-tech laboratories where scientists conduct research on the molecular genetics of cancer.

(Bottom) The Children's Hospital at Memorial University Medical Center offers more than 20 pediatric subspecialties including surgery, hematology/oncology, infectious disease, endocrinology, and neurosurgery.

Savannah State University

As the oldest public historically black university in Georgia and the oldest institution of higher learning in Savannah, Savannah State University is an enduring part of the state's history and a consistent contributor to its future. ■ *Originally established in Athens as Georgia State Industrial College for Colored Youth, SSU moved to its present*

location in Savannah in 1891 under the leadership of its first president, Major Richard R. Wright Sr. In the following years it became a full-time, degree-granting institution and was renamed Georgia State College, then Savannah State College. In 1996, the school achieved university status and was renamed Savannah State University.

The 201-acre campus of Savannah State University blends historic and modern architecture to create one of the most picturesque learning environments in the state of Georgia.

"The original founders believed that education and self-worth are keys to productive and successful lives," says Dr. Cheryl D. Dozier, president. "While they lacked material wealth, they believed that love and caring were necessary attributes in the educational process that would lead students to rewarding professional careers and potentially to positions of leadership in their professions."

Today, the 201-acre campus is by far the most picturesque in the state of Georgia. The moss-laden sweeping oak trees, expansive marsh and historic architecture create a resplendent yet tranquil atmosphere. Beneath the beauty and splendor is a vibrant residential campus bursting at the seams with the vigor of quality collegiate life: relevant academic majors, engaging lectures, cutting-edge research, quality student-faculty engagement and a nurturing environment.

DEGREE PROGRAMS OPEN
WORLD OF CAREER OPTIONS

Setting Savannah State apart is its focus on graduating students who are prepared to perform at higher levels of economic productivity, social responsibility and excellence in their chosen fields of endeavor in a changing global community. The university offers a broad array of undergraduate degree and graduate programs in its College of Business Administration, College of Liberal Arts and Social Sciences, College of Sciences and Technology and School of Teacher Education.

SSU is home to several unique and high-demand degree programs, including the only Bachelor and Master of Science in Marine Sciences program of its kind in Southeast Georgia. The program takes advantage of its campus location adjacent to

a salt marsh and is the only instructional unit in the University System of Georgia with direct ocean access and on-campus marine laboratory facilities. With three tracks of study—traditional marine science research, applied marine science and professional advancement, core courses provide a strong, broad and multi-disciplined investigation of marine sciences with emphasis on coastal oceanography.

SSU's Homeland Security and Emergency Management Program is the first bachelor's degree program of its kind in Georgia. As the home of numerous seaports and military installations, Savannah also gives SSU students access to hands-on training opportunities with local professionals and organizations in homeland security and emergency response.

The Mass Communications program is one of the top five in terms of student enrollment. Other than the University of Georgia, the Mass Communications degree at SSU is the only one in the state accredited by the Accrediting Council on Education in Journalism and Mass Communications.

One strategy that SSU has undertaken to prepare tomorrow's leaders is the Center for Leadership and Character Development. The center, located in the King-Frazier Student Center, is essentially a laboratory for the study and contemplation of leadership development, offering programs and services that help prepare principled students and citizens.

Programs of the center include the Fall Freshman Academy, the Distinguished Lecture Series, LEAD Workshops and the Alternative Spring Break Program, in which students are immersed in diverse cultures and environments across the country to engage in service-oriented learning.

INVOLVING EVERYONE

Living on campus in a close-knit, nurturing environment gives SSU students the opportunity to realize the complete college experience. They live and thrive in a supportive atmosphere surrounded by others sharing the same life-changing experiences, academically and socially, in an exciting university setting.

Convenient to all campus activities, Savannah State residential living options include two fully furnished apartment complexes—University Village and University Commons—as well as traditional residence halls and the modern, well-planned freshman suites, which are ideal for students new to the university. All residential buildings include laundry facilities and computer labs.

SSU offers an array of organized and informal co-curricular activities, including 75 student organizations, leadership

Combining top-flight talent with the top-notch resources that Savannah State has to offer, students and faculty inject endless energy and creativity into what they teach and how they learn.

workshops, 15 intramural activities, band, speech and theatre productions, student publications, honoraries, sororities, fraternities and student internships.

As a member of the NCAA Division I, the university also provides students the opportunity to compete in various sports on the intercollegiate level. Varsity sports include football, baseball, cross country, women's tennis, basketball, track and field, volleyball, cheerleading and golf.

Prospective students are encouraged to discover all that SSU has to offer by visiting the campus or the website. Tours are led by student Tiger Ambassadors, who also provide personal accounts of campus life through their own experiences and education.

"We welcome prospective students and their families to visit Savannah State University and experience campus life up close and personal," says Dr. Irvin Clark, SSU's Vice President of Student Affairs. "We ask our students, the Tiger Ambassadors, to lead tours so they can provide a direct connection to visitors that makes them feel welcomed, appreciated and at home on our campus." ∎

Tybee Island Tourism Council

Imagine five miles of inviting beaches, sea oats waving in the breeze and the smell of ocean air as dolphins and pelicans frolic offshore in the Atlantic. Welcome to Tybee Island, a laid-back barrier island off the Georgia coast that's rich in history and natural beauty.

Tybee Island, located approximately 18 miles east of Savannah, is a hospitable Southern beach town of a 3,650 residents that's known for its excellent seafood, comfortable accommodations and year-round recreational activities.

Like to fish? Choose from a pier, in the surf or off a deep sea charter. Enjoy shopping? Tybee's art galleries feature original paintings, jewelry and other handmade items. Best of all, visitors can dip their toes in the Atlantic Ocean and re-set their inner clocks to "Tybee time" to enjoy the ultimate island escape.

OUTDOOR ACTIVITIES ABOUND

Outdoor enthusiasts will enjoy kayaking through tidal salt marshes or paddling over to Little Tybee Island, an uninhabited nature preserve. Bicycling, paddleboarding, kite boarding, surfing and jet-skiing are other fun options.

Nature lovers can enjoy some of the best bird watching in the Southeast, plus the opportunity to observe Loggerhead Sea Turtles during their May through October nesting season on the beach. The Tybee Island Marine Science Center hosts a variety of programs to introduce visitors to indigenous marine life.

History buffs will enjoy touring the Tybee Island Light Station, Georgia's oldest and tallest lighthouse. Climb 178 steps to the top and enjoy the view! Originally built in 1736—three years after the 13th British colony was founded—this impressive structure has the distinction of being one of the most intact light stations in the United States.

HISTORIC MILITARY FORTS

Fort Pulaski is another "must see" attraction. Constructed to protect Savannah from naval attack, this brick fort was targeted by Union forces during the Civil War in early 1862 and finally captured on April 11. Large holes from the Union's rifled cannons can still be seen in the seven-foot-thick masonry walls. The picturesque Cockspur Lighthouse, which marks the entrance to the Savannah River's south channel, also is part of the Fort Pulaski National Monument.

Fort Screven was established in 1898 on Tybee Island's north end, to help guard the country during the Spanish-American War, World War I and World War II. The fort was closed in 1947 and sold to the City of Tybee Island. Today, its Battery Garland houses a history museum that tells the island's nearly 400-year-old story while other former fort structures serve as private residences.

A 'PERFECT LITTLE BEACH TOWN'

Enjoy an ice cream cone while strolling along the Tybee Island Pier and Pavilion, where people-watching remains an art. Sample fresh seafood and innovative coastal cuisine at the island's award-winning restaurants. Many of the local bars feature live music.

Come and find out why *Southern Living* magazine has called Tybee Island one of America's "Perfect Little Beach Towns"! ■

(Top) Kick off your shoes and relax. With five miles of uninterrupted public beach, you can stroll, swim or snooze to your heart's content.

(Inset left) Immerse yourself in Tybee's coastal wildlife, armed with just a paddle, a kayak and a personal guide. Beginners, families and experts welcome.

(Inset right) Tybee is one of the best places in Georgia to bird-watch. You may even spot Tybee's official bird, the Painted Bunting, also one of the continent's most colorful birds.

(Bottom) Can you climb 178 steps to the top? Tour Georgia's oldest and tallest lighthouse and check out the Tybee Island Museum to learn more about Tybee's rich history.

VISIT TYBEE ISLAND TOURISM COUNCIL ONLINE: www.tybeevisit.com

Rebuilt in 1996, today's TYBEE PIER & PAVILLION *is one of the island's most visited and visible attractions. Located on the south end of the island in the main business district, it is open and free to the public.*

STATEWIDE

Georgia

"GEORGIA—GEORGIA—GEORGIA ON my mind." What part of this beautiful state was the great Ray Charles thinking of when he wrote those lines? Was it the mountain music and tangy air in North Georgia? Perhaps it was the sound of the many waterfalls or the conviviality of the festivals held in the area. Could he have been thinking of an exquisite dinner in one of Atlanta's fine restaurants, pondering the choice of exotic cuisine or a homemade gumbo? Possibly it was of a successful business deal in that thriving and forward-looking city. Or perhaps he was remembering a swim in the warm salty waters of the coast. A service at the historic First African Baptist church or a carriage ride through the squares of Savannah? His hometown of Albany and the life-sized statue in Ray Charles Plaza that its citizens have erected in his honor? Or perhaps he was simply thinking of a cool spring morning and a walk beneath the massive live oaks that cover the state?

Georgia offers its citizens and visitors enough to satisfy any longing. Is it the energy of Atlanta, with its fine dining and exciting shopping? The graciousness and beauty of Savannah; its Southern hospitality and long history? Hiking and fishing in the mountains? Georgia has something for every wish. ▶

The largest **LIVE OAK** *in the state, rising 86 feet and over 300 years old, is found in Waycross. Photo by John Keith.*

BRASSTOWN BALD MOUNTAIN *is known to the Cherokee as Enotah, the sacred place where a giant canoe landed, saving a few Cherokee families from a great flood. Photo by Sean Pavone.*

The highest spot in Georgia, Brasstown Bald Mountain, is topped by a 5 story LOOKOUT TOWER *and offers superb views of the surrounding countryside. Photo by Sean Pavone.*

The graceful fountain at the north end of FORSYTHE PARK was added in 1858 in the style found in Parisian parks of the time. On St. Patrick's Day, the fountain turns green in honor of Savannah's Irish heritage. Photo by David Davis.

Georgians are enthusiastic fans whether the event is the TOUR DEGEORGIA
Bike Race in Ellijay (photo by Jeff Kinsey), a NASCAR event or a Falcons game.
(Photo courtesy of the Atlanta Falcons)

The falls, formed when the Tallulah River cut a 2 mile path through the
TALLULAH GORGE, *are a powerful challenge to kayakers and rafters.*

The **GEORGIA AQUARIUM** *in Atlanta, containing over 8.5 million gallons of marine and freshwater, is the world's largest aquarium, housing 500 different species of fish and sea creatures. Its exhibit tunnels provide visitors with unique views of the inhabitants, which include rare whale sharks and hammerheads. Photo by Sean Pavone.*

Profiles of Distinction

A look at the corporations, businesses and community service organizations that helped make this book possible. These forward-thinking companies and organizations are at the forefront of moving the state into a prosperous future.

Cancer Treatment Centers of America

Re/Max of Georgia

WellStar Health System

The quiet of the OKEFENOKEE SWAMP.
Photo by Nicola Keegan.

Cancer Treatment Centers of America
at Southeastern Regional Medical Center

Cancer Treatment Centers of America® (CTCA) at Southeastern Regional Medical Center opened in Newnan, Georgia, in August, 2012, to bring more state-of-the-art treatment options—and more hope—to patients fighting complex and advanced-stage cancer.

The metro Atlanta location joins CTCA® regional destination hospitals in Chicago, Philadelphia, Phoenix and Tulsa to provide fully integrated and personalized cancer care, delivered by a multidisciplinary care team focused on quality care, efficiency and absolute service excellence.

"At CTCA, patients are at the center of all that we do," says Kane Dawson, president and chief executive officer of CTCA at Southeastern Regional Medical Center. "We deliver innovative and compassionate care that empowers patients and focuses on the whole person to meet their individual needs."

In addition to providing high quality, comprehensive cancer care, Southeastern will provide a major boost to the local economy. Recognized by former Georgia Governor Sonny Perdue as one of the "State of Georgia's Top 10 Economic Development Projects," the hospital is expected to generate 500 new jobs and $500 million in economic activity over the first five years of operation.

CHANGING THE FACE OF CANCER CARE

Cancer Treatment Centers of America was founded in 1988 by Richard J Stephenson. Stephenson was disappointed with the impersonal and insensitive care his mother, Mary Brown Stephenson, received. When she lost her battle with cancer in 1982, Stephenson set out to change the face of cancer care. Stephenson's commitment to creating a truly patient-centered cancer treatment experience has been the organization's guiding principle ever since.

CTCA promises that the treatment, quality of life and service needs of every patient will be at the center of the hearts, minds and actions of its staff every day. At CTCA, patients find accomplished physicians who are experienced in caring for individuals living with advanced and complex cancer, along with experienced nutritionists, naturopathic doctors, chiropractors, mind-body therapists, spiritual counselors and other clinicians who provide integrative care and support.

Collectively, physicians and staff work to address the individual needs of patients, as if each patient was his or her own mother or loved one. They ask themselves: "If my mother had cancer, how would I want her to be treated?" That simple question has evolved into the CTCA Mother Standard® of care—a unique, vibrant approach that delivers a complete, quality treatment experience based on what cancer patients and their families value most.

TREATING THE WHOLE PERSON

Patients and their families travel hundreds of miles to access the unique care model found at CTCA hospitals, Patient Empowered Care®, that places patients at the center of their own care, encouraging and enabling them to take an active role in treatment decision making.

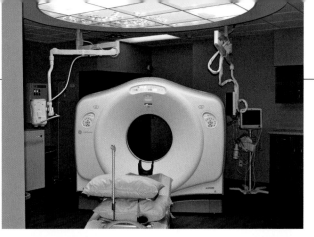

(Top left)
CT Scan with
skylight ceiling.

(Top right)
Dr. George Daneker
and Kane Dawson
with TomoTherapy®
machine.

(Bottom left)
Guest
accommodations.

(Bottom right)
Nursing staff in
Surgery
Department.

This innovative model combines leading clinical treatments and technologies with scientifically supported complementary therapies to help manage side effects and improve quality of life. All these services are delivered under one roof by a dedicated, multidisciplinary team of oncology care providers who personalize treatment plans based on the individual needs of each patient.

"My doctors and team at Cancer Treatment Centers of America gave me a plan that was right for me," said prostate cancer patient George Drennan of Canton, Georgia.

To support its commitment to provide clear information that helps patients and their families make informed treatment decisions, CTCA posts its length of life, quality of life, speed of care and patient experience data on its website.

PERSONALIZED TREATMENTS AND TECHNOLOGY

Using an integrated, patient-centered approach, CTCA combines advanced treatments and technologies with an array of complementary medical therapies. Oncologists work as a team with nutritionists, naturopathic doctors, mind-body therapists, rehabilitation therapists and spiritual support staff to treat the whole person. This means patients and caregivers enjoy the convenience of tests, treatments and supportive therapies all under one roof.

For CTCA Chief of Staff, Chief of Surgery and Surgical Oncologist Dr. George Daneker, it's an exclusive focus on cancer that sets CTCA apart. "At CTCA, we understand the urgency of bringing more options, more powerful and innovative therapies—and more hope—to patients and their families today. We're a team focused on bringing cancer treatment back to the needs of patients," he says.

METRO ATLANTA HOSPITAL
SERVES PATIENTS IN SOUTHEAST

Located about 25 miles southwest of Hartsfield-Jackson Atlanta International Airport, CTCA is a 226,000-square-foot, fully digital hospital focused exclusively on treating cancer.

Among the new hospital's features are 25 private inpatient treatment rooms, large surgical suites, specialized treatment suites for endoscopy and bronchoscopy, state-of-the-art radiation and therapy departments, rehabilitation and physical therapy, concierge services, a dining room, chapel and onsite guest accommodations. Advanced medical technologies include magnetic resonance imaging (MRI), positron emission tomography-computed tomography (PET-CT), Varian TrueBeam™, TomoTherapy®, Calypso®, TheraSphere, digital imaging, interventional angiography and more.

Outside the hospital is a swan pond visible from many guest rooms, with a peninsula and gazebo for relaxation. The outdoor patio area adjacent to the dining room has a koi pond and gazebo garden. Two rooftop terraces overlook the beautiful grounds and adjacent woods and fountains greet passersby at the main and outpatient entrances. Also available are 12 full-service RV parking spots for guests who prefer to travel by RV, bus or camper.

AVAILABLE AROUND THE CLOCK

Medical decisions are among the most important decisions patients and their families make in life. CTCA believes patients and their families should never have to wait to begin their journey toward finding the right treatment option. Oncology Information Specialists are available to discuss treatment options 24 hours a day, 365 days a year at 888-831-4493 or online at cancercenter.com.

For more information on Cancer Treatment Centers of America at Southeastern Regional Medical Center in Newnan, Georgia, please visit cancercenter.com/southeastern or call 855-848-5766 toll-free. ■

RE/MAX of Georgia

RE/MAX® of Georgia is a leader in customer satisfaction and sells more houses than any other real estate broker in the state. With more than 100 offices, it has a location that can serve its clients' needs in North, South, Central and Coastal Georgia.

(Top) RE/MAX Metro Atlanta Cityside is located in a historic home on Ponce de Leon Avenue, Atlanta, GA. Built in 1921 it is considered "The Hallmark of Druid Hills". They have great taste in office locations. Check out their Atlanta fine home collection.

(Middle) Beautiful homes are available in the Chateau Elan gated community.

(Bottom) Searching for a home with a spa, vineyard and winery in the backyard? Look no further with RE/MAX Town Square as they can guide your realization into a Chateau Elan property.

In 2011, RE/MAX® of Georgia was ranked number one in number of houses sold in all of Georgia, selling more than 25,000 houses. "We can sell houses faster than our competitors and, from a buyer's standpoint, we offer excellent service and top brand recognition," said Dane Ellison, CEO of RE/MAX® Regional Services.

CHANGING THE STATUS QUO

RE/MAX®, an acronym for Real Estate Maximums, was founded in 1973 by Dave and Gail Liniger. They wanted to change the status quo, which at that time meant agents forfeiting 50 percent of their earnings in exchange for an office and administrative services. The Linigers thought that business model was unfair since it meant that top earners were subsidizing bottom earners while perpetuating the idea that real estate professionals were amateur part-timers.

Their idea was to allow real estate professionals to earn all of their commissions and, in return, charge them a portion of overhead expenses. The Linigers believed that concept would attract the best, hardest-working entrepreneurs to their company—and it worked. Today, RE/MAX® is a global network of more than 100,000 sales associates in more than 87 countries.

RE/MAX® University offers continuing education classes and industry updates to its associates, as well as asset management, relocation, commercial investment, an international referral network, websites and introductions to the latest technological tools. With its red, white and blue colors and RE/MAX® balloon, the company has become globally recognized as a trustworthy leading force in real estate.

1,300 AGENTS THROUGHOUT GEORGIA

RE/MAX® of Georgia began in 1979 by Howard McPherson, a native Missourian who went on to expand the RE/MAX® brand throughout Georgia, Tennessee, Kentucky, Southern Ohio and Southeastern Michigan. Today, the Georgia company has almost 1,300 agents in 107 offices. In Georgia, their gross residential sales volume was $3.3 billion in 2011.

Those results equate to a great many happy customers! "Over the 50 years my husband and I have been married, we have bought and sold 13 houses," said Patty Day of Griffin, Georgia. "We closed on the sale of our 13th home this afternoon and if it weren't for our RE/MAX® agent, Linda Hilley with RE/MAX® Southern in Griffin, this day would not have occurred. Linda was able to have our home listed and closed in less than two months. We had our contract in 28 days. In today's market that is not only fabulous, but a dream!"

WINNER OF THE J.D. POWER AWARDS

Mrs. Day's rave review was echoed by a J.D. Power and Associates survey, which in 2011 recognized RE/MAX® agents

(Top) Luxury is located at Lake Burton Club. This exceptional property with lake and North Georgia mountain views is listed by RE/MAX of Rabun.

(Middle) St. Marys is a town graced by an abundance of water—the river, the Intracoastal Waterway, the Atlantic Ocean, and hundreds of tributaries. St. Marys is the Gateway to Cumberland Island, declared the nation's most beautiful wilderness beach. Her sunsets rival Key West. Find your St. Marys dream home with RE/MAX First Coast of Georgia.

for providing the "Highest Overall Customer Satisfaction for Home Buyers and Home Sellers among National Full-Service Real Estate Firms."

Another indication of RE/MAX's® results is that the Lake Burton Club, a private North Georgia club and community, named the RE/MAX of Rabun office as sole broker of its developer-owned properties. "Ed Poss, the owner-broker, is a recognized authority on real estate in Lake Burton and throughout Rabun County," said Buddy Parrish, general manager of Lake Burton Club. "His 40-year-old brokerage company has three office locations on Lake Burton itself, and we believe his representation will drive our sales for primary and vacation homes and home sites."

A WINNING FORMULA

RE/MAX® Metro Atlanta (www.RealEstateOfAtlanta.com) is one of the oldest franchises in the system, having opened in 1979. Broker/owner Donna Armstrong joined the business soon after. "Having the RE/MAX® brand, and the power behind that brand, is tremendous!" she says, "So this team wants to continue what we have been doing for 32 winning seasons."

RE/MAX® First Coast of GA Realty, based in southeastern Georgia, serves those who want to be coastal residents. In fact, *The Tribune* & *Georgian* newspaper voted it Camden County's "Best Real Estate Office" in 2011. "Our listings are in notable communities such as Osprey Cove in St Marys, listings range from $475,000 to $700,000, and in St Simons Island, from $300,000 to $1.8 million," said Broker Betty O'Shields.

RE/MAX® Towne Square, based in quickly expanding

(Bottom) The tee-to-green bentgrass golf course was listed as "one of the five 'Best of the Best' private golf courses in Georgia" by *Georgia Golf News*. Golf, water sports, athletic center, and the spa are a few of the amenities available at the 350 acre gated community, at the Lake Burton Club, exclusively sold by RE/MAX of Rabun.

Jackson County, specializes in helping buyers and sellers in the high-end golfing communities of Chateau Elan and Traditions of Braselton.

RE/MAX® associates love to work, but they also believe strongly in giving back to their communities. Since 1992, they have sponsored the Children's Miracle Network, raising more than $67 million for children's hospitals. In addition, RE/MAX® associates support the Susan B. Komen Breast Cancer Foundation and the Sentinels of Freedom Foundation. ∎

WellStar Health System begins with a vision. The physicians and team members believe in world-class care—state-of-the-art, compassionate care—right in the community. ■ From expert physicians, nurses and healthcare providers to the most advanced medical technology, WellStar delivers care far above the ordinary to patients at every stage of life.

WellStar is comprised of five hospitals, five urgent care centers, 14 satellite diagnostic-imaging centers, one adult congregate living facility, one skilled nursing facility and two inpatient community hospices. More than 500 primary care providers, specialists and advanced practitioners known collectively as the WellStar Medical Group provide care at more than 100 locations in metro Atlanta.

WELLSTAR FACILITIES CONVENIENTLY LOCATED

WellStar is conveniently available to more than 1 million metro Atlantans who are within a short driving distance from a WellStar medical facility. WellStar is one of only 42 health systems in the nation that has been accredited by the Joint Commission on Accreditation of Healthcare Organizations.

The system's five hospitals include WellStar Cobb in Austell, a 382-bed facility with cancer and cardiac programs as well as a private maternity center; WellStar Douglas in Douglasville, a 108-bed hospital with state of the art medical services and facilities and a medical staff of more than 350 providers; WellStar Kennestone, a 633-bed hospital that uses such advanced

technologies as da Vinci® robotic surgical and CyberKnife® systems; WellStar Paulding in Dallas, an 83-bed hospital specializing in emergency services, pain management and compassionate care for seniors; and WellStar Windy Hill in Marietta, a 115-bed long-term acute care hospital that is also home to one of the Southeast's largest sleep disorders clinic.

GOING BEYOND EXPECTATIONS

WellStar has one focus: providing care to its community that goes above and beyond expectations. As a not-for-profit, the system is dedicated to investing in the patients, not to paying stockholder dividends. That means providing the very best physicians and nurses, the latest medical technologies and treatments and the most comprehensive and compassionate care.

The main goal as a health system is to get—and keep—its patients well. A wide array of community health education programs and preventive/early detection screenings are readily available for that purpose. In FY2011, more than 200,000 community members took part in WellStar health classes and events.

WellStar's Cardiac Surgery Program received a "3 Star" rating

WellStar Kennestone Hospital is a 633-bed hospital that uses such advanced technologies as da Vinci® robotic surgical and CyberKnife® systems.

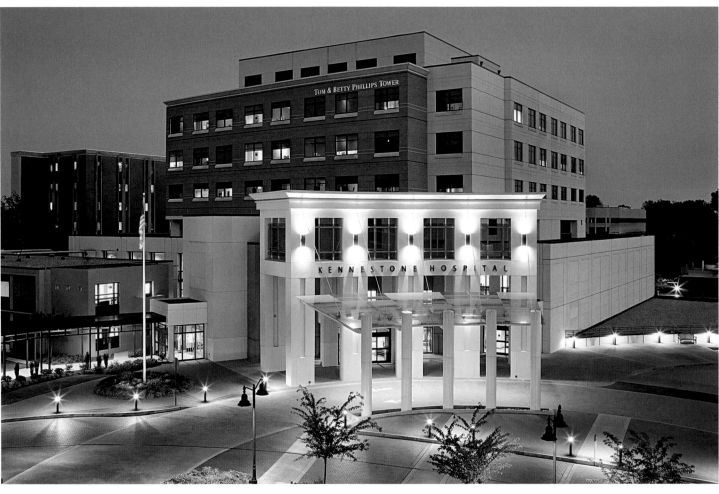

from the Society of Thoracic Surgeons. This rating denotes the highest category for clinical excellence and is held by only 12 to 15 percent of participating hospitals across the country. In the past year, WellStar's specialists performed 2,401 heart screenings and helped the more than 1,800 patients who had positive results receive care before they suffered heart attacks. In February 2011, a WellStar physician became one of the country's first doctors (and the first in the state) to implant an MRI-safe pacemaker.

TOPS IN EMERGENCY-ROOM TREATMENT

WellStar emergency departments took care of more than 300,000 patients in 2010, more than any other health system in Georgia. In 2011, WellStar Kennestone was approved as a Level II Trauma Center by the Georgia Department of Community Health. WellStar Kennestone improves access for Bartow, Cherokee, Cobb, Douglas and Paulding counties, providing critical, timely care for patients with serious injuries.

The nursing care delivery system has been redesigned and now encompasses a patient- and family-centered model with a lower nurse-to-patient ratio. Each hospital's nursing team is led by a Chief Nursing Officer who ensures the highest standards of practice are being met.

DA VINCI® SURGICAL SYSTEM ADDED

Other recent care enhancements include bringing the da Vinci® Surgical System to WellStar Cobb Hospital and the Therapeutic Cardiac Catheterization (PCI) procedures to WellStar Douglas Hospital.

The Specialty Center at WellStar Windy Hill Hospital is a dedicated long-term acute care (LTAC) program, providing advanced clinical and rehabilitation care for the medically complex patient who requires an average 25-day hospitalization.

Every day, in each of WellStar's hospitals, physician offices and other care centers provide care that goes above and beyond the patient's expectations to ensure that patients enjoy life, well-lived.

INNOVATIONS TO CONTINUE

As WellStar looks to a future of new technologies, new facilities and new treatment options, innovations continue. The patient- and family-centered nursing care, outstanding infection-reduction outcomes and robust clinical trials are just a few examples of the ways WellStar is providing world-class care.

The vision of WellStar Health System is to deliver world-class healthcare. WellStar, a not-for-profit health system, includes Cobb, Douglas, Kennestone, Paulding and Windy Hill hospitals; WellStar Medical Group; Urgent Care; Acworth Health Park; Health Place; Homecare; Hospice; Atherton Place; Paulding Nursing Center and WellStar Foundation. For more information, visit www.wellstar.org or call 770-956-STAR. ■

WellStar Health System's facilities are state-of-the-art. Its emergency department took care of more than 300,000 patients in 2010, more than any other health system in Georgia.

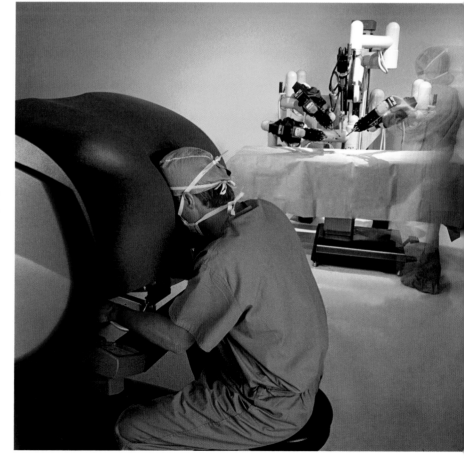

My Georgia Home/Introduction by Arthur Blank
ISBN 978-0-9747037-5-6

IMAGE PUBLISHING, INC.
901-756-5273
www.imagepublishinginc.com

Publisher:	Gigi Phillips, Image Publishing, Inc.
Editors:	Sanda Smith
	Nina Lockard
Project Manager:	Ann Ward
Creative Director/Designer:	Jencie LaVae Escue
Designer:	Ann Ward
Writers:	Annie Austin
	Zach Berry
	Kathy Brooks
	Matthew Fite
	Checky Herrington
	Terri Langley
	Nina Lockard
	Tim Sampson
	Sanda Smith
	Vicki Tyler
Proofreader:	David Ward
Marketing and Public Relations:	Amanda Stanfill
Digital Color Supervisor:	CueCreative

PRINTED IN THE USA

Index of Profiles

Index of Profiles

Index of Profiles

Index of Profiles

Index of Profiles

Index of Profiles